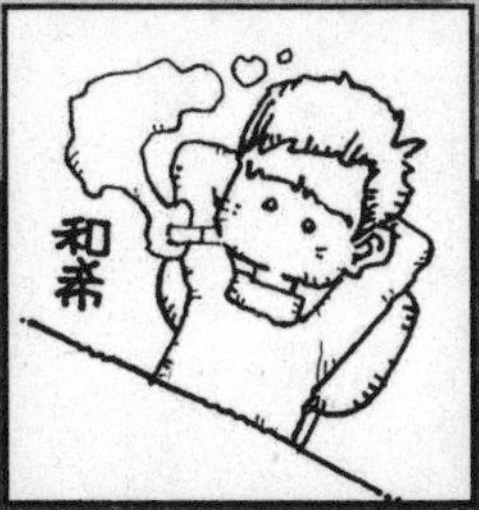
和希

KAZUKI TAKAHASHI

Mr. Miyoshi's art is, in a word, terrific. This guy is really good. I hope you'll all cheer for cheerful, energetic Yuma as he blasts through this manga version of *Yu-Gi-Oh! ZEXAL!*

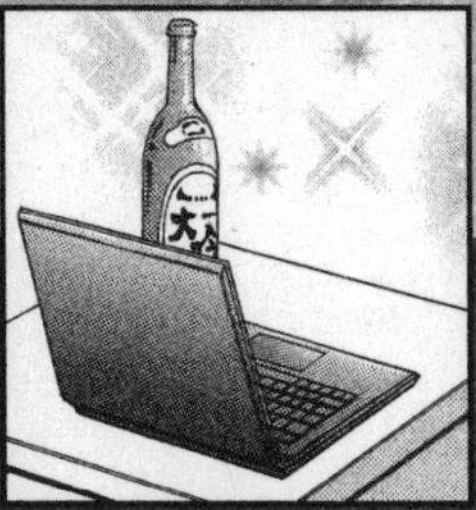

SHIN YOSHIDA

Thanks for checking out volume 1 of *Yu-Gi-Oh! ZEXAL*. Please keep supporting the comic version as well as the anime.

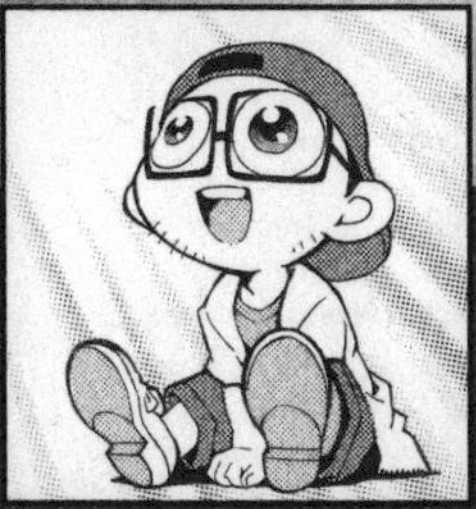

NAOHITO MIYOSHI

Hello, *Yu-Gi-Oh!* lovers! It's great to meet you. This is my first *Jump* comic! Yuma is gonna jet through his duels, and I'm gonna jet through this manga!

Volume 1
SHONEN JUMP Manga Edition

Original Concept by **KAZUKI TAKAHASHI**
Production Support: STUDIO DICE
Story by **SHIN YOSHIDA**
Art by **NAOHITO MIYOSHI**

Translation & English Adaptation **TAYLOR ENGEL AND IAN REID, HC LANGUAGE SOLUTIONS**
Touch-up Art & Lettering **JOHN HUNT**
Designer **FAWN LAU**
Editor **MIKE MONTESA**

YU-GI-OH! ZEXAL © 2010 by Kazuki Takahashi, Shin Yoshida, Naohito Miyoshi
All rights reserved.
First published in Japan in 2010 by SHUEISHA Inc., Tokyo.
English translation rights arranged by SHUEISHA Inc.

Based on Animation TV series YU-GI-OH! ZEXAL
© 1996 Kazuki Takahashi
© 2011 NAS · TV TOKYO

Printed in the U.S.A.

Published by VIZ Media, LLC
P.O. Box 77010
San Francisco, CA 94107

10 9 8 7 6 5 4 3 2 1
First printing, June 2012

www.viz.com

PARENTAL ADVISORY
YU-GI-OH! ZEXAL is rated T for Teen
and is recommended for ages 13 and up.
This volume contains fantasy violence.
ratings.viz.com

www.shonenjump.com

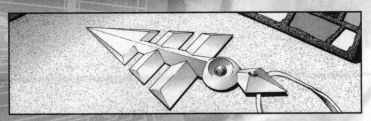

Yu-Gi-Oh! ZEXAL

VOLUME 1:
The Name's Yuma!!

Original Concept by **KAZUKI TAKAHASHI**
Production Support: **STUDIO DICE**
Story by **SHIN YOSHIDA**
Art by **NAOHITO MIYOSHI**

Yu-Gi-Oh! ZEXAL

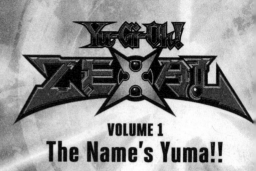

VOLUME 1
The Name's Yuma!!

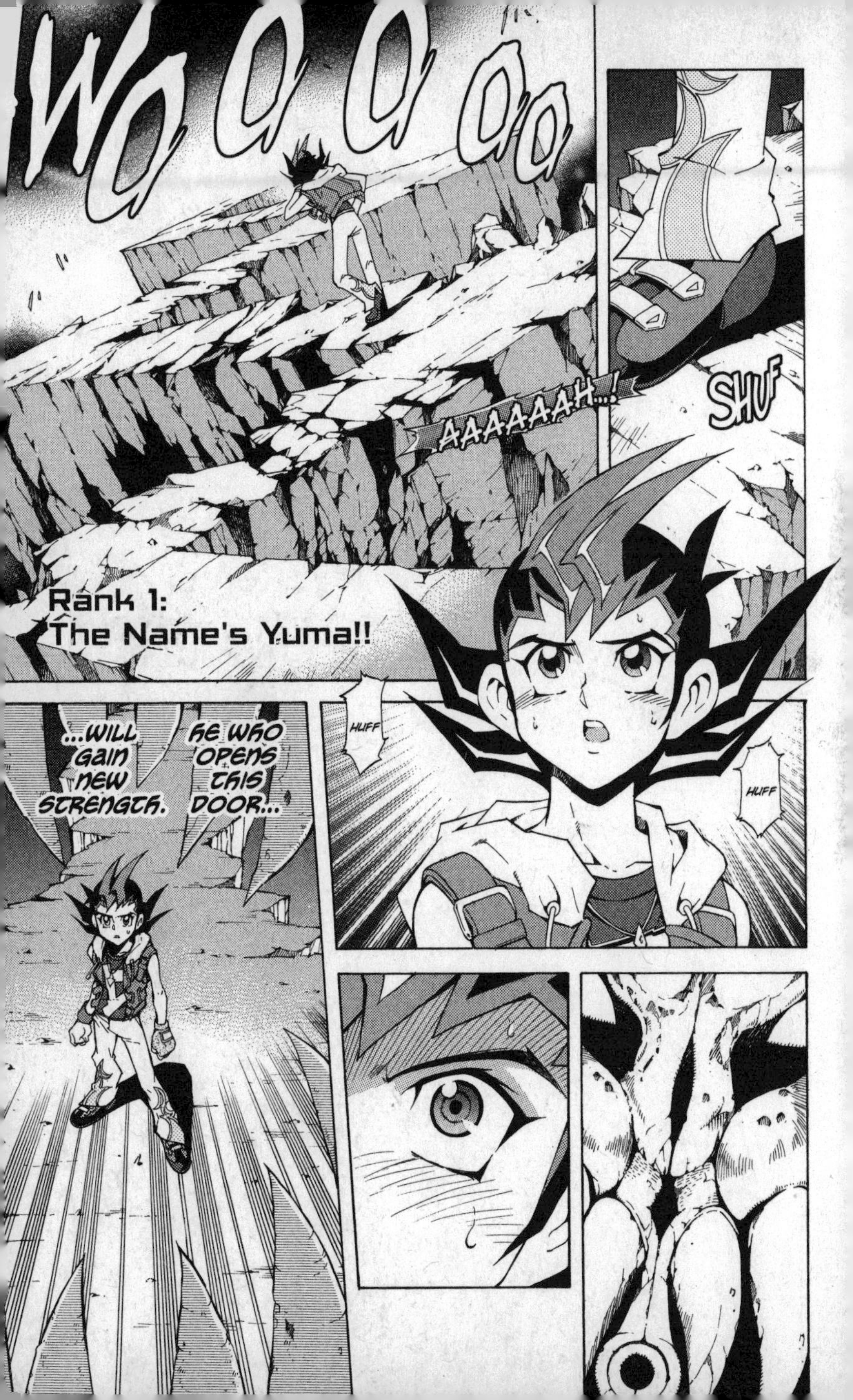
SHUF
WOAAAA
AAAAAAH...!
Rank 1:
The Name's Yuma!!
HUFF
HUFF
HE WHO OPENS THIS DOOR...
...WILL GAIN NEW STRENGTH.

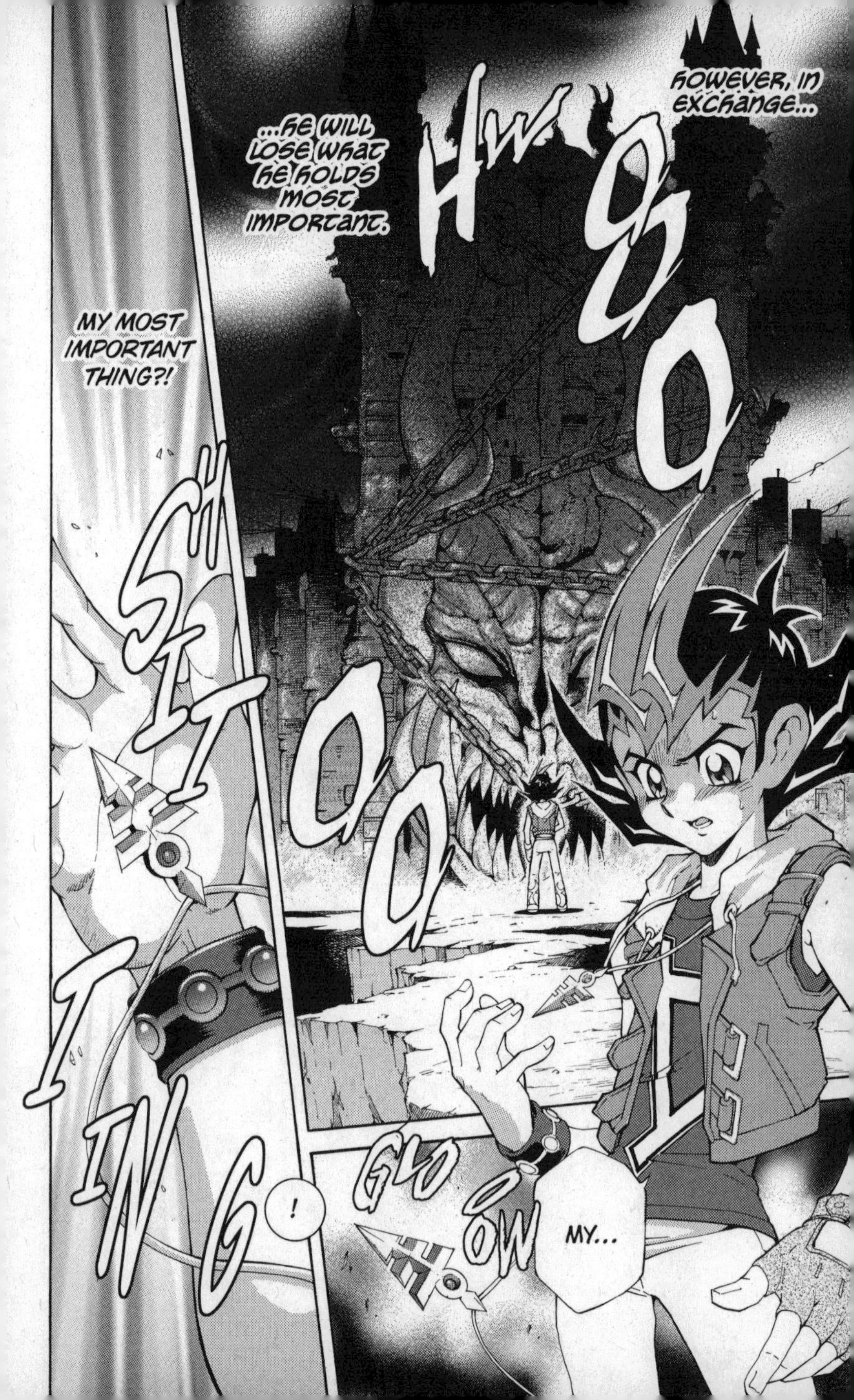
HOWEVER, IN EXCHANGE...
...HE WILL LOSE WHAT HE HOLDS MOST IMPORTANT.
HWOOOOO
GLOW
MY...
MY MOST IMPORTANT THING?!
SHIIING!

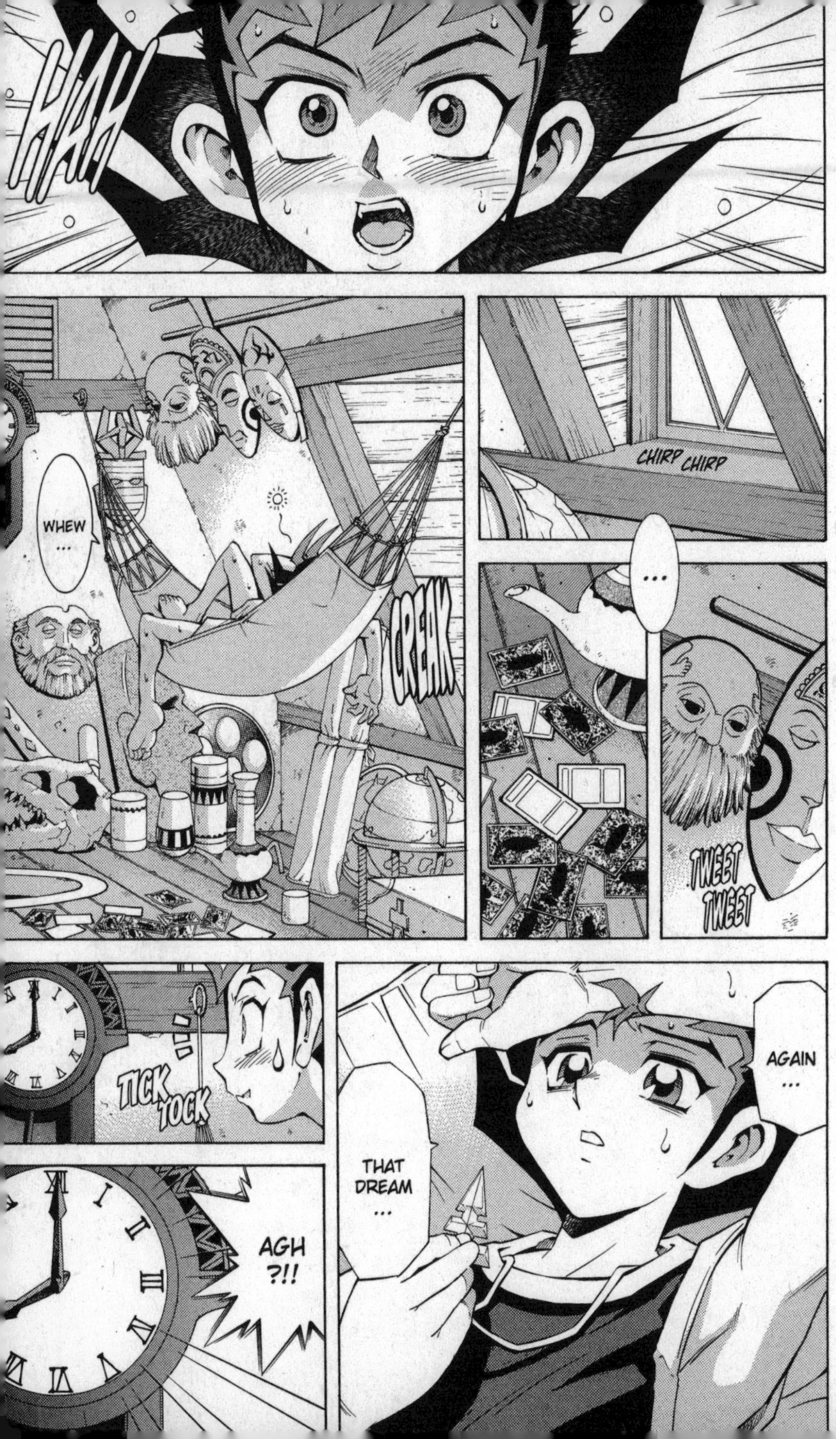
GYAH
CHIRP CHIRP
...
TWEET TWEET
WHEW ...
CREAK
AGAIN ...
THAT DREAM ...
TICK TOCK
AGH ?!!

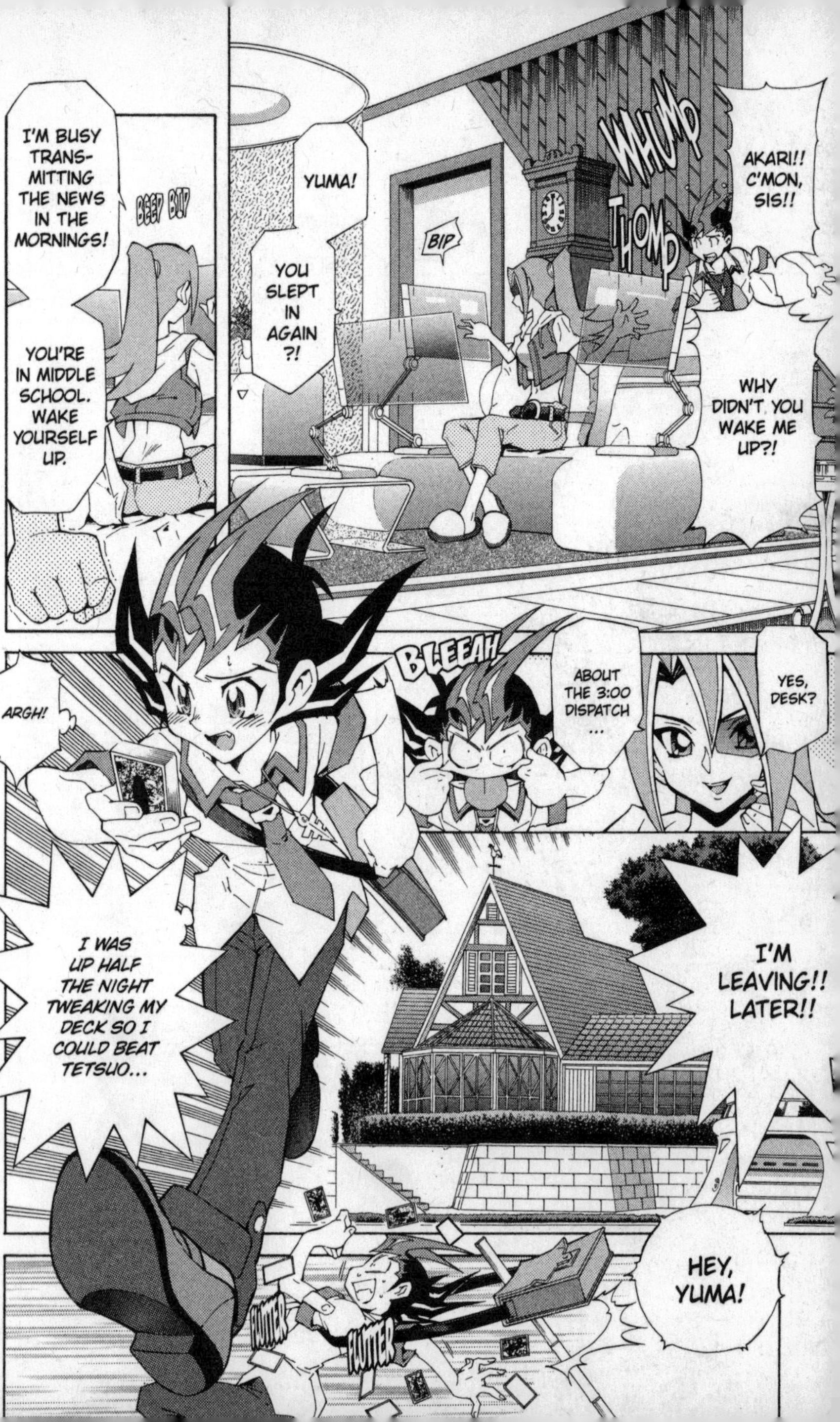
WHUMP
THOMP
AKARI!! C'MON, SIS!!
WHY DIDN'T YOU WAKE ME UP?!
YUMA!
BIP
YOU SLEPT IN AGAIN ?!
I'M BUSY TRANS-MITTING THE NEWS IN THE MORNINGS!
BEEP BIP
YOU'RE IN MIDDLE SCHOOL. WAKE YOURSELF UP.
YES, DESK?
ABOUT THE 3:00 DISPATCH ...
BLEEAH
ARGH!
I'M LEAVING!! LATER!!
I WAS UP HALF THE NIGHT TWEAKING MY DECK SO I COULD BEAT TETSUO...
HEY, YUMA!
FLUTTER
FLUTTER

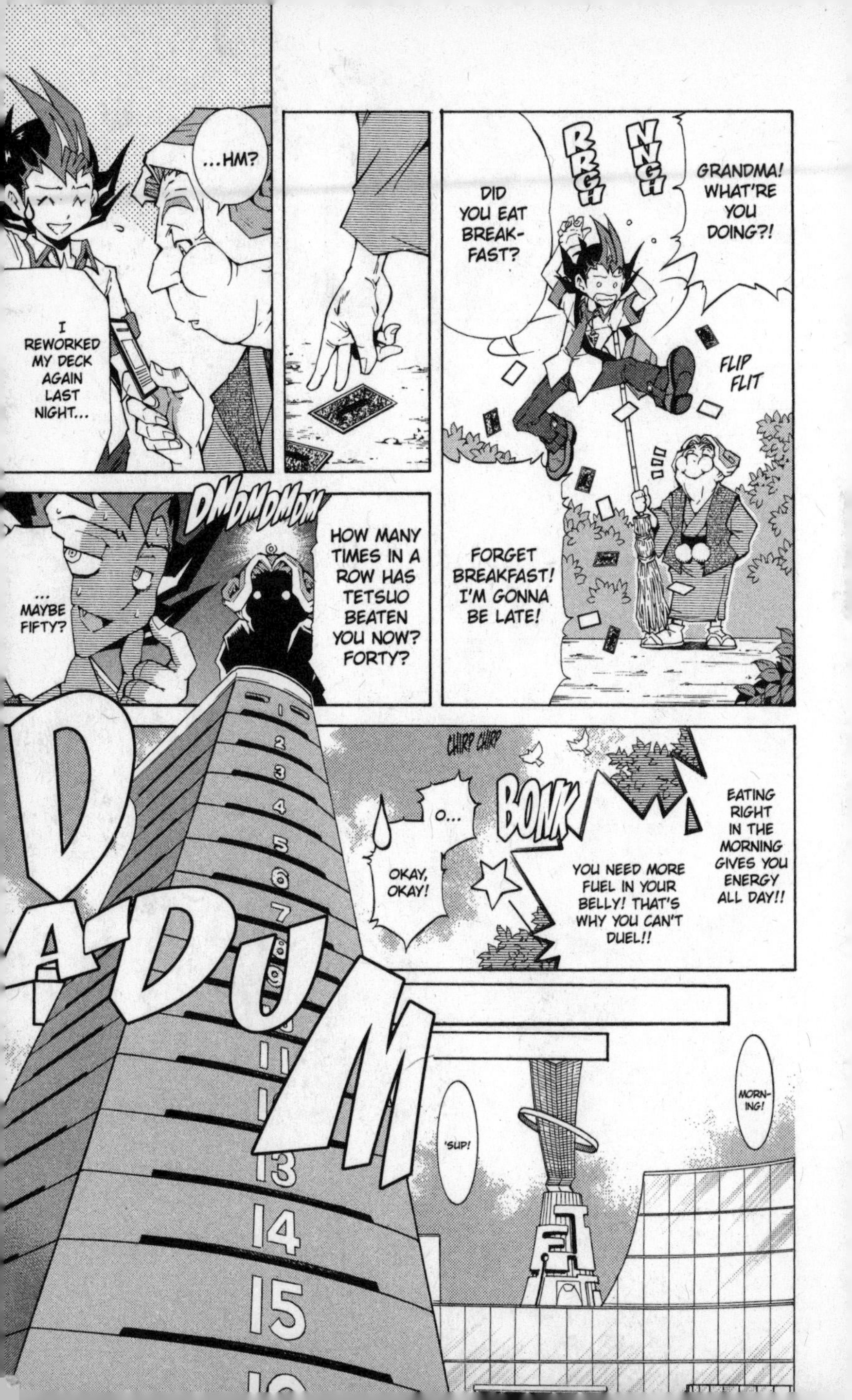
GRANDMA! WHAT'RE YOU DOING?!
NNGH
RRGH
DID YOU EAT BREAK-FAST?
FLIP FLIT
FORGET BREAKFAST! I'M GONNA BE LATE!
...HM?
I REWORKED MY DECK AGAIN LAST NIGHT...
DMDMDMDM
HOW MANY TIMES IN A ROW HAS TETSUO BEATEN YOU NOW? FORTY?
... MAYBE FIFTY?
EATING RIGHT IN THE MORNING GIVES YOU ENERGY ALL DAY!!
YOU NEED MORE FUEL IN YOUR BELLY! THAT'S WHY YOU CAN'T DUEL!!
BONK
CHIRP CHIRP
O...
OKAY, OKAY!
MORN-ING!
'SUP!
DADUM

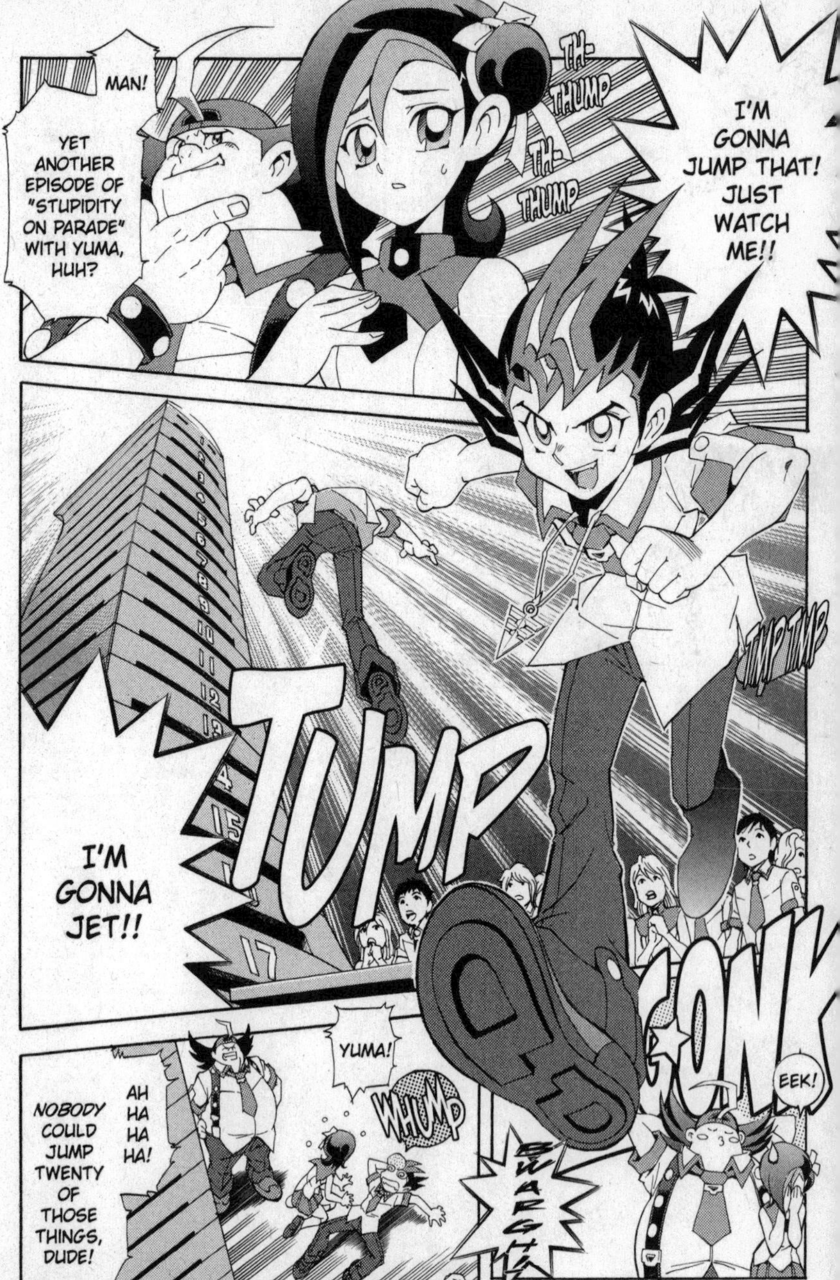
I'M GONNA JUMP THAT! JUST WATCH ME!!
TH-THUMP
TH-THUMP
MAN!
YET ANOTHER EPISODE OF "STUPIDITY ON PARADE" WITH YUMA, HUH?
TMP TMP
TUMP
I'M GONNA JET!!
GONK
EEK!
SWARGH!
YUMA!
WHUMP
AH HA HA HA!
NOBODY COULD JUMP TWENTY OF THOSE THINGS, DUDE!

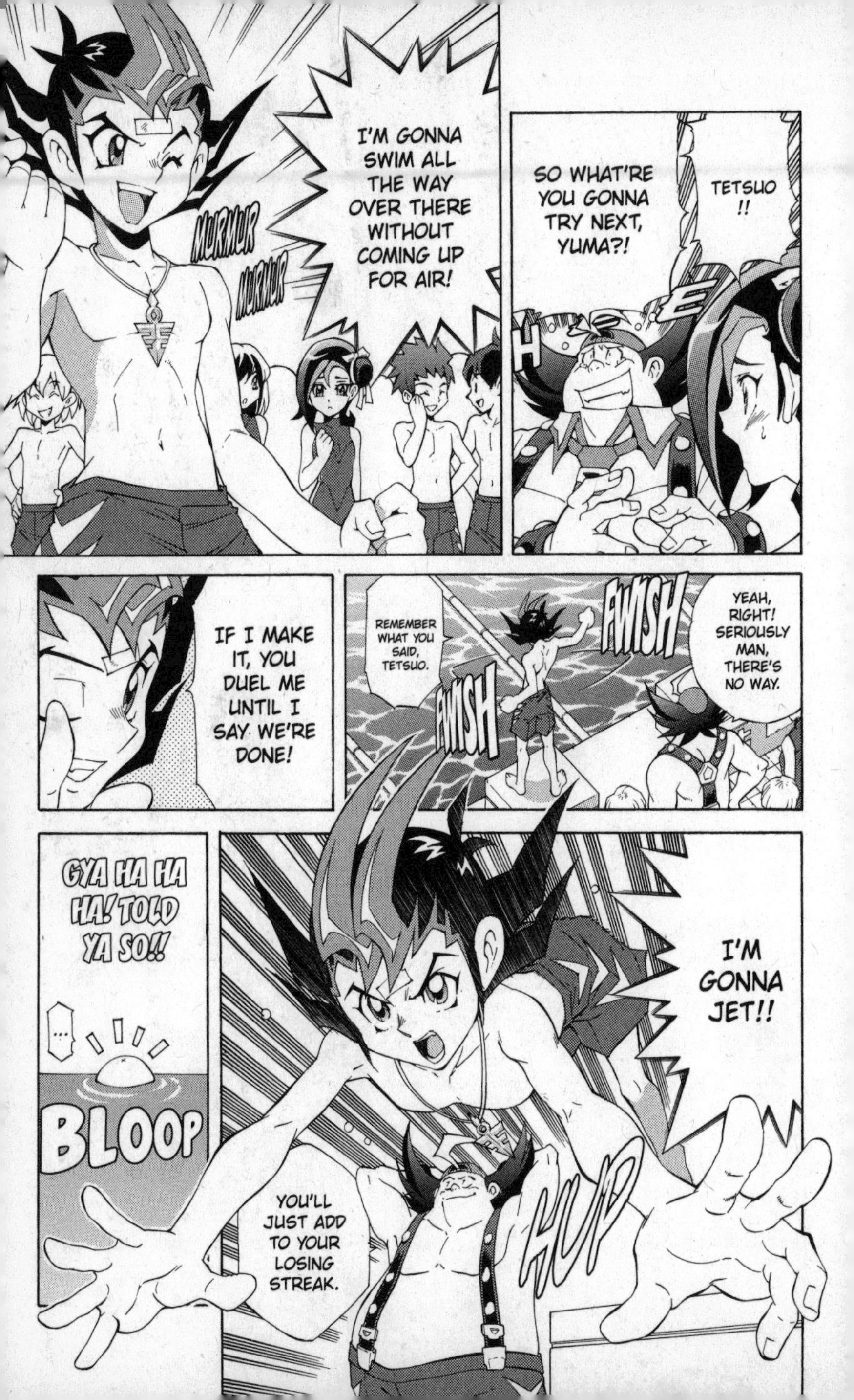
TETSUO !!
SO WHAT'RE YOU GONNA TRY NEXT, YUMA?!
I'M GONNA SWIM ALL THE WAY OVER THERE WITHOUT COMING UP FOR AIR!
MURMUR
MURMUR
YEAH, RIGHT! SERIOUSLY MAN, THERE'S NO WAY.
FWISH
REMEMBER WHAT YOU SAID, TETSUO.
FWISH
IF I MAKE IT, YOU DUEL ME UNTIL I SAY WE'RE DONE!
I'M GONNA JET!!
HUP
YOU'LL JUST ADD TO YOUR LOSING STREAK.
GYA HA HA HA! TOLD YA SO!!
...
BLOOP

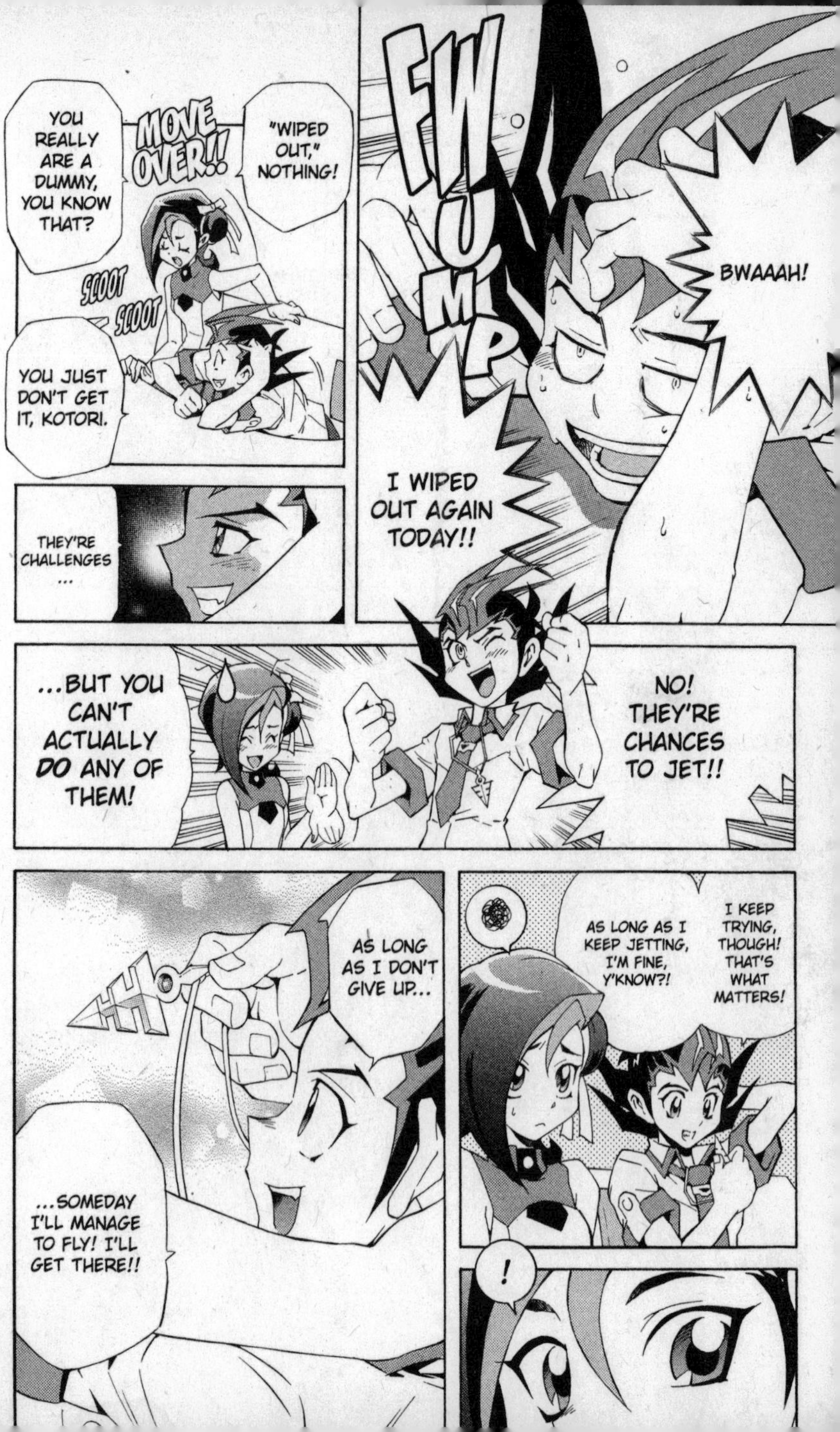
FWUMP
BWAAAH!
I WIPED OUT AGAIN TODAY!!
"WIPED OUT," NOTHING!
MOVE OVER!!
YOU REALLY ARE A DUMMY, YOU KNOW THAT?
SCOOT
SCOOT
YOU JUST DON'T GET IT, KOTORI.
THEY'RE CHALLENGES ...
NO! THEY'RE CHANCES TO JET!!
...BUT YOU CAN'T ACTUALLY DO ANY OF THEM!
I KEEP TRYING, THOUGH! THAT'S WHAT MATTERS!
AS LONG AS I KEEP JETTING, I'M FINE, Y'KNOW?!
!
AS LONG AS I DON'T GIVE UP...
HU
...SOMEDAY I'LL MANAGE TO FLY! I'LL GET THERE!!

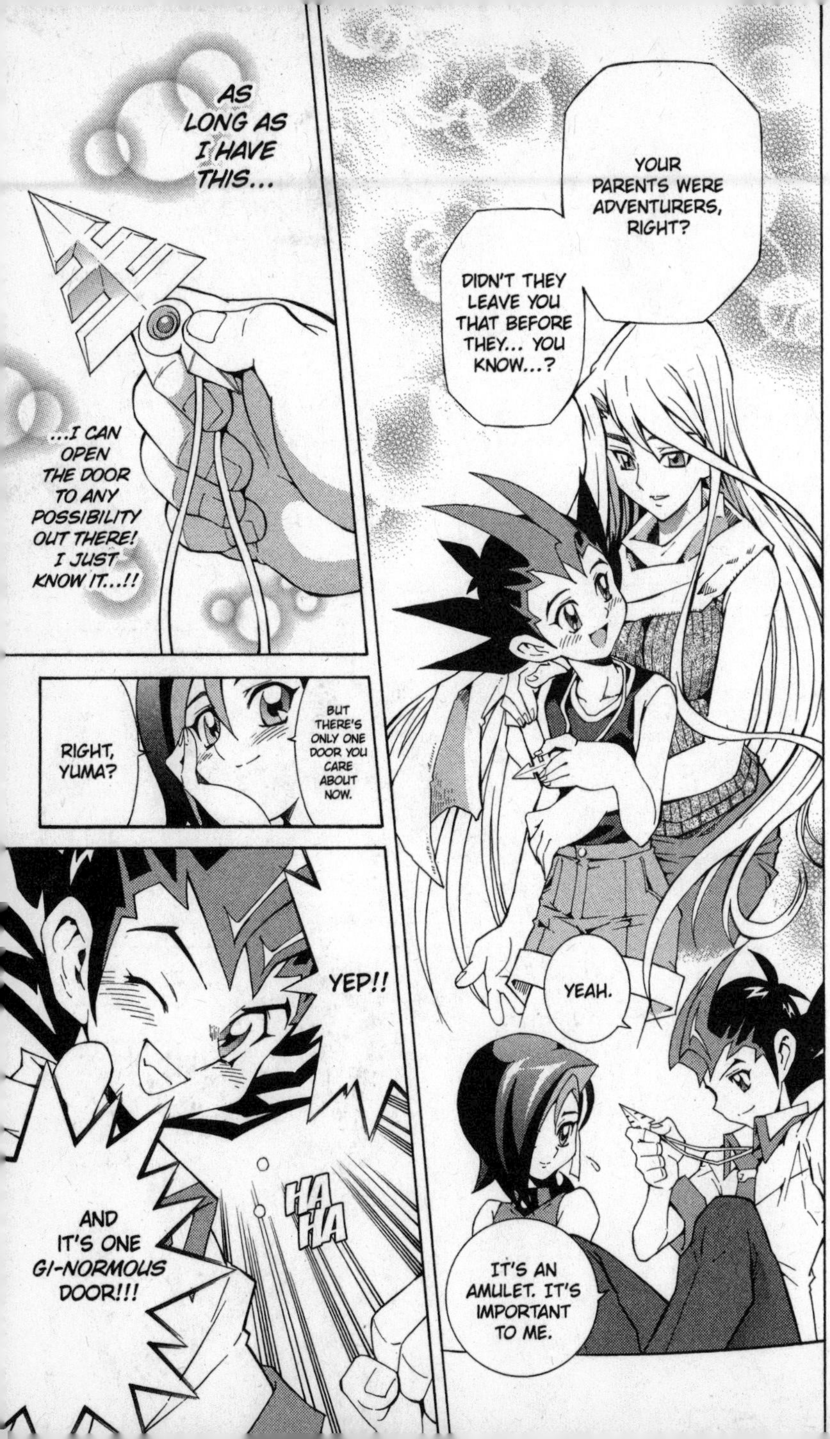
YOUR PARENTS WERE ADVENTURERS, RIGHT?
DIDN'T THEY LEAVE YOU THAT BEFORE THEY... YOU KNOW...?
YEAH.
IT'S AN AMULET. IT'S IMPORTANT TO ME.
AS LONG AS I HAVE THIS...
...I CAN OPEN THE DOOR TO ANY POSSIBILITY OUT THERE! I JUST KNOW IT...!!
BUT THERE'S ONLY ONE DOOR YOU CARE ABOUT NOW.
RIGHT, YUMA?
YEP!!
HA HA
AND IT'S ONE GI-NORMOUS DOOR!!!

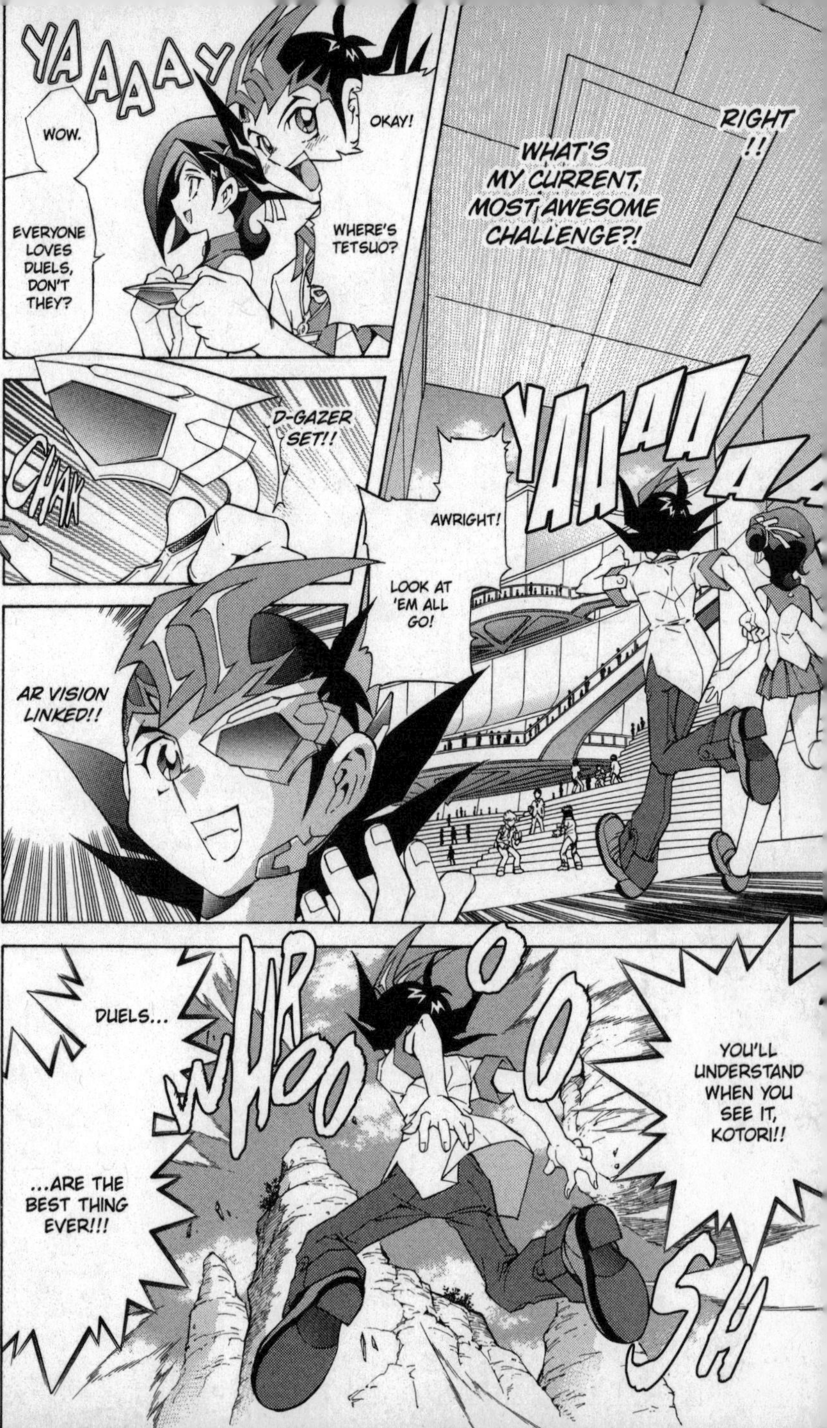
RIGHT!!
WHAT'S MY CURRENT, MOST AWESOME CHALLENGE?!
YAAAAAAA
AWRIGHT!
LOOK AT 'EM ALL GO!
YAAAAY
OKAY!
WOW.
WHERE'S TETSUO?
EVERYONE LOVES DUELS, DON'T THEY?
D-GAZER SET!!
CHAK
AR VISION LINKED!!
YOU'LL UNDERSTAND WHEN YOU SEE IT, KOTORI!!
WHOOOO
DUELS...
...ARE THE BEST THING EVER!!!
SH

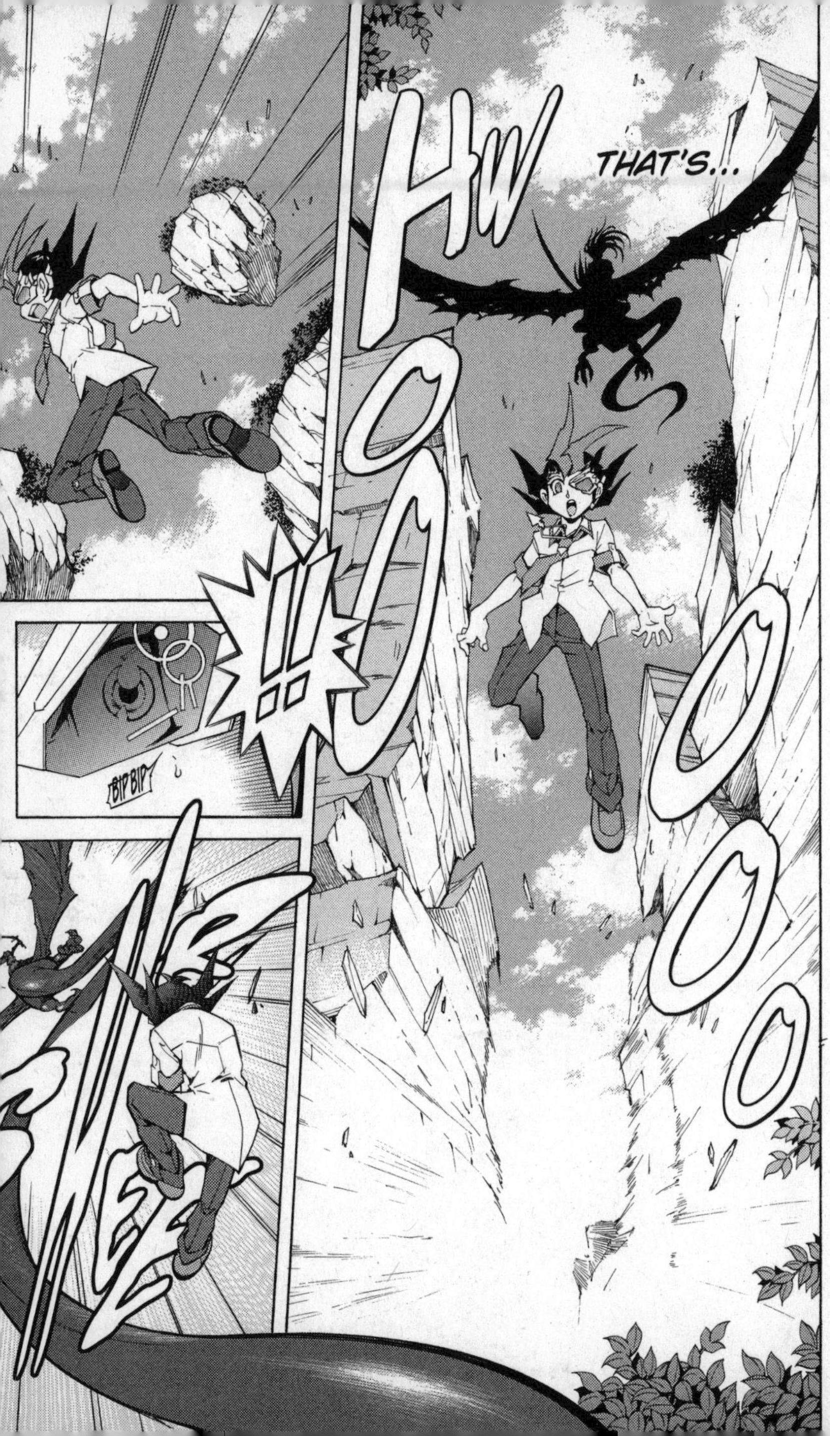
THAT'S...
HWOOOOOO
!!
BIP BIP

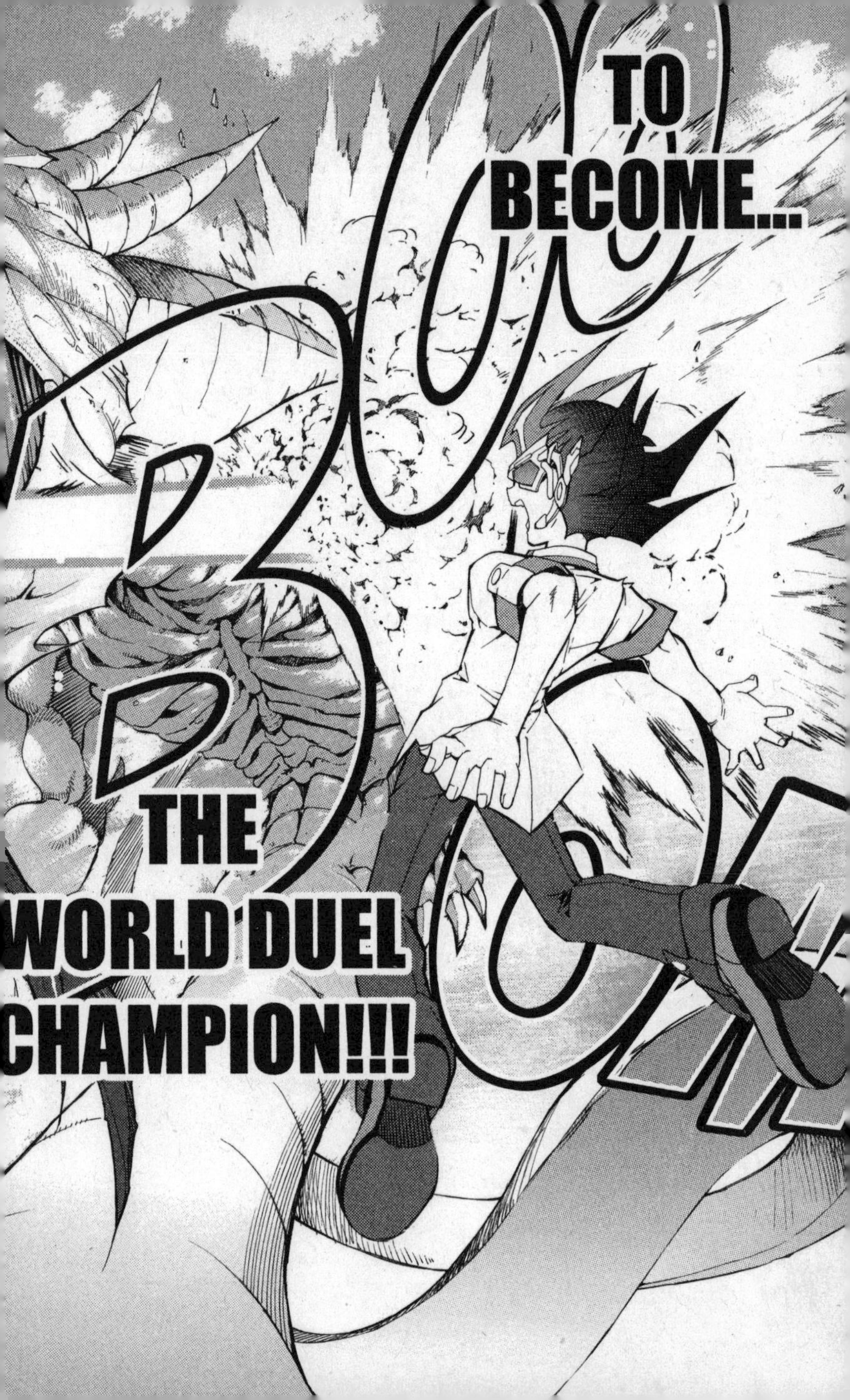
TO BECOME...
THE WORLD DUEL CHAMPION!!!

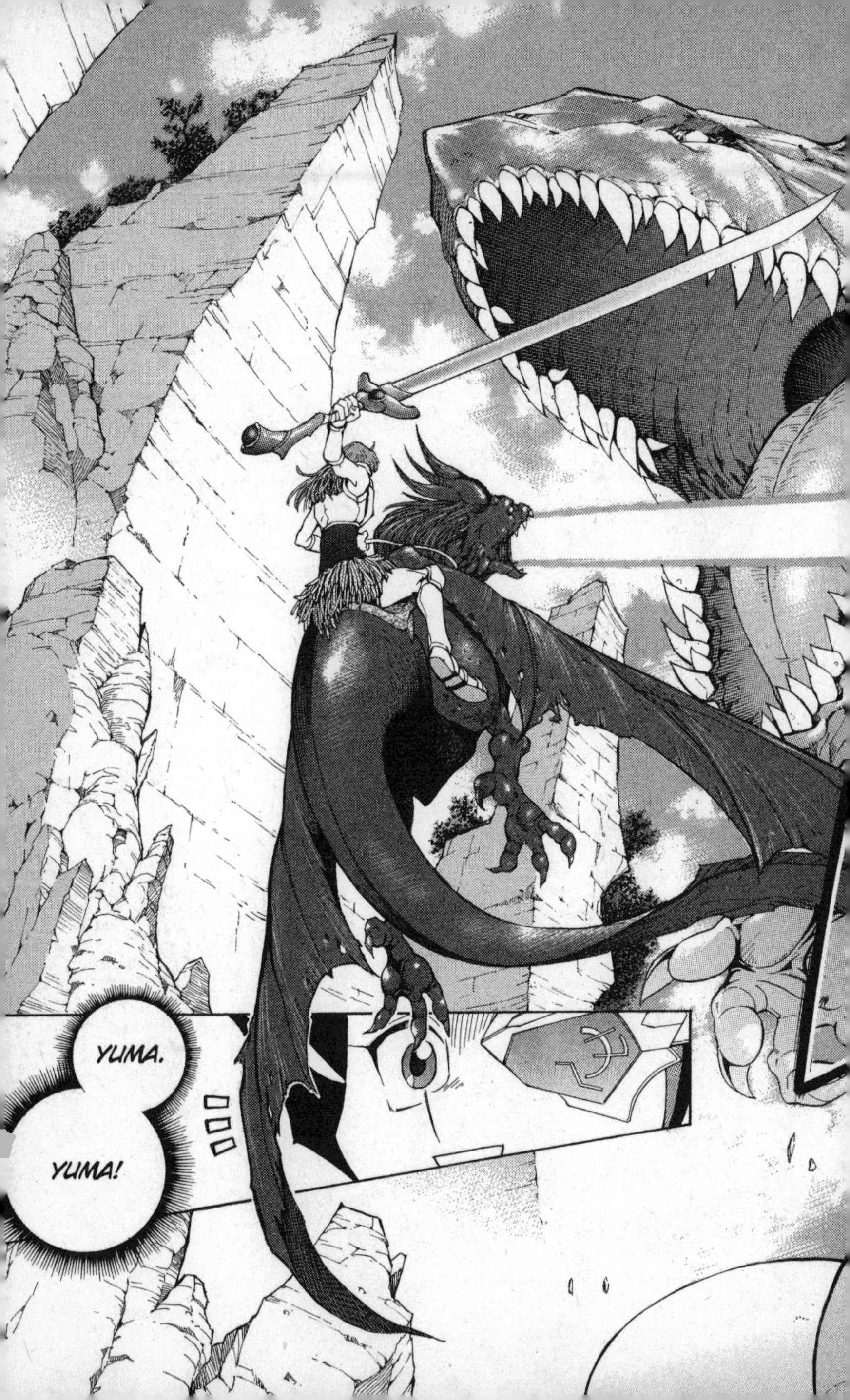
YUMA.
YUMA!

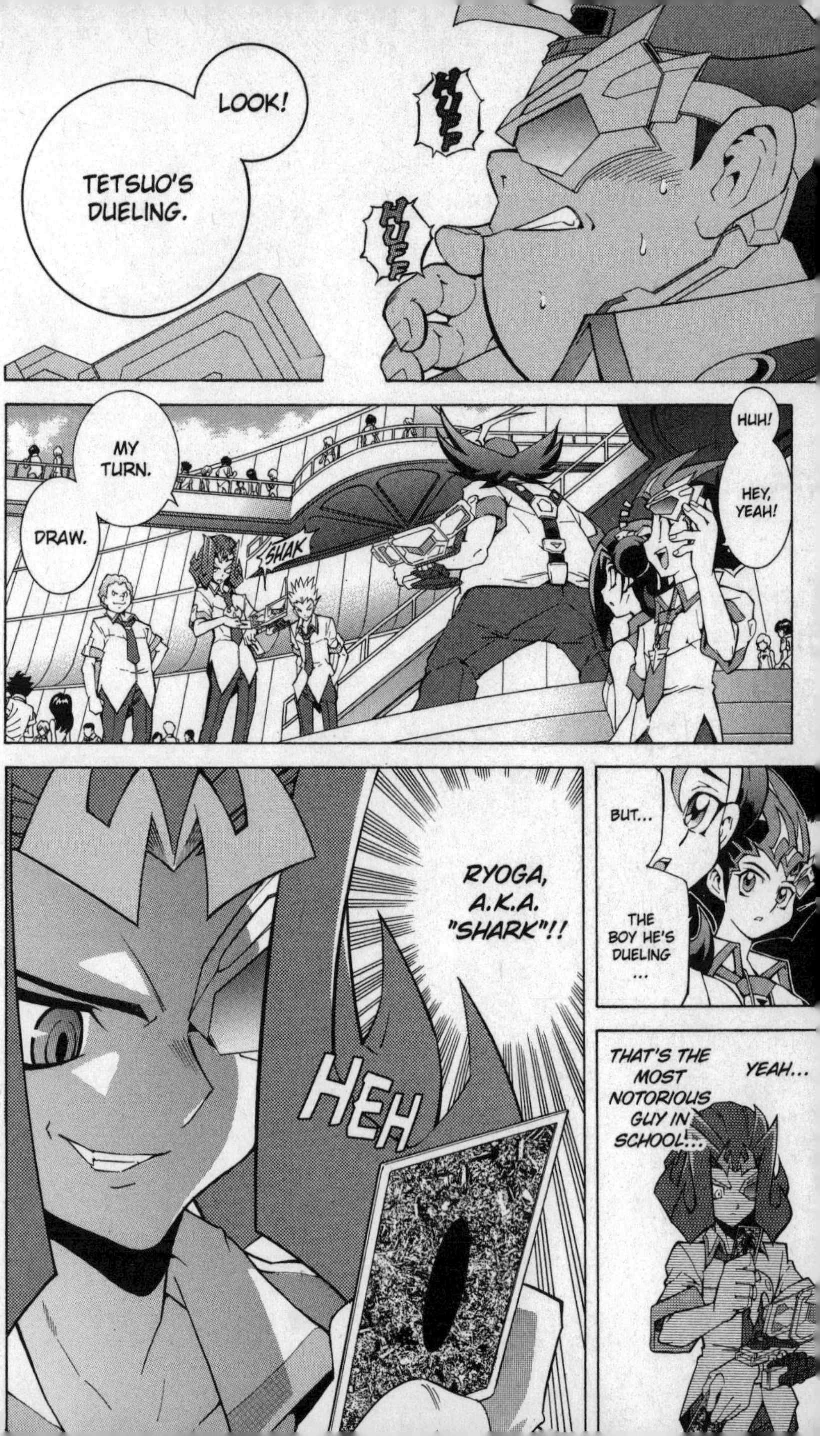
HUFF
HUFF
LOOK!
TETSUO'S DUELING.
HUH!
HEY, YEAH!
MY TURN.
DRAW.
SHAK
BUT...
THE BOY HE'S DUELING...
YEAH...
THAT'S THE MOST NOTORIOUS GUY IN SCHOOL...
RYOGA, A.K.A. "SHARK"!!
HEH

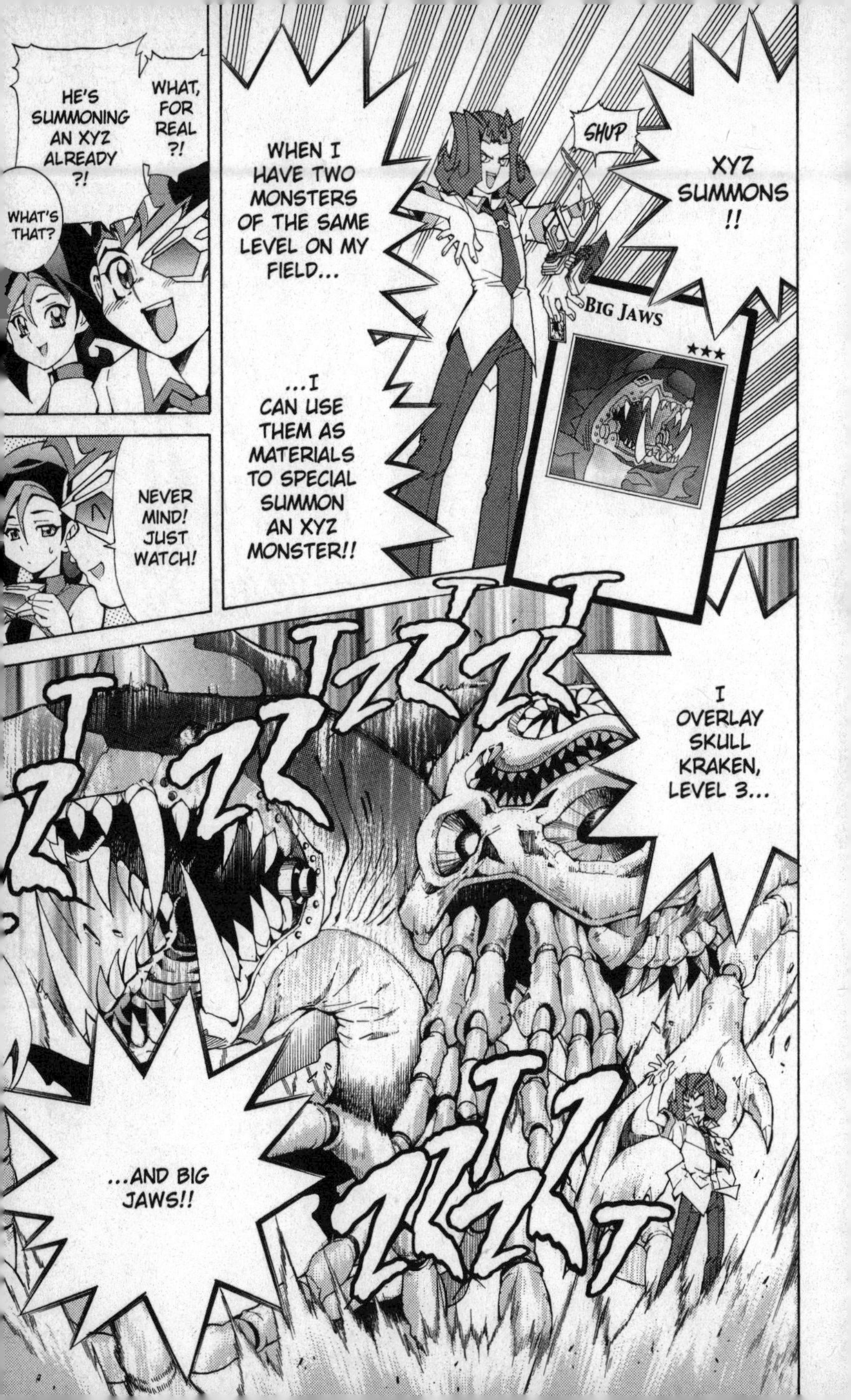
XYZ SUMMONS!!
SHUP
WHEN I HAVE TWO MONSTERS OF THE SAME LEVEL ON MY FIELD...
...I CAN USE THEM AS MATERIALS TO SPECIAL SUMMON AN XYZ MONSTER!!
BIG JAWS
WHAT, FOR REAL?!
HE'S SUMMONING AN XYZ ALREADY?!
WHAT'S THAT?
NEVER MIND! JUST WATCH!
I OVERLAY SKULL KRAKEN, LEVEL 3...
...AND BIG JAWS!!

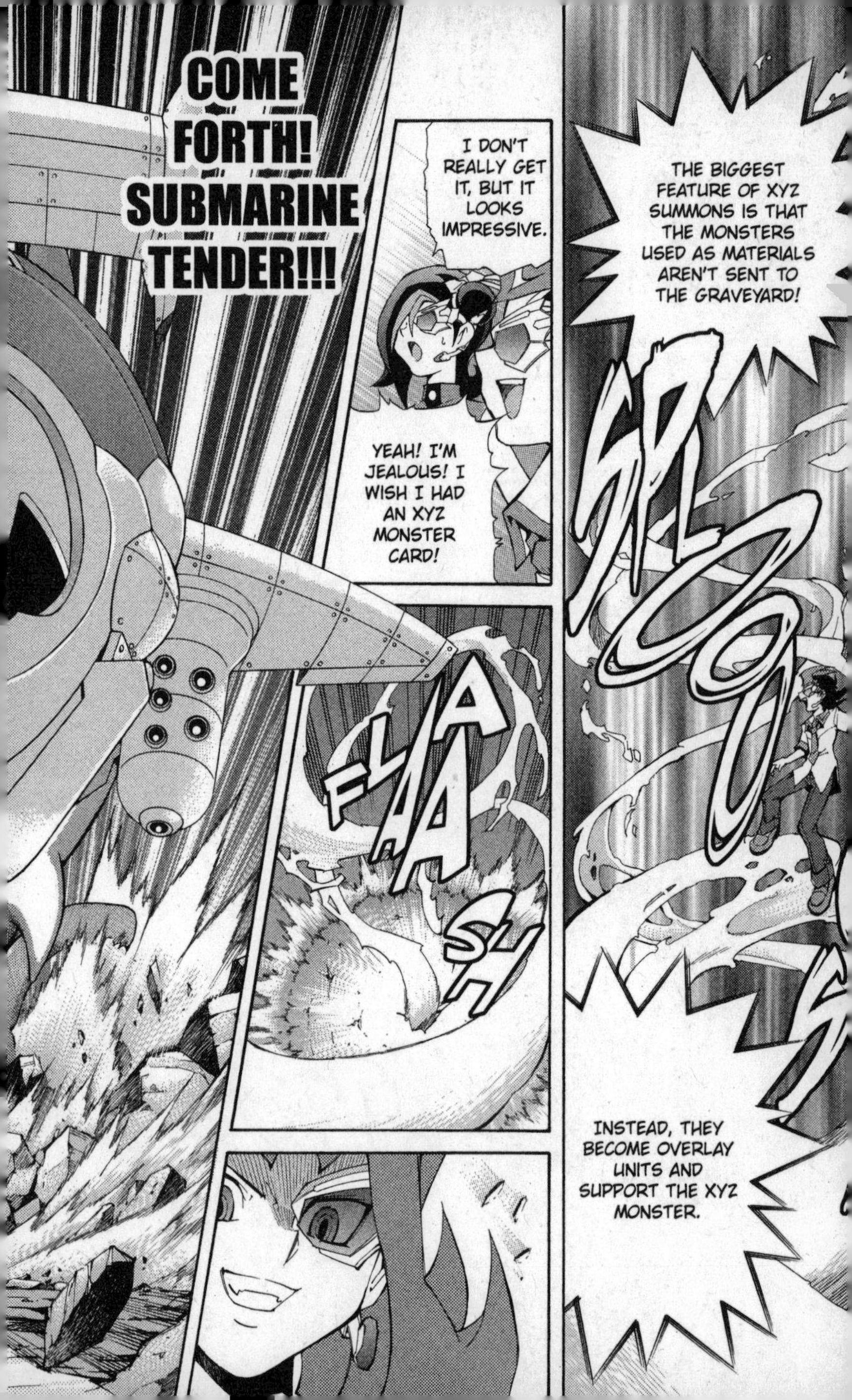
THE BIGGEST FEATURE OF XYZ SUMMONS IS THAT THE MONSTERS USED AS MATERIALS AREN'T SENT TO THE GRAVEYARD!
SPLOOSH
INSTEAD, THEY BECOME OVERLAY UNITS AND SUPPORT THE XYZ MONSTER.
I DON'T REALLY GET IT, BUT IT LOOKS IMPRESSIVE.
YEAH! I'M JEALOUS! I WISH I HAD AN XYZ MONSTER CARD!
FLAAASH
COME FORTH! SUBMARINE TENDER!!!

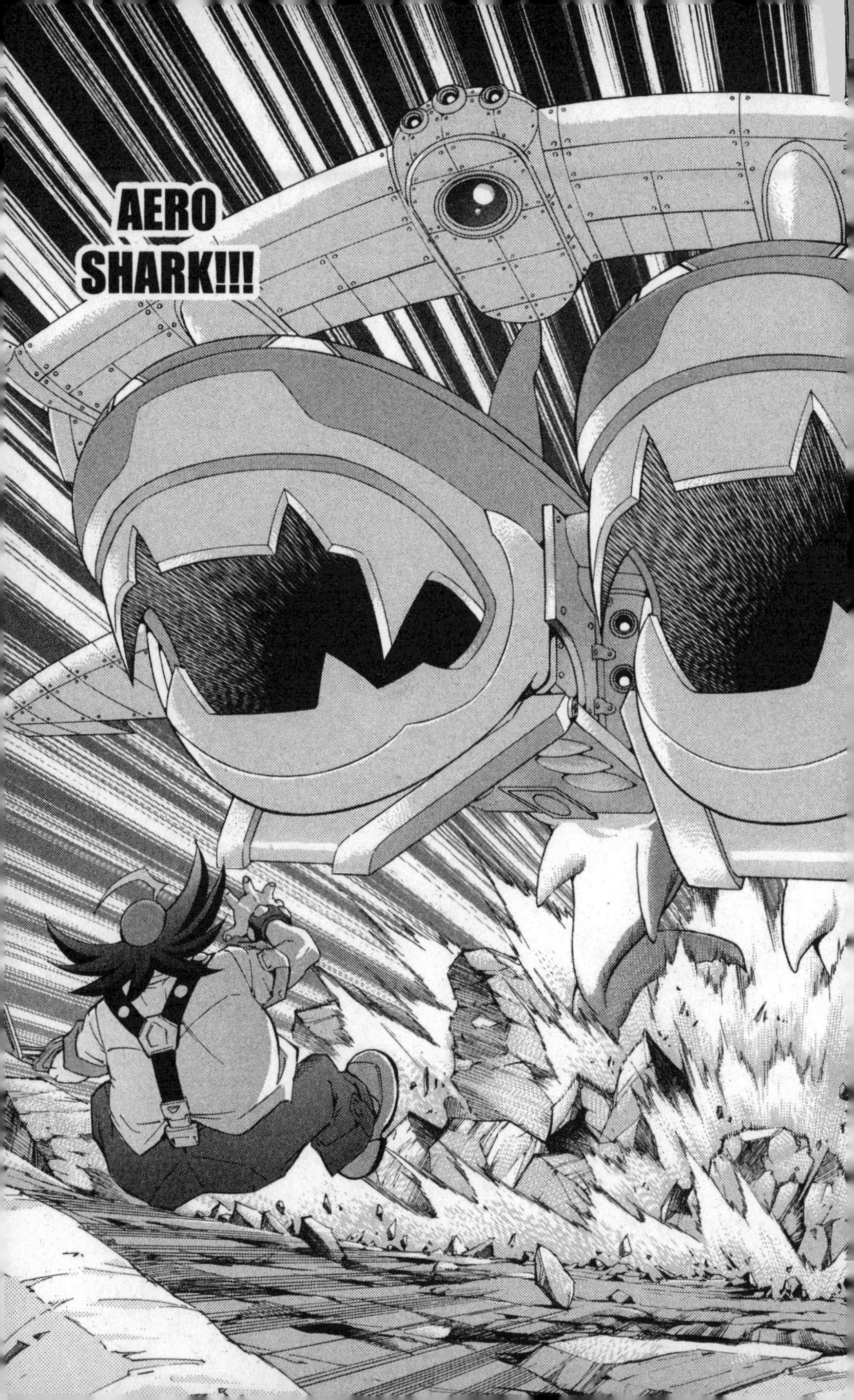
AERO
SHARK!!!

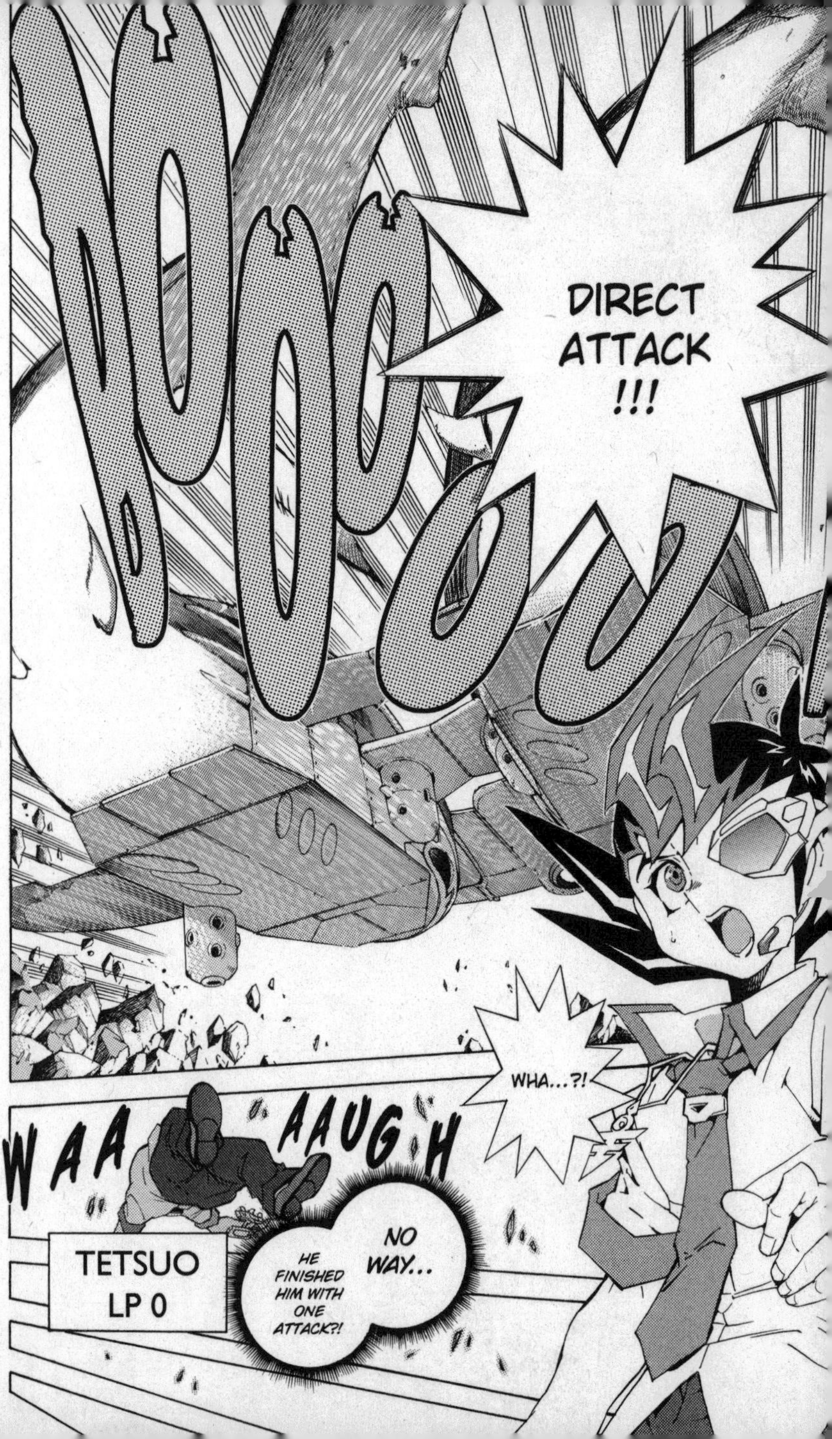
DIRECT ATTACK!!!
WHA...?!
WAAAAUGH
NO WAY...
HE FINISHED HIM WITH ONE ATTACK?!
TETSUO LP 0

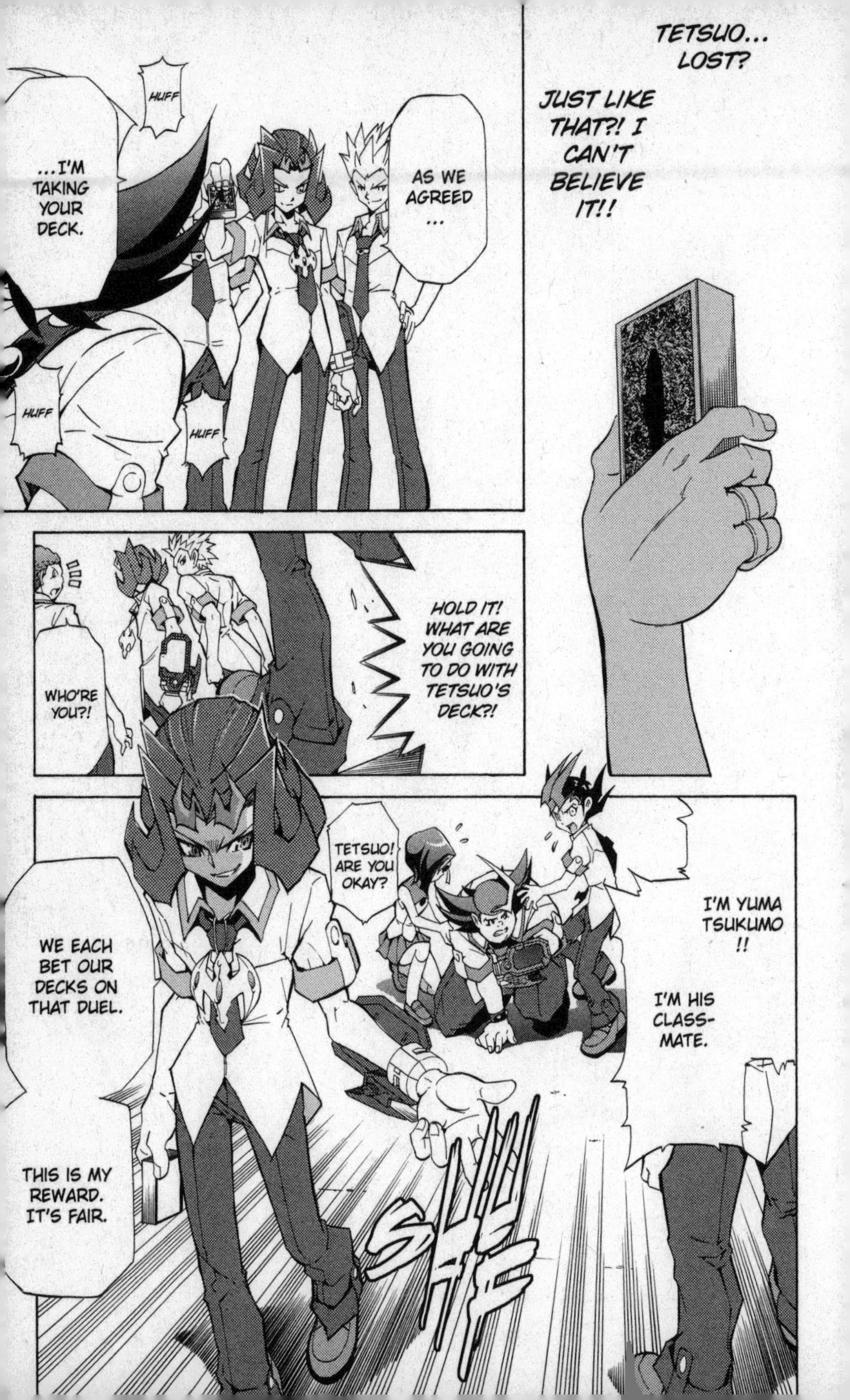
TETSUO... LOST?
JUST LIKE THAT?! I CAN'T BELIEVE IT!!
AS WE AGREED ...
HUFF
...I'M TAKING YOUR DECK.
HUFF
HUFF
HOLD IT! WHAT ARE YOU GOING TO DO WITH TETSUO'S DECK?!
WHO'RE YOU?!
I'M YUMA TSUKUMO !!
I'M HIS CLASSMATE.
TETSUO! ARE YOU OKAY?
WE EACH BET OUR DECKS ON THAT DUEL.
THIS IS MY REWARD. IT'S FAIR.

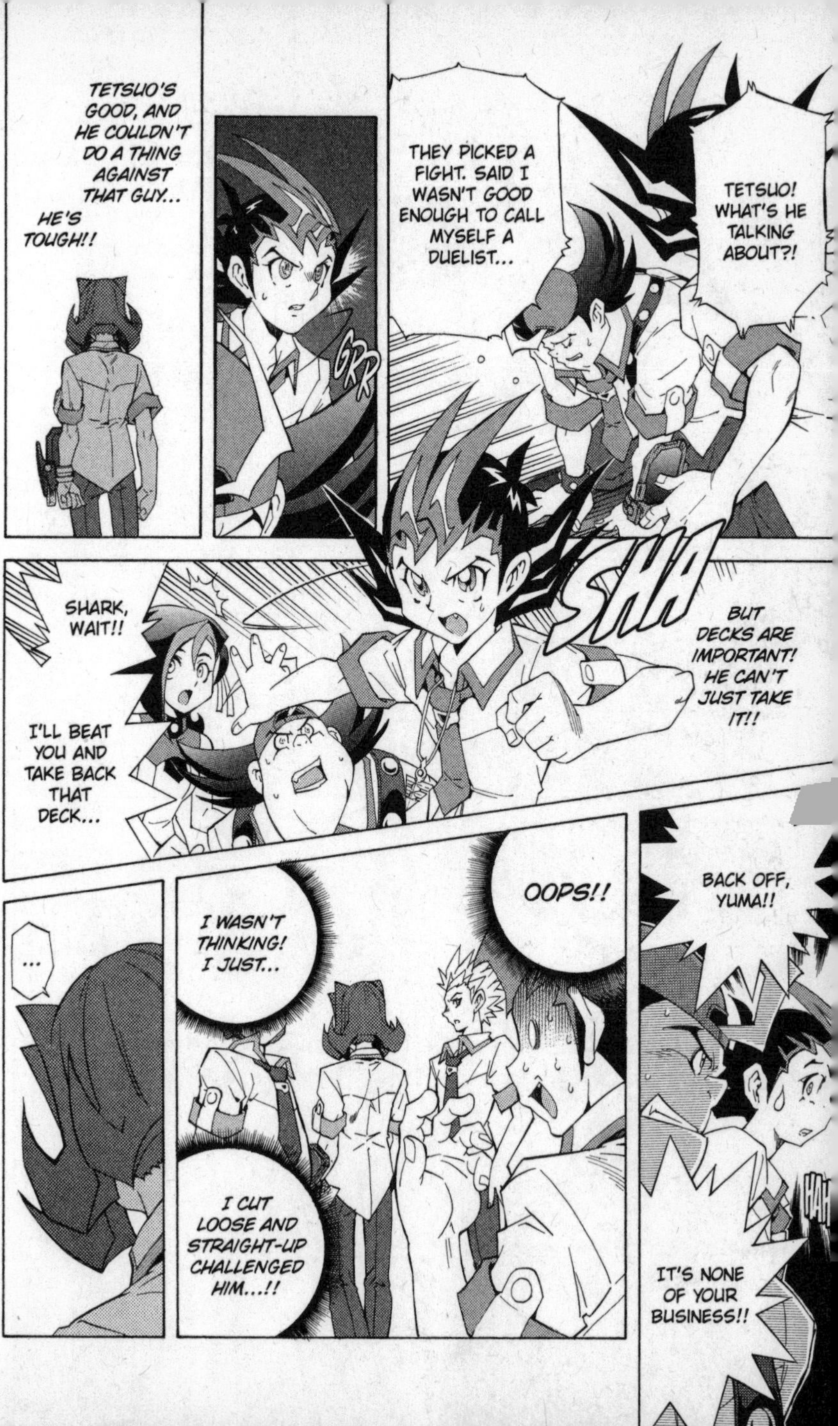
TETSUO! WHAT'S HE TALKING ABOUT?!
THEY PICKED A FIGHT. SAID I WASN'T GOOD ENOUGH TO CALL MYSELF A DUELIST...
GRR
TETSUO'S GOOD, AND HE COULDN'T DO A THING AGAINST THAT GUY...
HE'S TOUGH!!
SHA
BUT DECKS ARE IMPORTANT! HE CAN'T JUST TAKE IT!!
SHARK, WAIT!!
I'LL BEAT YOU AND TAKE BACK THAT DECK...
BACK OFF, YUMA!!
HAH
IT'S NONE OF YOUR BUSINESS!!
OOPS!!
I WASN'T THINKING! I JUST...
I CUT LOOSE AND STRAIGHT-UP CHALLENGED HIM...!!
...

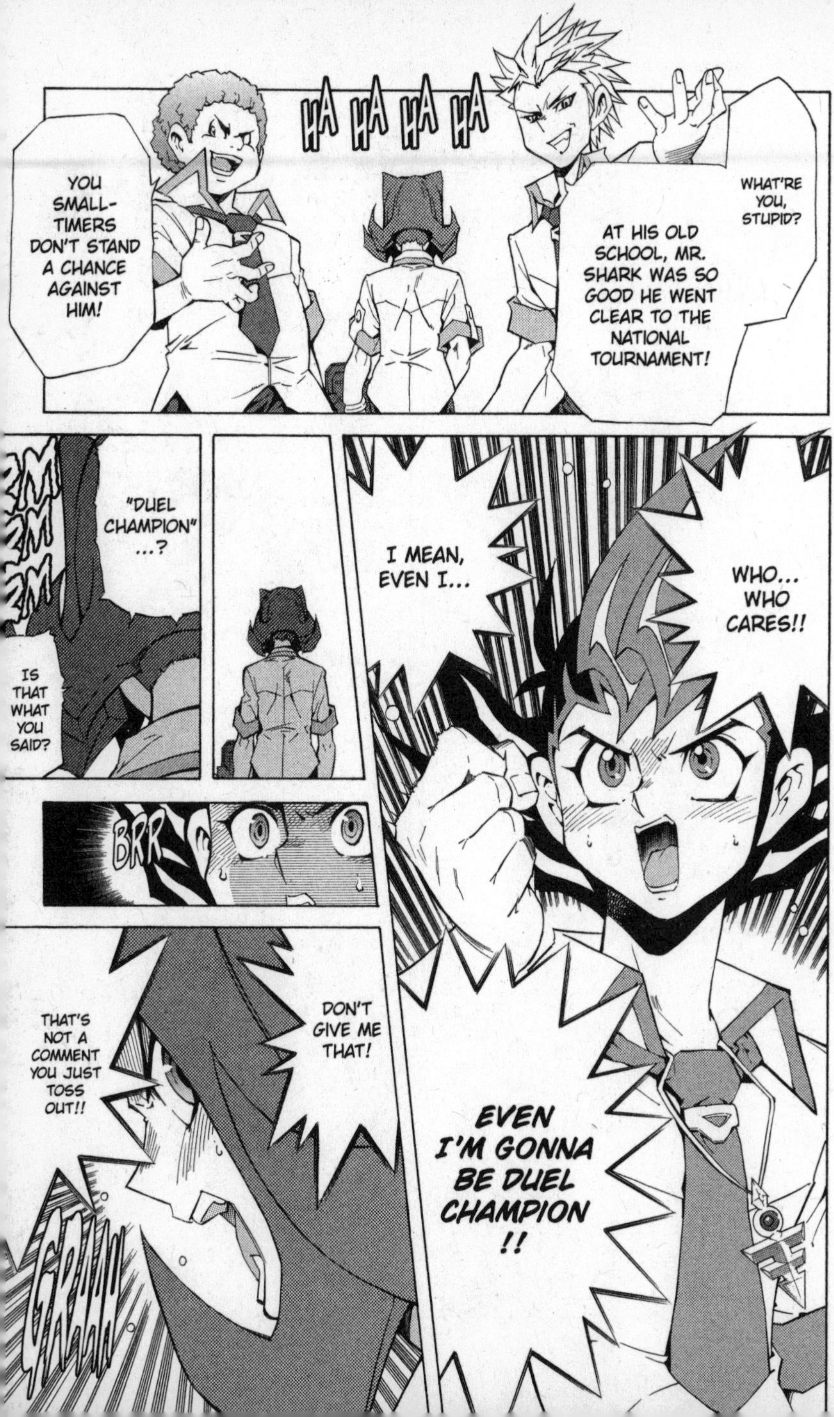
WHAT'RE YOU, STUPID?
HA HA HA HA
AT HIS OLD SCHOOL, MR. SHARK WAS SO GOOD HE WENT CLEAR TO THE NATIONAL TOURNAMENT!
YOU SMALL-TIMERS DON'T STAND A CHANCE AGAINST HIM!
WHO... WHO CARES!!
I MEAN, EVEN I...
EVEN I'M GONNA BE DUEL CHAMPION!!
"DUEL CHAMPION"...?
IS THAT WHAT YOU SAID?
BRR
DON'T GIVE ME THAT!
THAT'S NOT A COMMENT YOU JUST TOSS OUT!!

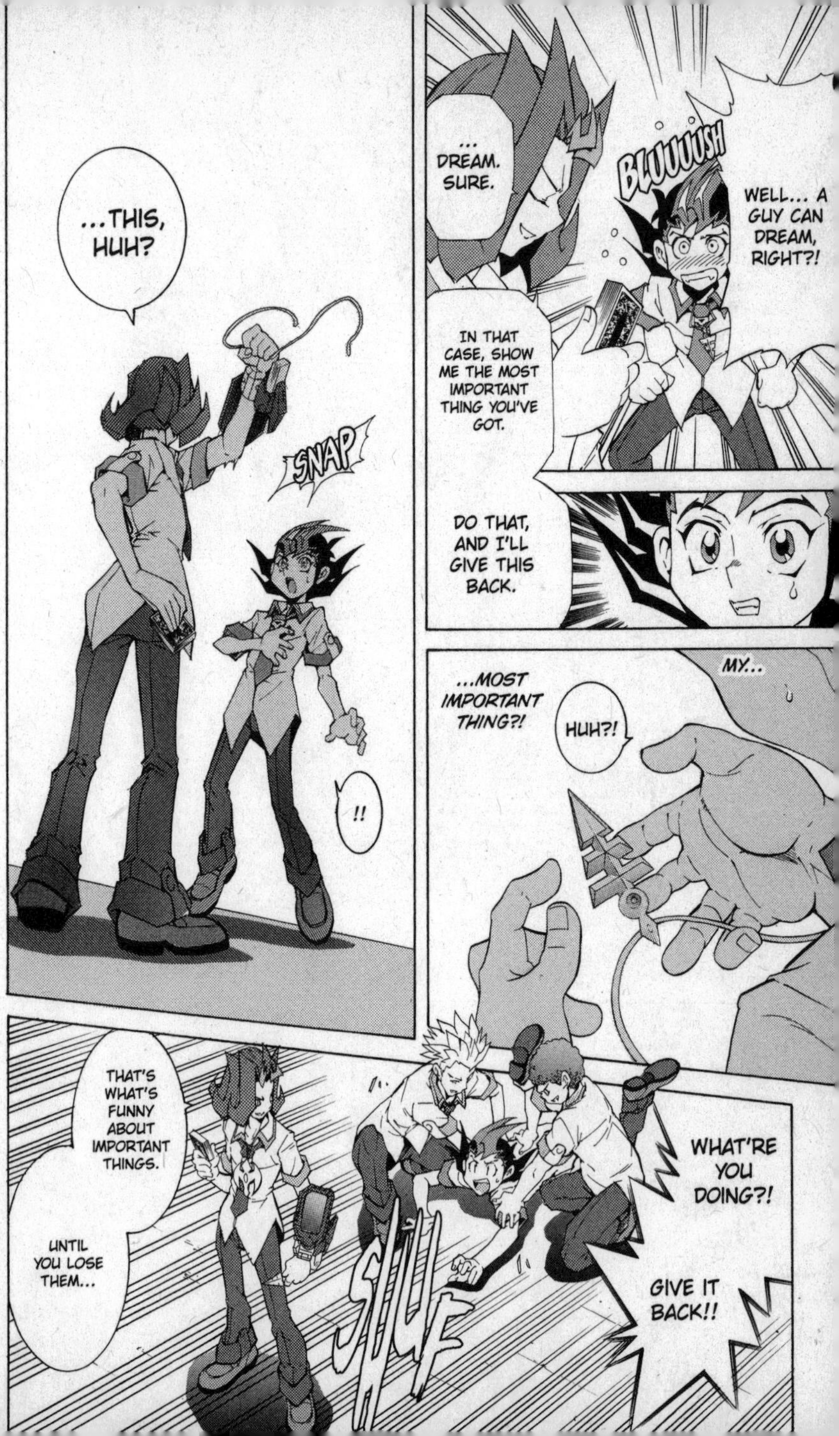

WELL... A GUY CAN DREAM, RIGHT?!
BLUUUUSH
... DREAM. SURE.
IN THAT CASE, SHOW ME THE MOST IMPORTANT THING YOU'VE GOT.
DO THAT, AND I'LL GIVE THIS BACK.
MY...
HUH?!
...MOST IMPORTANT THING?!
...THIS, HUH?
SNAP
!!
WHAT'RE YOU DOING?!
GIVE IT BACK!!
SHUF
THAT'S WHAT'S FUNNY ABOUT IMPORTANT THINGS.
UNTIL YOU LOSE THEM...

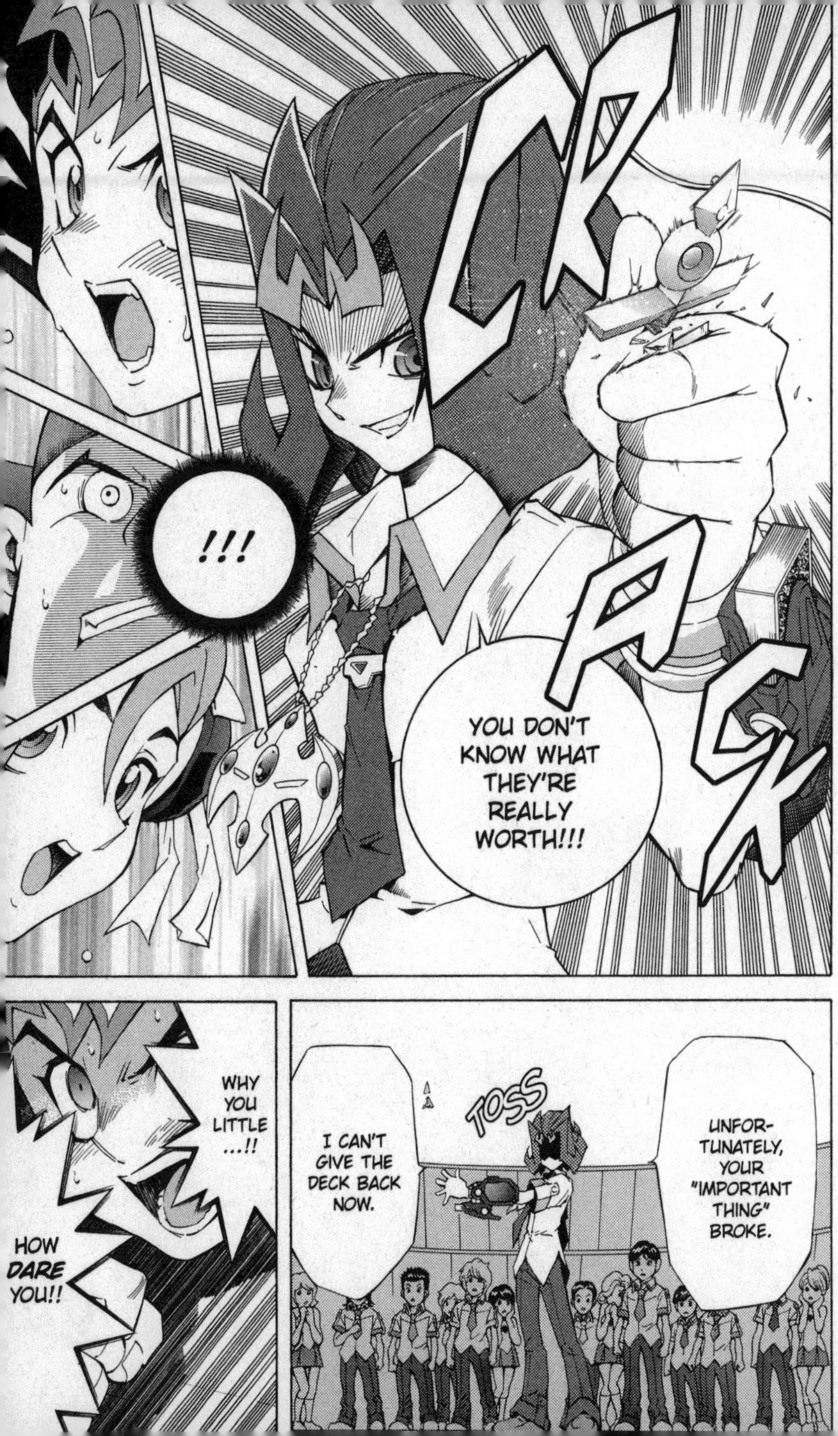
CRACK
YOU DON'T KNOW WHAT THEY'RE REALLY WORTH!!!
!!!
UNFOR-TUNATELY, YOUR "IMPORTANT THING" BROKE.
TOSS
I CAN'T GIVE THE DECK BACK NOW.
WHY YOU LITTLE ...!!
HOW DARE YOU!!

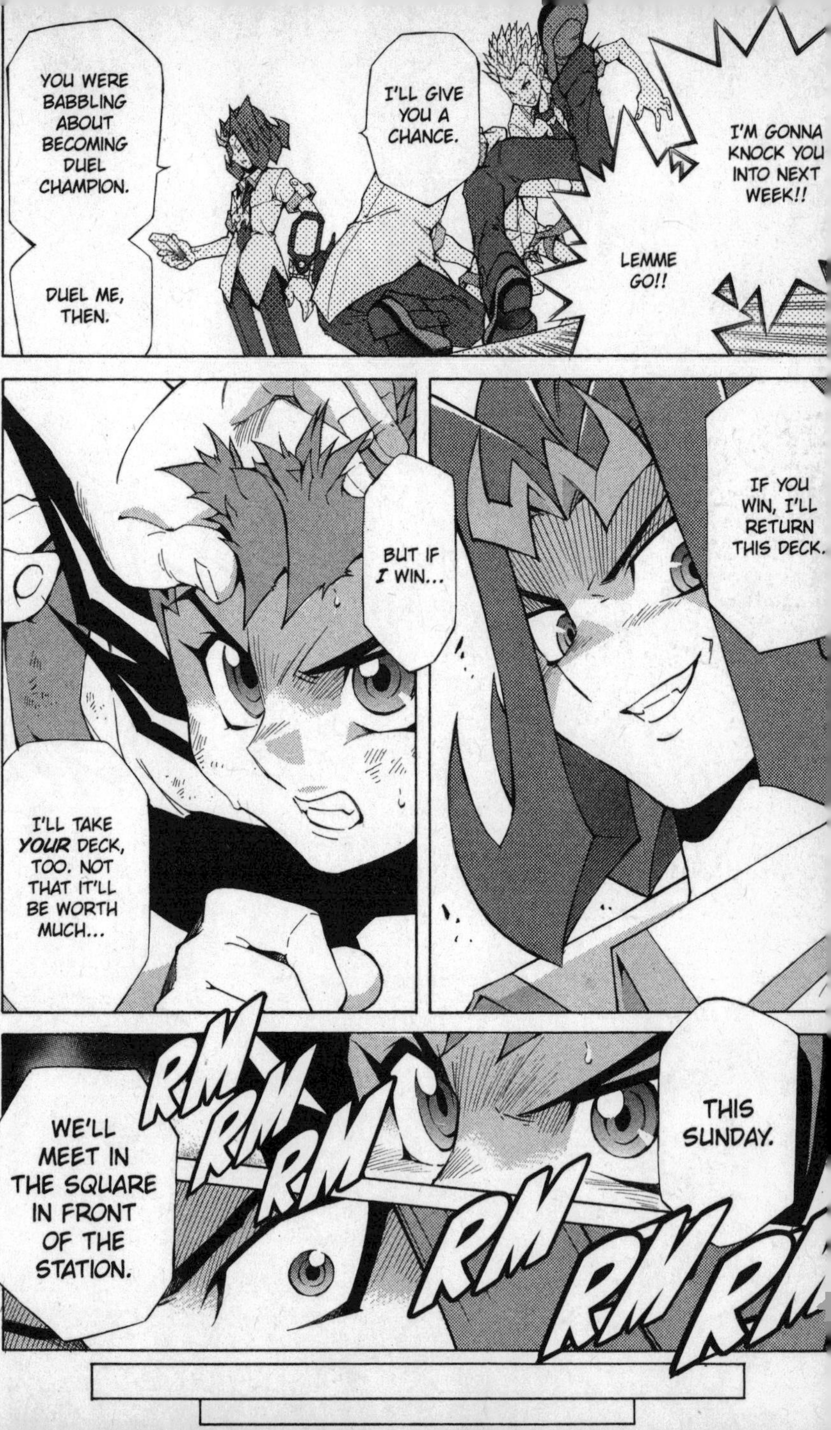
I'M GONNA KNOCK YOU INTO NEXT WEEK!!
LEMME GO!!
I'LL GIVE YOU A CHANCE.
YOU WERE BABBLING ABOUT BECOMING DUEL CHAMPION.
DUEL ME, THEN.
IF YOU WIN, I'LL RETURN THIS DECK.
BUT IF *I* WIN...
I'LL TAKE ***YOUR*** DECK, TOO. NOT THAT IT'LL BE WORTH MUCH...
THIS SUNDAY.
RM RM RM
RM RM RM
WE'LL MEET IN THE SQUARE IN FRONT OF THE STATION.

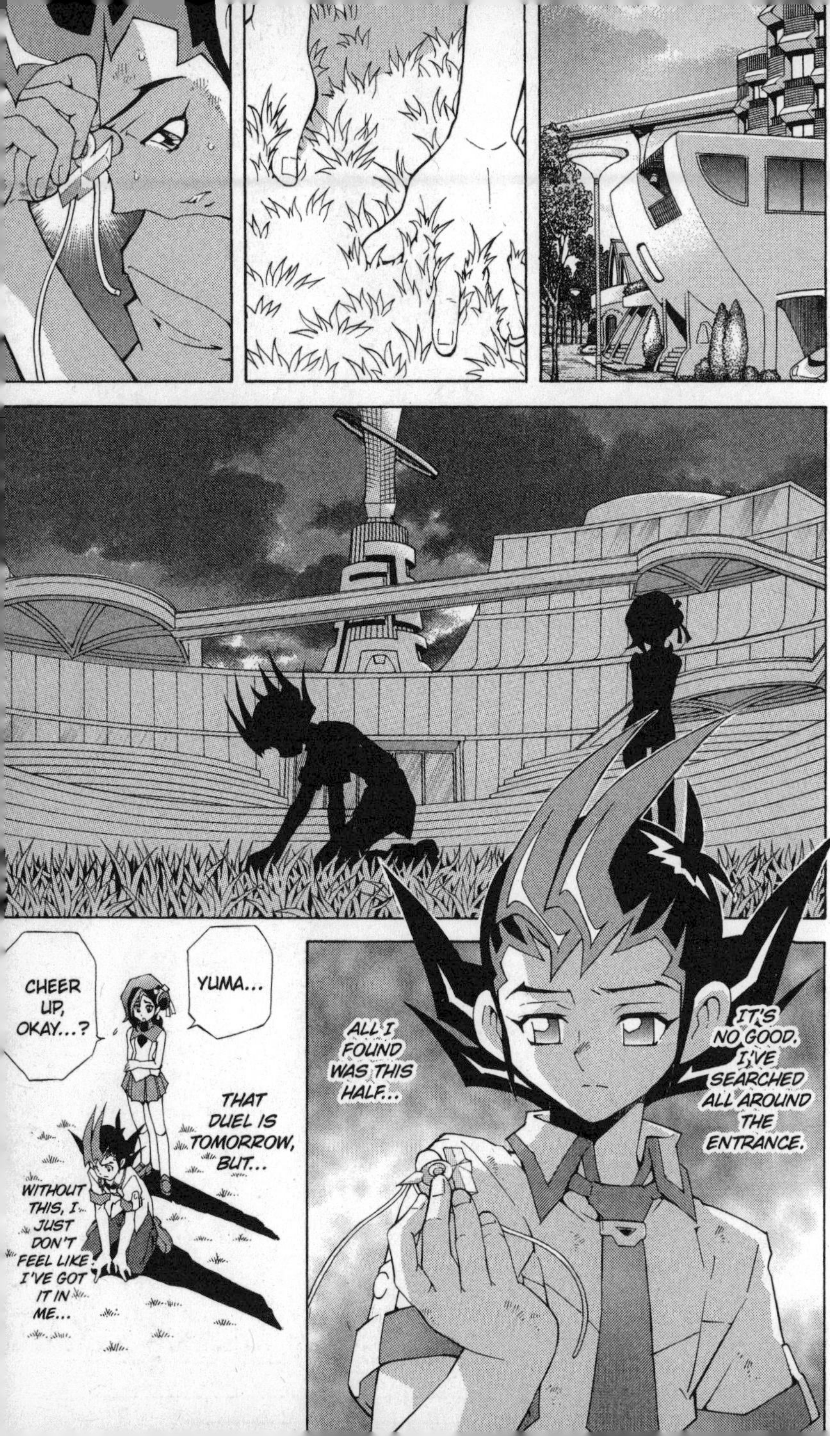
IT'S NO GOOD. I'VE SEARCHED ALL AROUND THE ENTRANCE.
ALL I FOUND WAS THIS HALF...
YUMA...
CHEER UP, OKAY...?
THAT DUEL IS TOMORROW, BUT...
WITHOUT THIS, I JUST DON'T FEEL LIKE I'VE GOT IT IN ME...

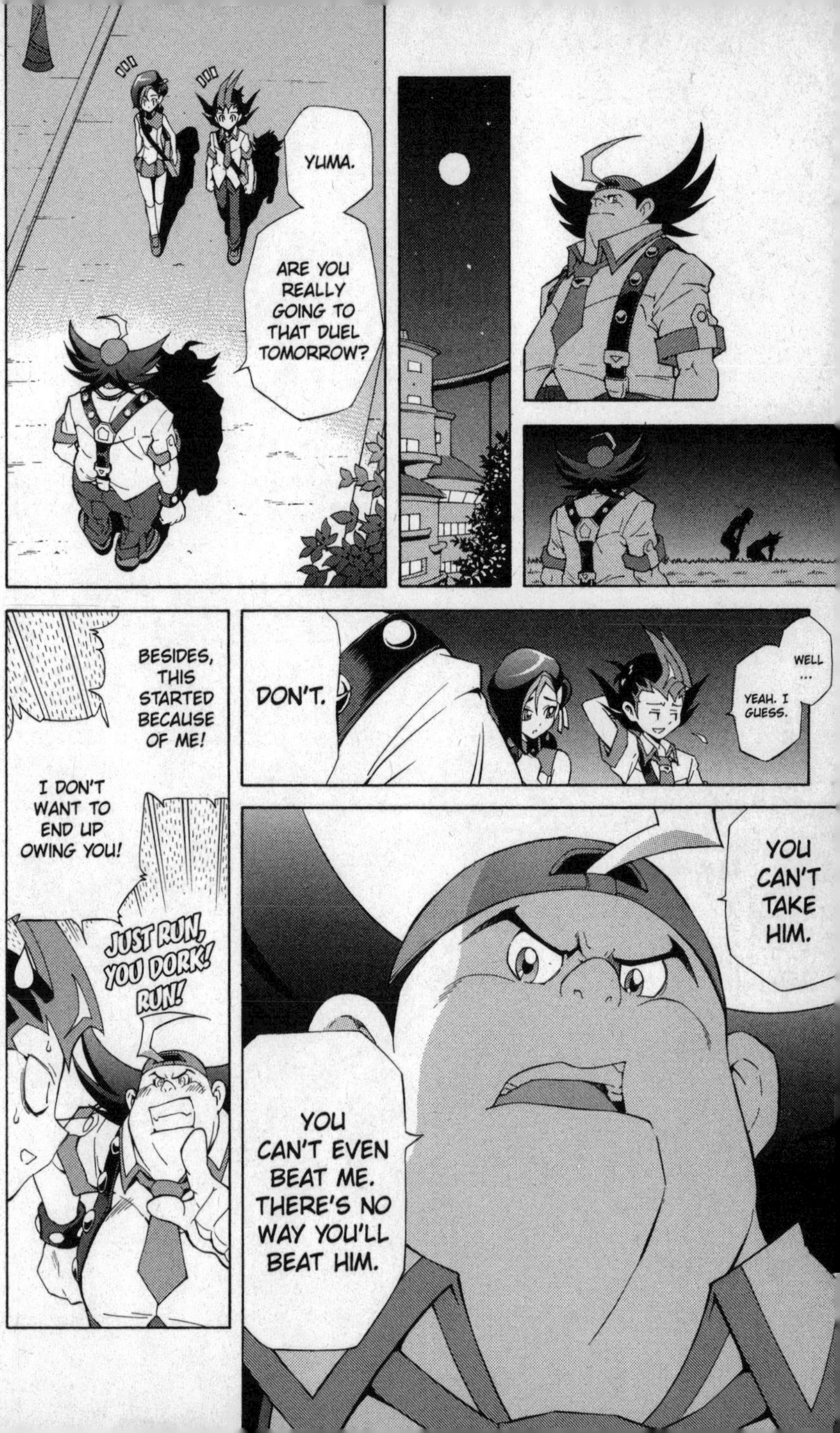
YUMA.
ARE YOU REALLY GOING TO THAT DUEL TOMORROW?
WELL... YEAH. I GUESS.
DON'T.
YOU CAN'T TAKE HIM.
YOU CAN'T EVEN BEAT ME. THERE'S NO WAY YOU'LL BEAT HIM.
BESIDES, THIS STARTED BECAUSE OF ME!
I DON'T WANT TO END UP OWING YOU!
JUST RUN, YOU DORK! RUN!

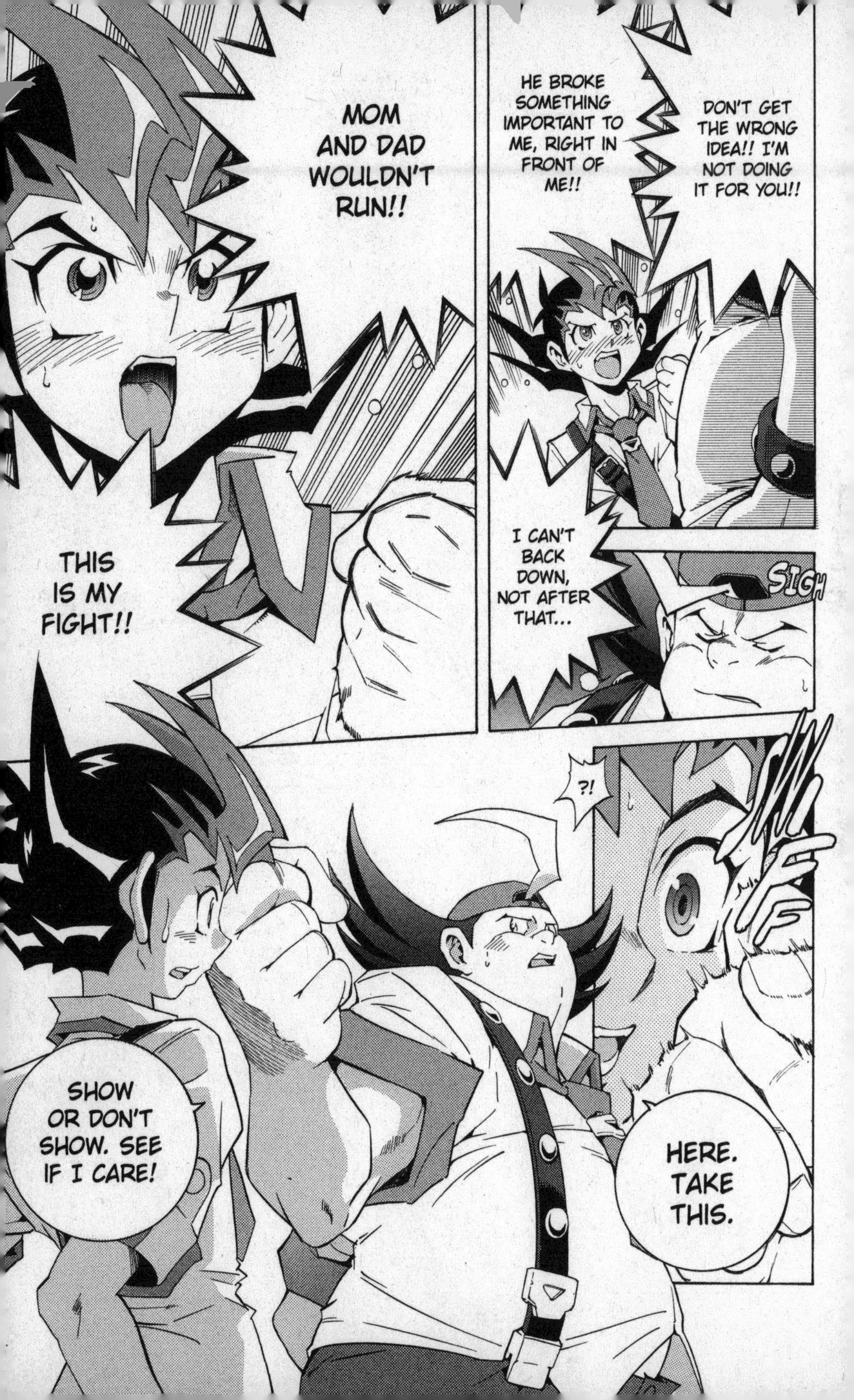
DON'T GET THE WRONG IDEA!! I'M NOT DOING IT FOR YOU!!
HE BROKE SOMETHING IMPORTANT TO ME, RIGHT IN FRONT OF ME!!
SIGH
I CAN'T BACK DOWN, NOT AFTER THAT...
MOM AND DAD WOULDN'T RUN!!
THIS IS MY FIGHT!!
?!
HERE. TAKE THIS.
SHOW OR DON'T SHOW. SEE IF I CARE!

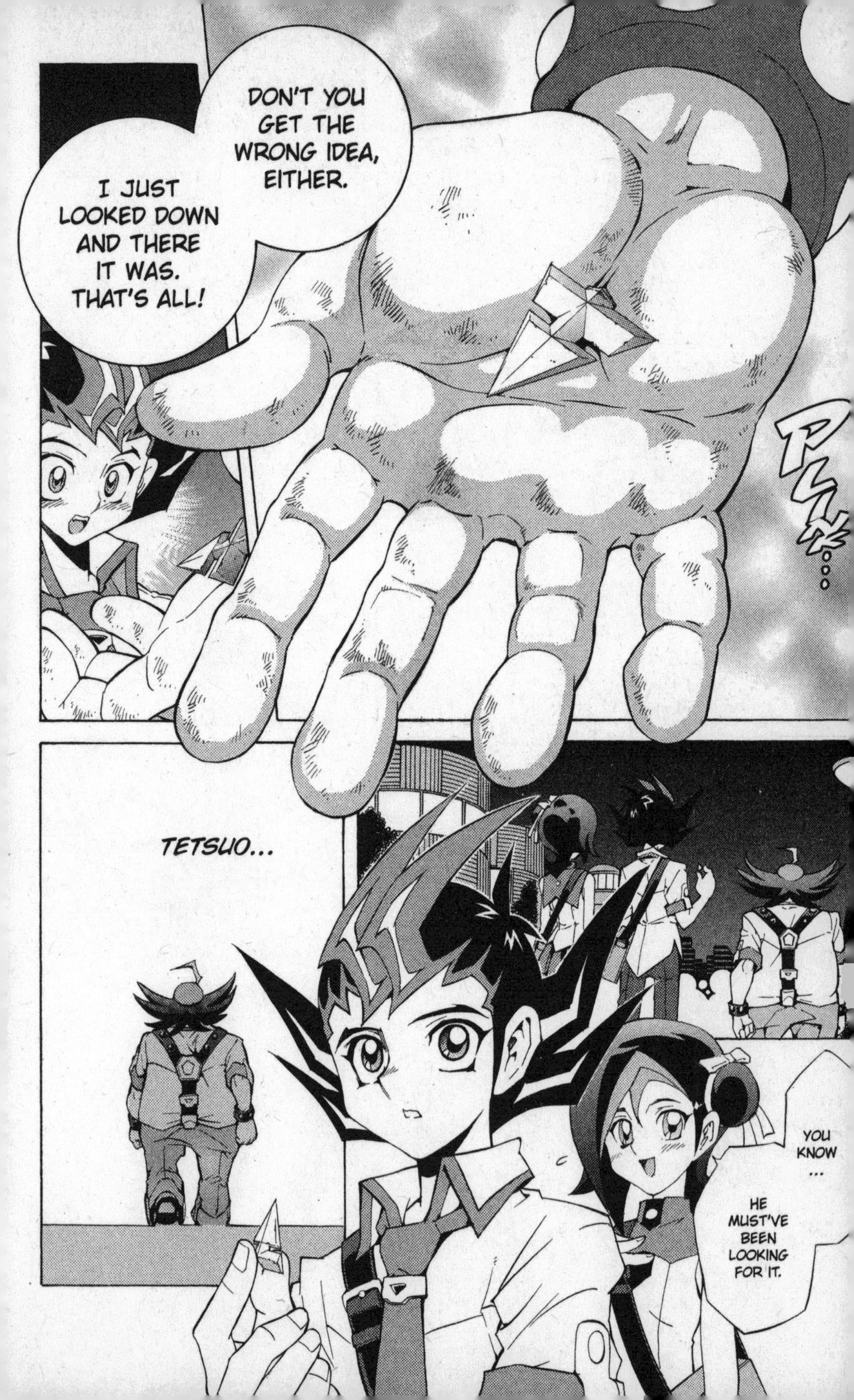
DON'T YOU GET THE WRONG IDEA, EITHER.
I JUST LOOKED DOWN AND THERE IT WAS. THAT'S ALL!
PLUK...
YOU KNOW...
HE MUST'VE BEEN LOOKING FOR IT.
TETSUO...

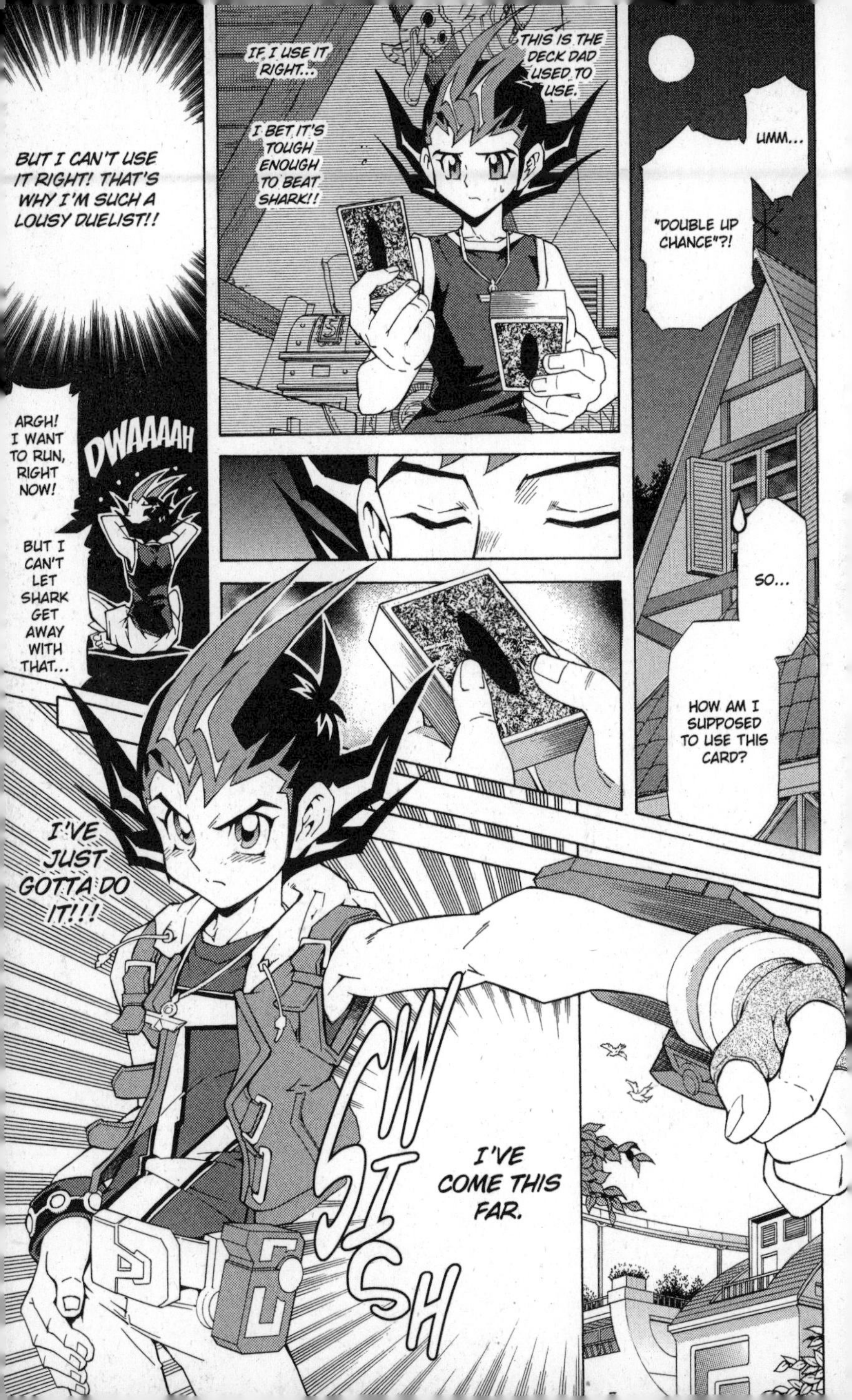
UMM...
"DOUBLE UP CHANCE"?!
SO...
HOW AM I SUPPOSED TO USE THIS CARD?
THIS IS THE DECK DAD USED TO USE.
IF I USE IT RIGHT...
I BET IT'S TOUGH ENOUGH TO BEAT SHARK!!
BUT I CAN'T USE IT RIGHT! THAT'S WHY I'M SUCH A LOUSY DUELIST!!
ARGH! I WANT TO RUN, RIGHT NOW!
DWAAAAH
BUT I CAN'T LET SHARK GET AWAY WITH THAT...
I'VE COME THIS FAR.
SWISH
I'VE JUST GOTTA DO IT!!!

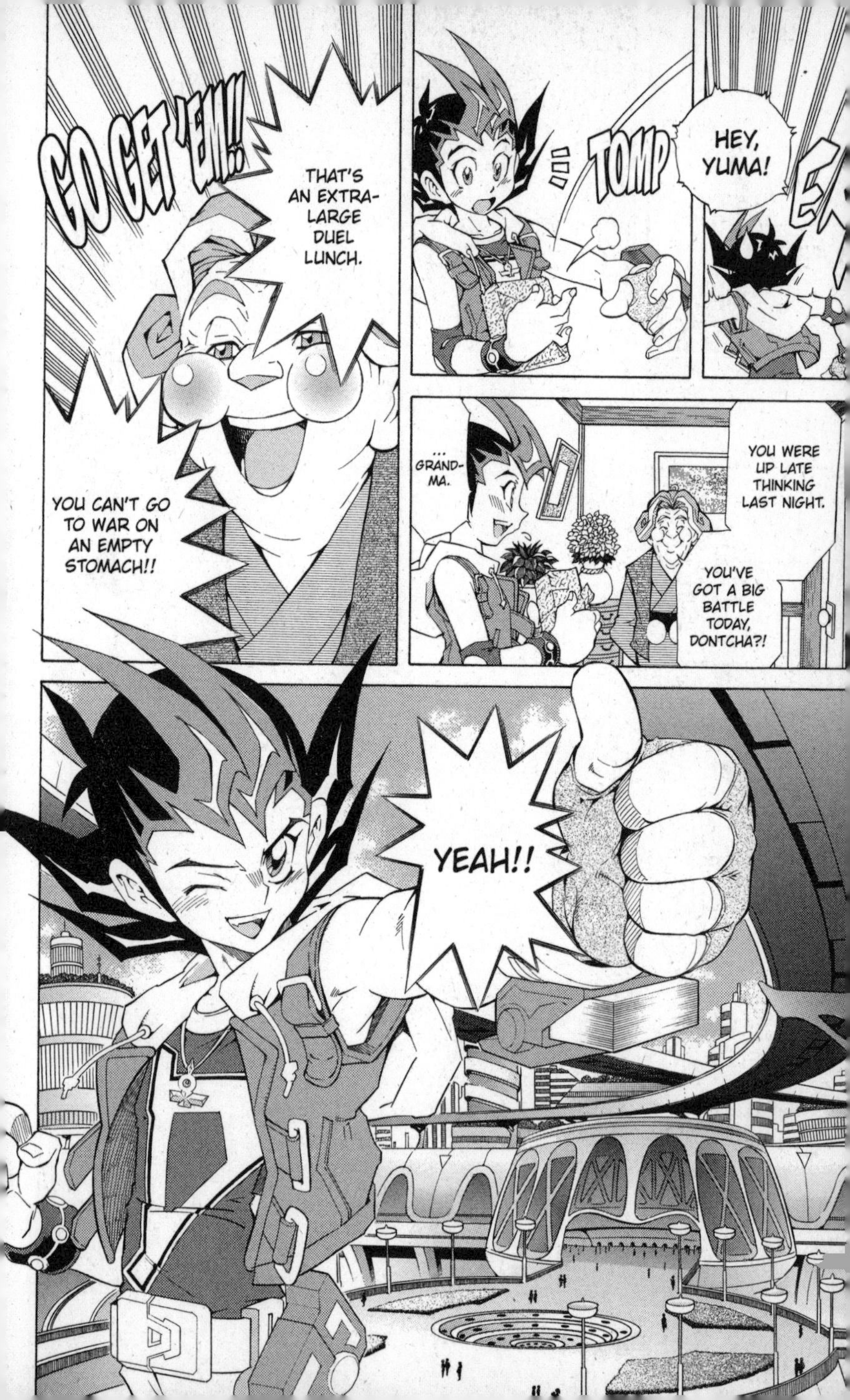
HEY, YUMA!
TOMP
!!
YOU WERE UP LATE THINKING LAST NIGHT.
YOU'VE GOT A BIG BATTLE TODAY, DONTCHA?!
... GRAND-MA.
GO GET 'EM!!
THAT'S AN EXTRA-LARGE DUEL LUNCH.
YOU CAN'T GO TO WAR ON AN EMPTY STOMACH!!
YEAH!!

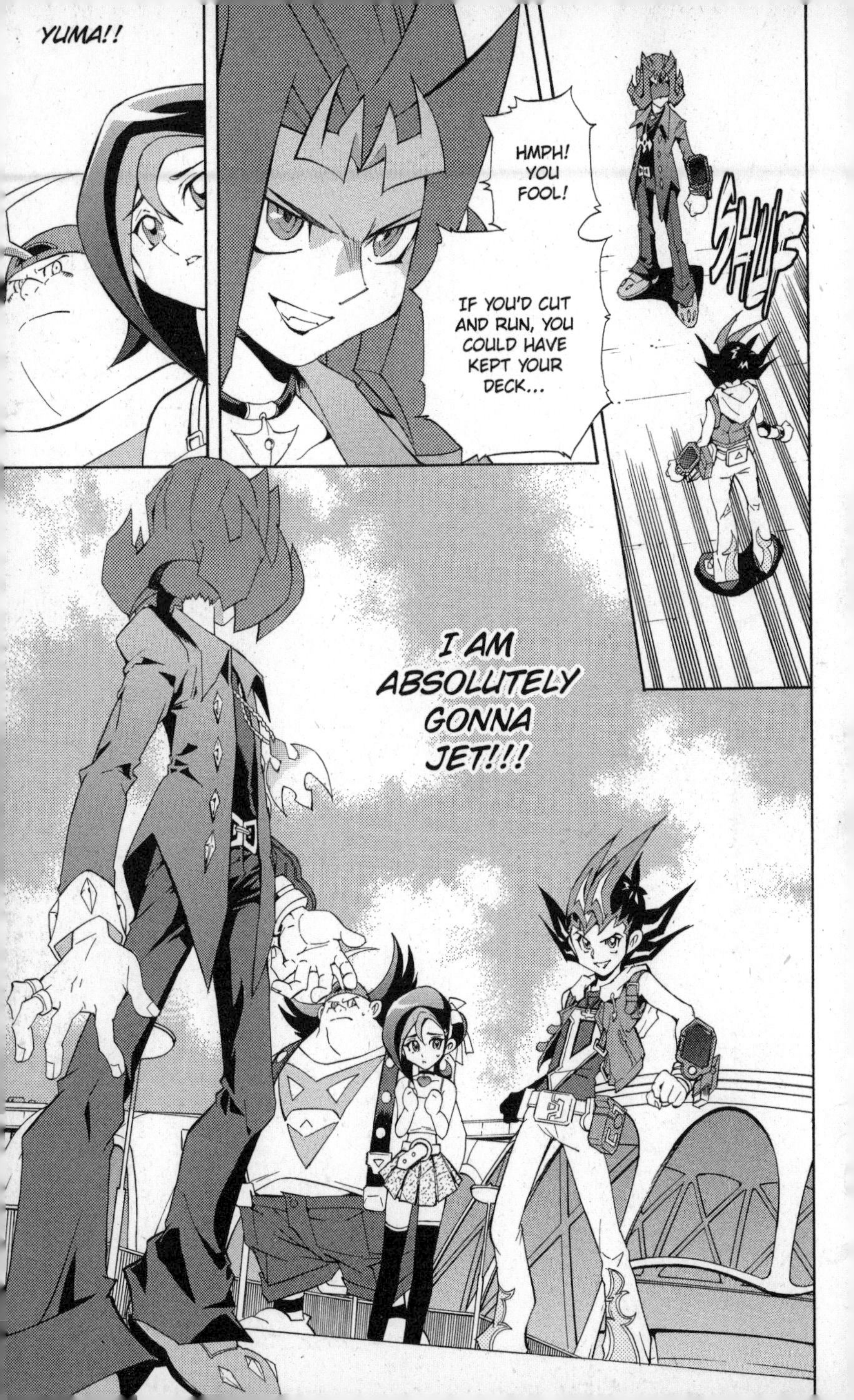
SHUF
HMPH! YOU FOOL!
IF YOU'D CUT AND RUN, YOU COULD HAVE KEPT YOUR DECK...
YUMA!!
I AM ABSOLUTELY GONNA JET!!!

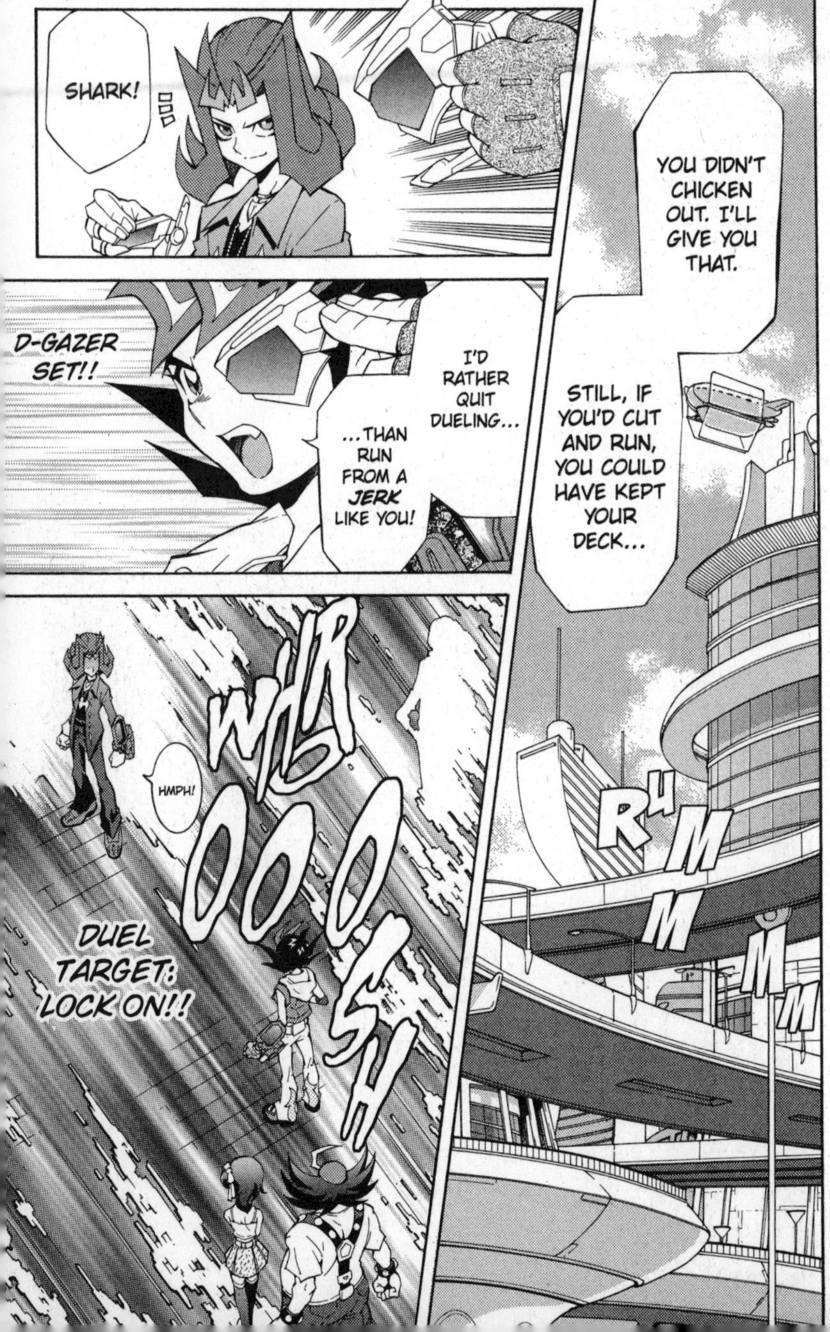
YOU DIDN'T CHICKEN OUT. I'LL GIVE YOU THAT.
STILL, IF YOU'D CUT AND RUN, YOU COULD HAVE KEPT YOUR DECK...
RUMMMMM
SHARK!
D-GAZER SET!!
I'D RATHER QUIT DUELING...
...THAN RUN FROM A JERK LIKE YOU!
WHOOOSH
HMPH!
DUEL TARGET: LOCK ON!!

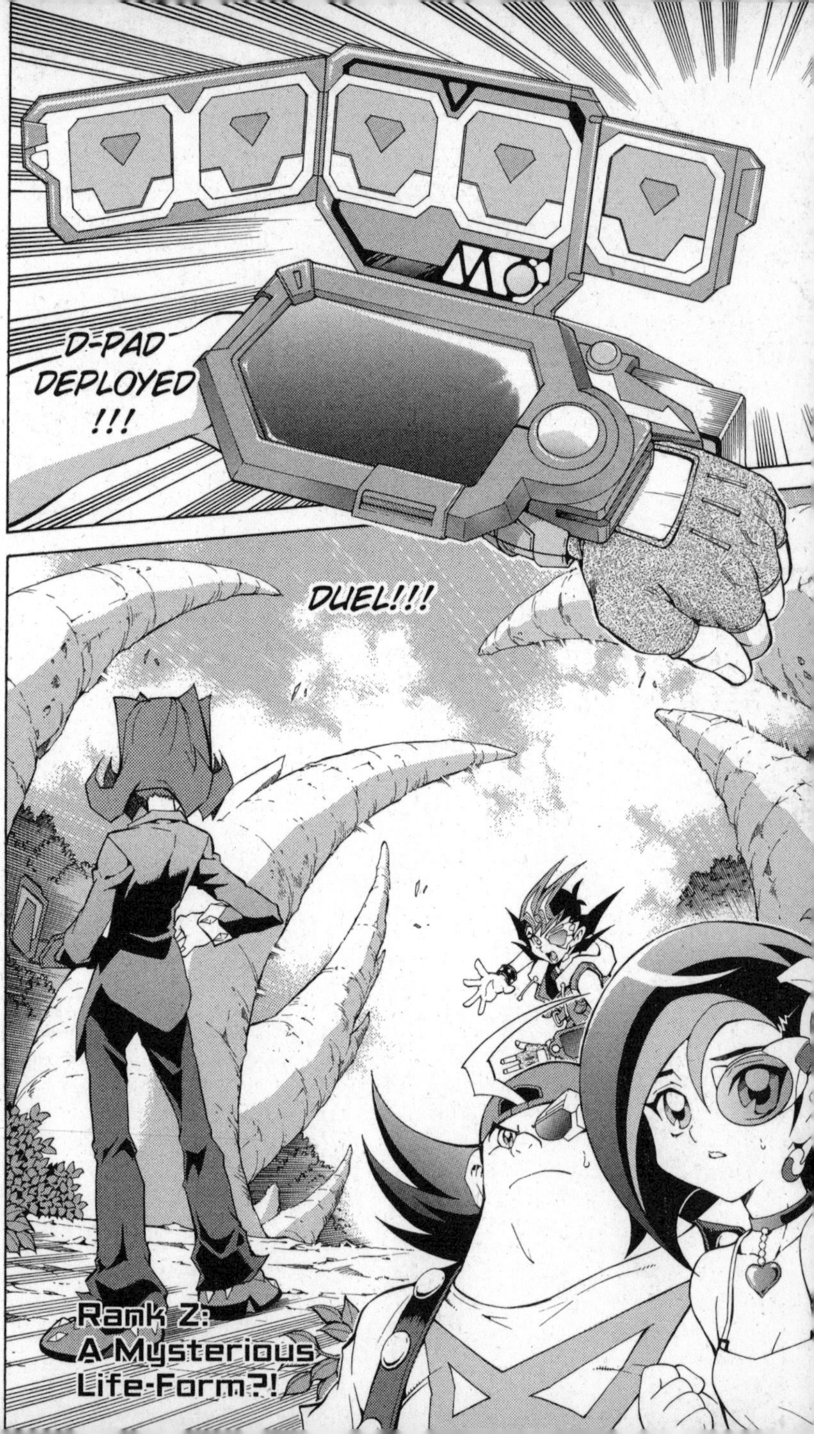
D-PAD DEPLOYED !!!
DUEL!!!
Rank 2: A Mysterious Life-Form?!

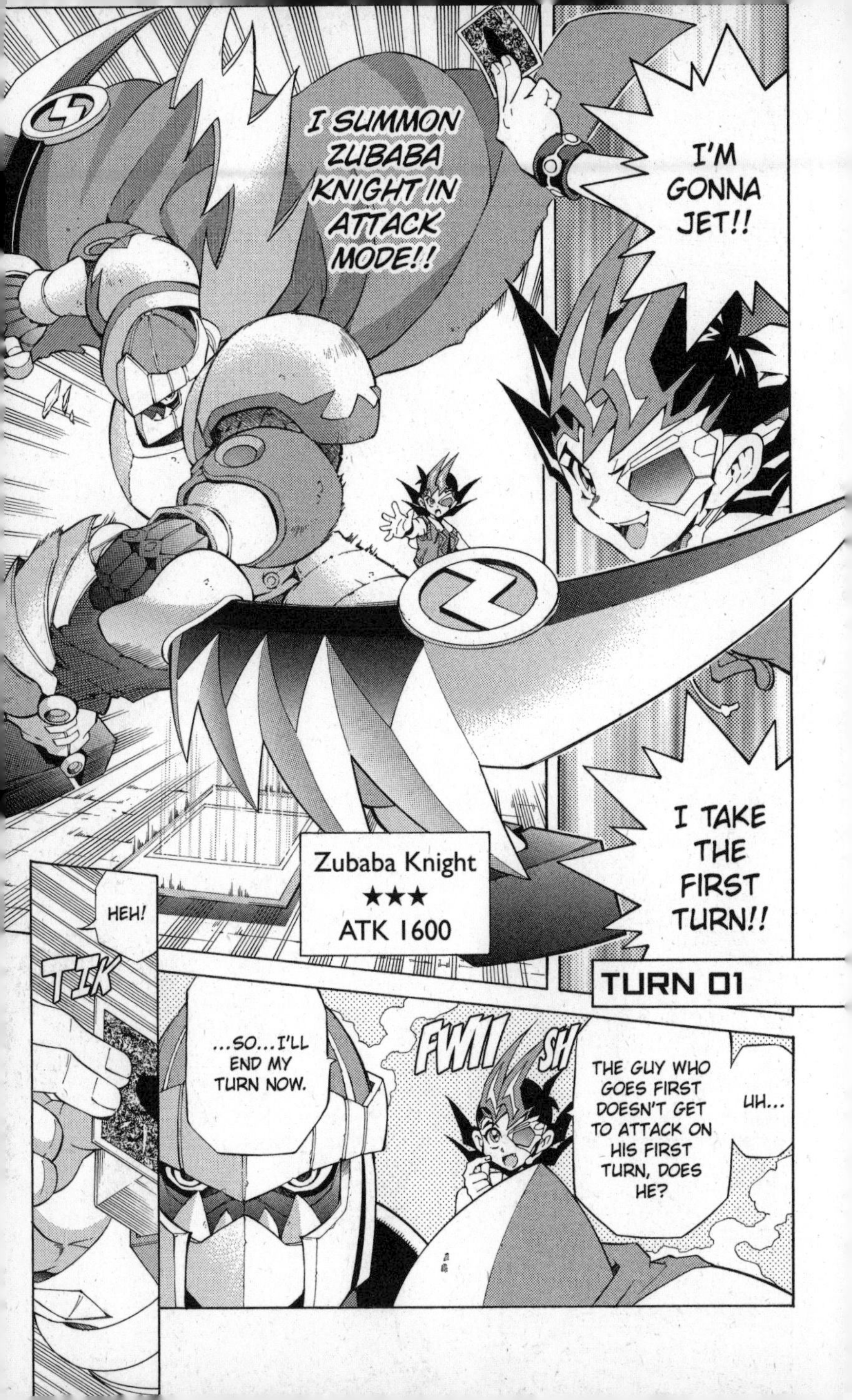

I'M GONNA JET!!
I TAKE THE FIRST TURN!!
TURN 01
I SUMMON ZUBABA KNIGHT IN ATTACK MODE!!
Zubaba Knight
★★★
ATK 1600
UH...
THE GUY WHO GOES FIRST DOESN'T GET TO ATTACK ON HIS FIRST TURN, DOES HE?
FWISH
...SO...I'LL END MY TURN NOW.
HEH!
TIK

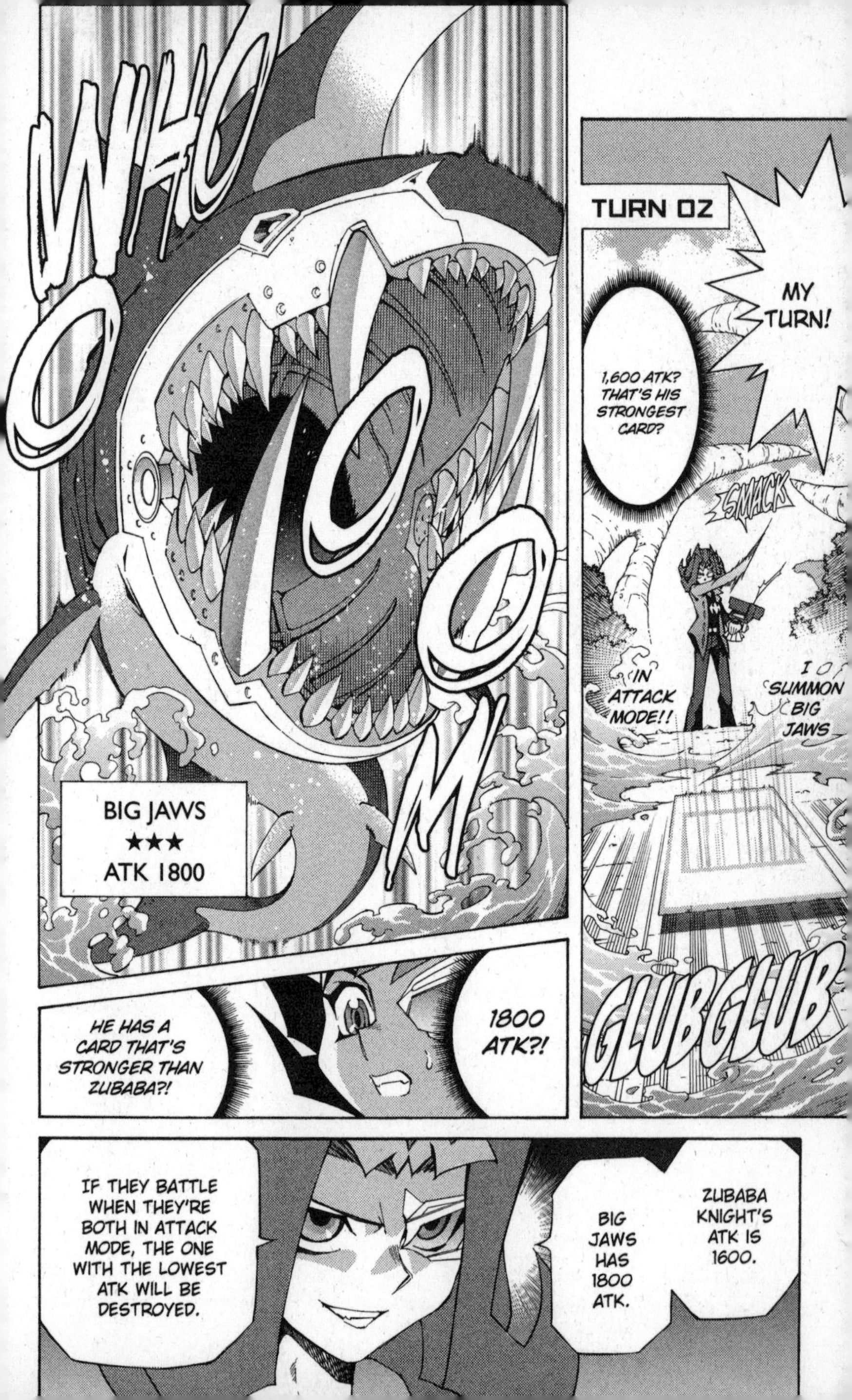

TURN 02
MY TURN!
1,600 ATK? THAT'S HIS STRONGEST CARD?
SMACK
I SUMMON BIG JAWS
IN ATTACK MODE!!
GLUBGLUB
WHOOOOOM
BIG JAWS ★★★ ATK 1800
1800 ATK?!
HE HAS A CARD THAT'S STRONGER THAN ZUBABA?!
ZUBABA KNIGHT'S ATK IS 1600.
BIG JAWS HAS 1800 ATK.
IF THEY BATTLE WHEN THEY'RE BOTH IN ATTACK MODE, THE ONE WITH THE LOWEST ATK WILL BE DESTROYED.

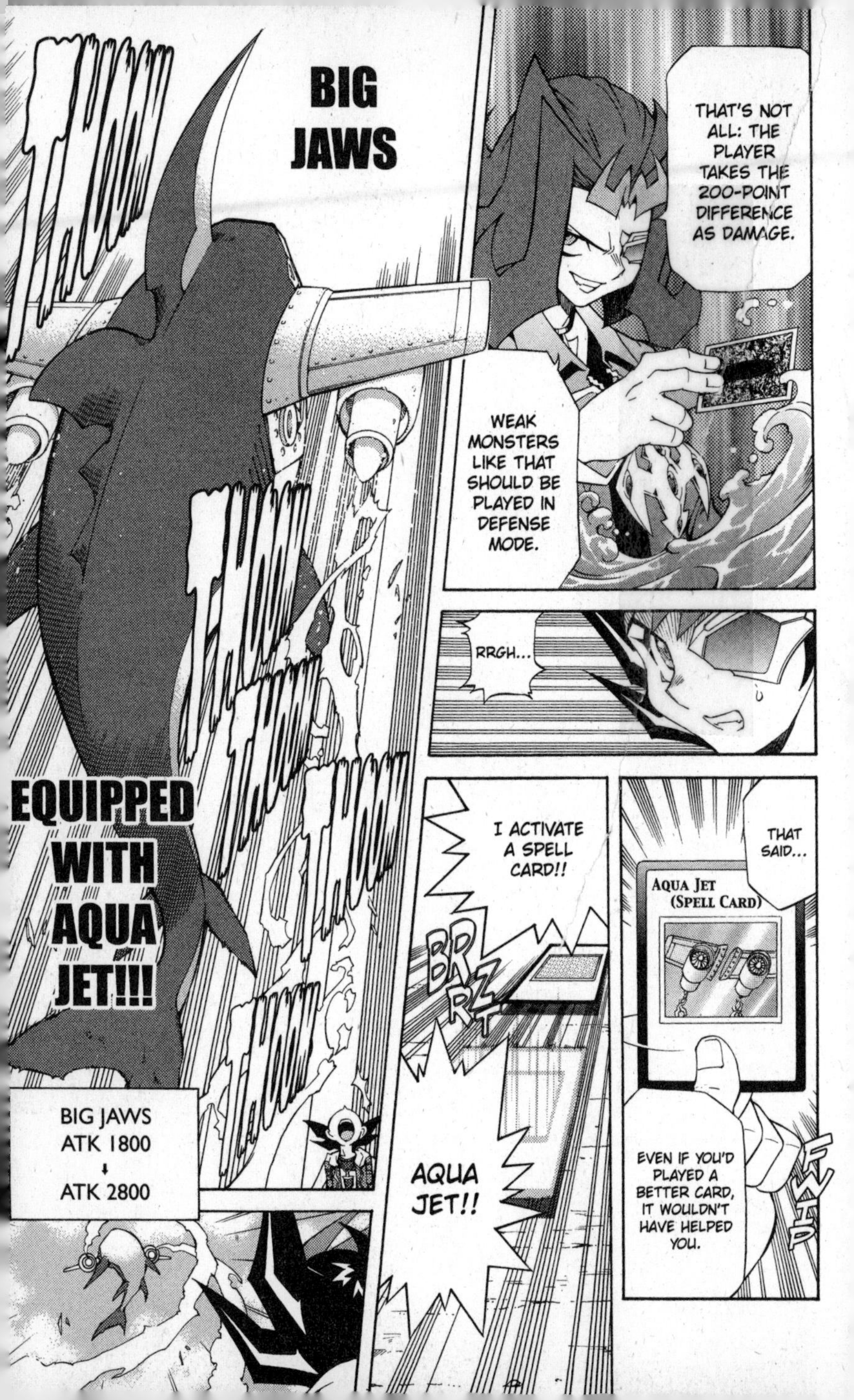
THAT'S NOT ALL: THE PLAYER TAKES THE 200-POINT DIFFERENCE AS DAMAGE.
WEAK MONSTERS LIKE THAT SHOULD BE PLAYED IN DEFENSE MODE.
RRGH...
THAT SAID...
AQUA JET (SPELL CARD)
EVEN IF YOU'D PLAYED A BETTER CARD, IT WOULDN'T HAVE HELPED YOU.
FWIP
I ACTIVATE A SPELL CARD!!
BRRZT
AQUA JET!!
BIG JAWS
EQUIPPED WITH AQUA JET!!!
BIG JAWS ATK 1800 ↓ ATK 2800

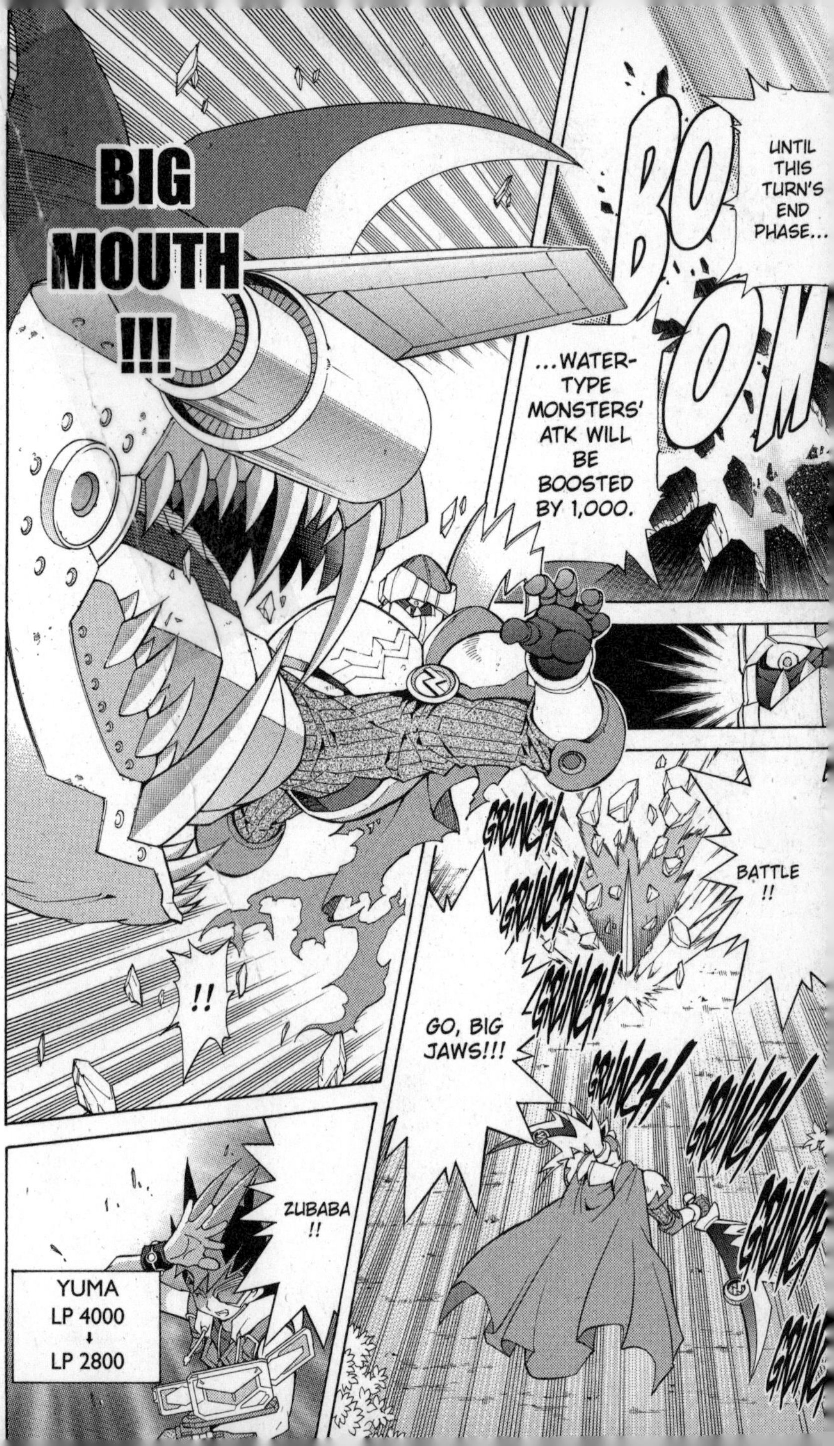
UNTIL THIS TURN'S END PHASE...
...WATER-TYPE MONSTERS' ATK WILL BE BOOSTED BY 1,000.
BOOOM
BIG MOUTH !!!
BATTLE !!
GO, BIG JAWS!!!
GRUNCH GRUNCH GRUNCH GRUNCH GRUNCH GRUNCH GRUNCH
!!
ZUBABA !!
YUMA
LP 4000
↓
LP 2800

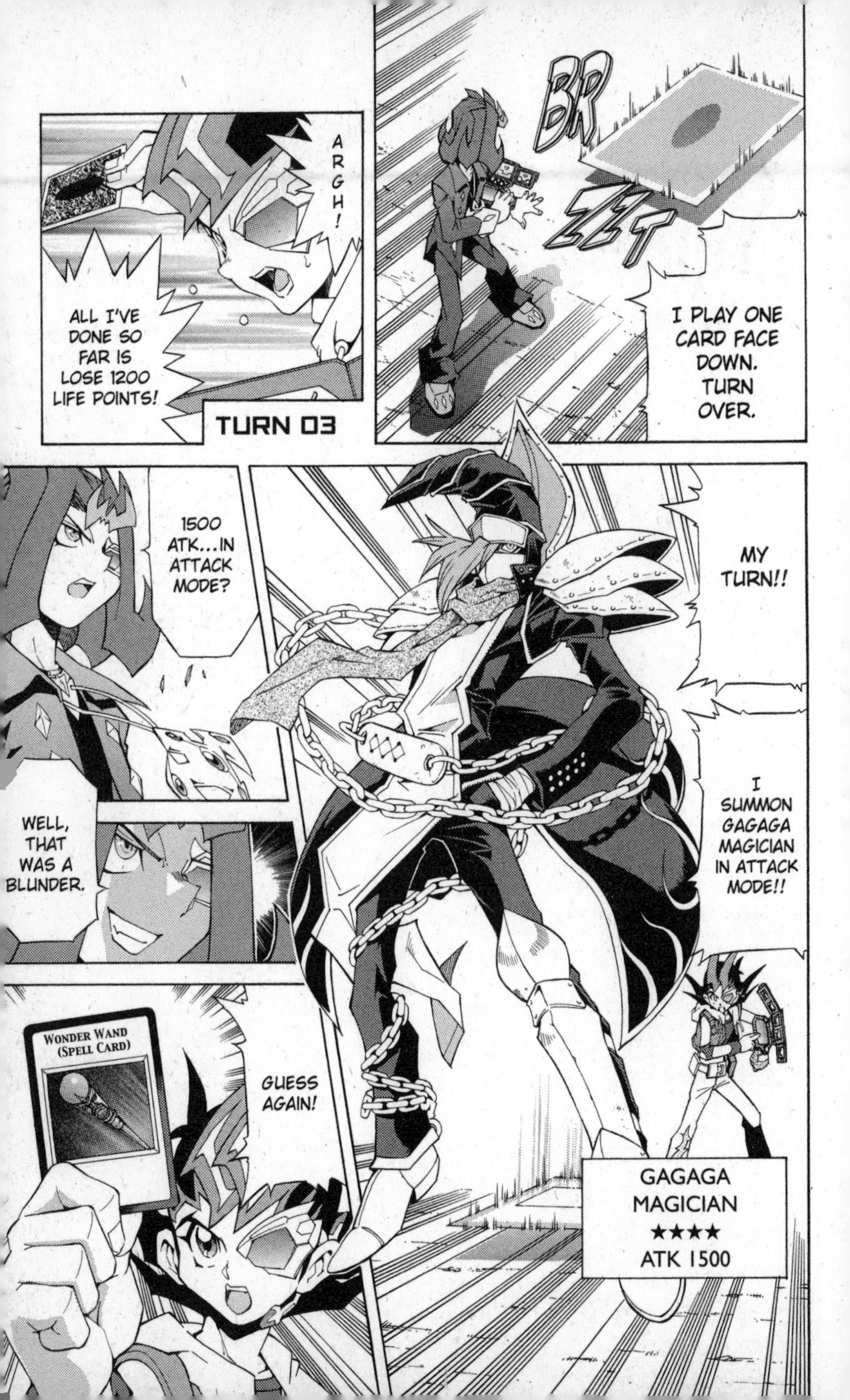
BRZZT
I PLAY ONE CARD FACE DOWN. TURN OVER.
ARGH!
ALL I'VE DONE SO FAR IS LOSE 1200 LIFE POINTS!
TURN 03
MY TURN!!
I SUMMON GAGAGA MAGICIAN IN ATTACK MODE!!
GAGAGA MAGICIAN
★★★★
ATK 1500
1500 ATK...IN ATTACK MODE?
WELL, THAT WAS A BLUNDER.
WONDER WAND (SPELL CARD)
GUESS AGAIN!

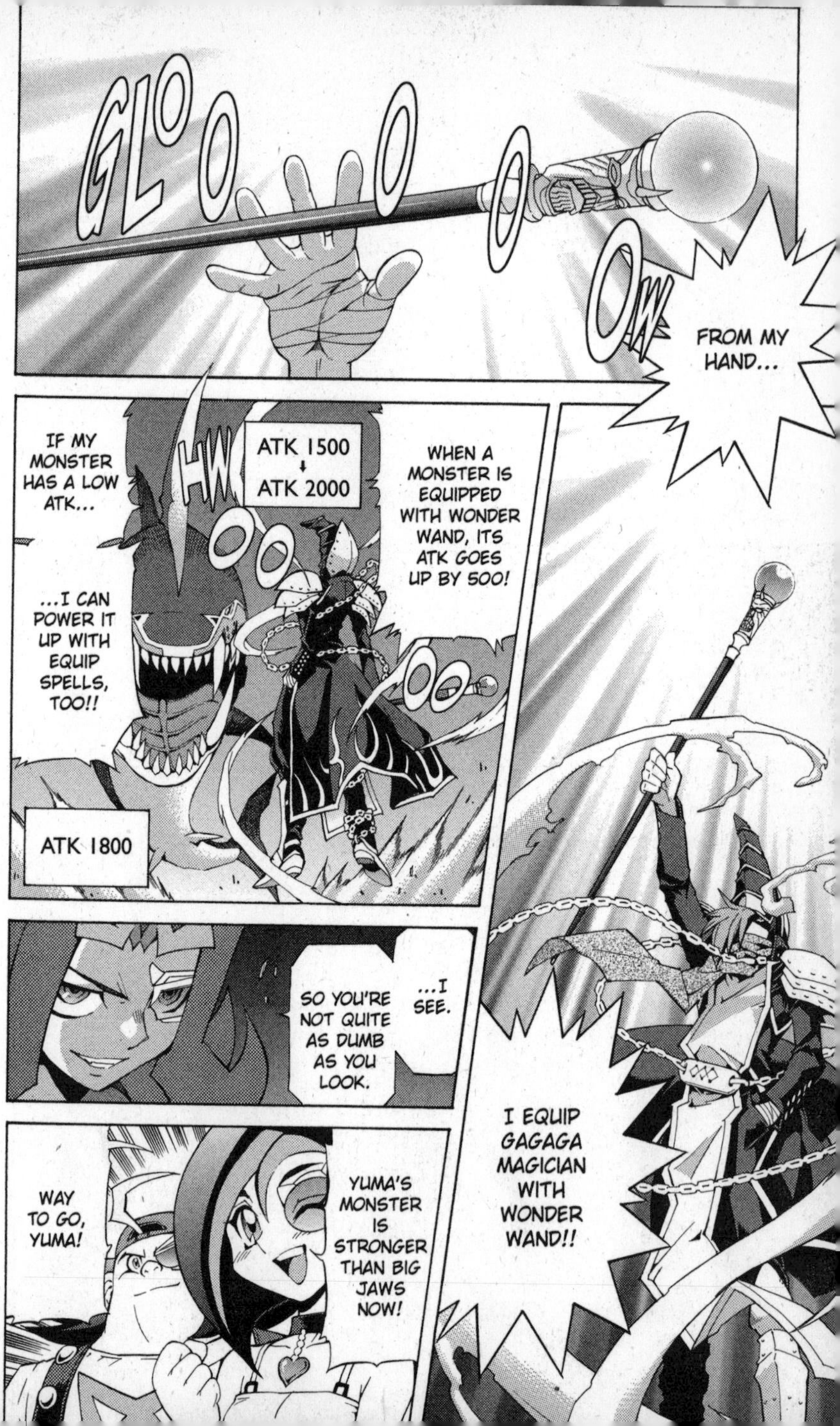
GLOOOOOOOW
FROM MY HAND...
I EQUIP GAGAGA MAGICIAN WITH WONDER WAND!!
WHEN A MONSTER IS EQUIPPED WITH WONDER WAND, ITS ATK GOES UP BY 500!
ATK 1500 → ATK 2000
HWOOOO
IF MY MONSTER HAS A LOW ATK...
...I CAN POWER IT UP WITH EQUIP SPELLS, TOO!!
ATK 1800
...I SEE.
SO YOU'RE NOT QUITE AS DUMB AS YOU LOOK.
YUMA'S MONSTER IS STRONGER THAN BIG JAWS NOW!
WAY TO GO, YUMA!

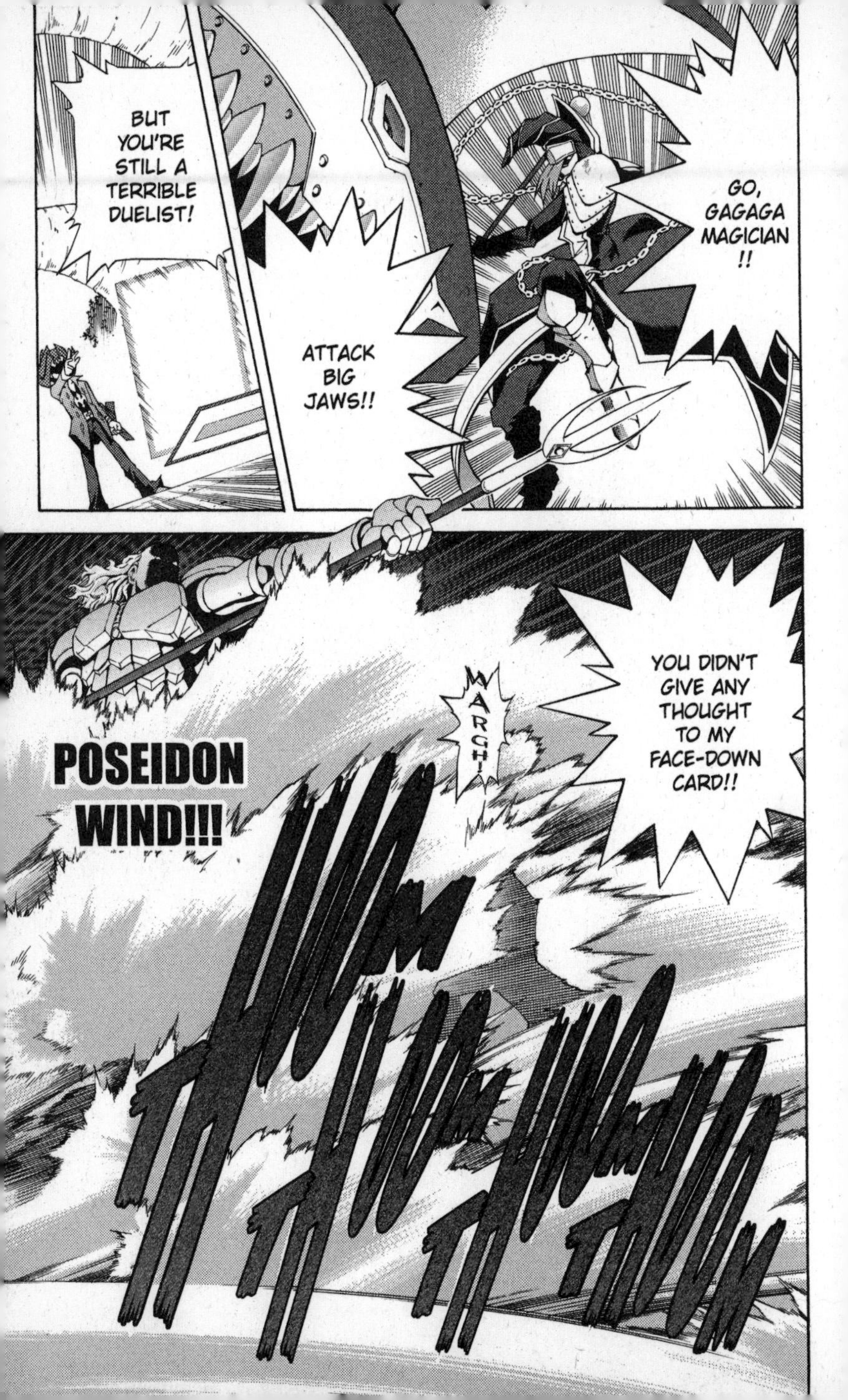
GO, GAGAGA MAGICIAN!!
ATTACK BIG JAWS!!
BUT YOU'RE STILL A TERRIBLE DUELIST!
YOU DIDN'T GIVE ANY THOUGHT TO MY FACE-DOWN CARD!!
WARGH!
POSEIDON WIND!!!

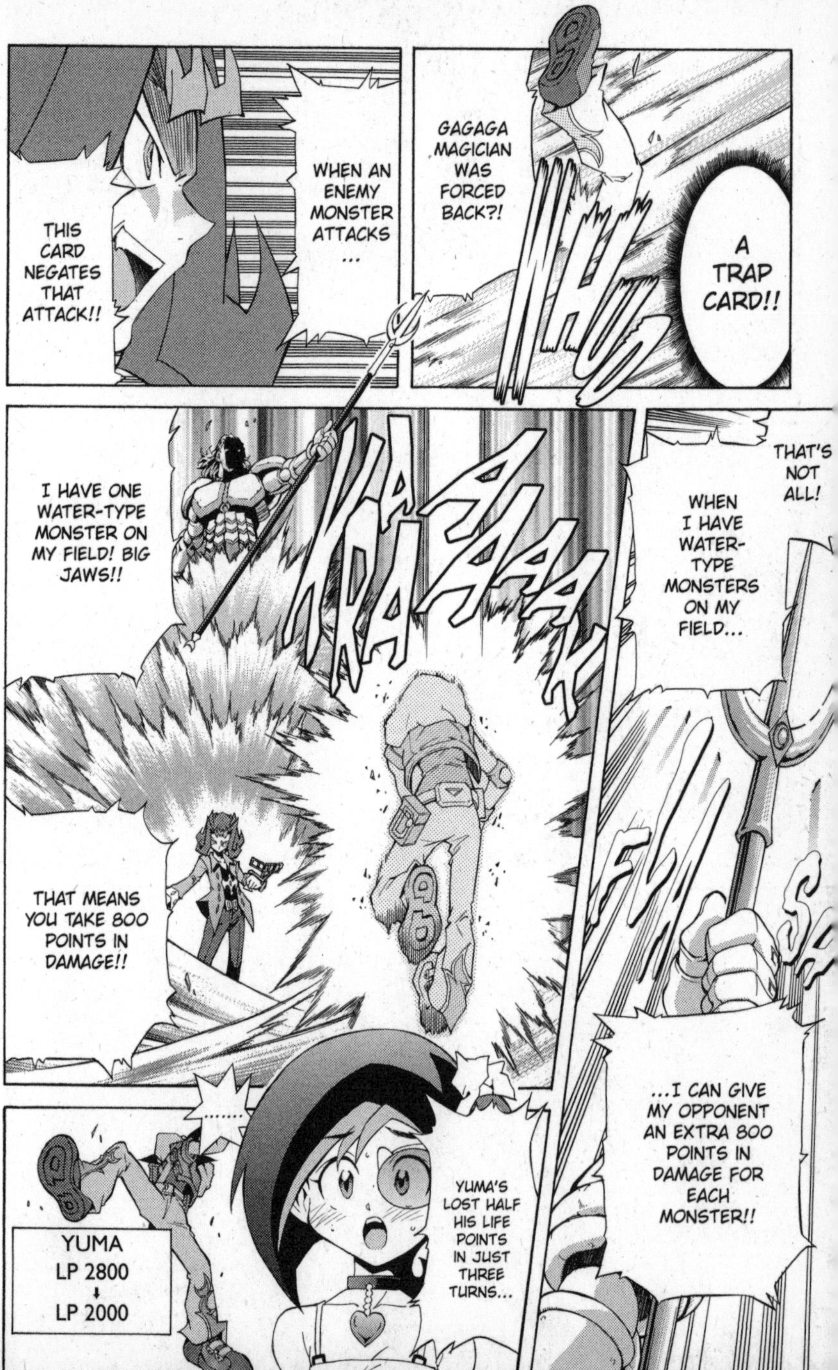
A TRAP CARD!!
GAGAGA MAGICIAN WAS FORCED BACK?!
WHEN AN ENEMY MONSTER ATTACKS ...
THIS CARD NEGATES THAT ATTACK!!
THAT'S NOT ALL!
WHEN I HAVE WATER-TYPE MONSTERS ON MY FIELD...
I HAVE ONE WATER-TYPE MONSTER ON MY FIELD! BIG JAWS!!
THAT MEANS YOU TAKE 800 POINTS IN DAMAGE!!
...I CAN GIVE MY OPPONENT AN EXTRA 800 POINTS IN DAMAGE FOR EACH MONSTER!!
YUMA'S LOST HALF HIS LIFE POINTS IN JUST THREE TURNS...
....
YUMA
LP 2800
↓
LP 2000

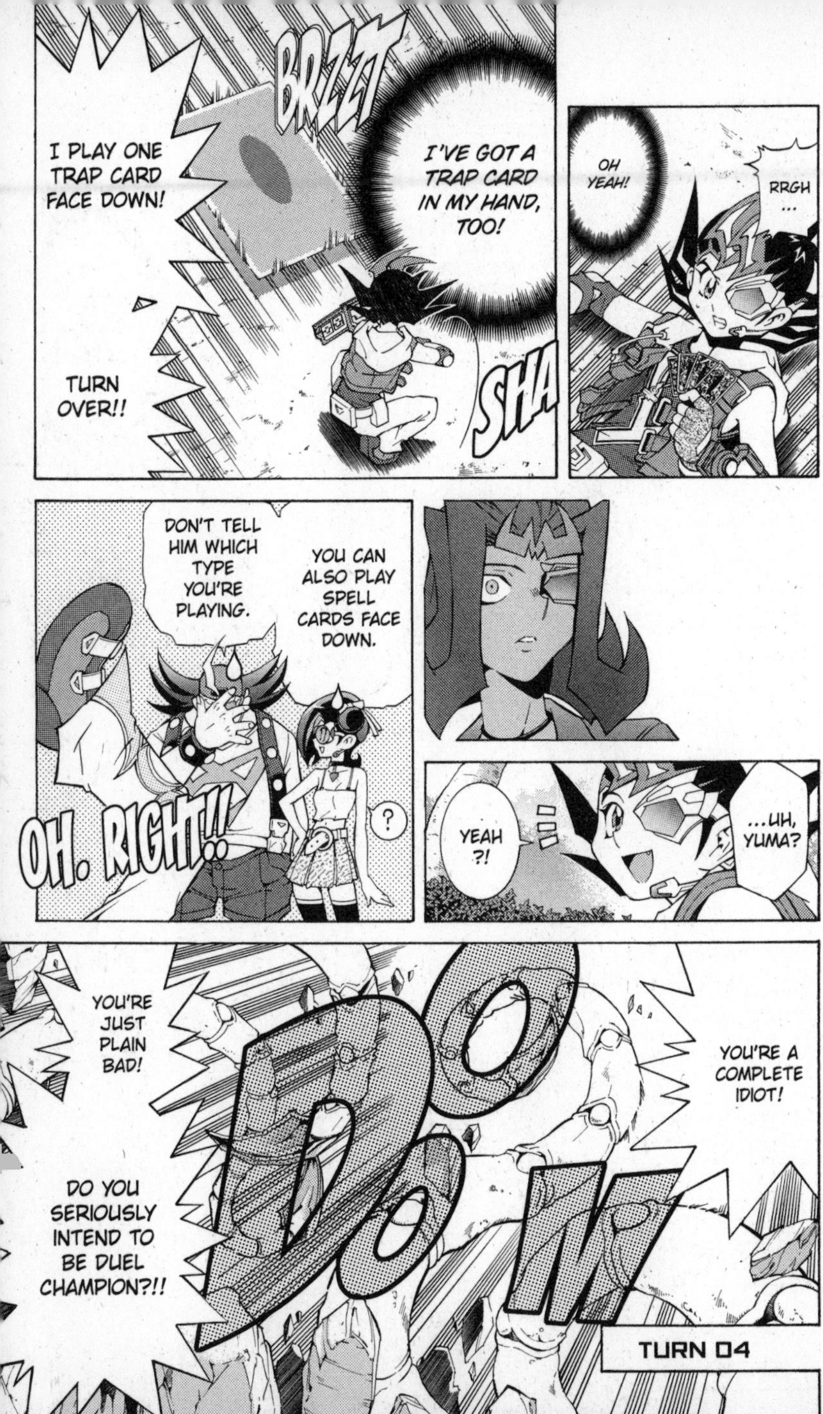
RRGH ...
OH YEAH!
BRZZT
I'VE GOT A TRAP CARD IN MY HAND, TOO!
I PLAY ONE TRAP CARD FACE DOWN!
SHA
TURN OVER!!
...UH, YUMA?
YEAH ?!
YOU CAN ALSO PLAY SPELL CARDS FACE DOWN.
DON'T TELL HIM WHICH TYPE YOU'RE PLAYING.
?
OH. RIGHT!!
YOU'RE A COMPLETE IDIOT!
DOOOM
YOU'RE JUST PLAIN BAD!
DO YOU SERIOUSLY INTEND TO BE DUEL CHAMPION?!!
TURN 04

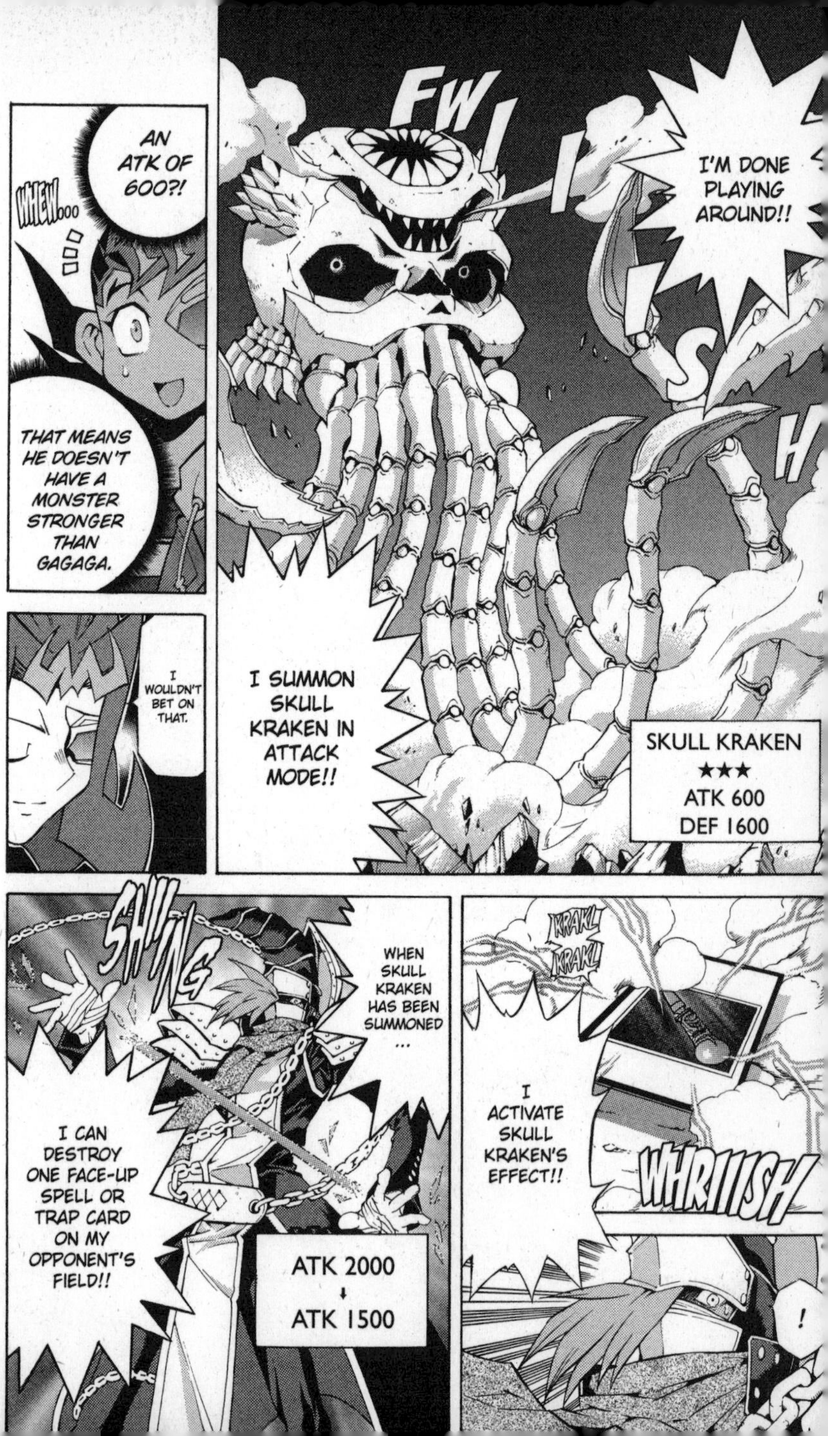
FWIISH
I'M DONE PLAYING AROUND!!
I SUMMON SKULL KRAKEN IN ATTACK MODE!!
SKULL KRAKEN ★★★ ATK 600 DEF 1600
AN ATK OF 600?!
WHEW...
THAT MEANS HE DOESN'T HAVE A MONSTER STRONGER THAN GAGAGA.
I WOULDN'T BET ON THAT.
KRAKL
KRAKL
I ACTIVATE SKULL KRAKEN'S EFFECT!!
WHRIIISH
!
SHING
WHEN SKULL KRAKEN HAS BEEN SUMMONED...
I CAN DESTROY ONE FACE-UP SPELL OR TRAP CARD ON MY OPPONENT'S FIELD!!
ATK 2000 ↓ ATK 1500

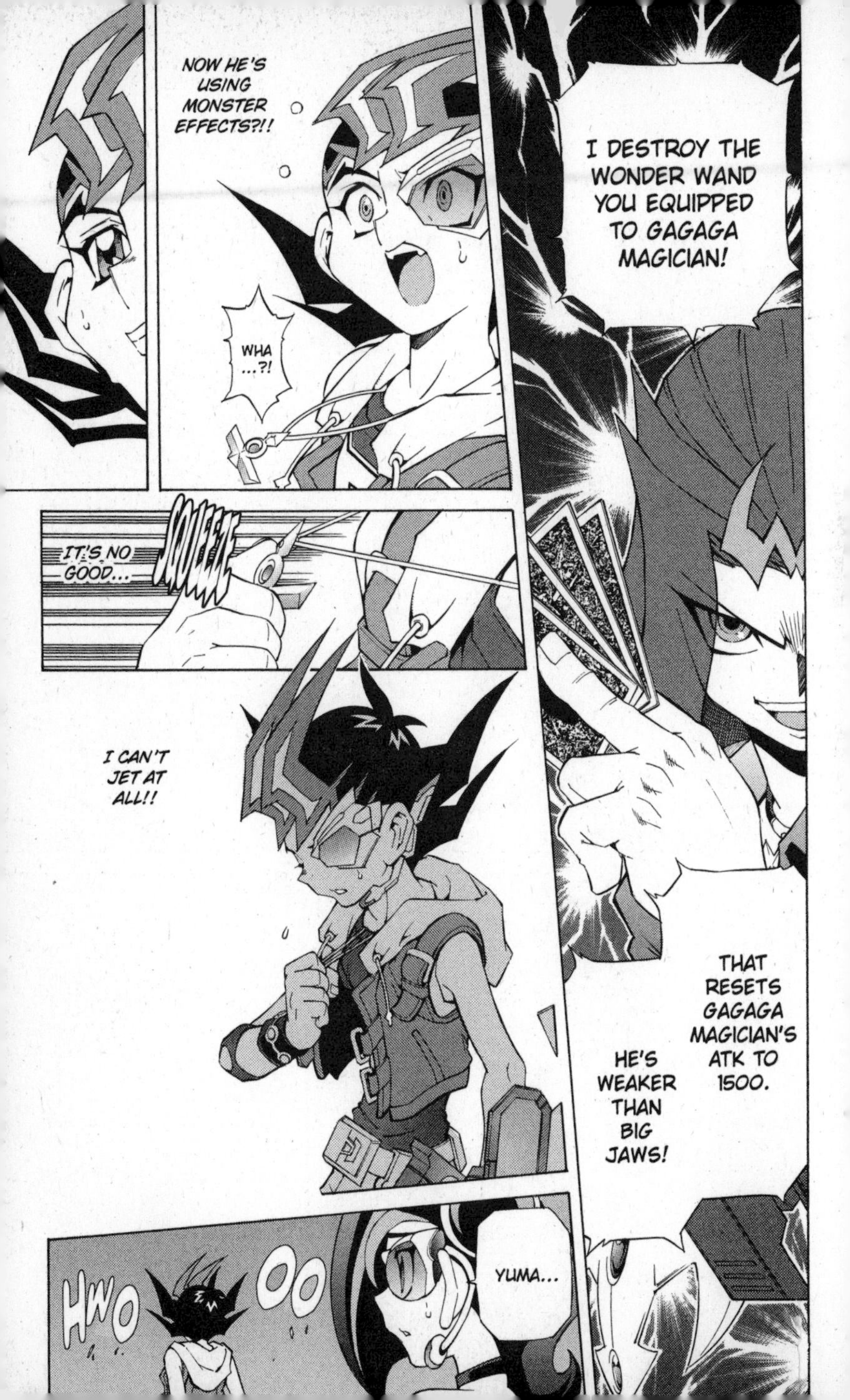

I DESTROY THE WONDER WAND YOU EQUIPPED TO GAGAGA MAGICIAN!
THAT RESETS GAGAGA MAGICIAN'S ATK TO 1500.
HE'S WEAKER THAN BIG JAWS!
NOW HE'S USING MONSTER EFFECTS?!!
WHA ...?!
SQUEEZE
IT'S NO GOOD...
I CAN'T JET AT ALL!!
YUMA...
HWOO

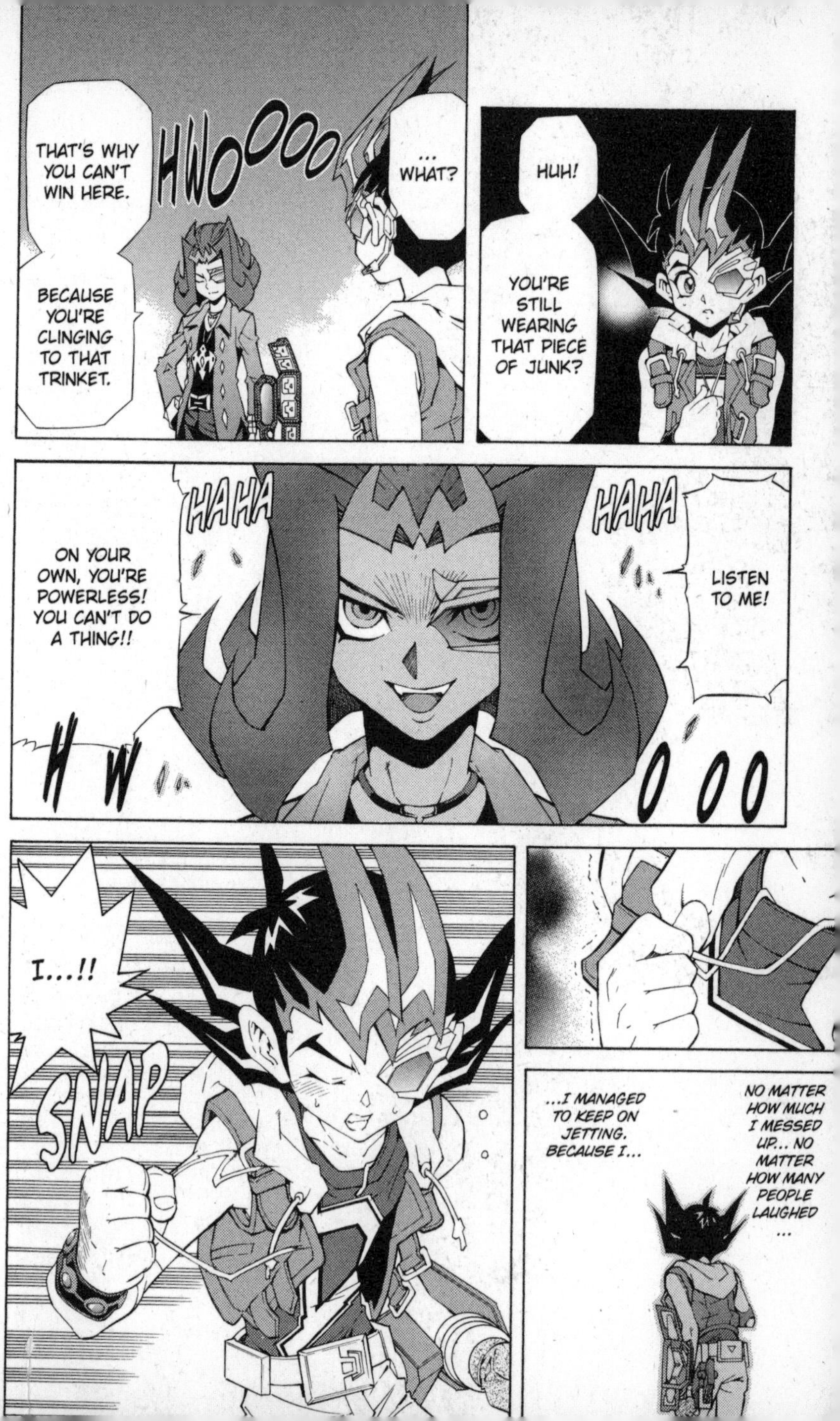
HUH!
YOU'RE STILL WEARING THAT PIECE OF JUNK?
... WHAT?
HWOOOOO
THAT'S WHY YOU CAN'T WIN HERE.
BECAUSE YOU'RE CLINGING TO THAT TRINKET.
LISTEN TO ME!
HAHA
ON YOUR OWN, YOU'RE POWERLESS! YOU CAN'T DO A THING!!
HAHA
H W O O O
NO MATTER HOW MUCH I MESSED UP... NO MATTER HOW MANY PEOPLE LAUGHED ...
...I MANAGED TO KEEP ON JETTING. BECAUSE I...
I...!!
SNAP

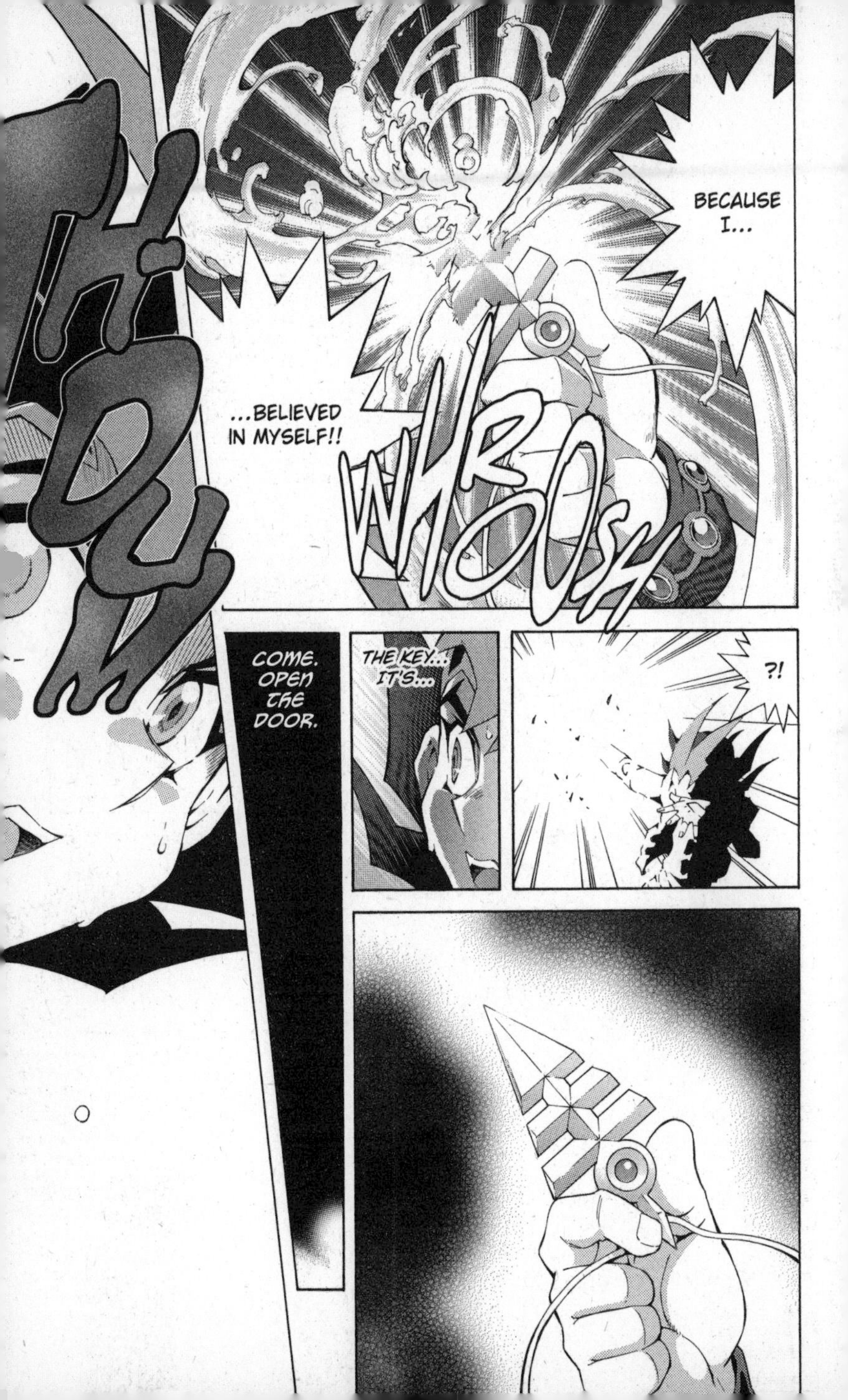
BECAUSE I...
...BELIEVED IN MYSELF!!
WHROOSH
?!
THE KEY... IT'S...
COME. OPEN THE DOOR.

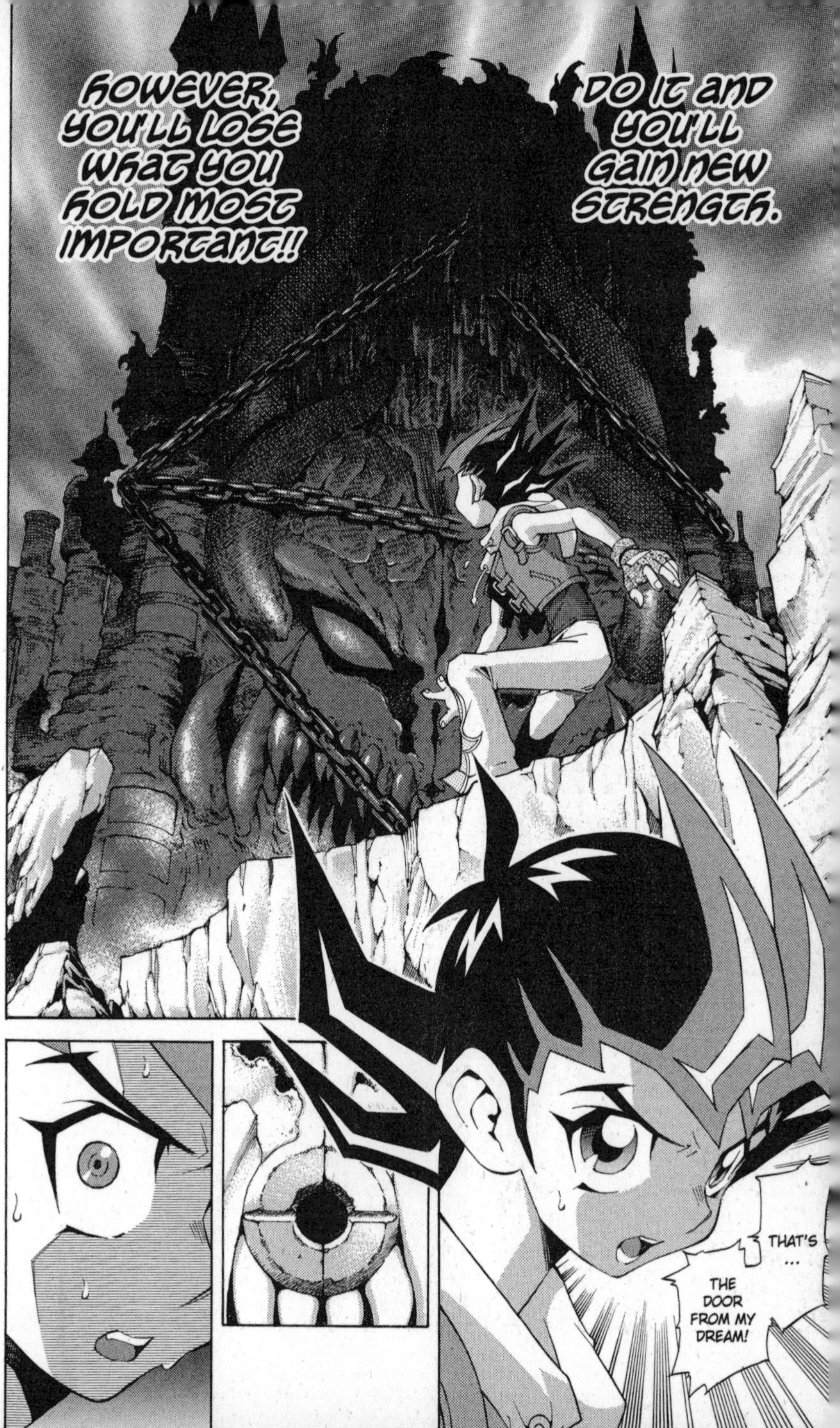
DO IT AND YOU'LL GAIN NEW STRENGTH.
HOWEVER, YOU'LL LOSE WHAT YOU HOLD MOST IMPORTANT!!
THAT'S ...
THE DOOR FROM MY DREAM!

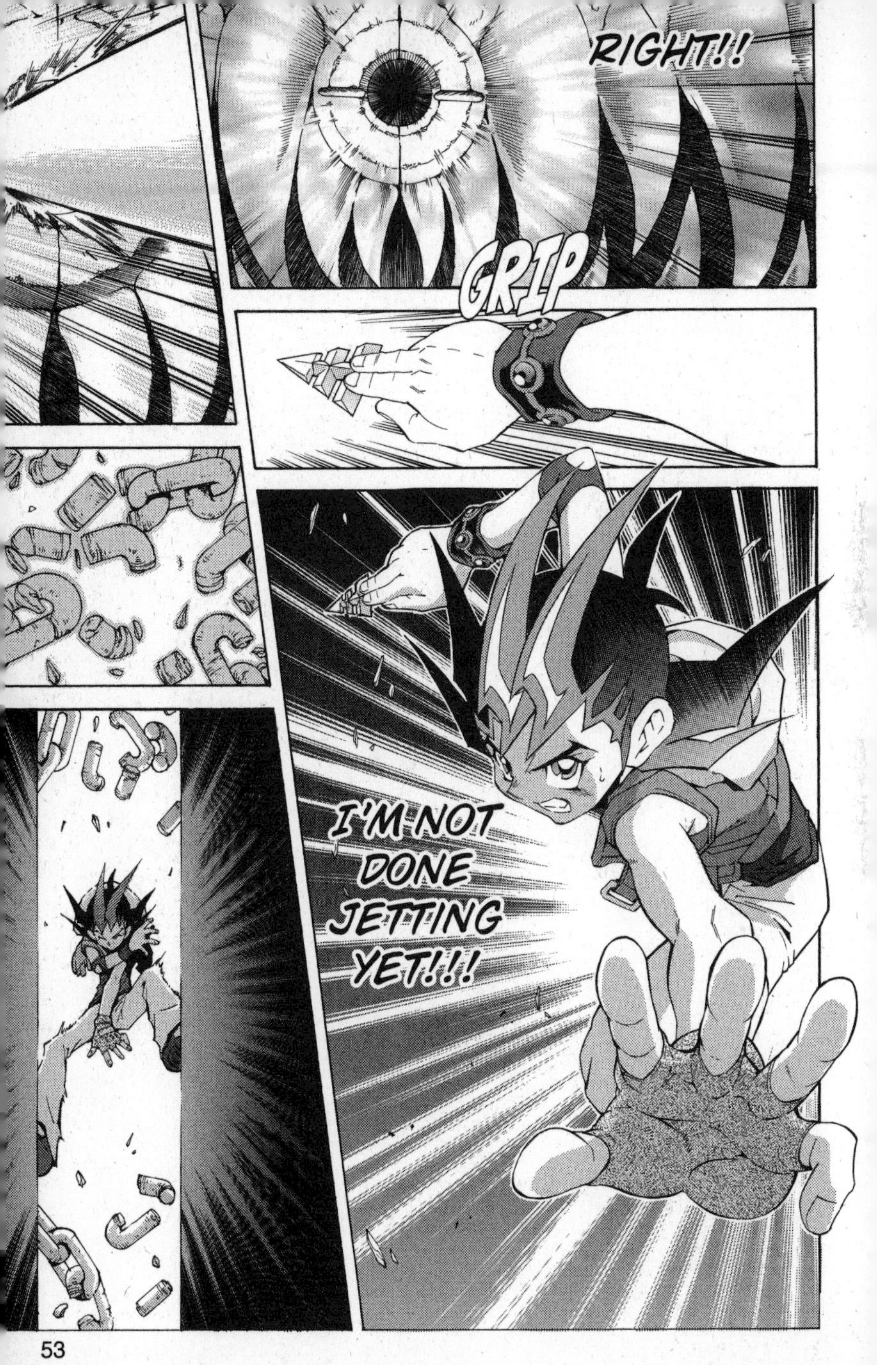
RIGHT!!
GRIP
I'M NOT DONE JETTING YET!!!

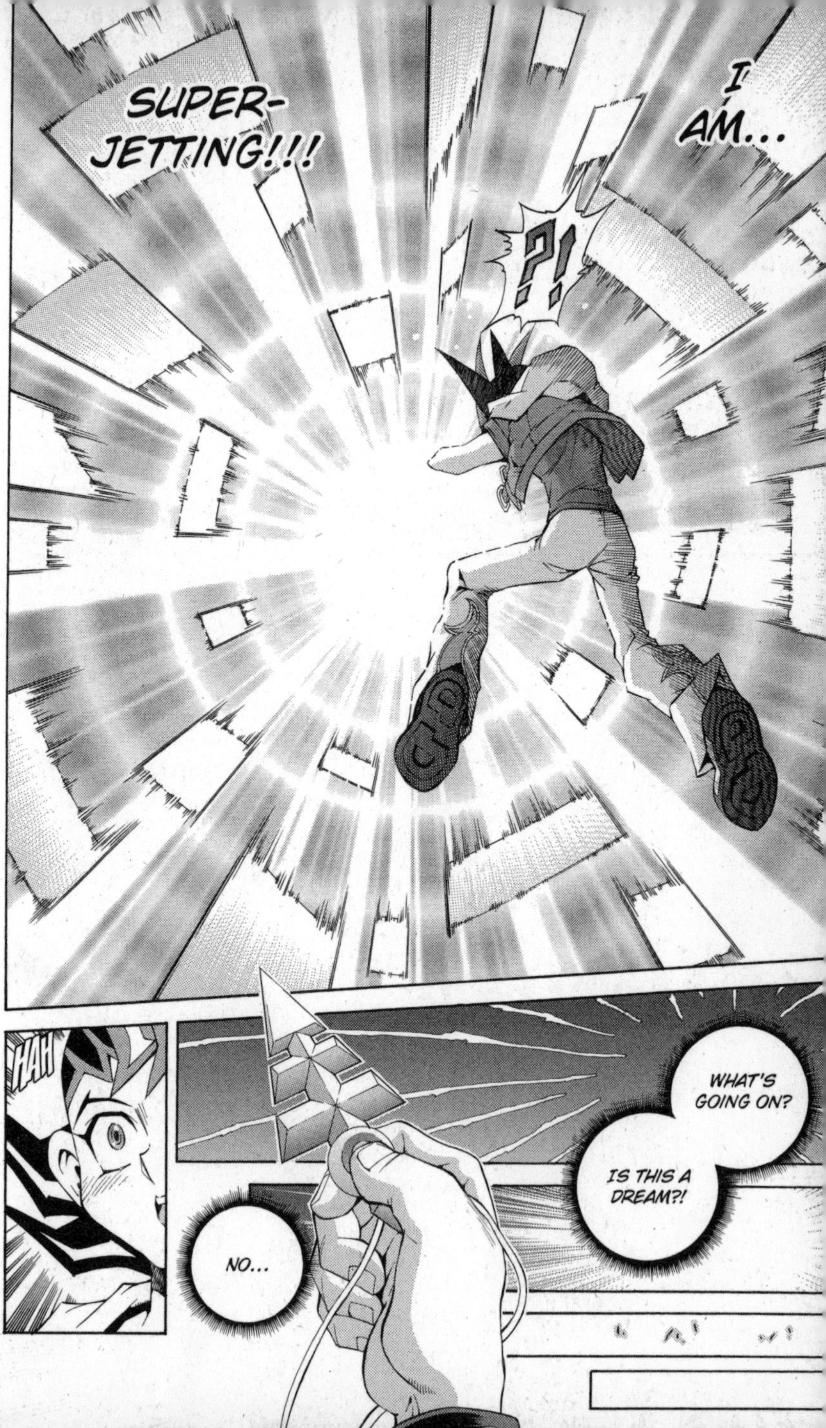
I AM...
SUPER-JETTING!!!
?!
WHAT'S GOING ON?
IS THIS A DREAM?!
NO...
HAH

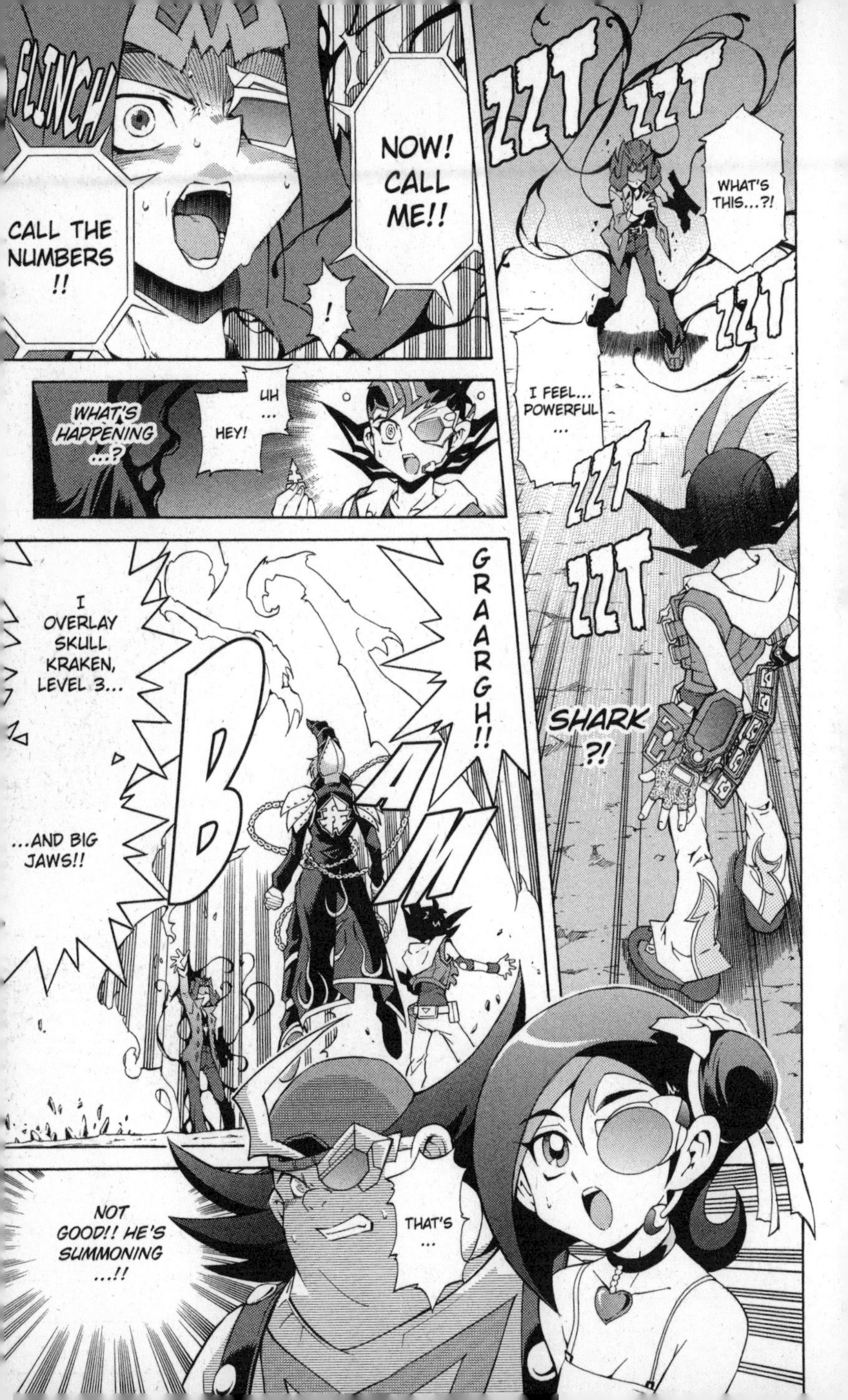
ZZT ZZT
WHAT'S THIS...?!
ZZT
I FEEL... POWERFUL...
ZZT
ZZT
SHARK?!
NOW! CALL ME!!
!
CALL THE NUMBERS!!
FLINCH
UH...
HEY!
WHAT'S HAPPENING...?
GRAARGH!!
BAM
I OVERLAY SKULL KRAKEN, LEVEL 3...
...AND BIG JAWS!!
THAT'S...
NOT GOOD!! HE'S SUMMONING...!!

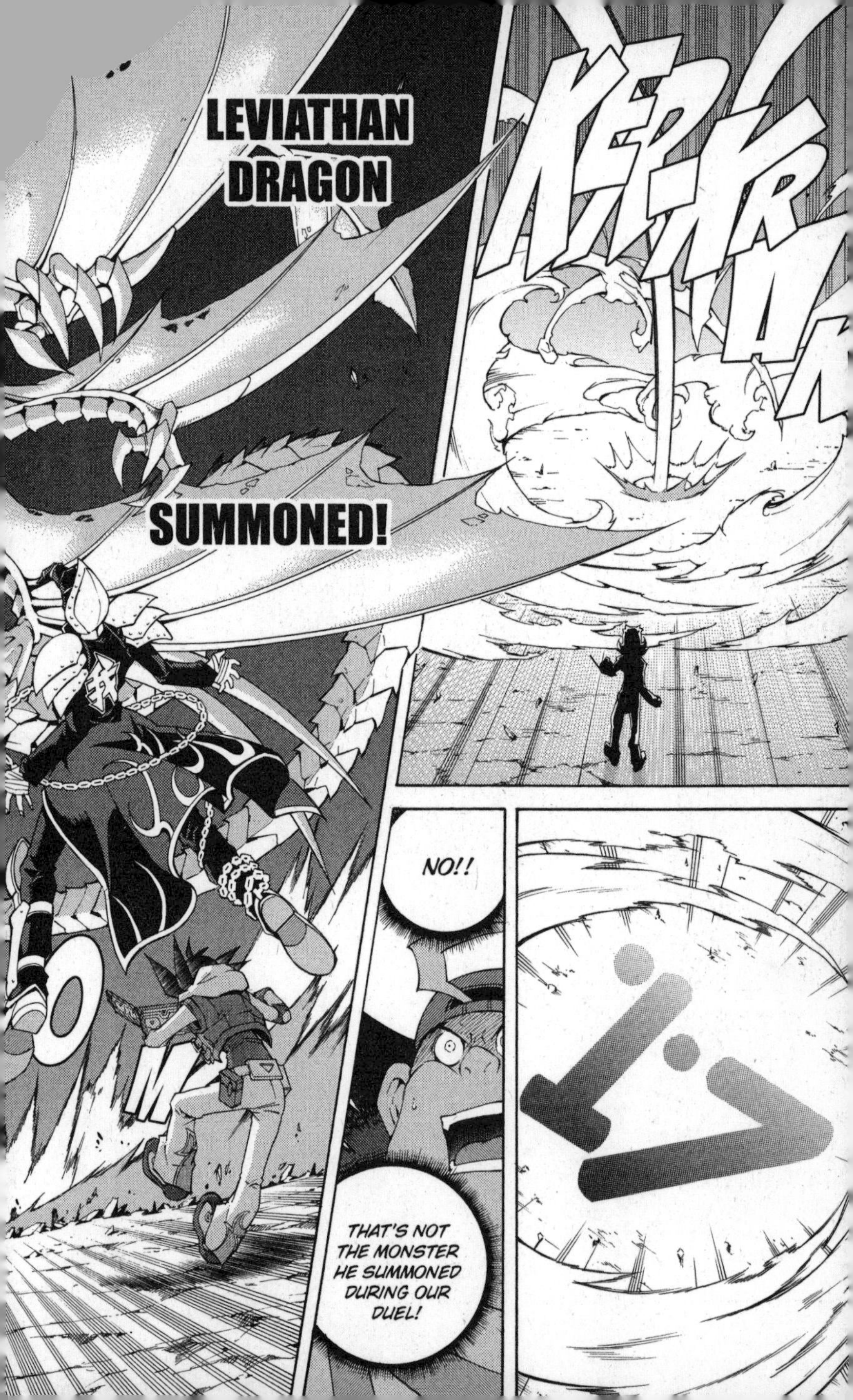
KER-RA
LEVIATHAN DRAGON
SUMMONED!
NO!!
THAT'S NOT THE MONSTER HE SUMMONED DURING OUR DUEL!

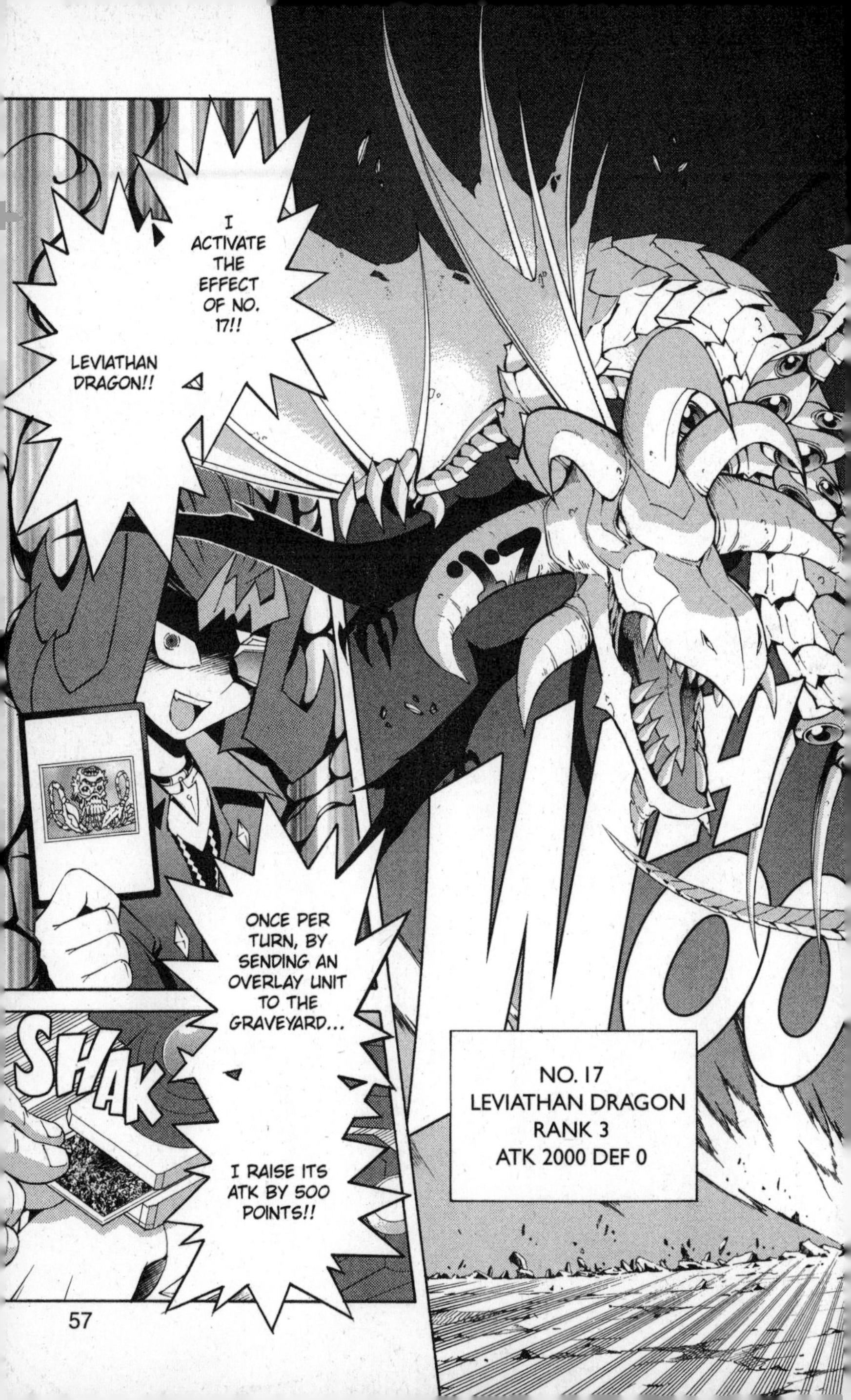
WHOOO
NO. 17
LEVIATHAN DRAGON
RANK 3
ATK 2000 DEF 0
I ACTIVATE THE EFFECT OF NO. 17!!
LEVIATHAN DRAGON!!
ONCE PER TURN, BY SENDING AN OVERLAY UNIT TO THE GRAVEYARD...
SHAK
I RAISE ITS ATK BY 500 POINTS!!

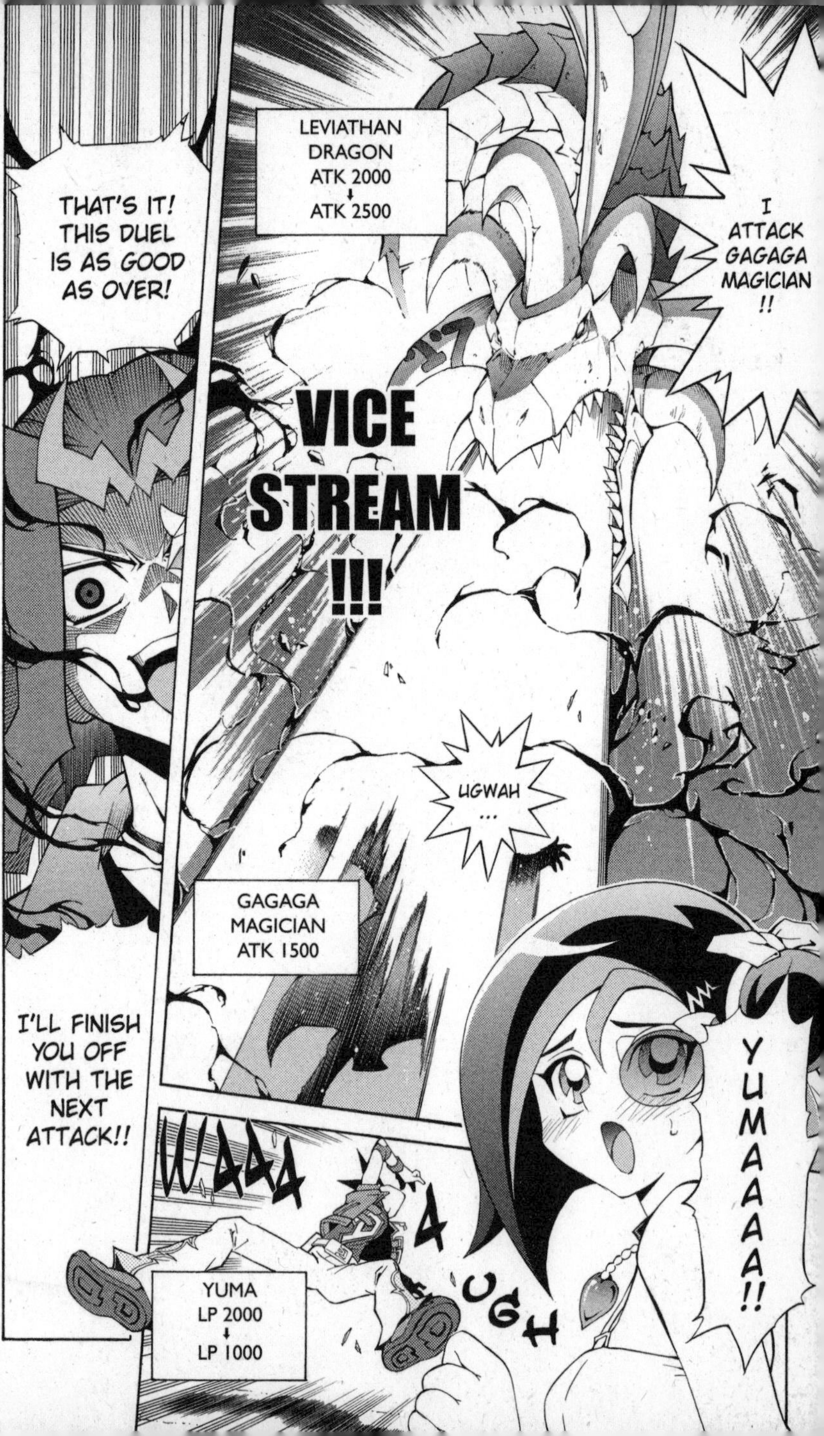
I ATTACK GAGAGA MAGICIAN!!
LEVIATHAN DRAGON ATK 2000 ↓ ATK 2500
VICE STREAM!!!
UGWAH...
GAGAGA MAGICIAN ATK 1500
YUMAAAAAA!!
WAAAA
UGH
YUMA LP 2000 ↓ LP 1000
THAT'S IT! THIS DUEL IS AS GOOD AS OVER!
I'LL FINISH YOU OFF WITH THE NEXT ATTACK!!

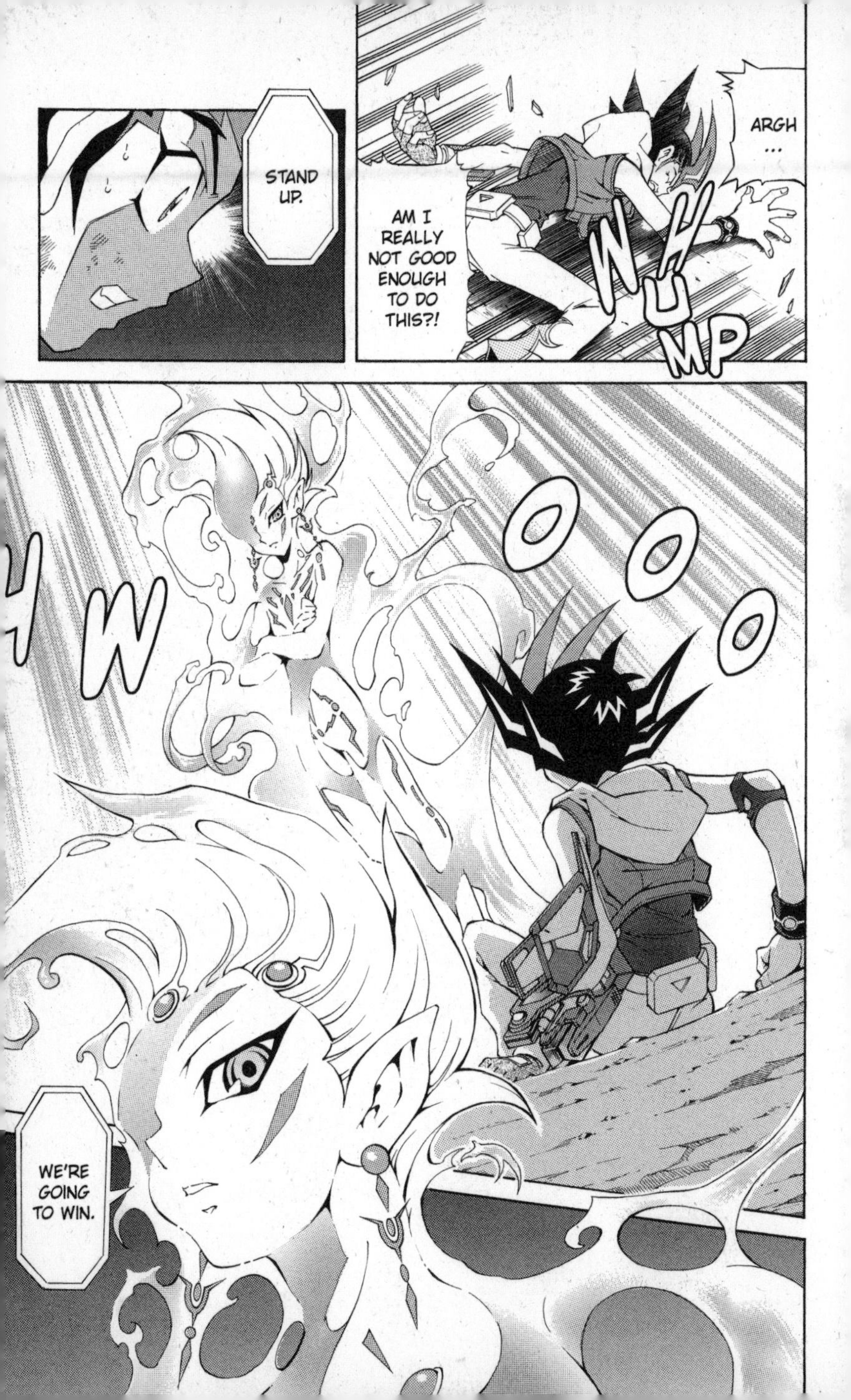
ARGH ...
AM I REALLY NOT GOOD ENOUGH TO DO THIS?!
WHUMP
STAND UP.
HW
OOO
WE'RE GOING TO WIN.

astral's journal
#1
DAY
SCRITCH
SCRITCH
NIGHT
SNOOOOORE
OBSERVATION RECORD 1
(AGAIN)
DAY
SCRITCH
SCRITCH
MIYOSHI'S DAYS ARE REPETITIVE AND MONOTONOUS.
HOWEVER...
SNOOOORE
They grew again this month...
EVEN IN MONOTONY, THERE IS CHANGE...
I'LL REMEMBER THAT.

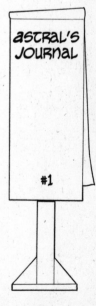

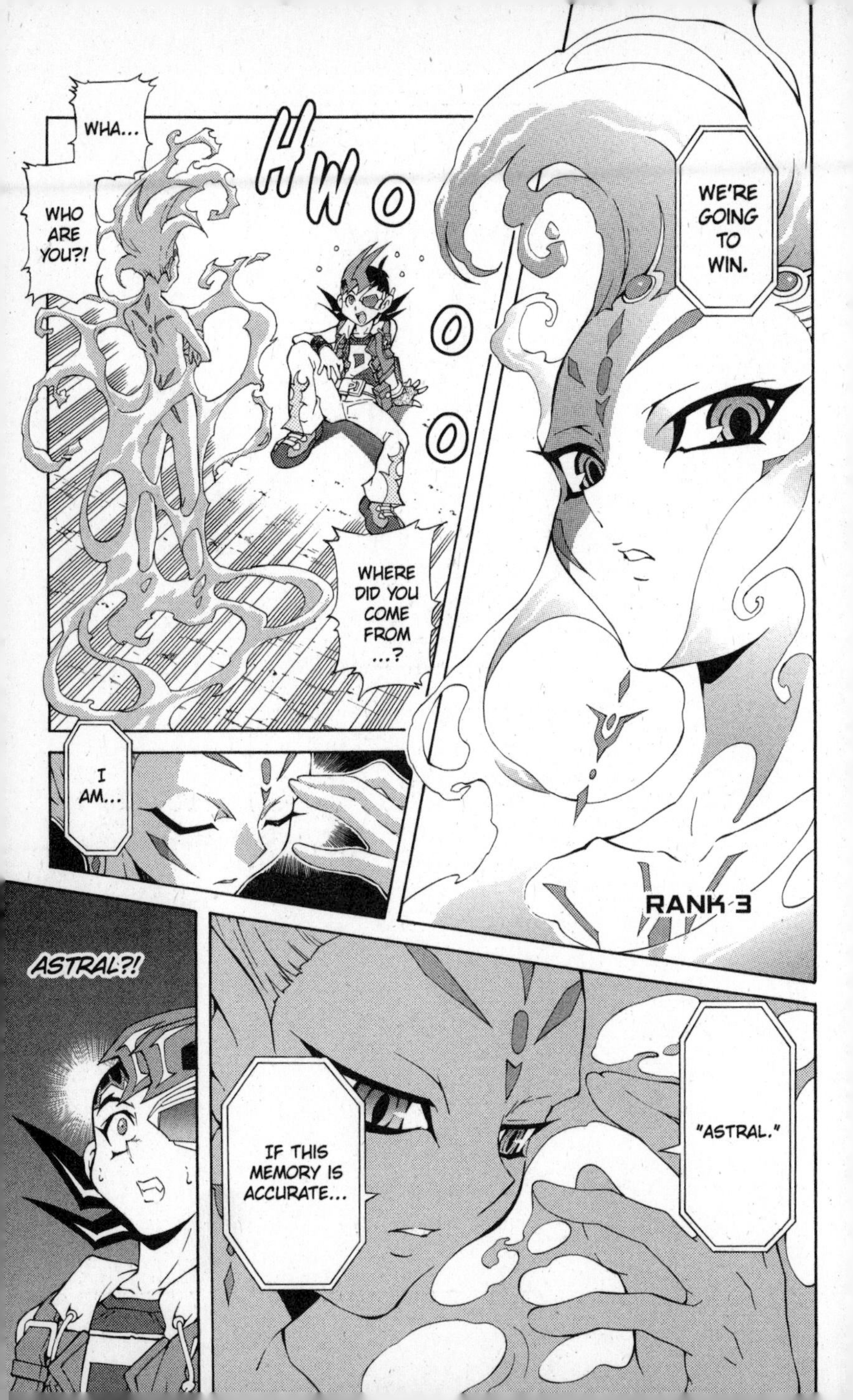
WE'RE GOING TO WIN.
RANK 3
HWOOOOO
WHA...
WHO ARE YOU?!
WHERE DID YOU COME FROM ...?
I AM...
"ASTRAL."
IF THIS MEMORY IS ACCURATE...
ASTRAL?!

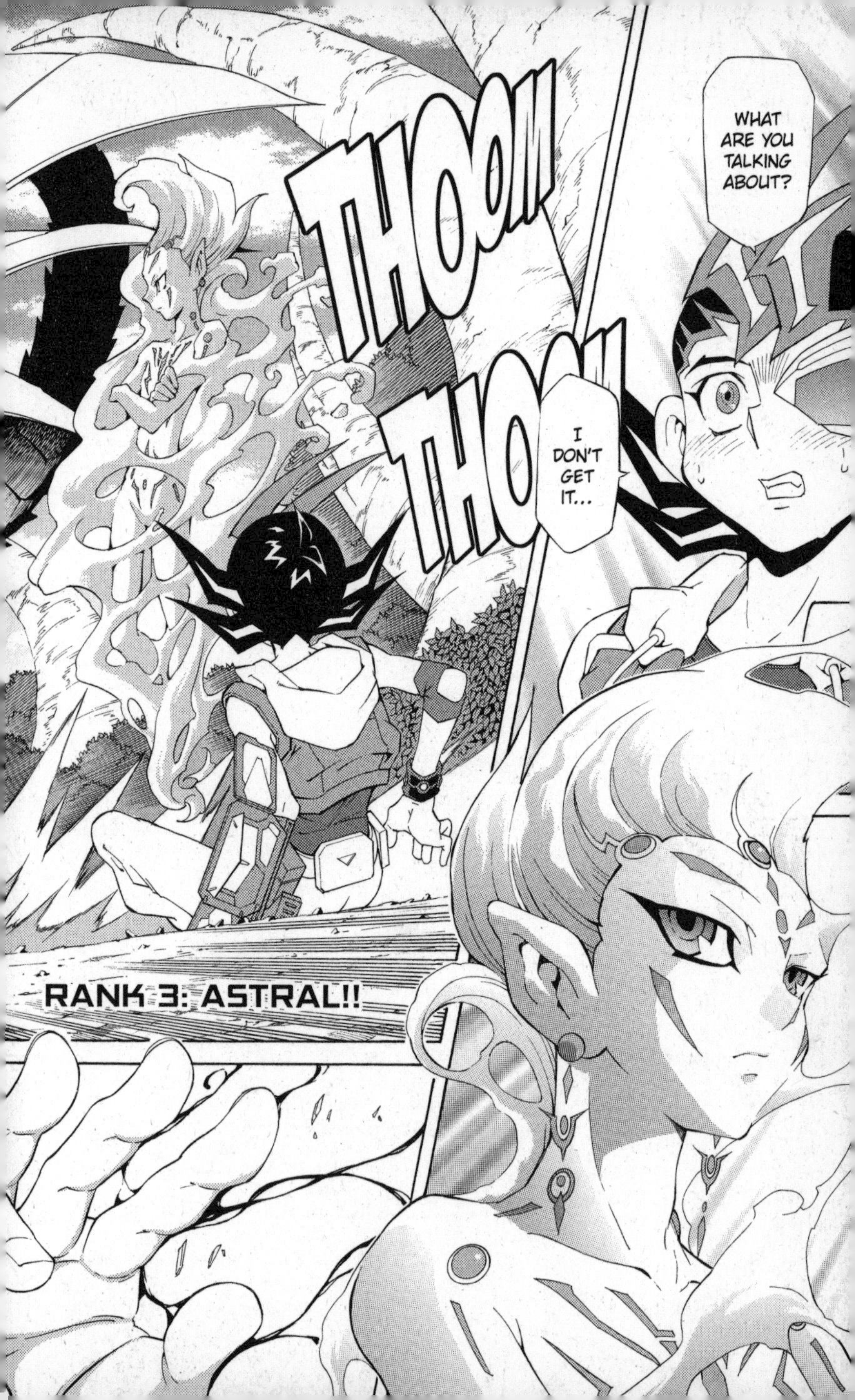
WHAT ARE YOU TALKING ABOUT?
THOOM
I DON'T GET IT...
THOOM
RANK 3: ASTRAL!!

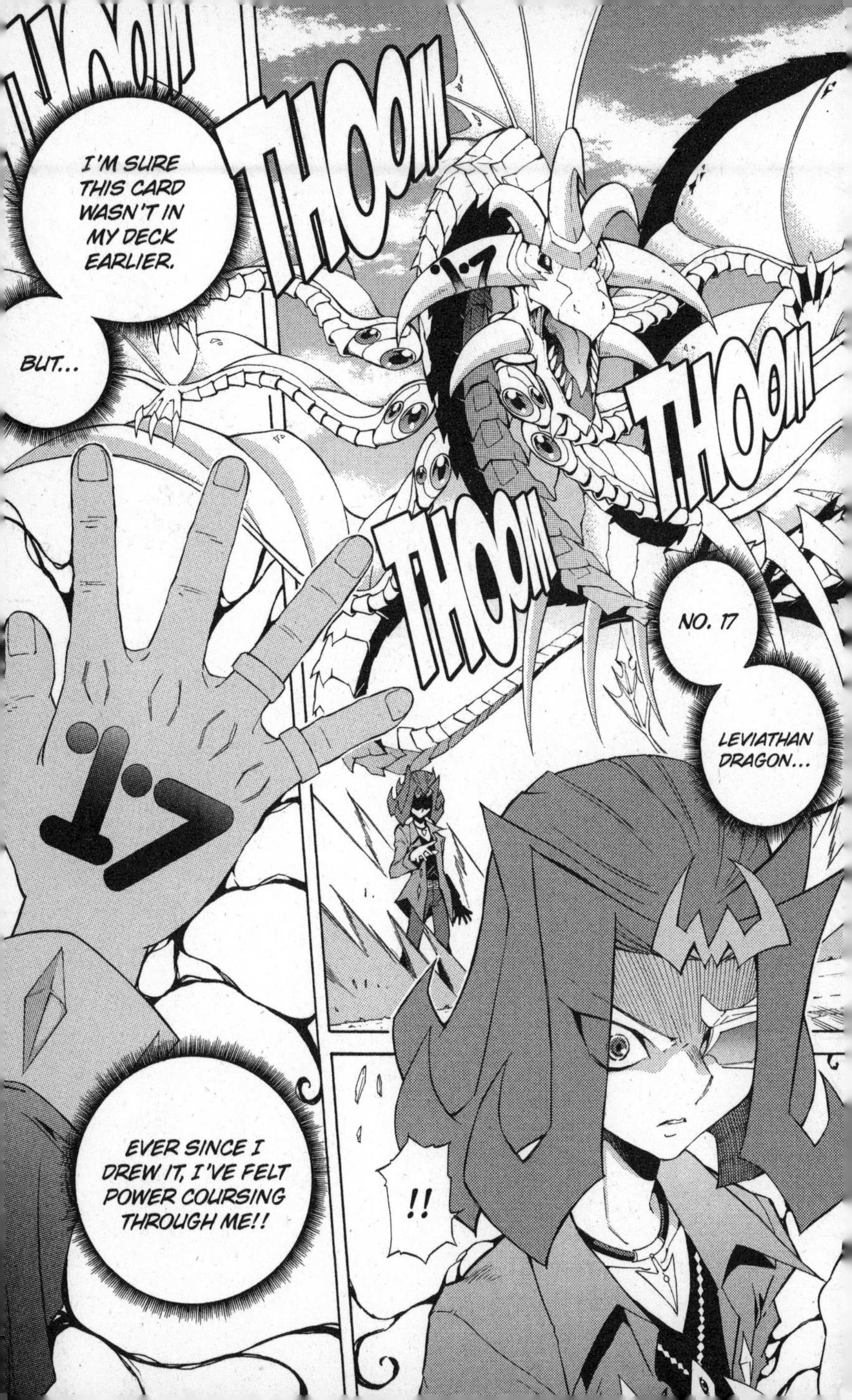
THOOM
I'M SURE THIS CARD WASN'T IN MY DECK EARLIER.
BUT...
THOOM
THOOM
NO. 17
LEVIATHAN DRAGON...
!!
EVER SINCE I DREW IT, I'VE FELT POWER COURSING THROUGH ME!!

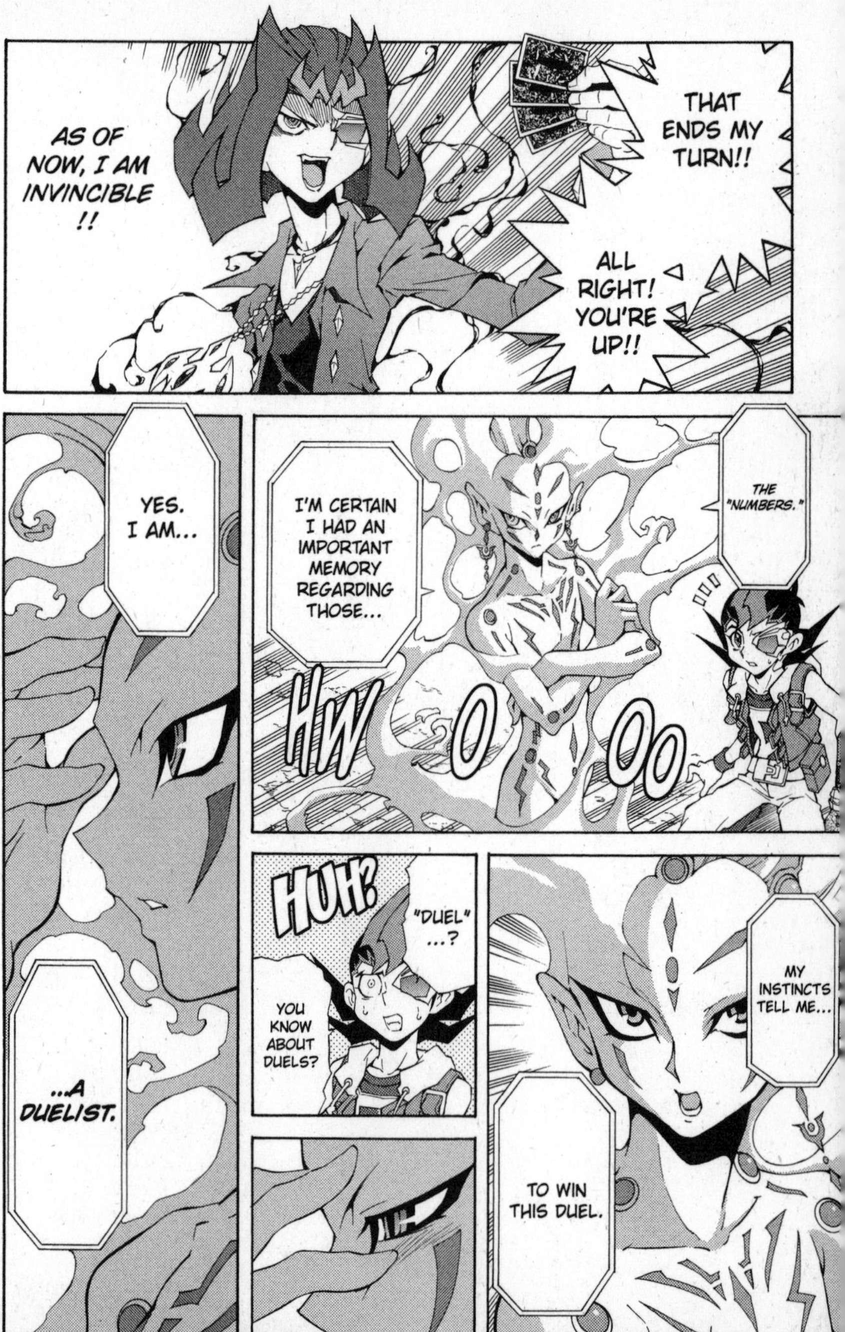
THAT ENDS MY TURN!!
ALL RIGHT! YOU'RE UP!!
AS OF NOW, I AM INVINCIBLE !!
THE "NUMBERS."
I'M CERTAIN I HAD AN IMPORTANT MEMORY REGARDING THOSE...
HWOOOO
MY INSTINCTS TELL ME...
TO WIN THIS DUEL.
HUH?
"DUEL" ...?
YOU KNOW ABOUT DUELS?
YES. I AM...
...A DUELIST.

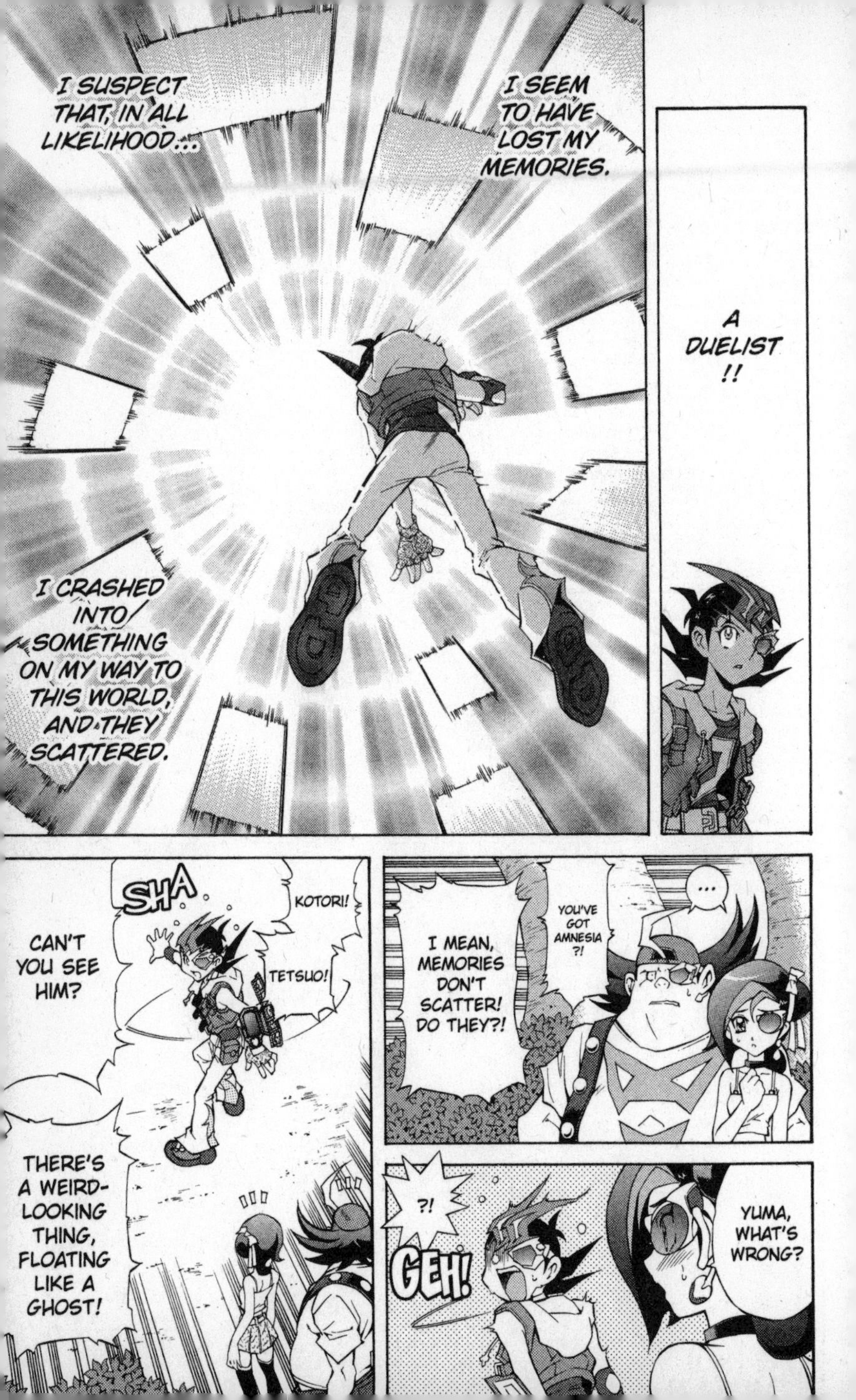
A DUELIST!!
I SEEM TO HAVE LOST MY MEMORIES.
I SUSPECT THAT, IN ALL LIKELIHOOD...
I CRASHED INTO SOMETHING ON MY WAY TO THIS WORLD, AND THEY SCATTERED.
...
YOU'VE GOT AMNESIA?!
I MEAN, MEMORIES DON'T SCATTER! DO THEY?!
YUMA, WHAT'S WRONG?
?!
GEH!
KOTORI!
TETSUO!
SHA
CAN'T YOU SEE HIM?
THERE'S A WEIRD-LOOKING THING, FLOATING LIKE A GHOST!

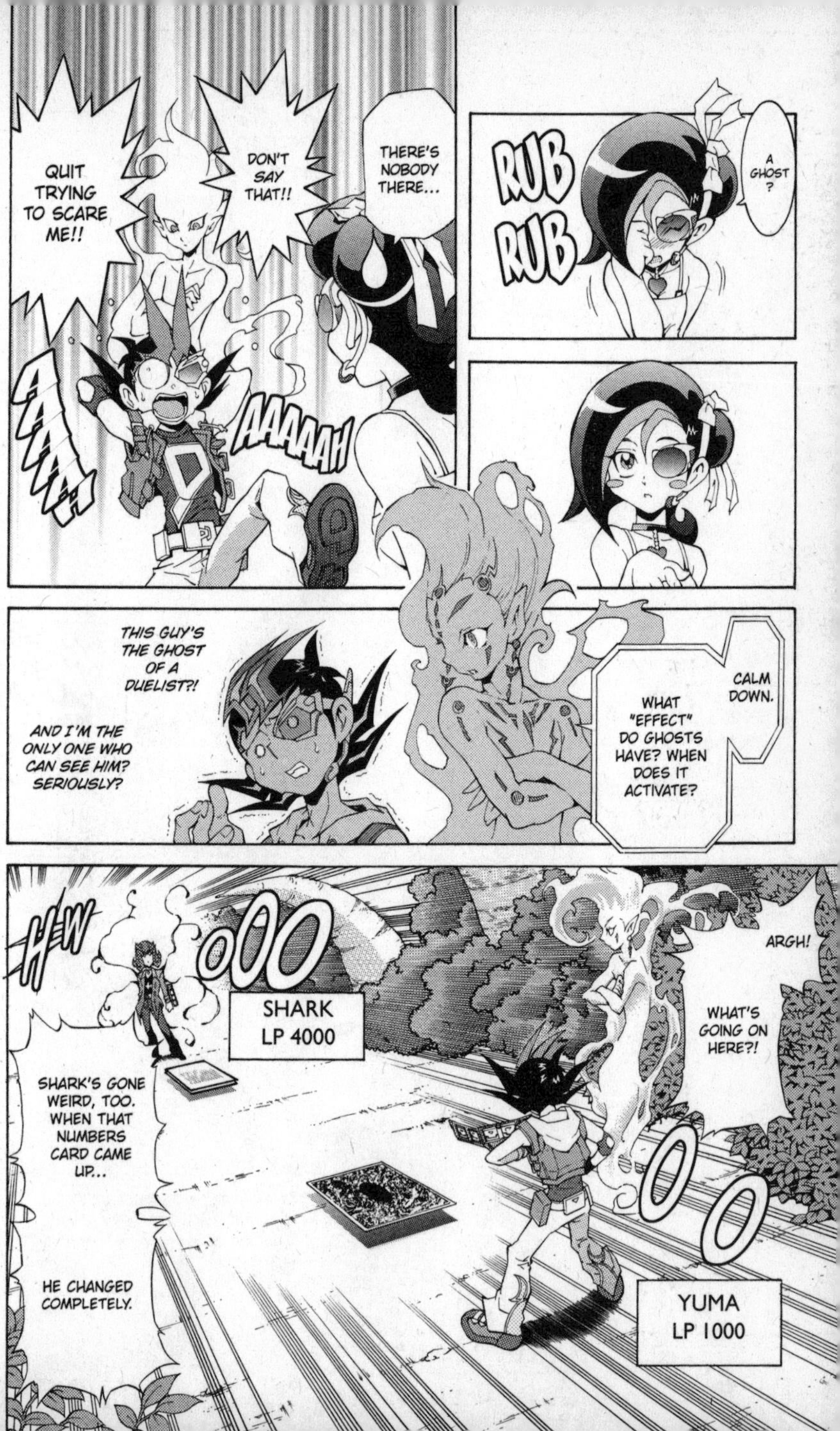
RUB RUB
A GHOST?
THERE'S NOBODY THERE...
DON'T SAY THAT!!
QUIT TRYING TO SCARE ME!!
AAAAAH
CALM DOWN.
WHAT "EFFECT" DO GHOSTS HAVE? WHEN DOES IT ACTIVATE?
THIS GUY'S THE GHOST OF A DUELIST?!
AND I'M THE ONLY ONE WHO CAN SEE HIM? SERIOUSLY?
ARGH!
WHAT'S GOING ON HERE?!
OO
YUMA LP 1000
HWOOO
SHARK LP 4000
SHARK'S GONE WEIRD, TOO. WHEN THAT NUMBERS CARD CAME UP...
HE CHANGED COMPLETELY.

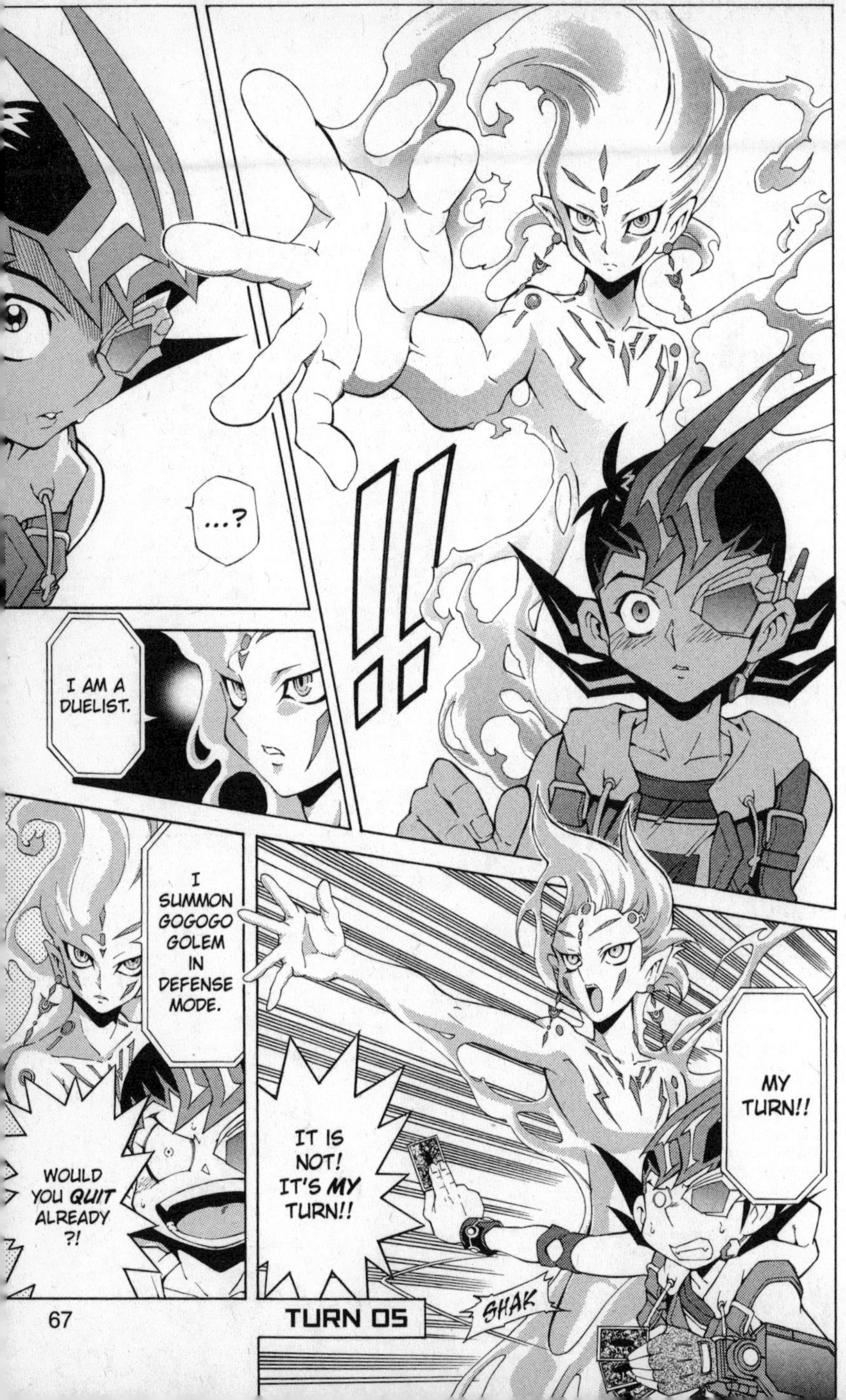
!!
...?
I AM A DUELIST.
MY TURN!!
IT IS NOT! IT'S *MY* TURN!!
SHAK
I SUMMON GOGOGO GOLEM IN DEFENSE MODE.
WOULD YOU *QUIT* ALREADY?!
TURN 05

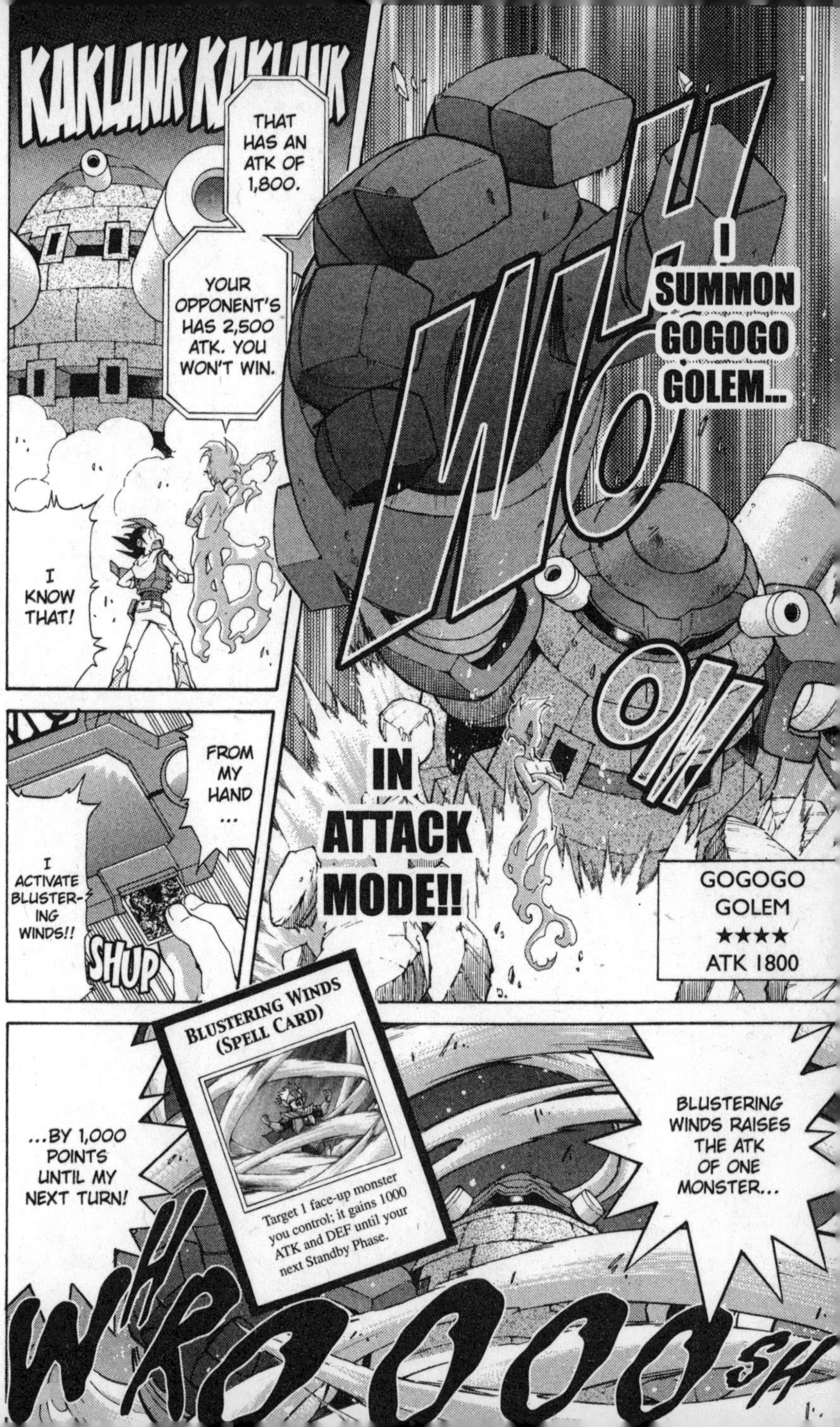

WHOH!
OM
I SUMMON GOGOGO GOLEM...
IN ATTACK MODE!!
GOGOGO GOLEM ★★★★ ATK 1800
KAKLANK KAKLANK
THAT HAS AN ATK OF 1,800.
YOUR OPPONENT'S HAS 2,500 ATK. YOU WON'T WIN.
I KNOW THAT!
FROM MY HAND ...
I ACTIVATE BLUSTER-ING WINDS!!
SHUP
BLUSTERING WINDS RAISES THE ATK OF ONE MONSTER...
BLUSTERING WINDS (SPELL CARD)
Target 1 face-up monster you control; it gains 1000 ATK and DEF until your next Standby Phase.
...BY 1,000 POINTS UNTIL MY NEXT TURN!
WHOOOOOSH

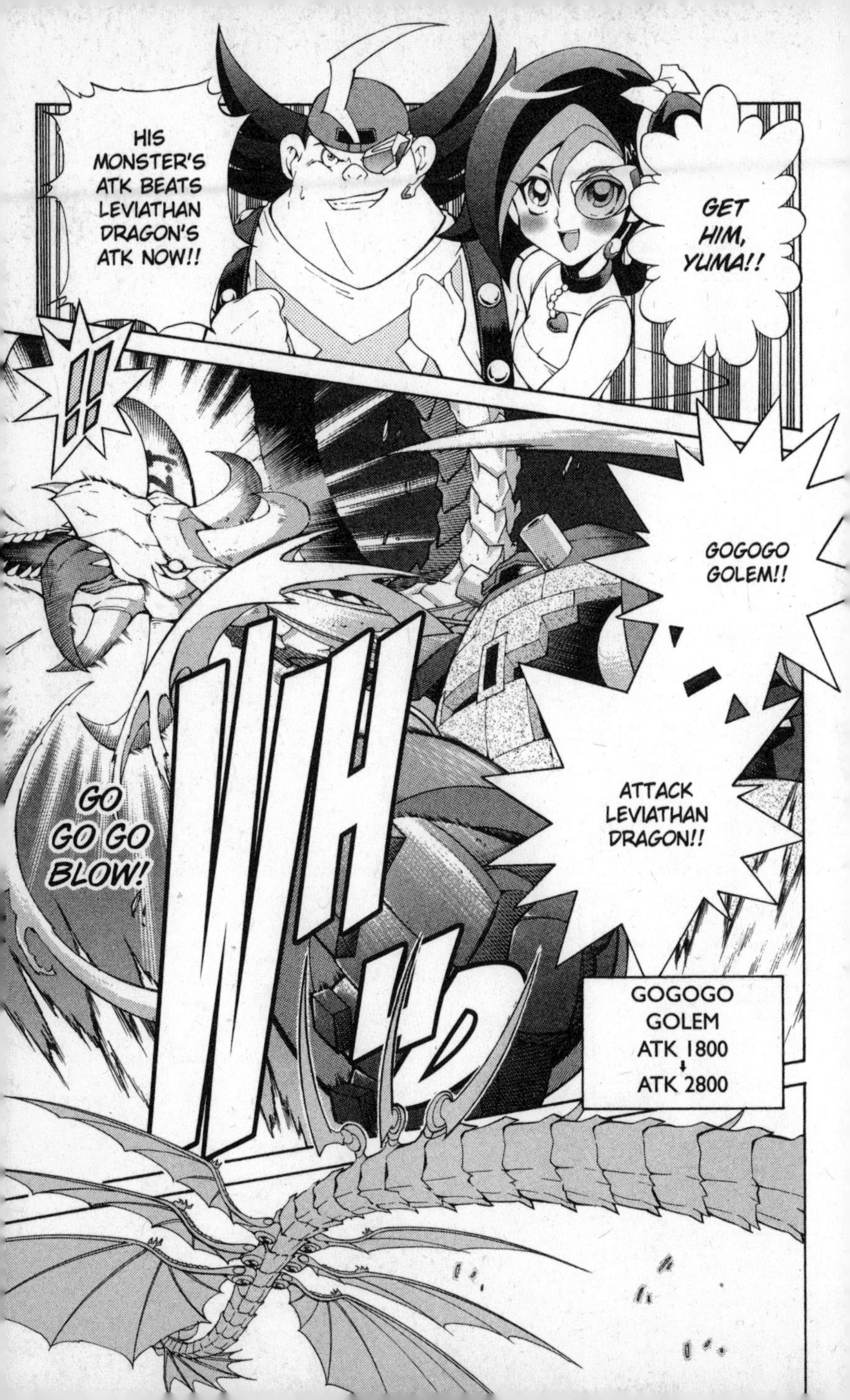
GET HIM, YUMA!!
HIS MONSTER'S ATK BEATS LEVIATHAN DRAGON'S ATK NOW!!
!!
GOGOGO GOLEM!!
ATTACK LEVIATHAN DRAGON!!
GO GO GO BLOW!
GOGOGO GOLEM ATK 1800 ↓ ATK 2800

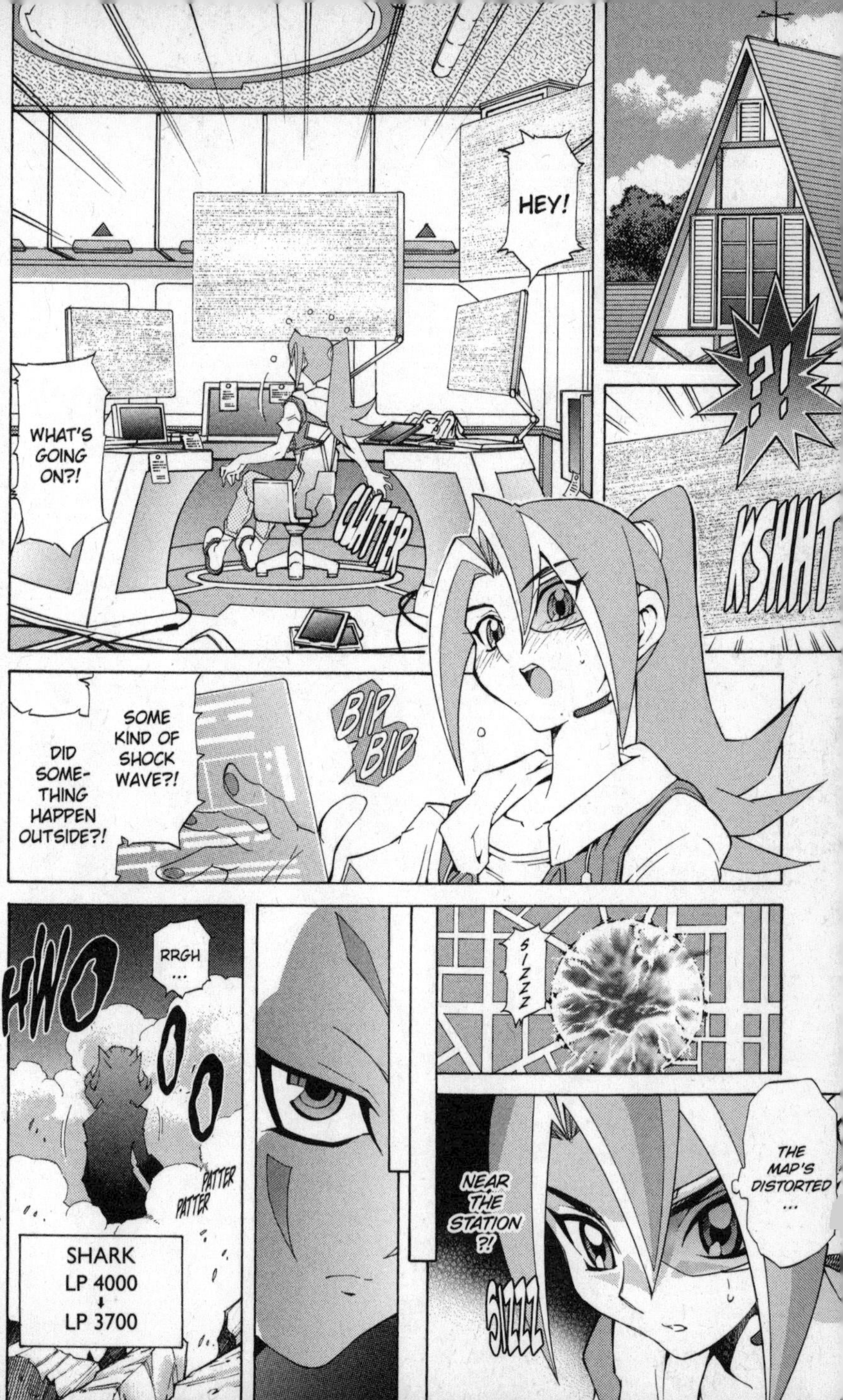
?!
KSHHT
HEY!
CLATTER
WHAT'S GOING ON?!
BIP BIP
SOME KIND OF SHOCK WAVE?!
DID SOME-THING HAPPEN OUTSIDE?!
SIZZZ
THE MAP'S DISTORTED...
NEAR THE STATION?!
SIZZZ
RRGH...
HWOOO
PATTER PATTER
SHARK LP 4000 ↓ LP 3700

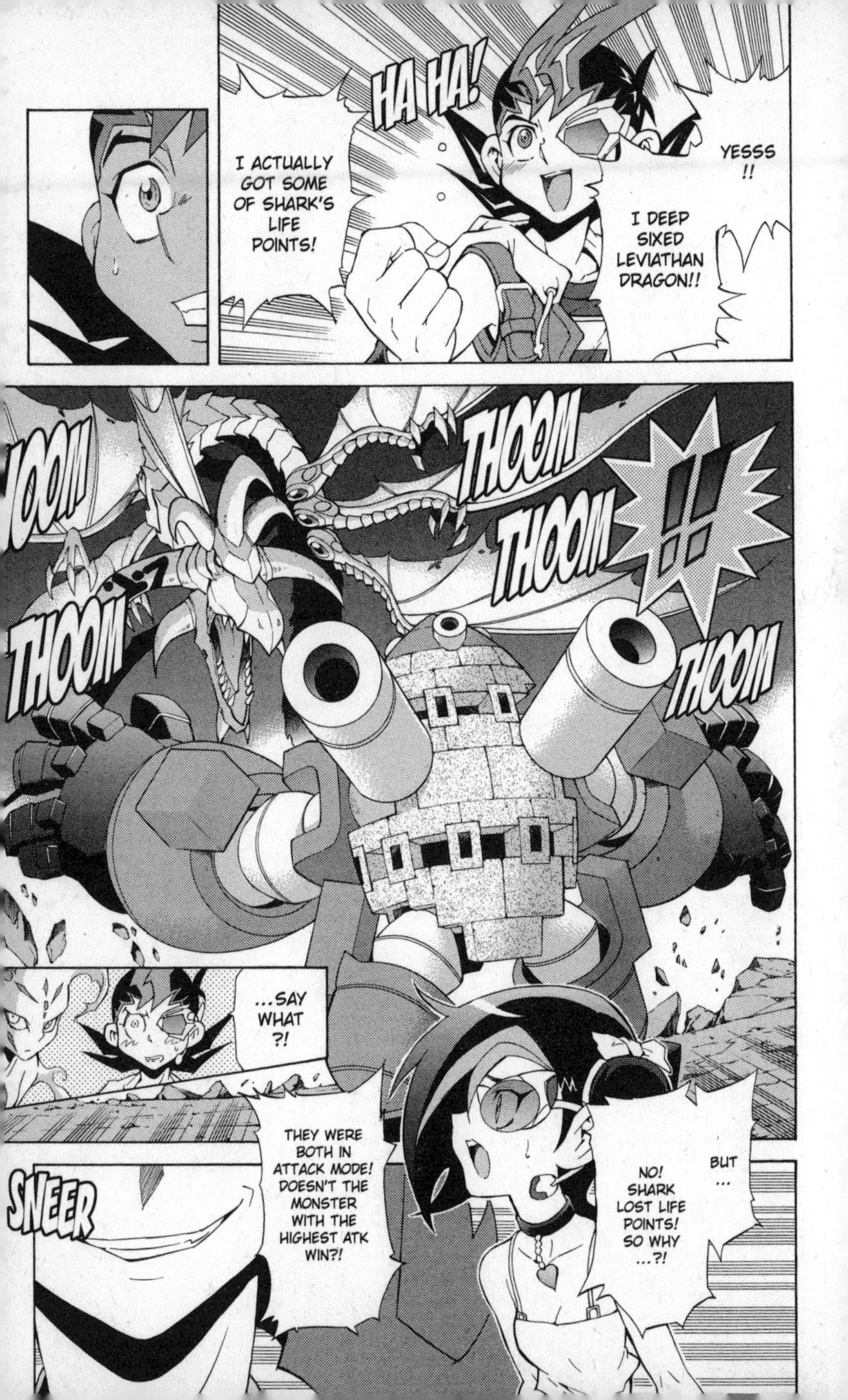
HA HA!
YESSS !!
I DEEP SIXED LEVIATHAN DRAGON!!
I ACTUALLY GOT SOME OF SHARK'S LIFE POINTS!
THOOM
THOOM
THOOM
!!
THOOM
BUT ...
NO! SHARK LOST LIFE POINTS! SO WHY ...?!
THEY WERE BOTH IN ATTACK MODE! DOESN'T THE MONSTER WITH THE HIGHEST ATK WIN?!
...SAY WHAT ?!
SNEER

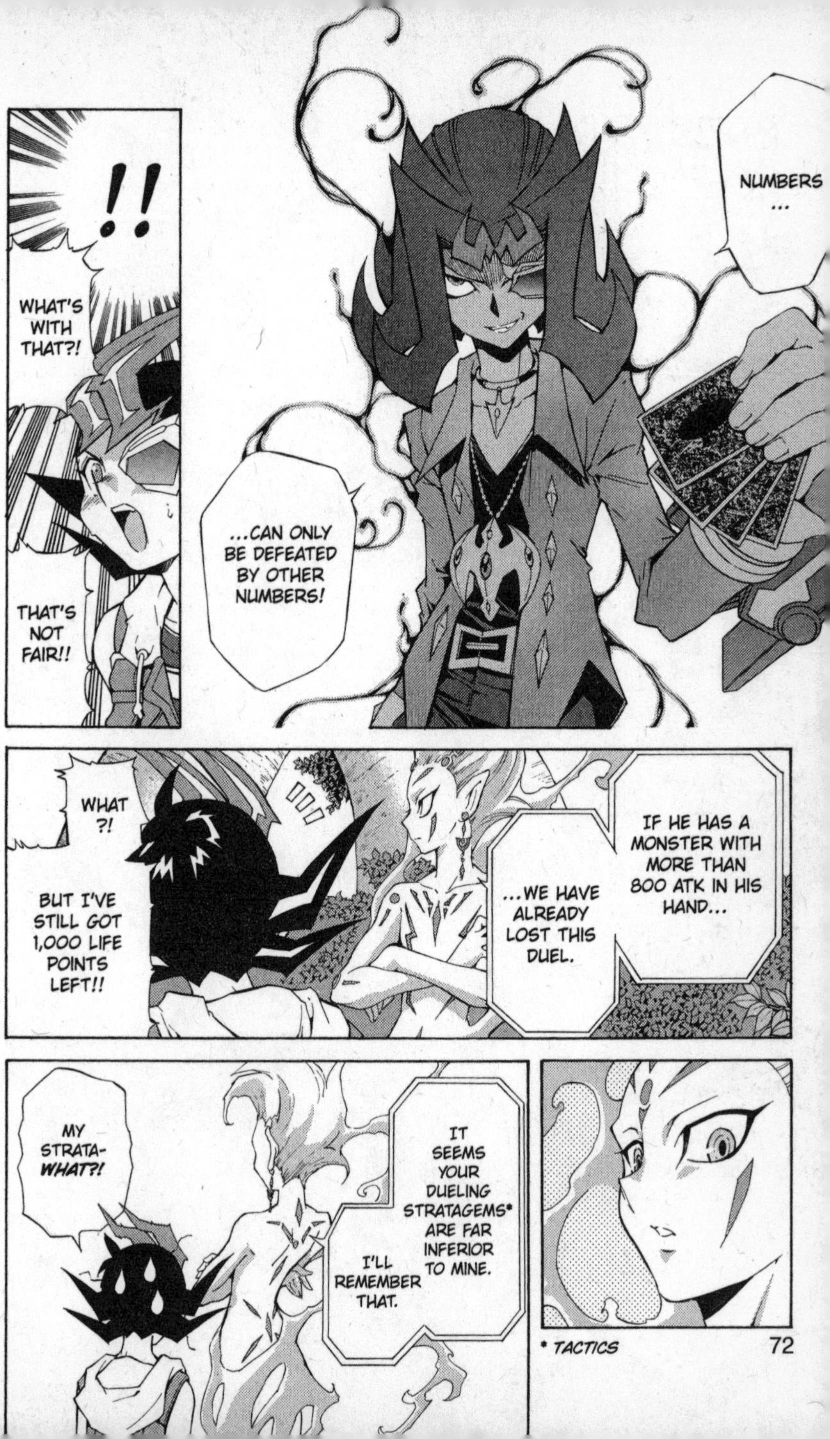
NUMBERS ...
...CAN ONLY BE DEFEATED BY OTHER NUMBERS!
!!
WHAT'S WITH THAT?!
THAT'S NOT FAIR!!
IF HE HAS A MONSTER WITH MORE THAN 800 ATK IN HIS HAND...
...WE HAVE ALREADY LOST THIS DUEL.
WHAT ?!
BUT I'VE STILL GOT 1,000 LIFE POINTS LEFT!!
IT SEEMS YOUR DUELING STRATAGEMS* ARE FAR INFERIOR TO MINE.
I'LL REMEMBER THAT.
MY STRATA-*WHAT?!*

* *TACTICS*

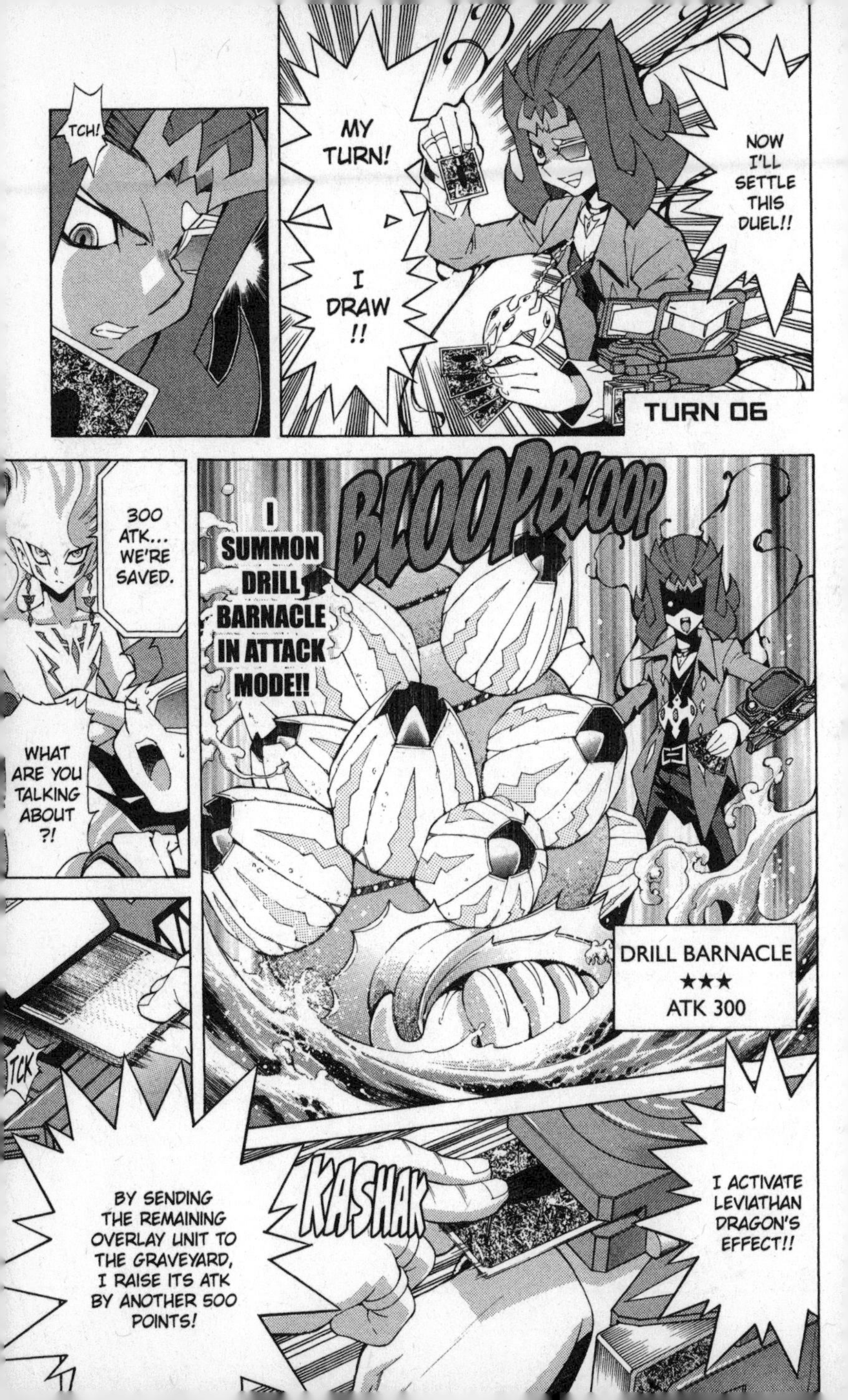
NOW I'LL SETTLE THIS DUEL!!
MY TURN!
I DRAW!!
TURN 06
TCH!
BLOOP BLOOP
I SUMMON DRILL BARNACLE IN ATTACK MODE!!
DRILL BARNACLE
★★★
ATK 300
300 ATK... WE'RE SAVED.
WHAT ARE YOU TALKING ABOUT?!
TCK
I ACTIVATE LEVIATHAN DRAGON'S EFFECT!!
KASHAK
BY SENDING THE REMAINING OVERLAY UNIT TO THE GRAVEYARD, I RAISE ITS ATK BY ANOTHER 500 POINTS!

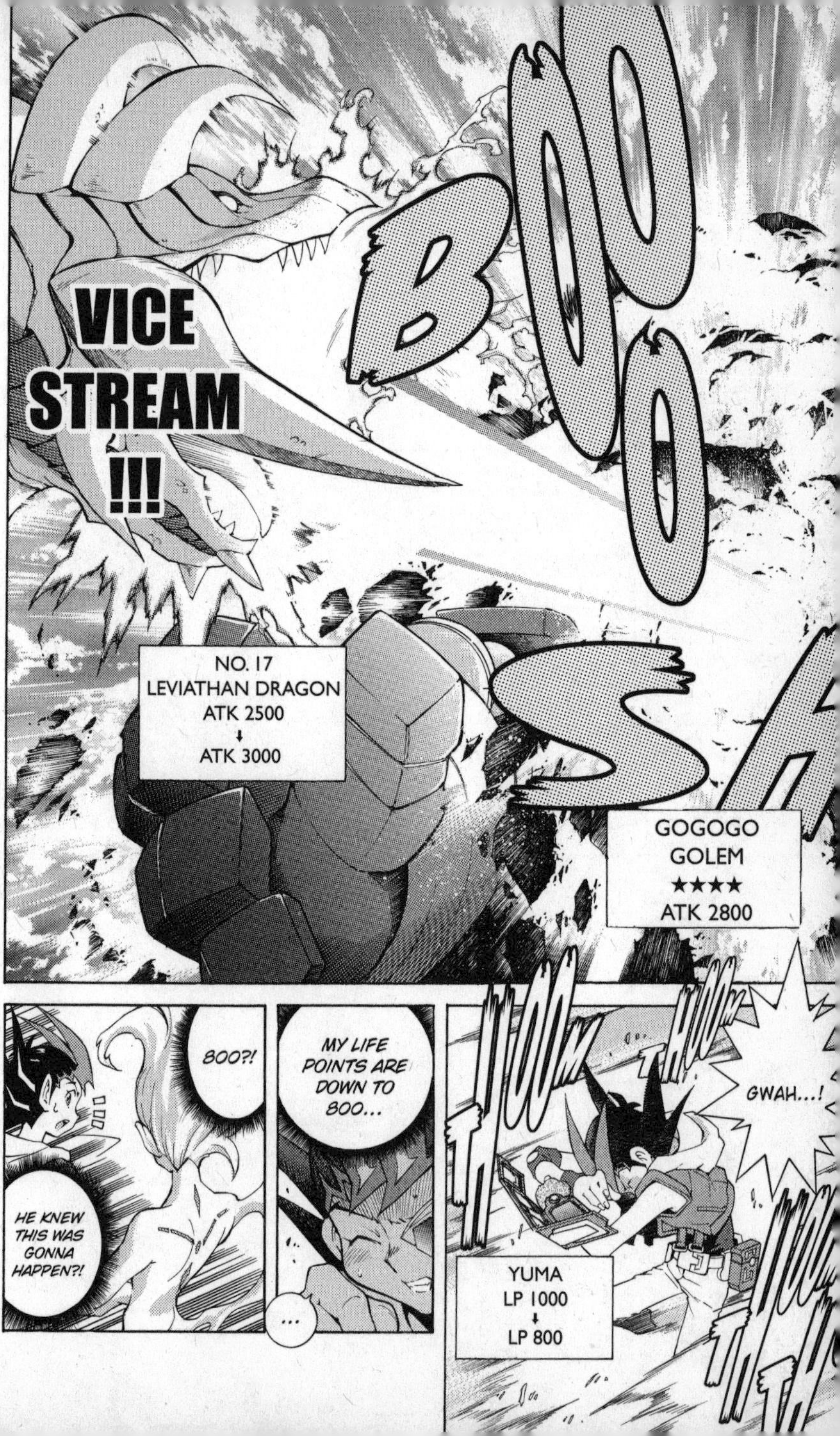
VICE STREAM !!!
NO. 17
LEVIATHAN DRAGON
ATK 2500
↓
ATK 3000
GOGOGO
GOLEM
★★★★
ATK 2800
GWAH...!
YUMA
LP 1000
↓
LP 800
MY LIFE POINTS ARE DOWN TO 800...
...
800?!
HE KNEW THIS WAS GONNA HAPPEN?!

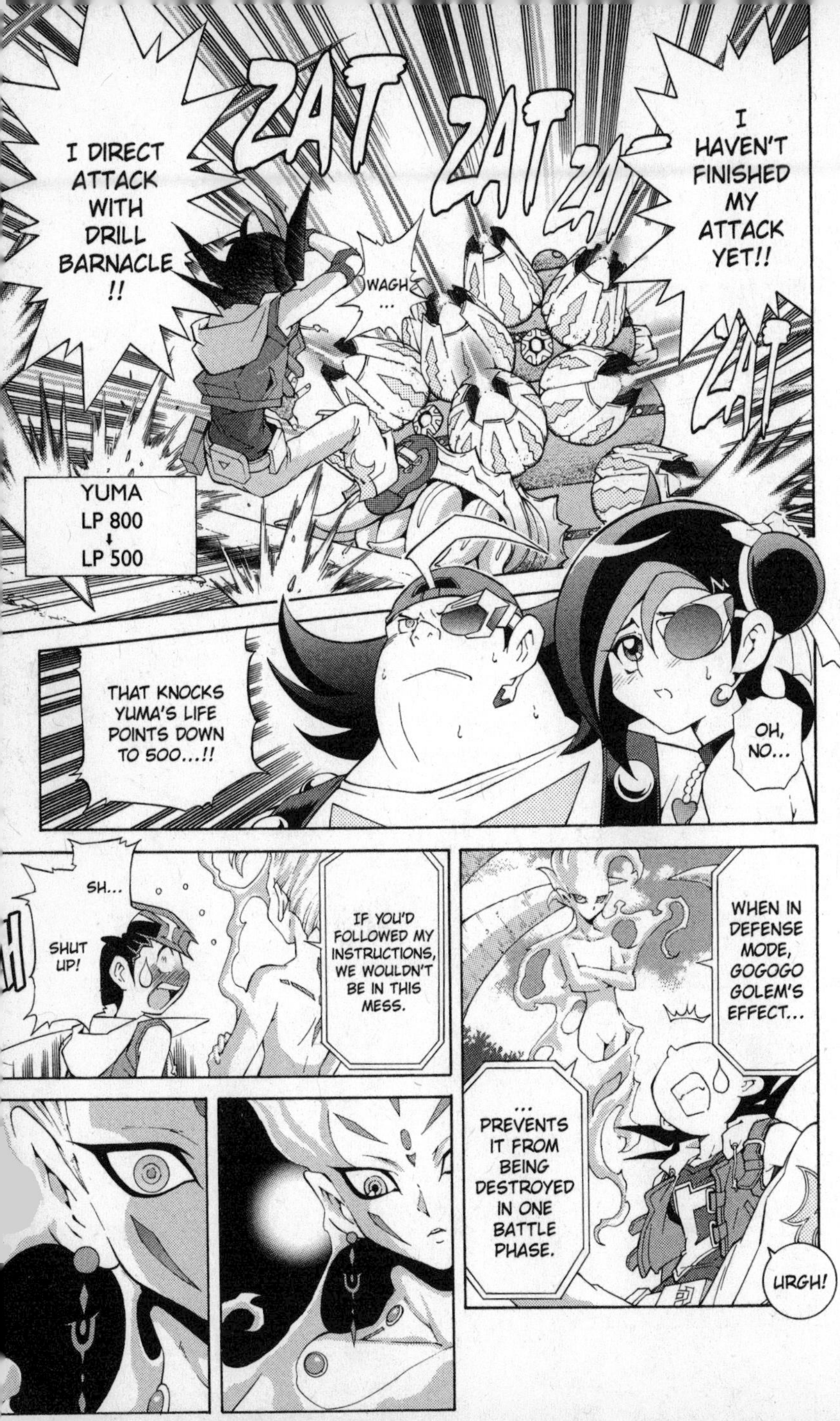
I HAVEN'T FINISHED MY ATTACK YET!!
ZAT ZAT ZAT
I DIRECT ATTACK WITH DRILL BARNACLE!!
WAGH...
ZAT
YUMA LP 800 ↓ LP 500
OH, NO...
THAT KNOCKS YUMA'S LIFE POINTS DOWN TO 500...!!
WHEN IN DEFENSE MODE, GOGOGO GOLEM'S EFFECT...
...PREVENTS IT FROM BEING DESTROYED IN ONE BATTLE PHASE.
URGH!
IF YOU'D FOLLOWED MY INSTRUCTIONS, WE WOULDN'T BE IN THIS MESS.
SH...
SHUT UP!

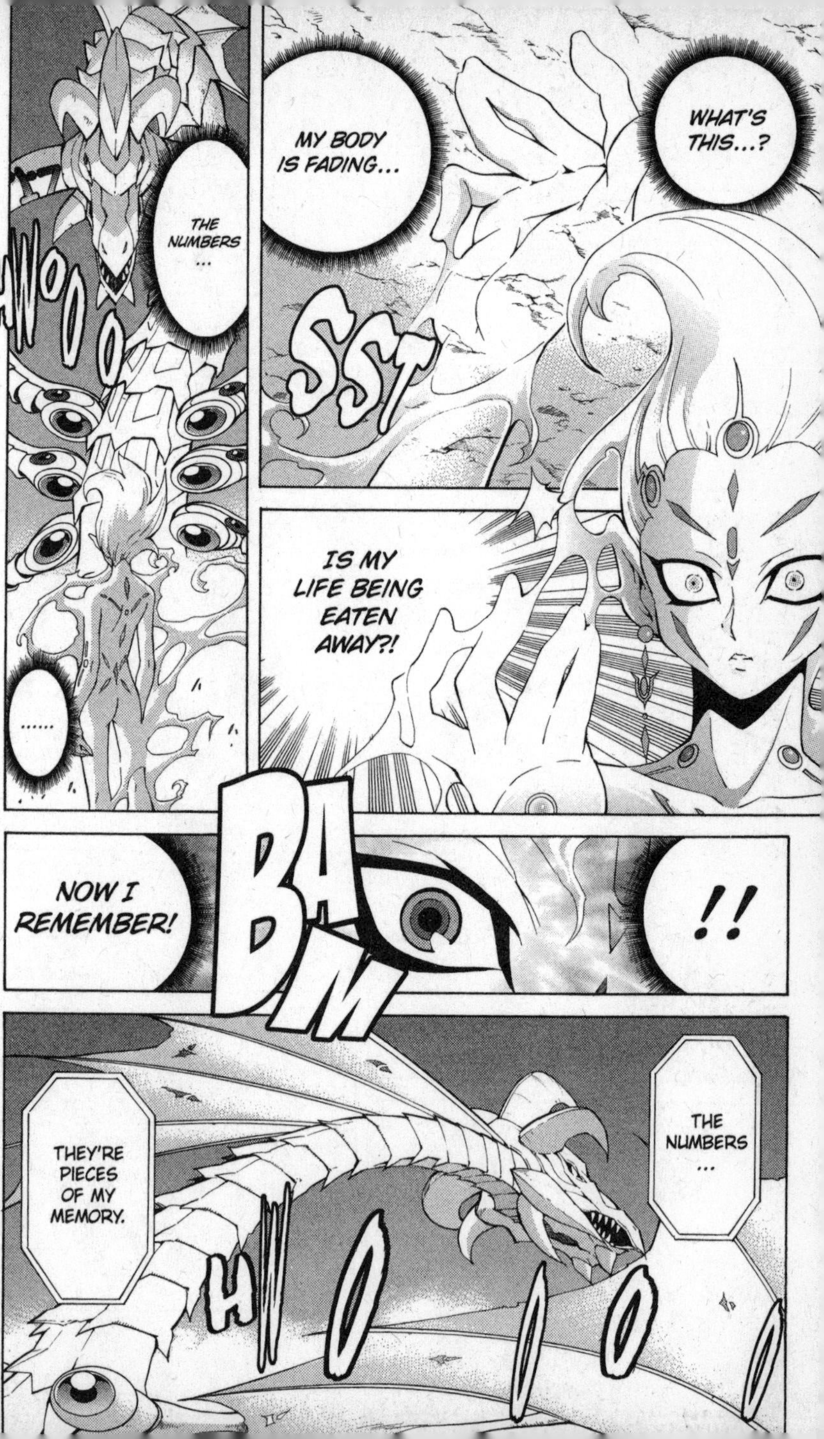
WHAT'S THIS...?
MY BODY IS FADING...
SST
IS MY LIFE BEING EATEN AWAY?!
THE NUMBERS...
HWOOO
......
!!
BAM
NOW I REMEMBER!
THE NUMBERS...
THEY'RE PIECES OF MY MEMORY.
HOOOOO

EVEN AMONG XYZ MONSTERS, NUMBERS ARE SPECIAL.
12345
67890
CARDS OF THIS WORLD CAN'T DEFEAT THEM.
AND IN A DUEL OF NUMBERS, THE WINNER ABSORBS THE NUMBER OF THE LOSER!!
?
?
UNLESS I WIN THIS DUEL, I WILL VANISH.
I MUST WIN... I ABSOLUTELY CANNOT LOSE THIS DUEL.

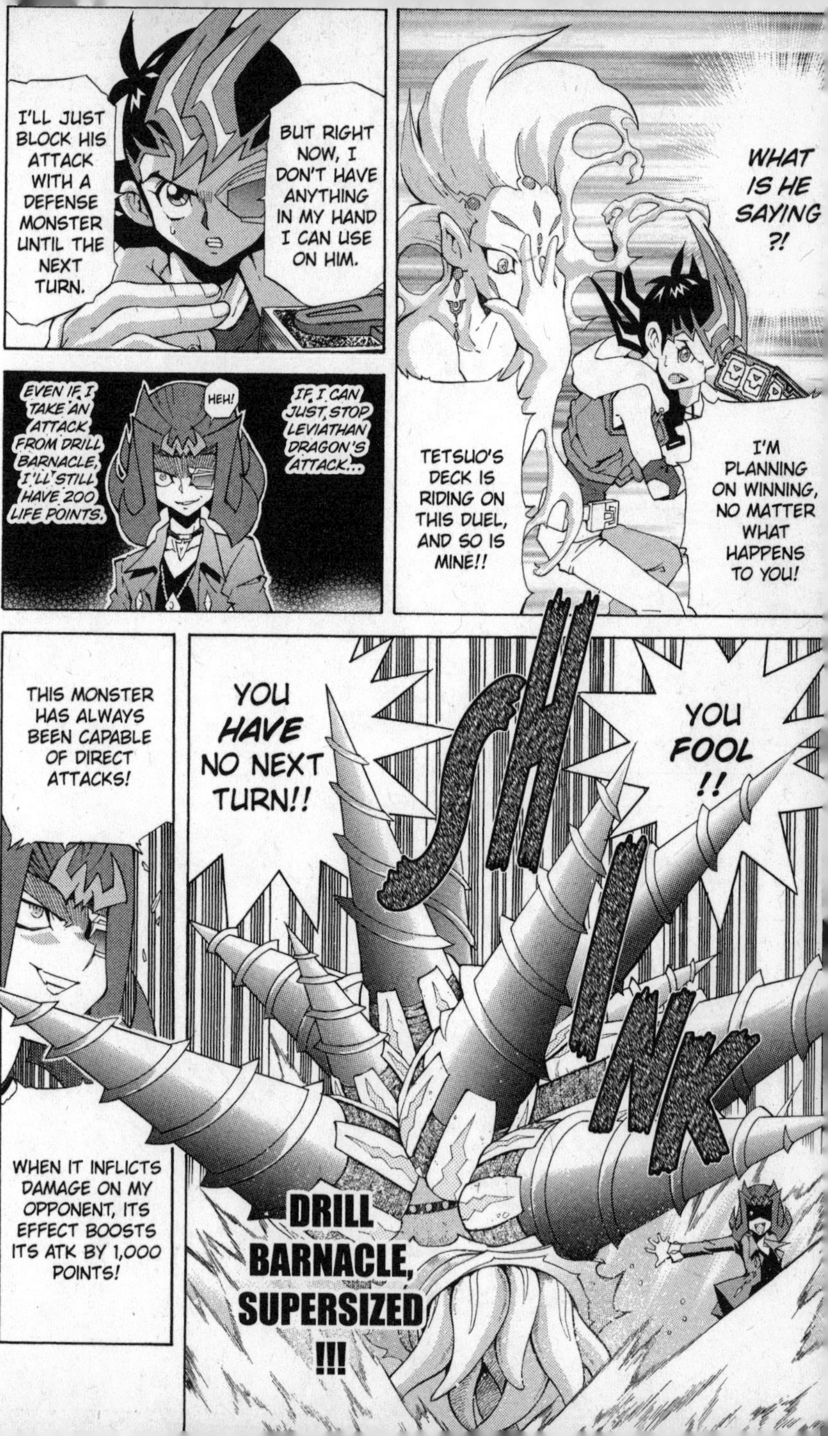
WHAT IS HE SAYING?!
I'M PLANNING ON WINNING, NO MATTER WHAT HAPPENS TO YOU!
TETSUO'S DECK IS RIDING ON THIS DUEL, AND SO IS MINE!!
BUT RIGHT NOW, I DON'T HAVE ANYTHING IN MY HAND I CAN USE ON HIM.
I'LL JUST BLOCK HIS ATTACK WITH A DEFENSE MONSTER UNTIL THE NEXT TURN.
IF I CAN JUST STOP LEVIATHAN DRAGON'S ATTACK...
HEH!
EVEN IF I TAKE AN ATTACK FROM DRILL BARNACLE, I'LL STILL HAVE 200 LIFE POINTS.
SHINK
YOU FOOL!!
YOU HAVE NO NEXT TURN!!
DRILL BARNACLE, SUPERSIZED!!!
THIS MONSTER HAS ALWAYS BEEN CAPABLE OF DIRECT ATTACKS!
WHEN IT INFLICTS DAMAGE ON MY OPPONENT, ITS EFFECT BOOSTS ITS ATK BY 1,000 POINTS!

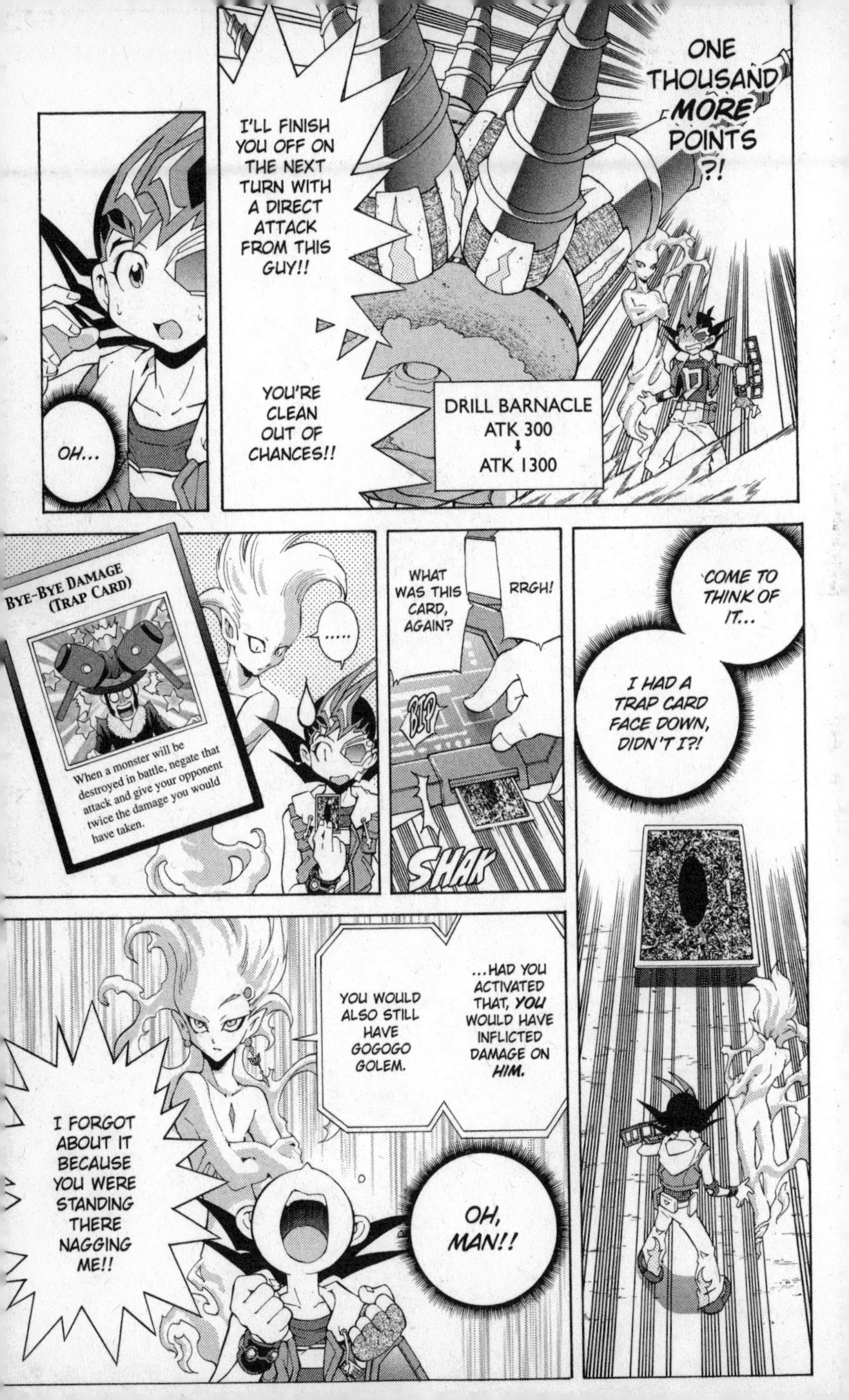

ONE THOUSAND MORE POINTS ?!
I'LL FINISH YOU OFF ON THE NEXT TURN WITH A DIRECT ATTACK FROM THIS GUY!!
YOU'RE CLEAN OUT OF CHANCES!!
DRILL BARNACLE ATK 300 ATK 1300
OH...
COME TO THINK OF IT...
I HAD A TRAP CARD FACE DOWN, DIDN'T I?!
RRGH!
WHAT WAS THIS CARD, AGAIN?
BLIP
SHAK
......
BYE-BYE DAMAGE (TRAP CARD)
When a monster will be destroyed in battle, negate that attack and give your opponent twice the damage you would have taken.
...HAD YOU ACTIVATED THAT, YOU WOULD HAVE INFLICTED DAMAGE ON HIM.
YOU WOULD ALSO STILL HAVE GOGOGO GOLEM.
OH, MAN!!
I FORGOT ABOUT IT BECAUSE YOU WERE STANDING THERE NAGGING ME!!

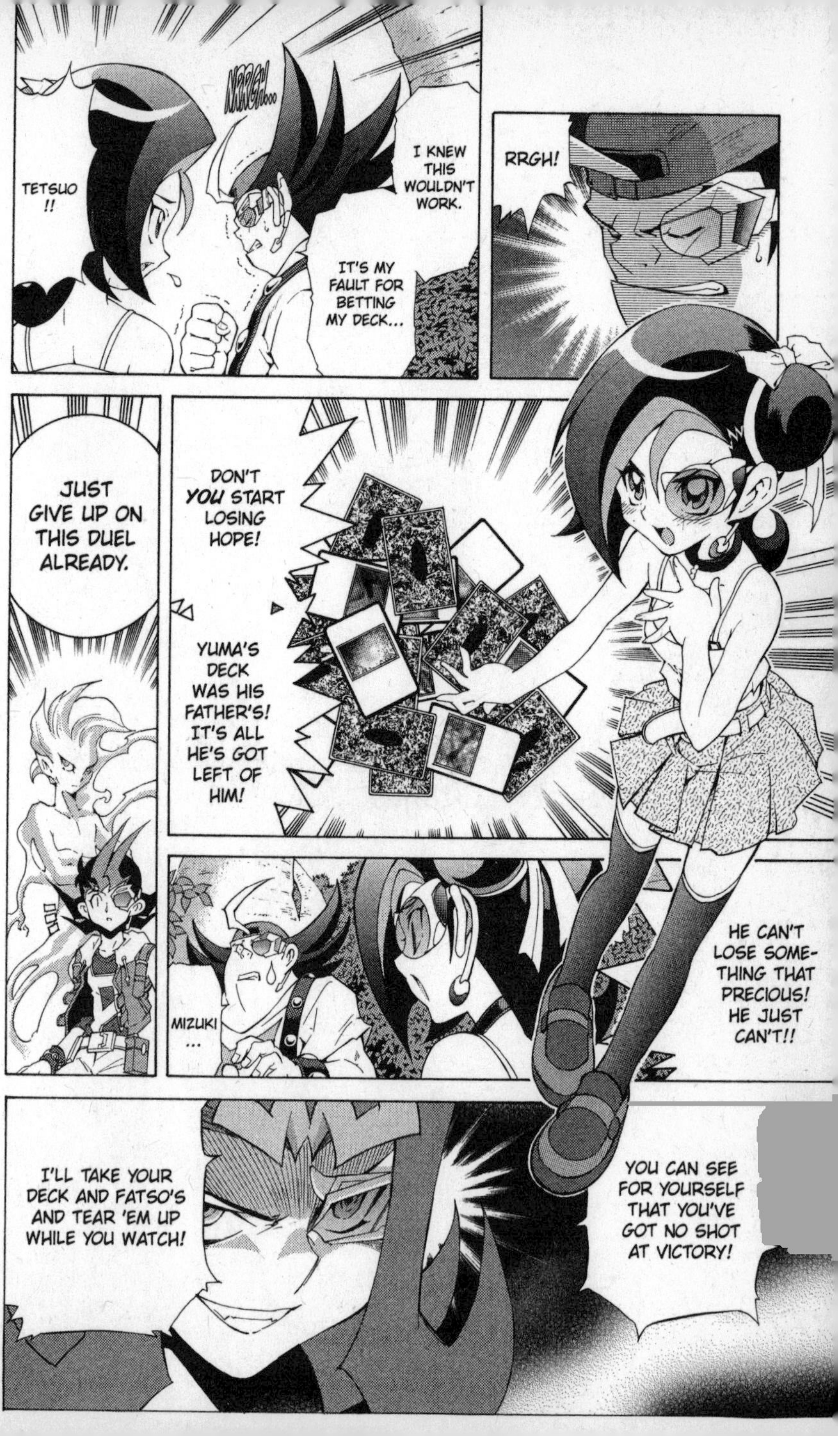

RRGH!
NRRGH...
I KNEW THIS WOULDN'T WORK.
IT'S MY FAULT FOR BETTING MY DECK...
TETSUO !!
DON'T *YOU* START LOSING HOPE!
YUMA'S DECK WAS HIS FATHER'S! IT'S ALL HE'S GOT LEFT OF HIM!
HE CAN'T LOSE SOME-THING THAT PRECIOUS! HE JUST CAN'T!!
MIZUKI ...
JUST GIVE UP ON THIS DUEL ALREADY.
YOU CAN SEE FOR YOURSELF THAT YOU'VE GOT NO SHOT AT VICTORY!
I'LL TAKE YOUR DECK AND FATSO'S AND TEAR 'EM UP WHILE YOU WATCH!

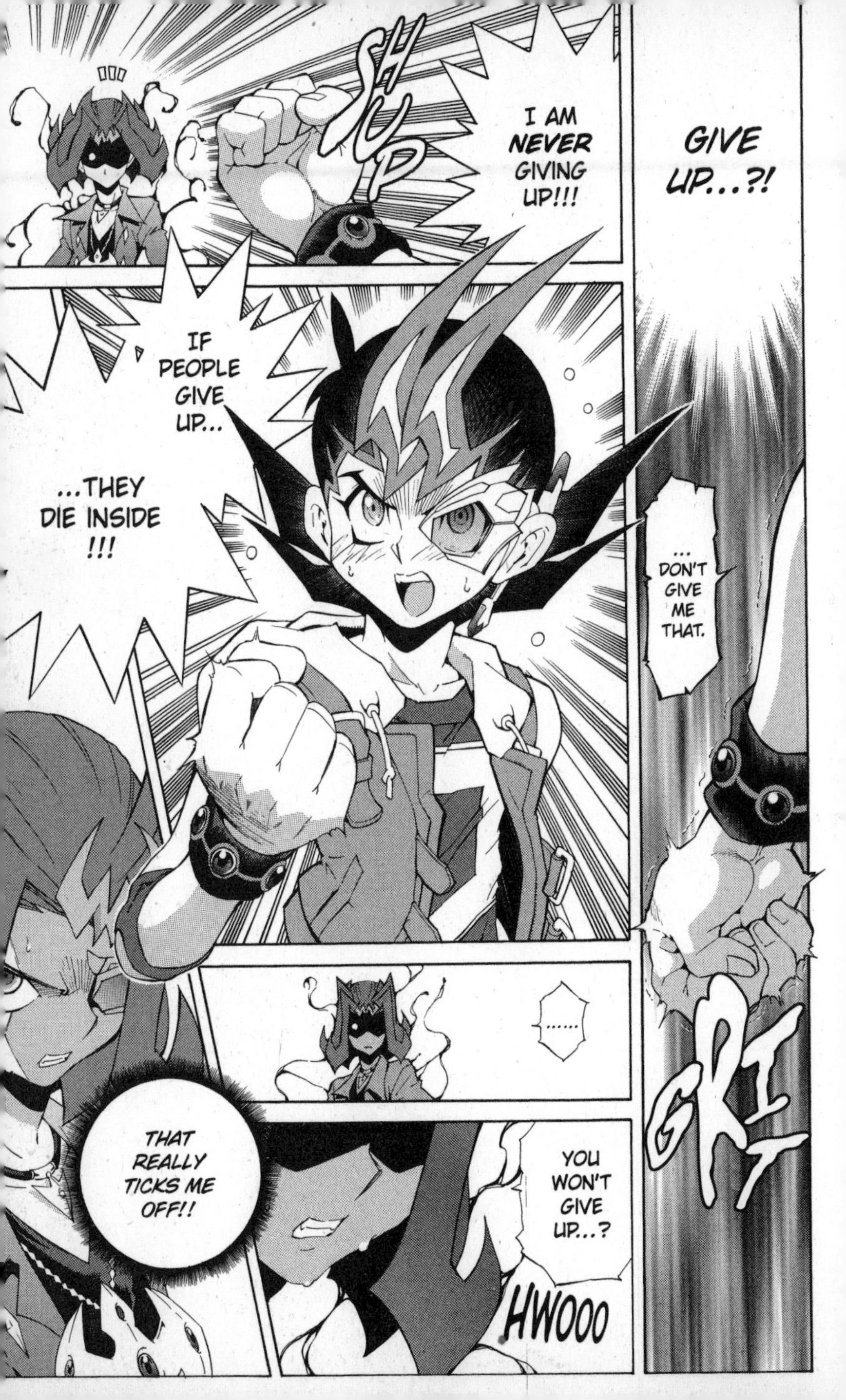
GIVE UP...?!
...DON'T GIVE ME THAT.
GRIT
SHUP
I AM NEVER GIVING UP!!!
IF PEOPLE GIVE UP...
...THEY DIE INSIDE!!!
......
YOU WON'T GIVE UP...?
HWOOO
THAT REALLY TICKS ME OFF!!

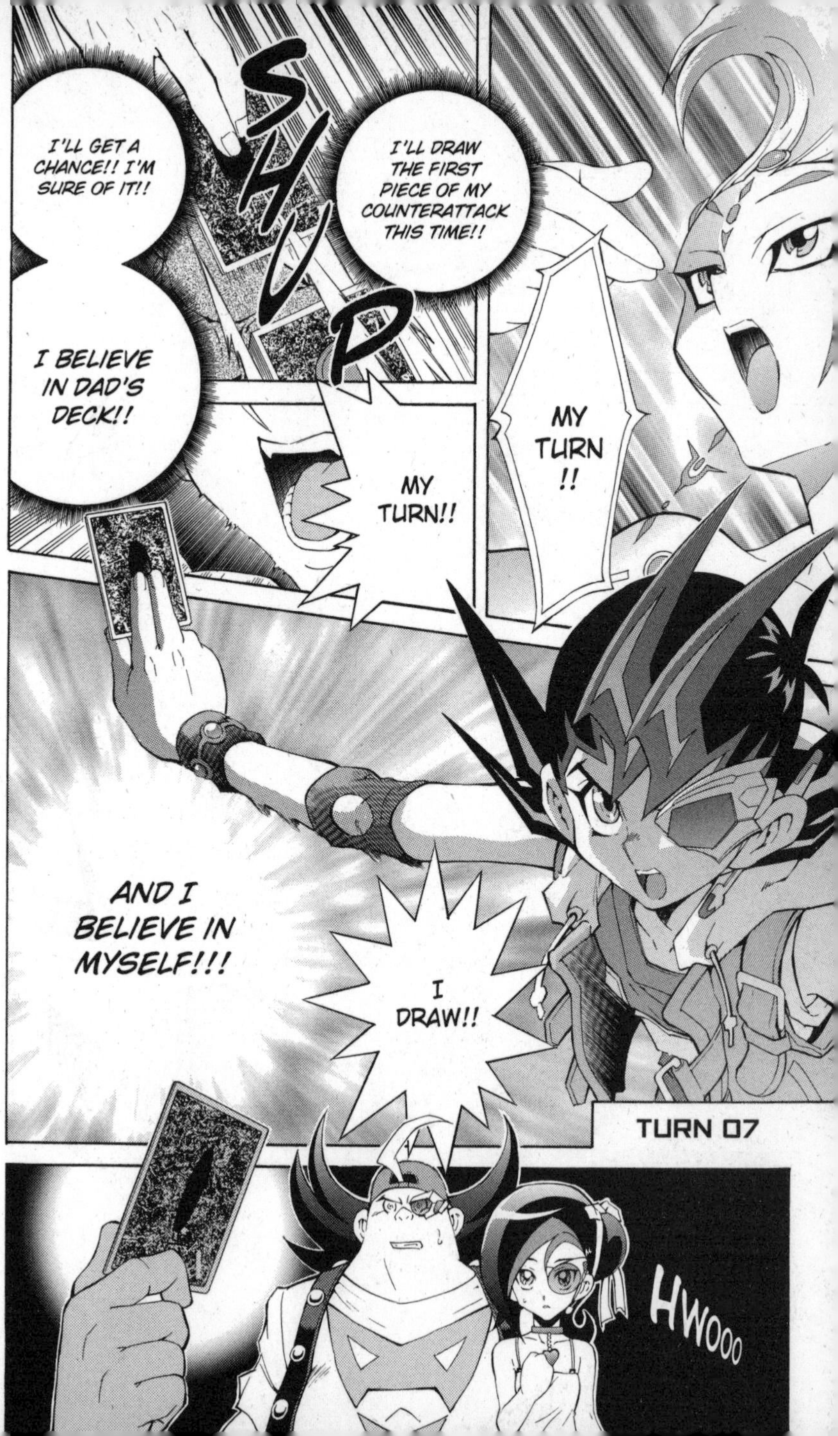
MY TURN!!
I'LL DRAW THE FIRST PIECE OF MY COUNTERATTACK THIS TIME!!
I'LL GET A CHANCE!! I'M SURE OF IT!!
SHUD
I BELIEVE IN DAD'S DECK!!
MY TURN!!
I DRAW!!
AND I BELIEVE IN MYSELF!!!
TURN 07
HWOOO

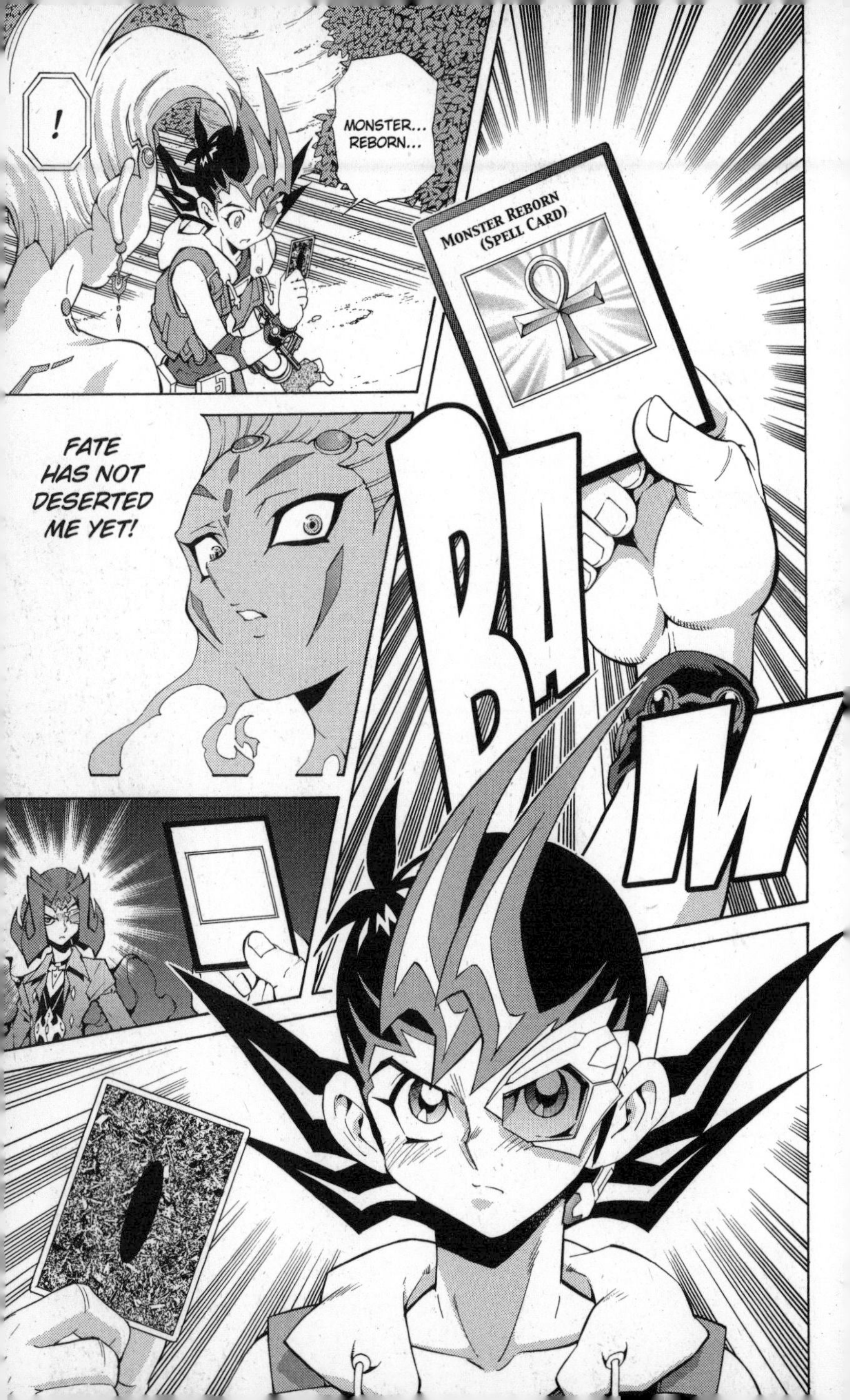
MONSTER REBORN (SPELL CARD)
BAM
MONSTER... REBORN...
!
FATE HAS NOT DESERTED ME YET!

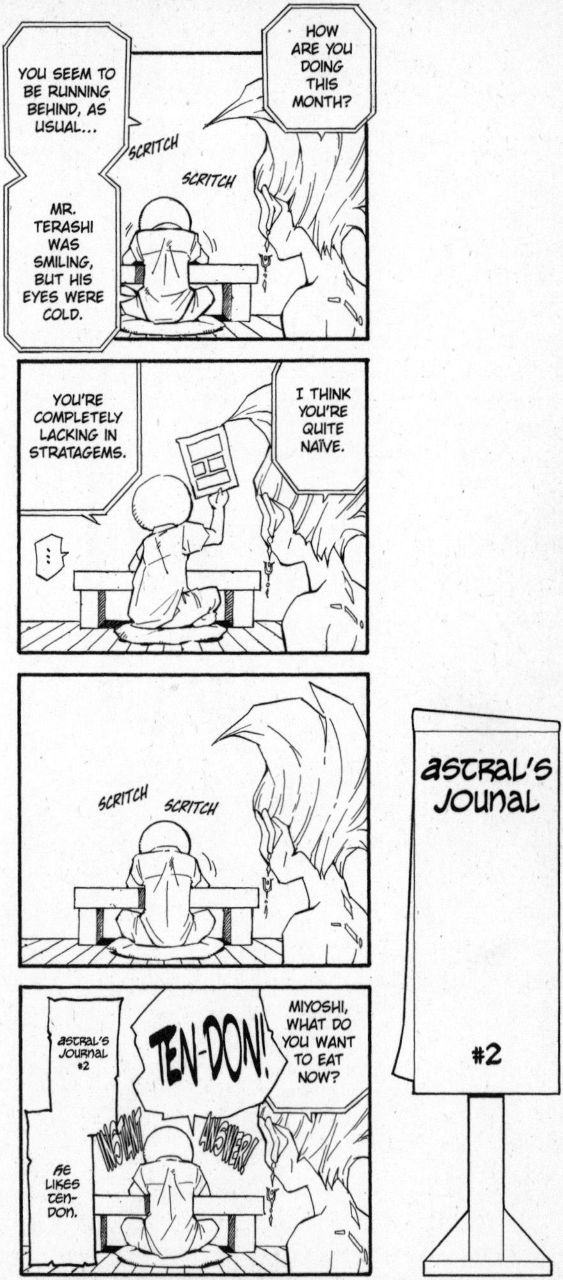
astral's
Jounal
#2
HOW ARE YOU DOING THIS MONTH?
YOU SEEM TO BE RUNNING BEHIND, AS USUAL...
SCRITCH
SCRITCH
MR. TERASHI WAS SMILING, BUT HIS EYES WERE COLD.
I THINK YOU'RE QUITE NAÏVE.
YOU'RE COMPLETELY LACKING IN STRATAGEMS.
...
SCRITCH
SCRITCH
MIYOSHI, WHAT DO YOU WANT TO EAT NOW?
TEN-DON!
astral's Journal #2
INSTANT
ANSWER!
HE LIKES TEN-DON.

*TEN-DON IS SHORT FOR "TEMPURA DONBURI", WHICH IS SHRIMP OR VEGETABLES FRIED IN LIGHT BATTER AND SERVED OVER RICE IN A BOWL.

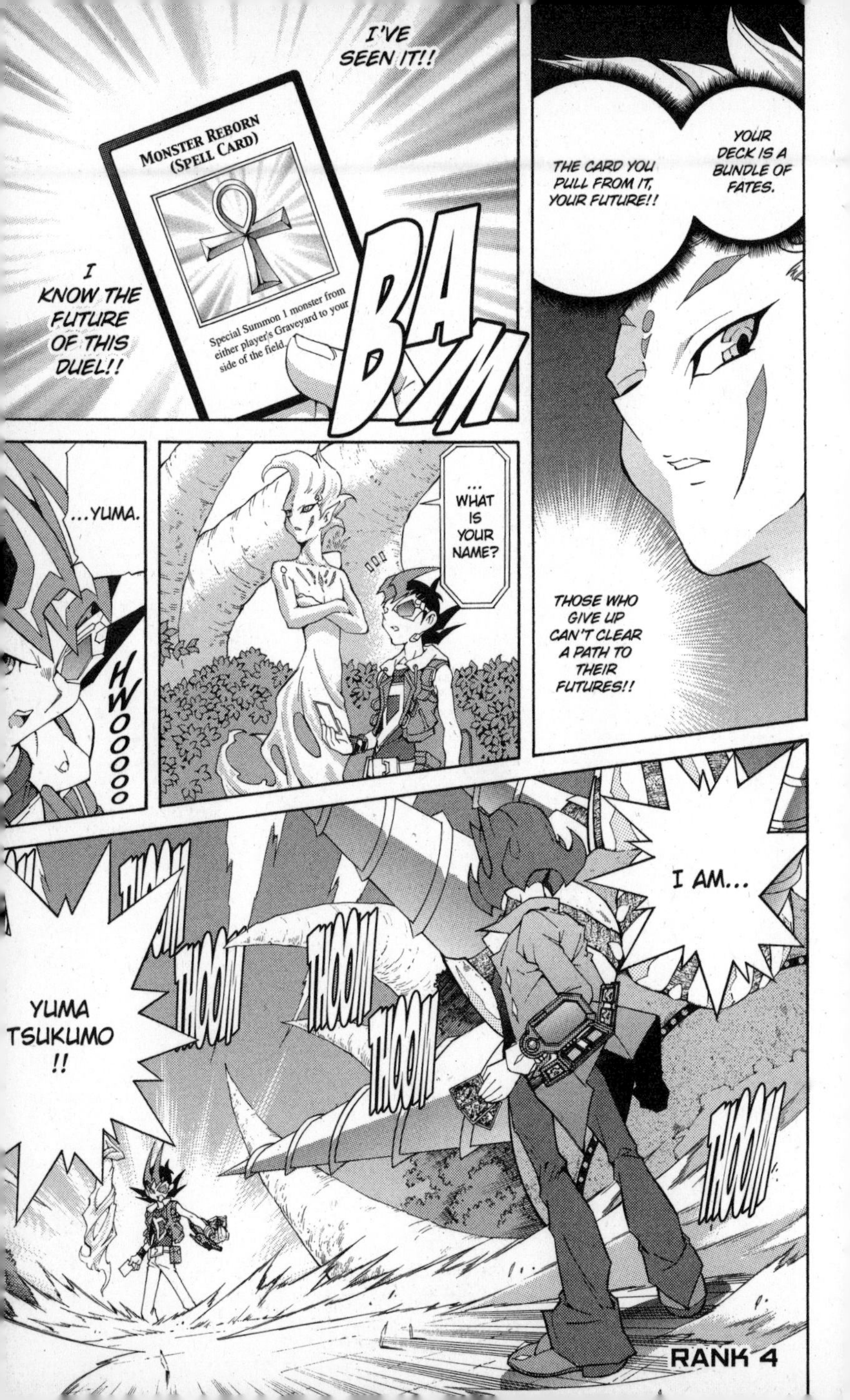
YOUR DECK IS A BUNDLE OF FATES.
THE CARD YOU PULL FROM IT, YOUR FUTURE!!
THOSE WHO GIVE UP CAN'T CLEAR A PATH TO THEIR FUTURES!!
I'VE SEEN IT!!
MONSTER REBORN (SPELL CARD)
Special Summon 1 monster from either player's Graveyard to your side of the field.
BAM
I KNOW THE FUTURE OF THIS DUEL!!
... WHAT IS YOUR NAME?
...YUMA.
HWOOOOOO
I AM...
THOOM
THOOM
THOOM
THOOM
THOOM
THOOM
YUMA TSUKUMO !!

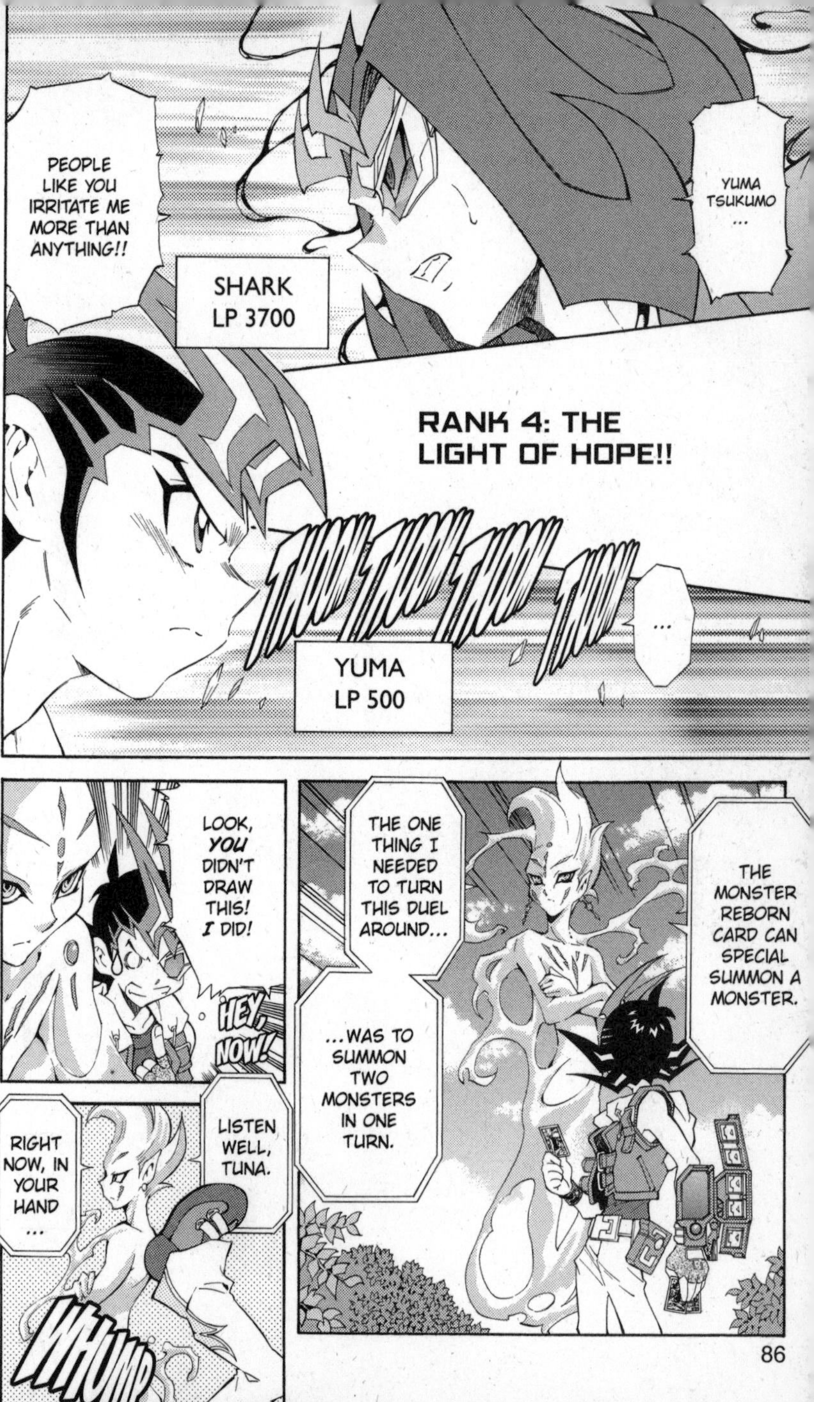
YUMA TSUKUMO ...
PEOPLE LIKE YOU IRRITATE ME MORE THAN ANYTHING!!
SHARK LP 3700
RANK 4: THE LIGHT OF HOPE!!
...
YUMA LP 500
THE MONSTER REBORN CARD CAN SPECIAL SUMMON A MONSTER.
THE ONE THING I NEEDED TO TURN THIS DUEL AROUND...
...WAS TO SUMMON TWO MONSTERS IN ONE TURN.
LOOK, *YOU* DIDN'T DRAW THIS! *I* DID!
HEY, NOW!
LISTEN WELL, TUNA.
RIGHT NOW, IN YOUR HAND ...
WHUMP

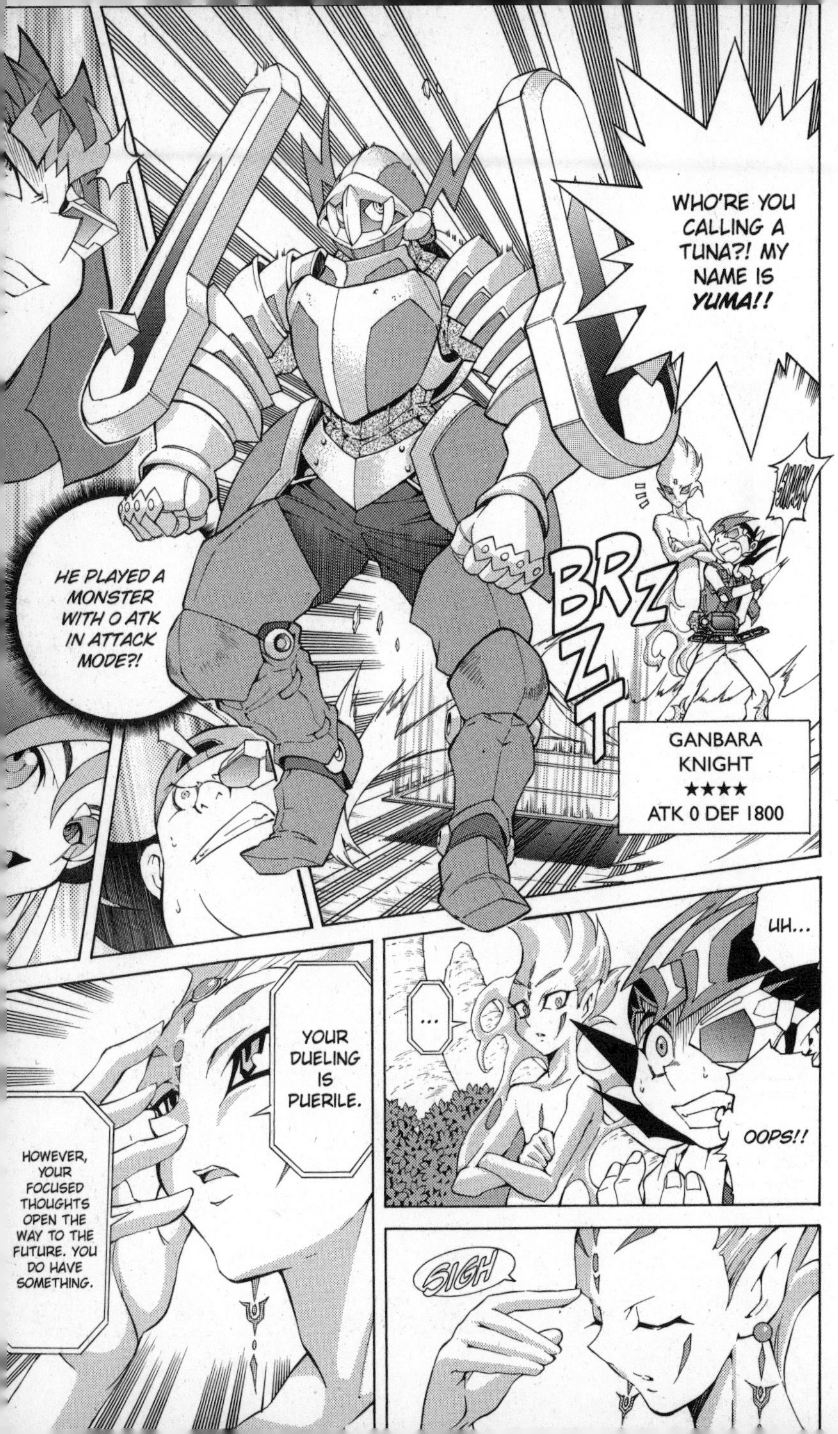

WHO'RE YOU CALLING A TUNA?! MY NAME IS *YUMA!!*
BRZZT
GANBARA KNIGHT
★★★★
ATK 0 DEF 1800
HE PLAYED A MONSTER WITH 0 ATK IN ATTACK MODE?!
UH...
...
OOPS!!
SIGH
YOUR DUELING IS PUERILE.
HOWEVER, YOUR FOCUSED THOUGHTS OPEN THE WAY TO THE FUTURE. YOU DO HAVE SOMETHING.

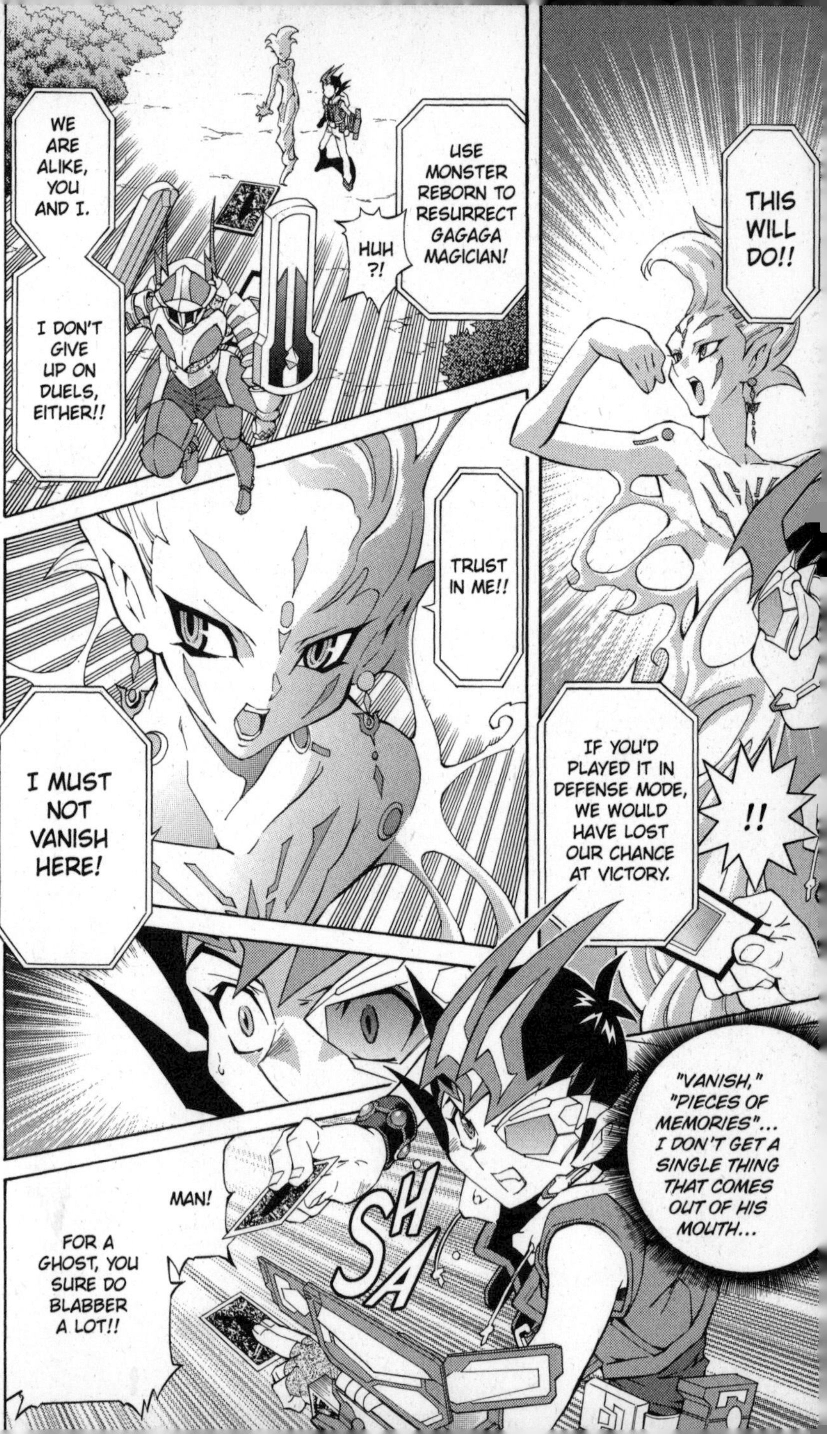
THIS WILL DO!!
IF YOU'D PLAYED IT IN DEFENSE MODE, WE WOULD HAVE LOST OUR CHANCE AT VICTORY.
!!
USE MONSTER REBORN TO RESURRECT GAGAGA MAGICIAN!
HUH?!
WE ARE ALIKE, YOU AND I.
I DON'T GIVE UP ON DUELS, EITHER!!
TRUST IN ME!!
I MUST NOT VANISH HERE!
"VANISH," "PIECES OF MEMORIES"... I DON'T GET A SINGLE THING THAT COMES OUT OF HIS MOUTH...
SHSA
MAN!
FOR A GHOST, YOU SURE DO BLABBER A LOT!!

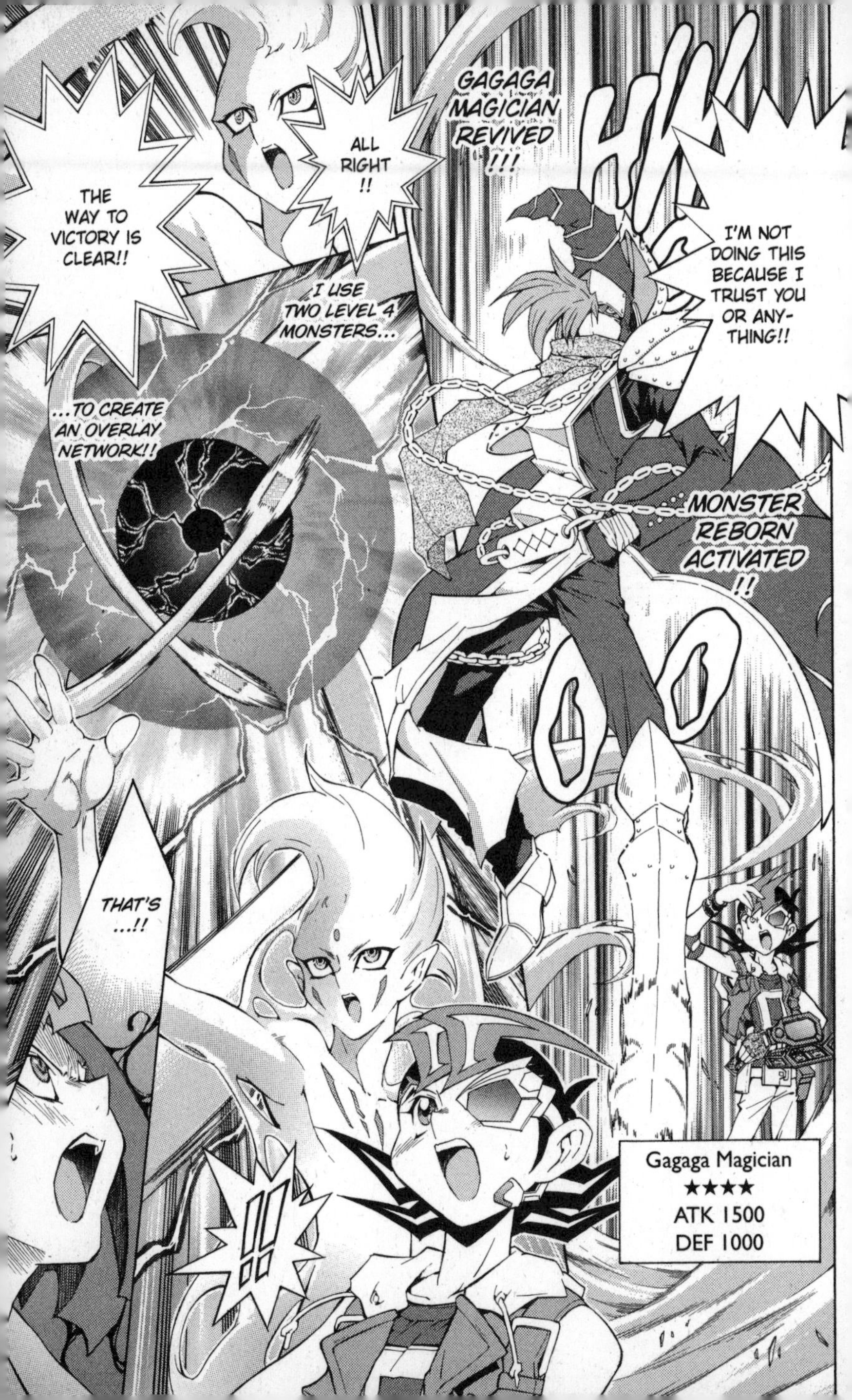
GAGAGA MAGICIAN REVIVED!!!
I'M NOT DOING THIS BECAUSE I TRUST YOU OR ANY-THING!!
ALL RIGHT!!
THE WAY TO VICTORY IS CLEAR!!
I USE TWO LEVEL 4 MONSTERS...
MONSTER REBORN ACTIVATED!!
...TO CREATE AN OVERLAY NETWORK!!
THAT'S...!!
Gagaga Magician
★★★★
ATK 1500
DEF 1000
!!

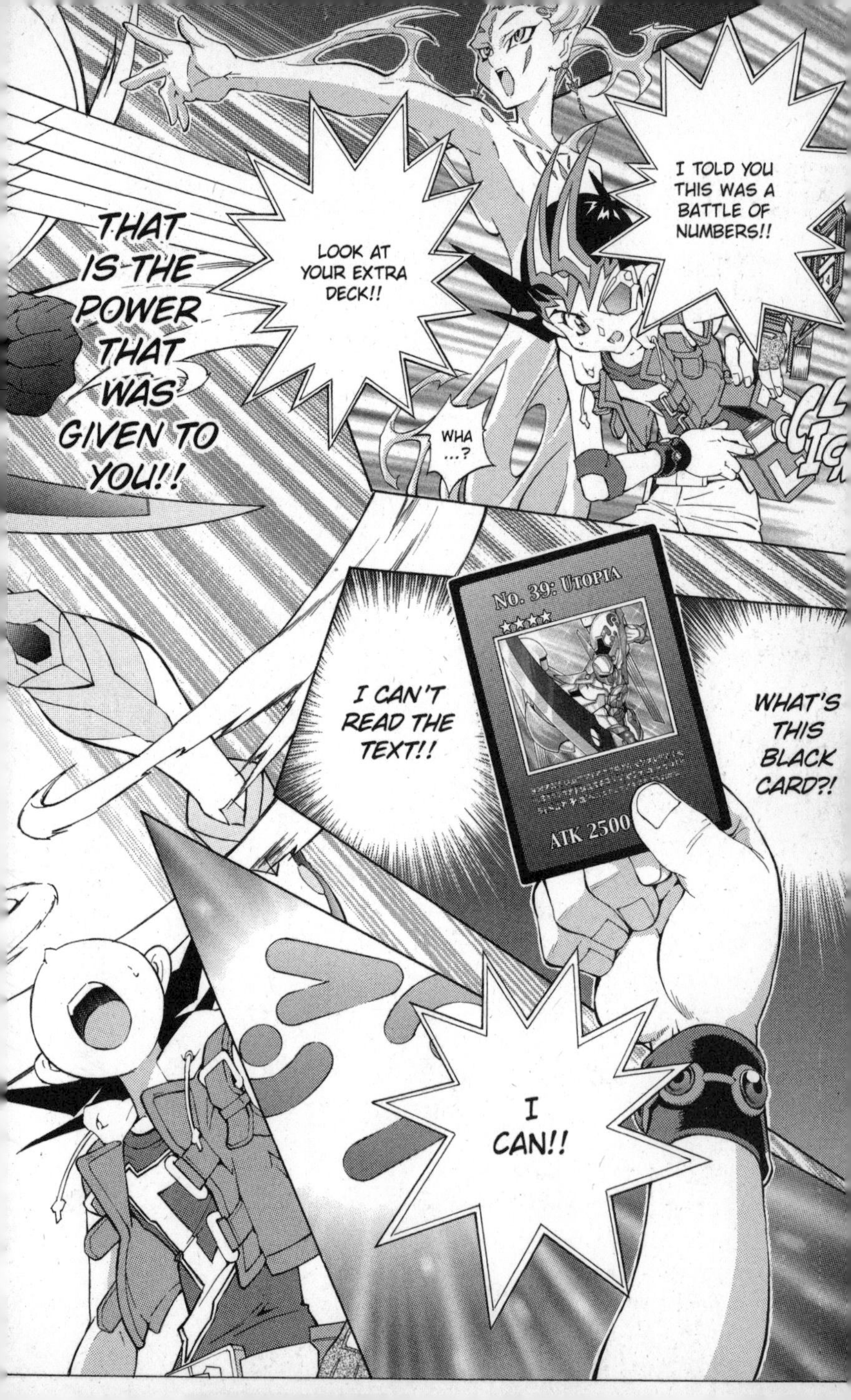
I TOLD YOU THIS WAS A BATTLE OF NUMBERS!!
LOOK AT YOUR EXTRA DECK!!
THAT IS THE POWER THAT WAS GIVEN TO YOU!!
WHA ...?
WHAT'S THIS BLACK CARD?!
No. 39: UTOPIA
ATK 2500
I CAN'T READ THE TEXT!!
I CAN!!

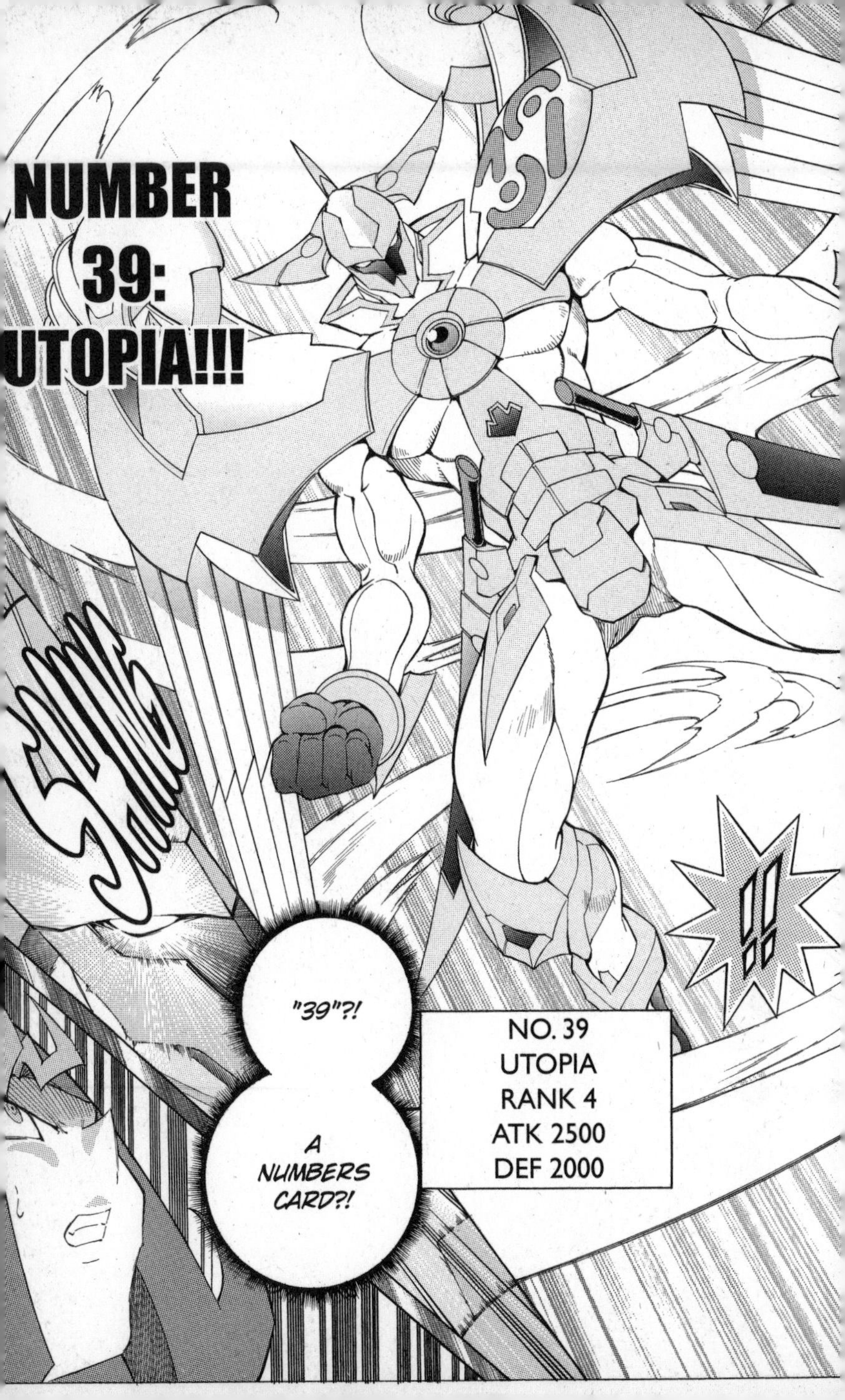
NUMBER 39: UTOPIA!!!
!!
NO. 39 UTOPIA RANK 4 ATK 2500 DEF 2000
"39"?!
A NUMBERS CARD?!

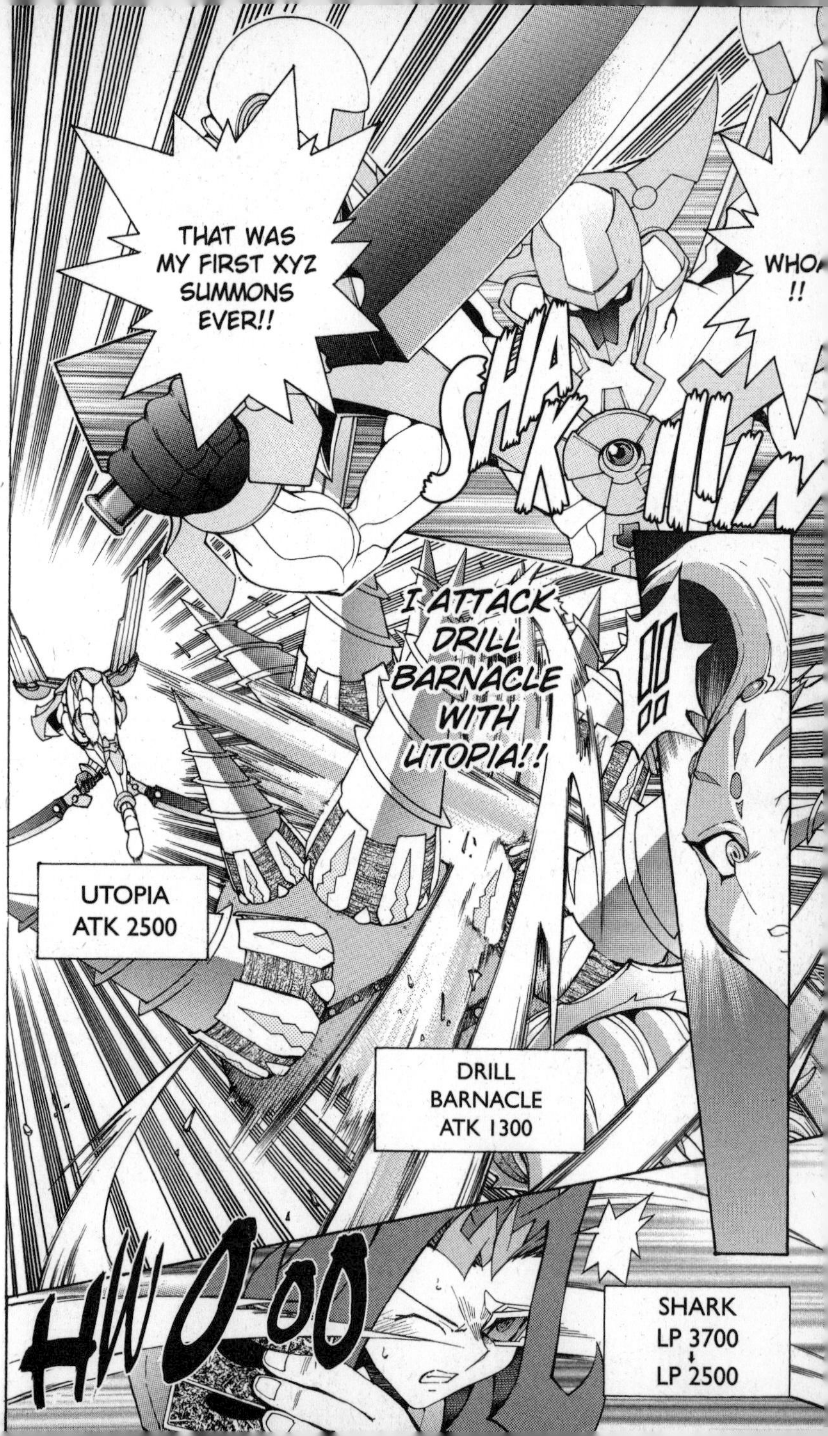
WHOA !!
SHAKIIIN
THAT WAS MY FIRST XYZ SUMMONS EVER!!
!!
I ATTACK DRILL BARNACLE WITH UTOPIA!!
UTOPIA ATK 2500
DRILL BARNACLE ATK 1300
SHARK LP 3700 ↓ LP 2500
HWOOO

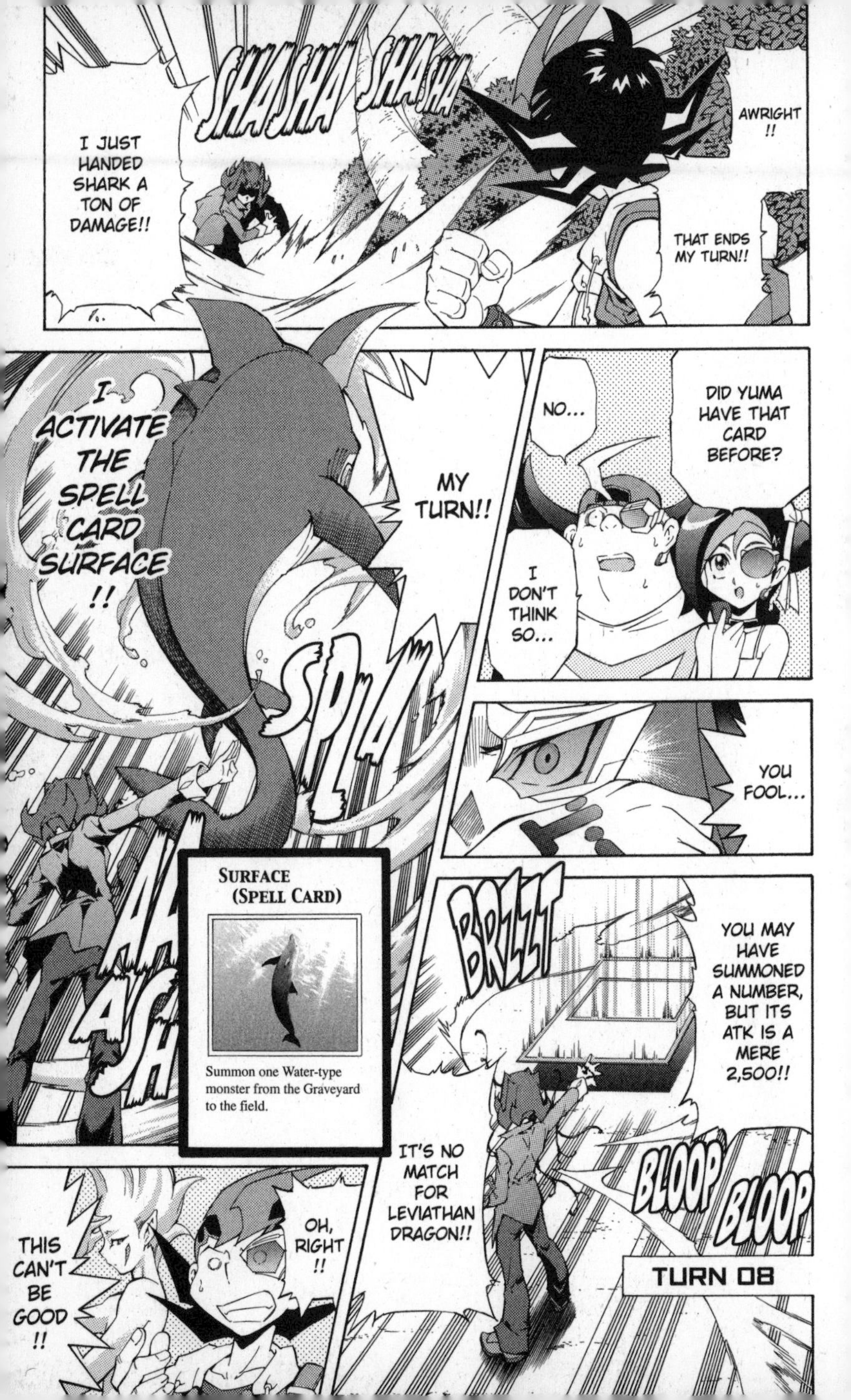
AWRIGHT!!
SHASHA SHASHA
THAT ENDS MY TURN!!
I JUST HANDED SHARK A TON OF DAMAGE!!
DID YUMA HAVE THAT CARD BEFORE?
NO...
I DON'T THINK SO...
YOU FOOL...
YOU MAY HAVE SUMMONED A NUMBER, BUT ITS ATK IS A MERE 2,500!!
BRZZT
IT'S NO MATCH FOR LEVIATHAN DRAGON!!
BLOOP BLOOP
TURN 08
MY TURN!!
I ACTIVATE THE SPELL CARD SURFACE!!
SPLA
AAAH
SURFACE (SPELL CARD)
Summon one Water-type monster from the Graveyard to the field.
OH, RIGHT!!
THIS CAN'T BE GOOD!!

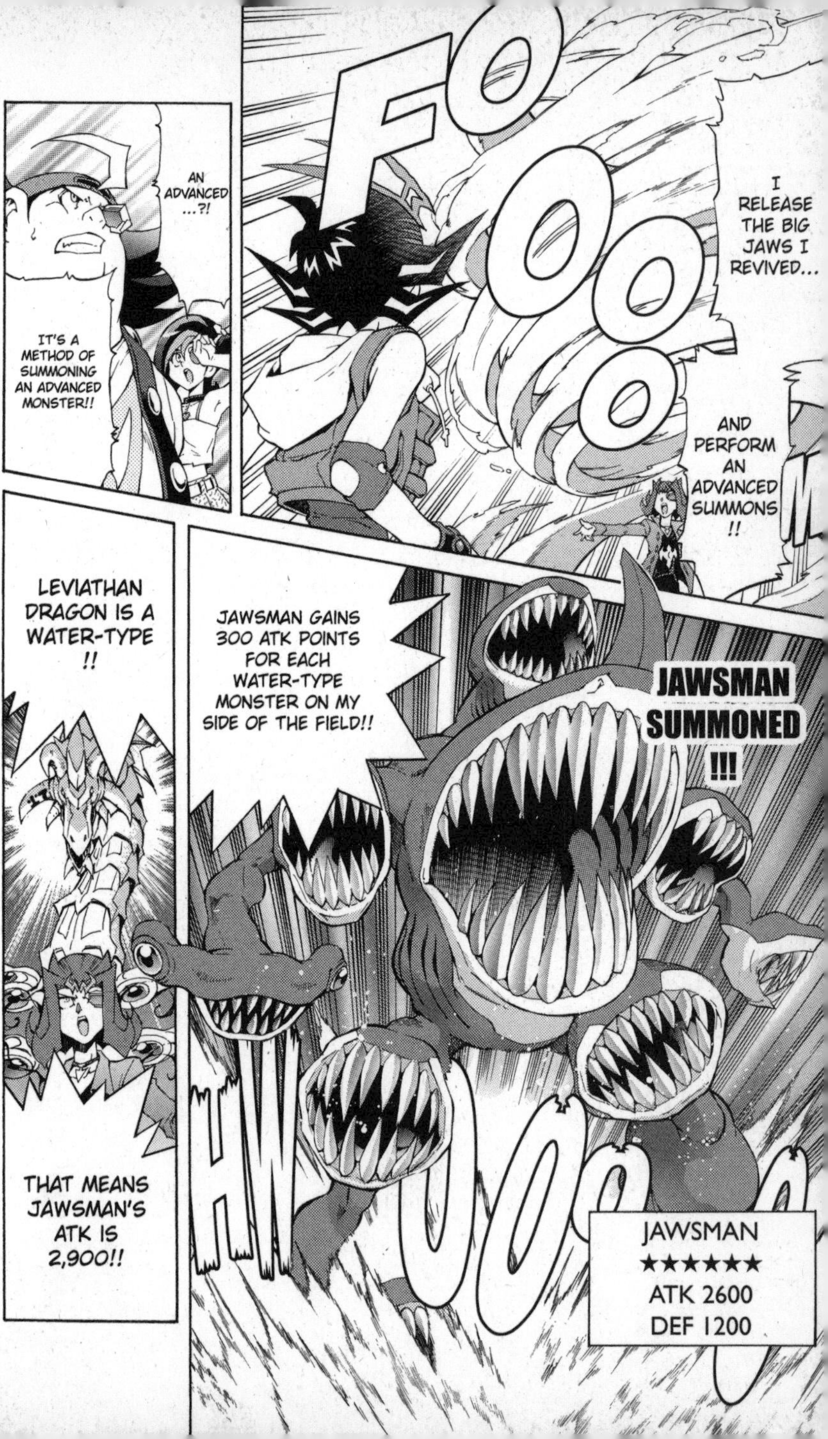
FOOOOO
I RELEASE THE BIG JAWS I REVIVED...
AND PERFORM AN ADVANCED SUMMONS!!
AN ADVANCED...?!
IT'S A METHOD OF SUMMONING AN ADVANCED MONSTER!!
JAWSMAN SUMMONED!!!
JAWSMAN GAINS 300 ATK POINTS FOR EACH WATER-TYPE MONSTER ON MY SIDE OF THE FIELD!!
HWOOOO
JAWSMAN ★★★★★★ ATK 2600 DEF 1200
LEVIATHAN DRAGON IS A WATER-TYPE!!
THAT MEANS JAWSMAN'S ATK IS 2,900!!

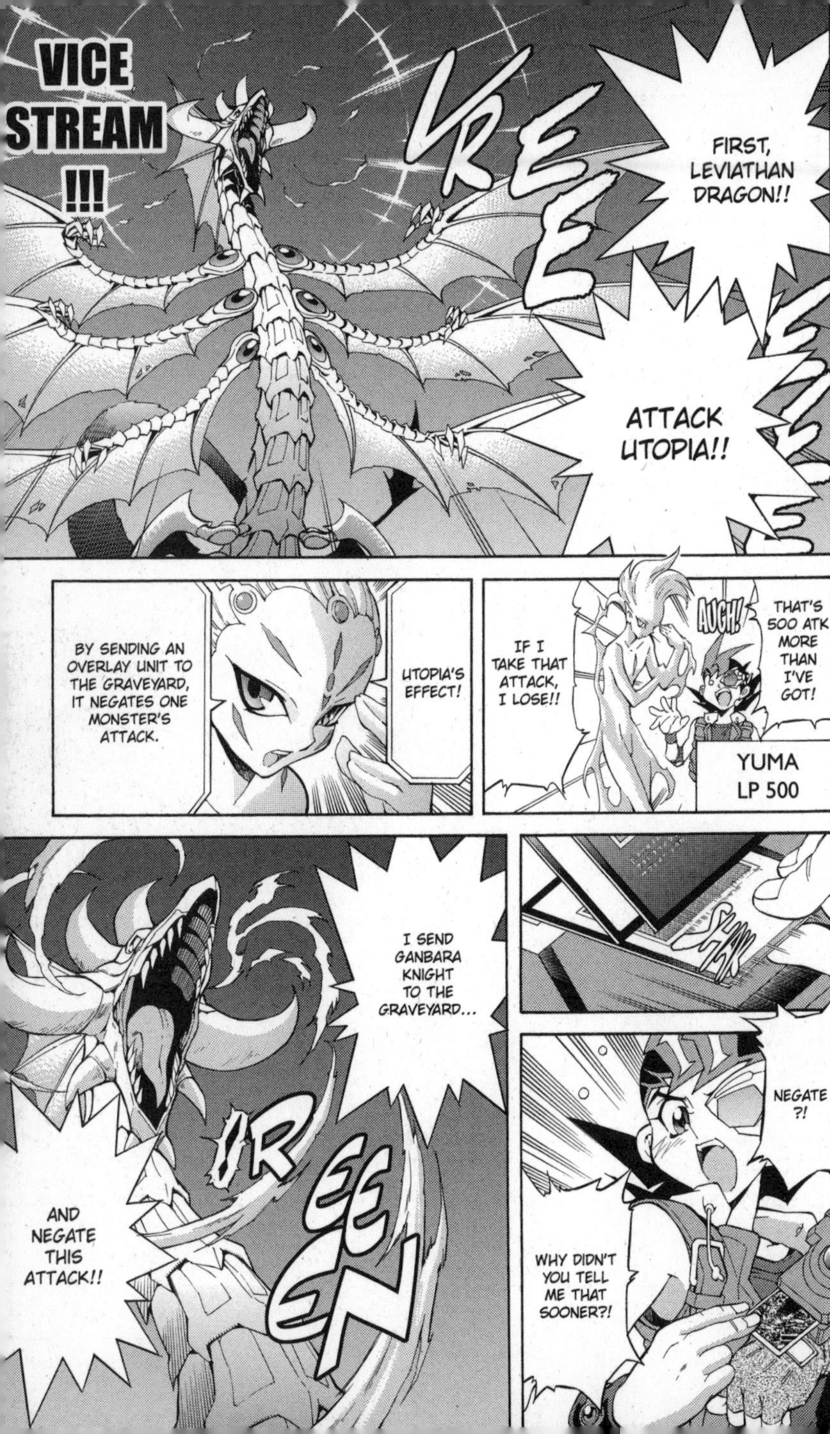
FIRST, LEVIATHAN DRAGON!!
ATTACK UTOPIA!!
VICE STREAM!!!
THAT'S 500 ATK MORE THAN I'VE GOT!
AUGH!
IF I TAKE THAT ATTACK, I LOSE!!
YUMA LP 500
UTOPIA'S EFFECT!
BY SENDING AN OVERLAY UNIT TO THE GRAVEYARD, IT NEGATES ONE MONSTER'S ATTACK.
NEGATE?!
WHY DIDN'T YOU TELL ME THAT SOONER?!
I SEND GANBARA KNIGHT TO THE GRAVEYARD...
AND NEGATE THIS ATTACK!!

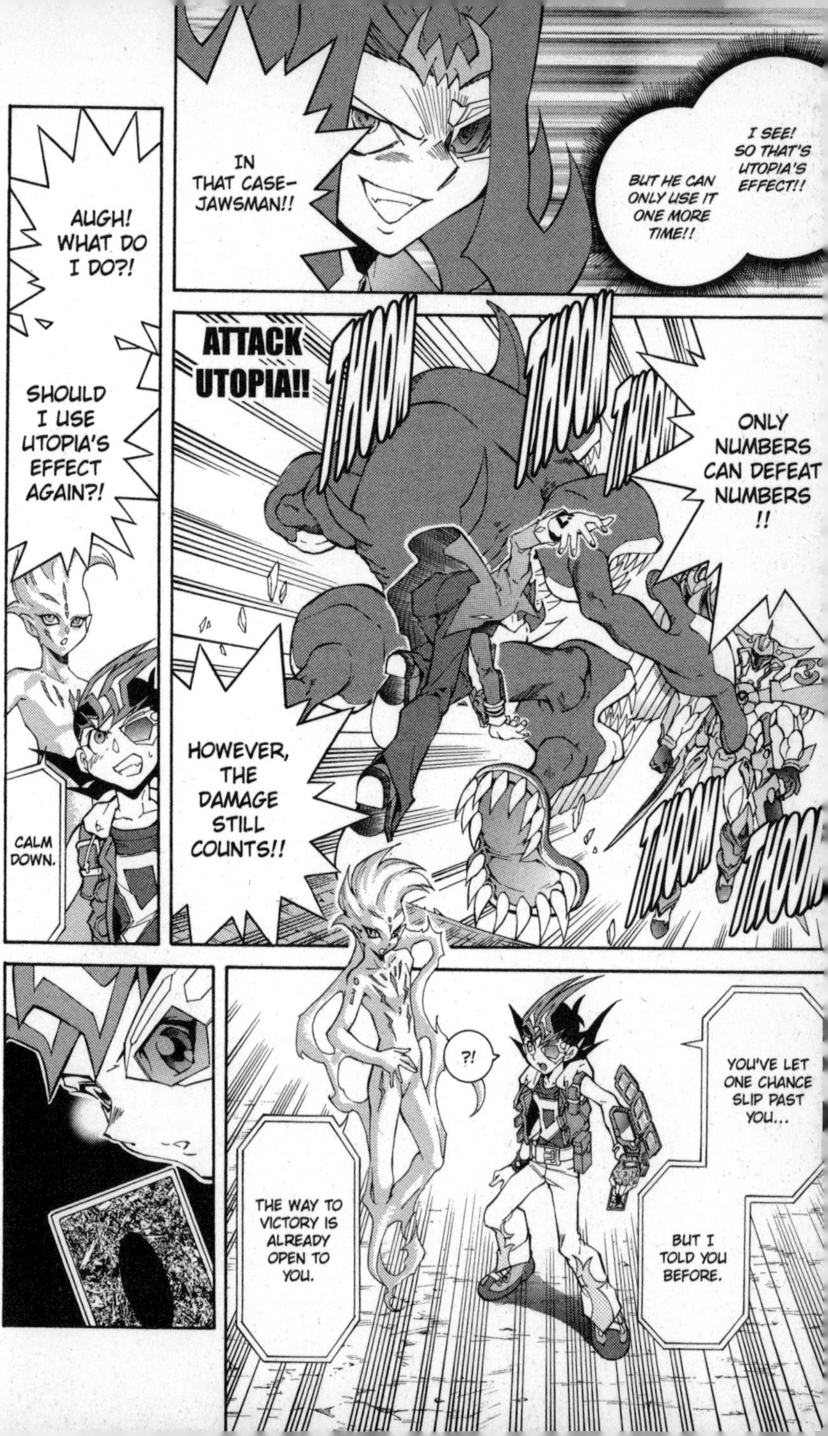
I SEE! SO THAT'S UTOPIA'S EFFECT!!
BUT HE CAN ONLY USE IT ONE MORE TIME!!
IN THAT CASE- JAWSMAN!!
ONLY NUMBERS CAN DEFEAT NUMBERS!!
THOOM THOOM THOOM
ATTACK UTOPIA!!
HOWEVER, THE DAMAGE STILL COUNTS!!
THOOM THOOM
AUGH! WHAT DO I DO?!
SHOULD I USE UTOPIA'S EFFECT AGAIN?!
CALM DOWN.
?!
YOU'VE LET ONE CHANCE SLIP PAST YOU...
BUT I TOLD YOU BEFORE.
THE WAY TO VICTORY IS ALREADY OPEN TO YOU.

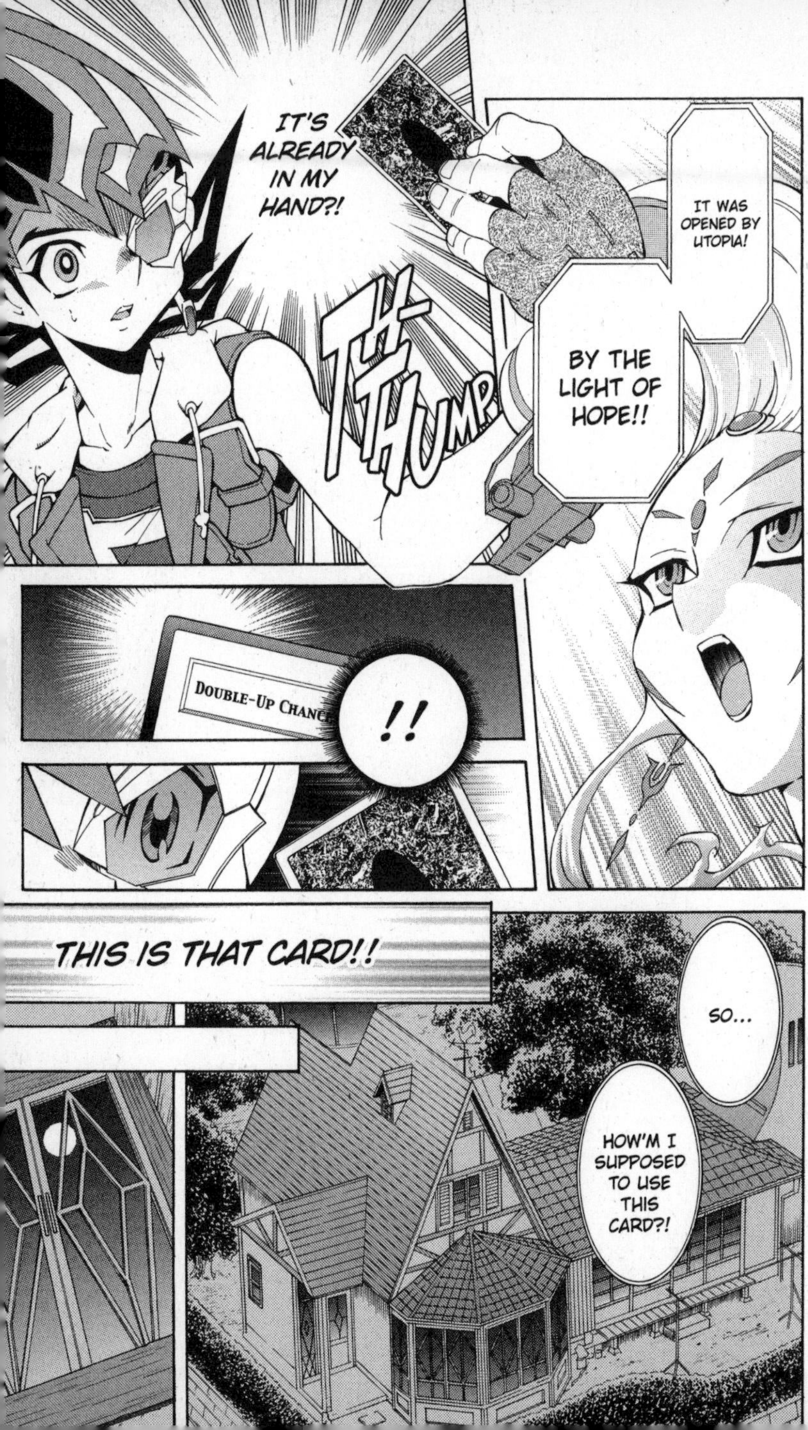
IT WAS OPENED BY UTOPIA!
BY THE LIGHT OF HOPE!!
IT'S ALREADY IN MY HAND?!
TH-THUMP
DOUBLE-UP CHANC
!!
THIS IS THAT CARD!!
SO...
HOW'M I SUPPOSED TO USE THIS CARD?!

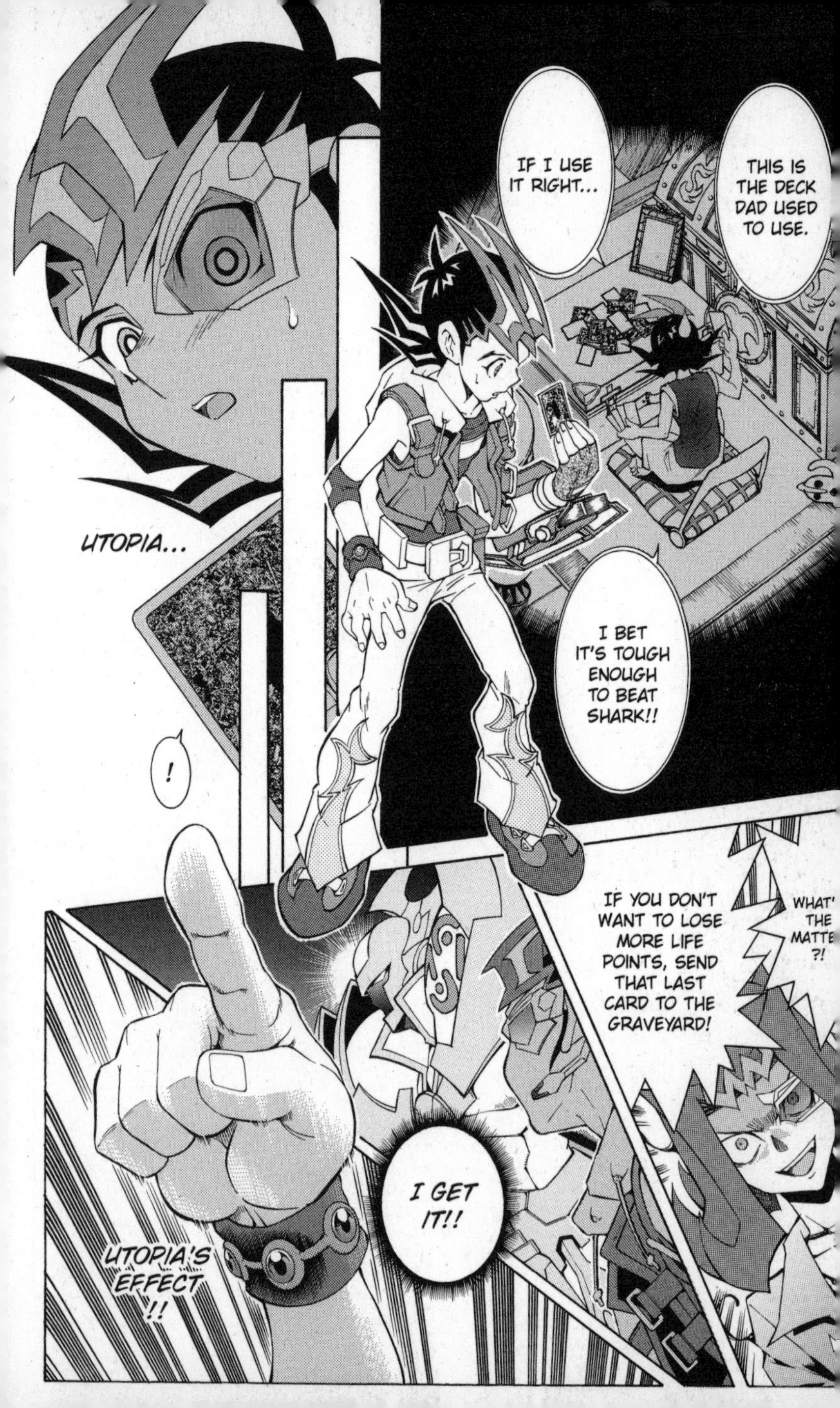
THIS IS THE DECK DAD USED TO USE.
IF I USE IT RIGHT...
I BET IT'S TOUGH ENOUGH TO BEAT SHARK!!
UTOPIA...
!
WHAT' THE MATTE ?!
IF YOU DON'T WANT TO LOSE MORE LIFE POINTS, SEND THAT LAST CARD TO THE GRAVEYARD!
I GET IT!!
UTOPIA'S EFFECT!!

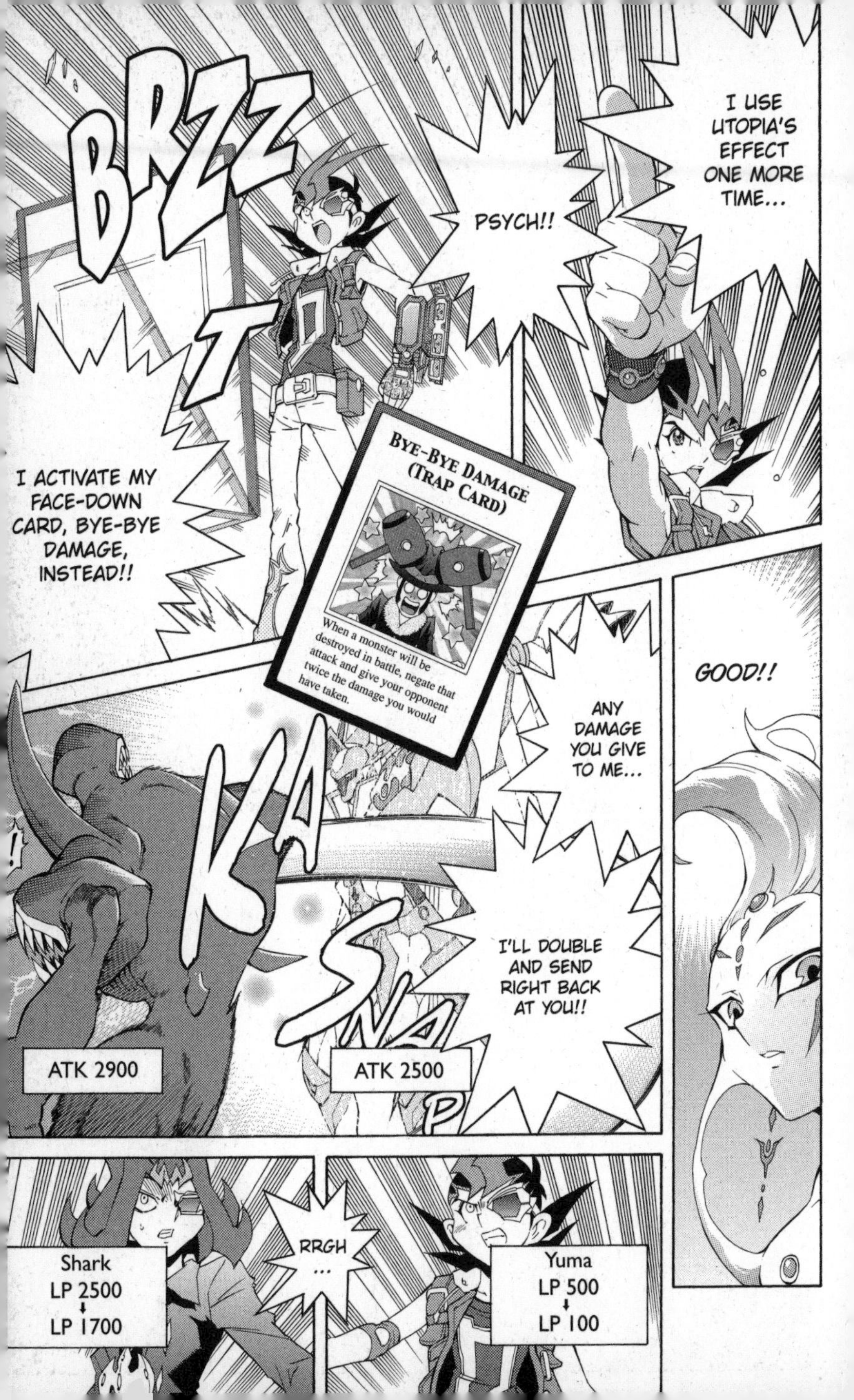
I USE UTOPIA'S EFFECT ONE MORE TIME...
PSYCH!!
BRZZT
I ACTIVATE MY FACE-DOWN CARD, BYE-BYE DAMAGE, INSTEAD!!
BYE-BYE DAMAGE (TRAP CARD)
When a monster will be destroyed in battle, negate that attack and give your opponent twice the damage you would have taken.
GOOD!!
ANY DAMAGE YOU GIVE TO ME...
I'LL DOUBLE AND SEND RIGHT BACK AT YOU!!
KA
SNAP
ATK 2500
ATK 2900
Yuma LP 500 ↓ LP 100
RRGH ...
Shark LP 2500 ↓ LP 1700

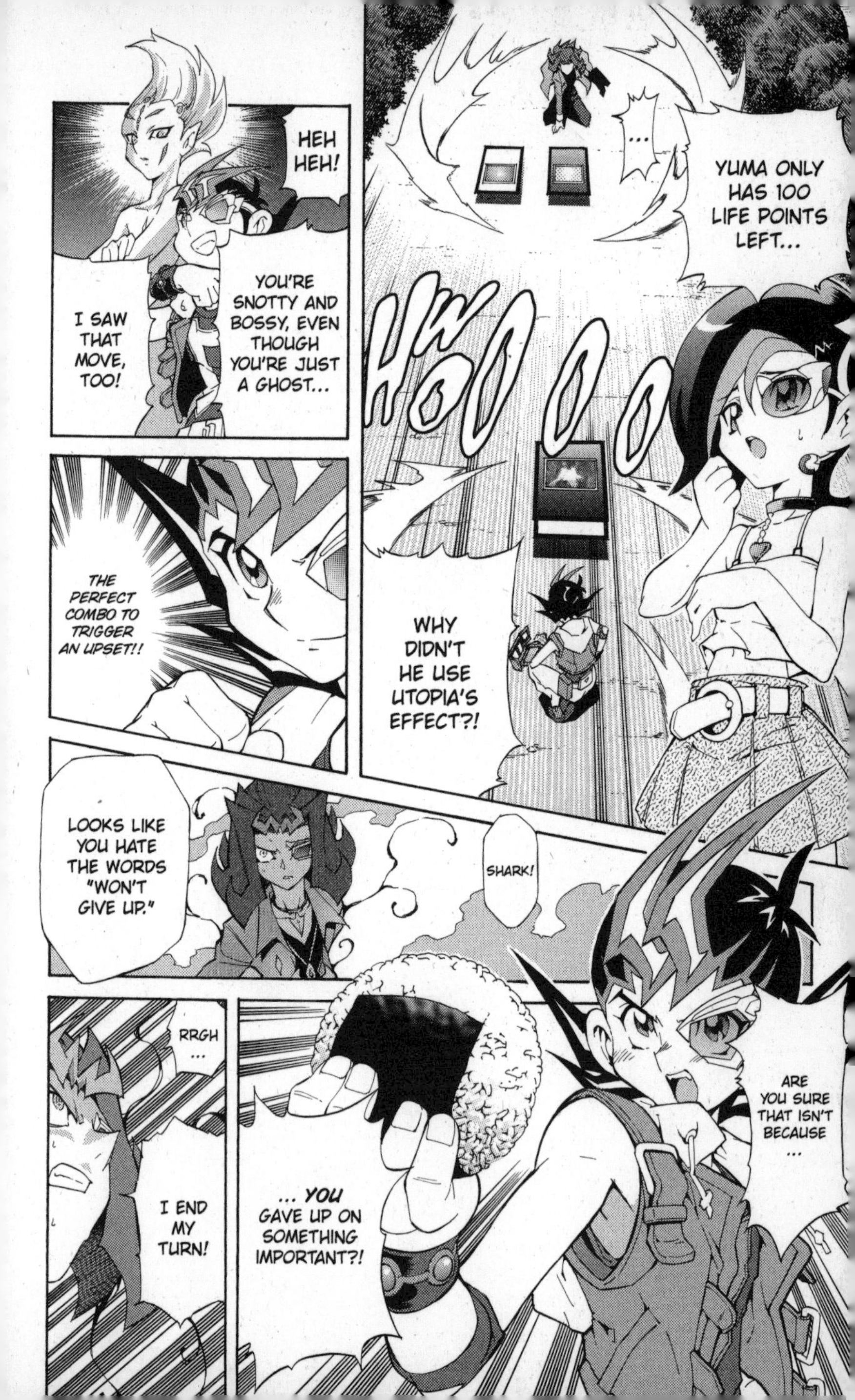
...
YUMA ONLY HAS 100 LIFE POINTS LEFT...
WHOOOO
WHY DIDN'T HE USE UTOPIA'S EFFECT?!
HEH HEH!
YOU'RE SNOTTY AND BOSSY, EVEN THOUGH YOU'RE JUST A GHOST...
I SAW THAT MOVE, TOO!
THE PERFECT COMBO TO TRIGGER AN UPSET!!
SHARK!
LOOKS LIKE YOU HATE THE WORDS "WON'T GIVE UP."
ARE YOU SURE THAT ISN'T BECAUSE...
...YOU GAVE UP ON SOMETHING IMPORTANT?!
RRGH...
I END MY TURN!

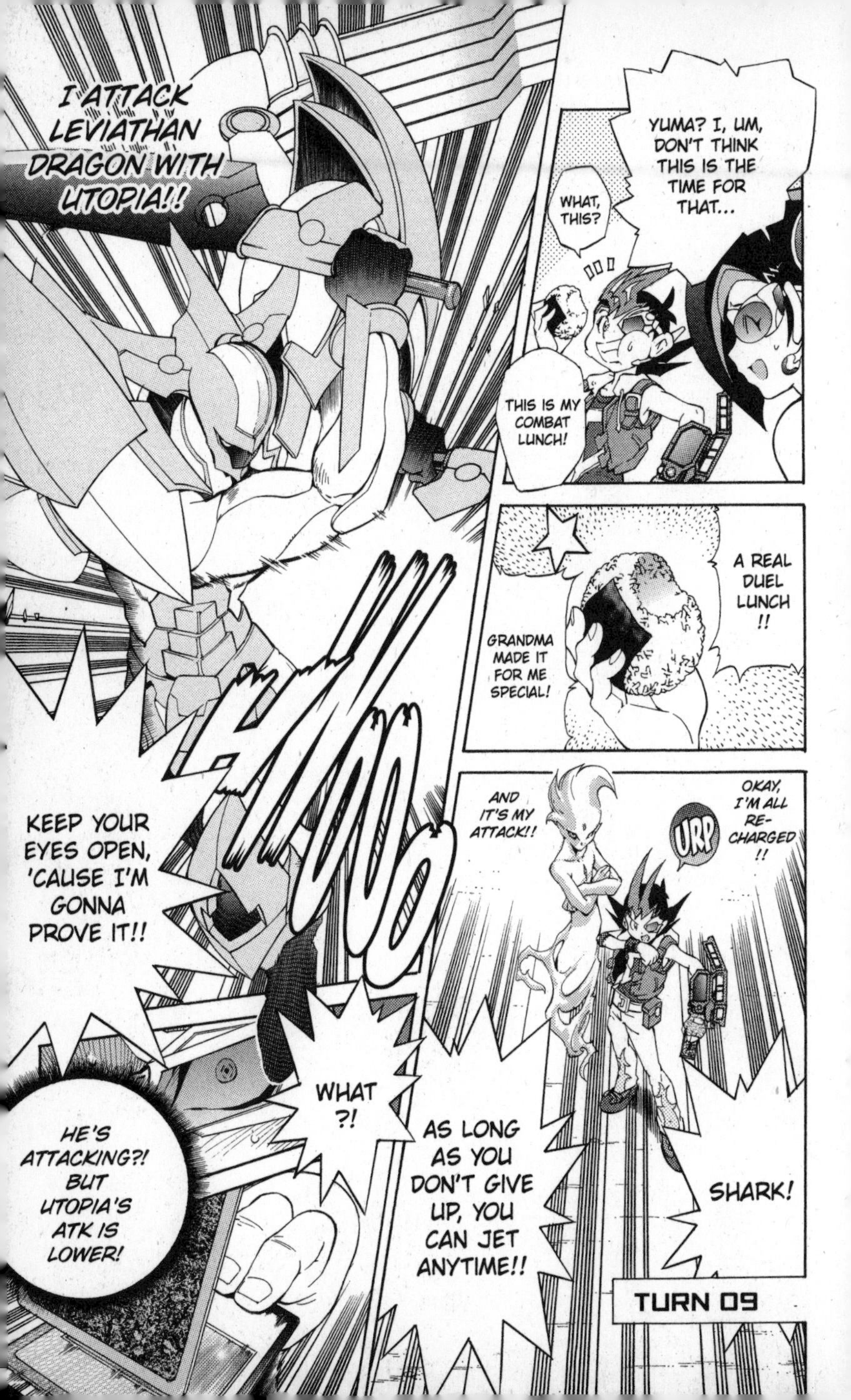
YUMA? I, UM, DON'T THINK THIS IS THE TIME FOR THAT...
WHAT, THIS?
THIS IS MY COMBAT LUNCH!
A REAL DUEL LUNCH!!
GRANDMA MADE IT FOR ME SPECIAL!
OKAY, I'M ALL RE-CHARGED!!
URP
AND IT'S MY ATTACK!!
SHARK!
AS LONG AS YOU DON'T GIVE UP, YOU CAN JET ANYTIME!!
TURN 09
I ATTACK LEVIATHAN DRAGON WITH UTOPIA!!
KEEP YOUR EYES OPEN, 'CAUSE I'M GONNA PROVE IT!!
WHAT?!
HE'S ATTACKING?! BUT UTOPIA'S ATK IS LOWER!

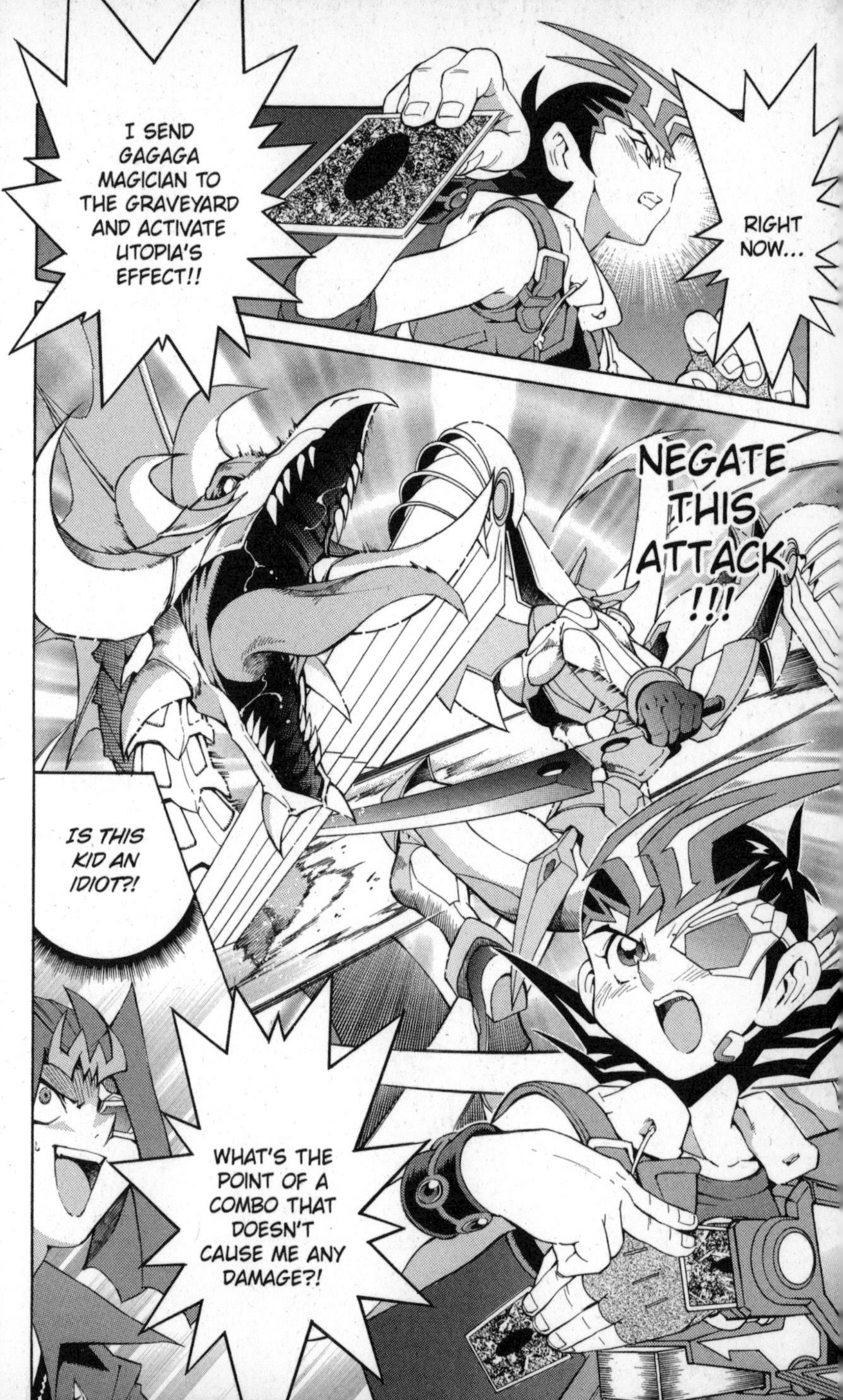
RIGHT NOW...
I SEND GAGAGA MAGICIAN TO THE GRAVEYARD AND ACTIVATE UTOPIA'S EFFECT!!
NEGATE THIS ATTACK!!!
IS THIS KID AN IDIOT?!
WHAT'S THE POINT OF A COMBO THAT DOESN'T CAUSE ME ANY DAMAGE?!

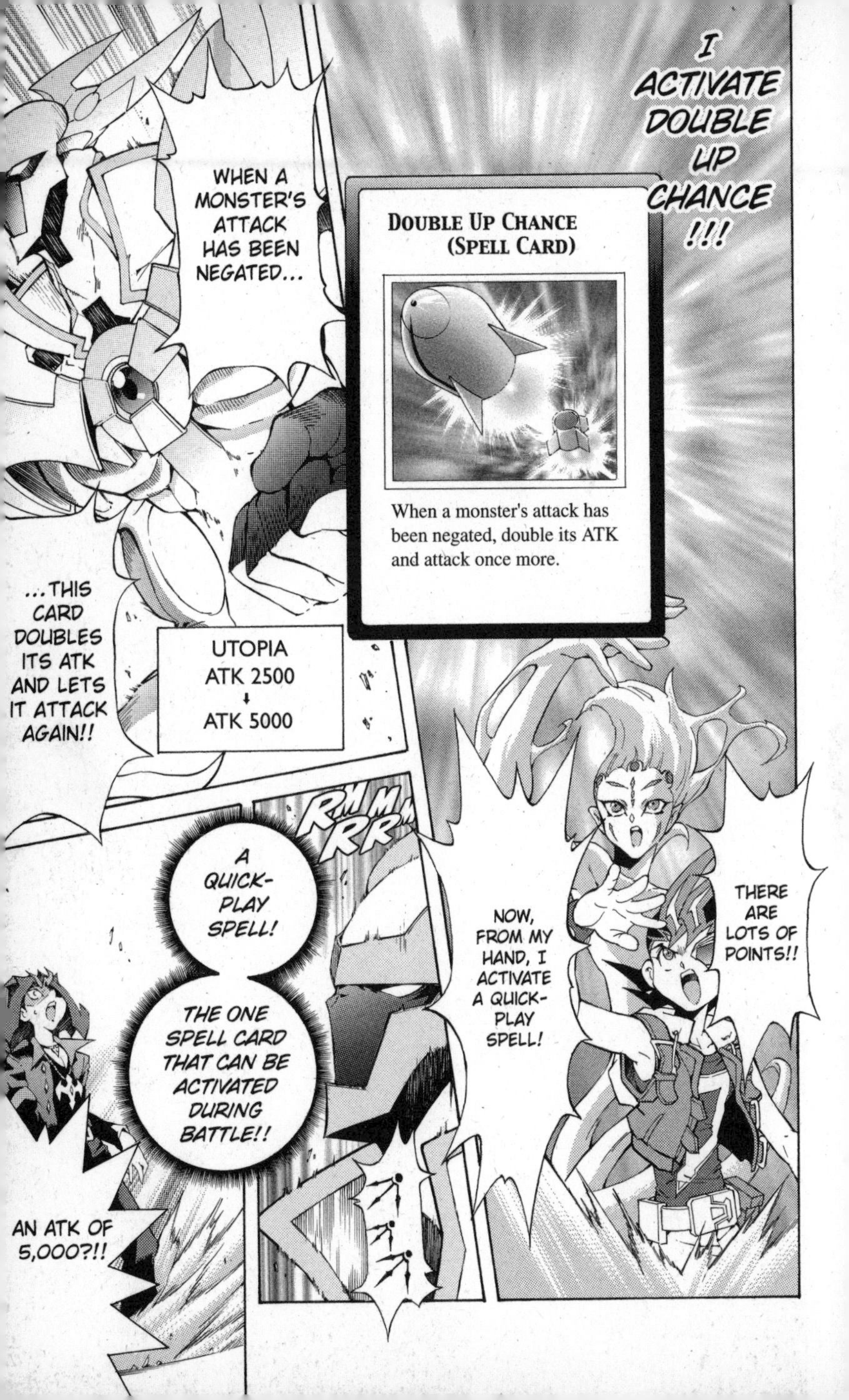
I ACTIVATE DOUBLE UP CHANCE!!!
DOUBLE UP CHANCE (SPELL CARD)
When a monster's attack has been negated, double its ATK and attack once more.
WHEN A MONSTER'S ATTACK HAS BEEN NEGATED...
...THIS CARD DOUBLES ITS ATK AND LETS IT ATTACK AGAIN!!
UTOPIA ATK 2500 ↓ ATK 5000
THERE ARE LOTS OF POINTS!!
NOW, FROM MY HAND, I ACTIVATE A QUICK-PLAY SPELL!
RMMMRR
A QUICK-PLAY SPELL!
THE ONE SPELL CARD THAT CAN BE ACTIVATED DURING BATTLE!!
AN ATK OF 5,000?!!

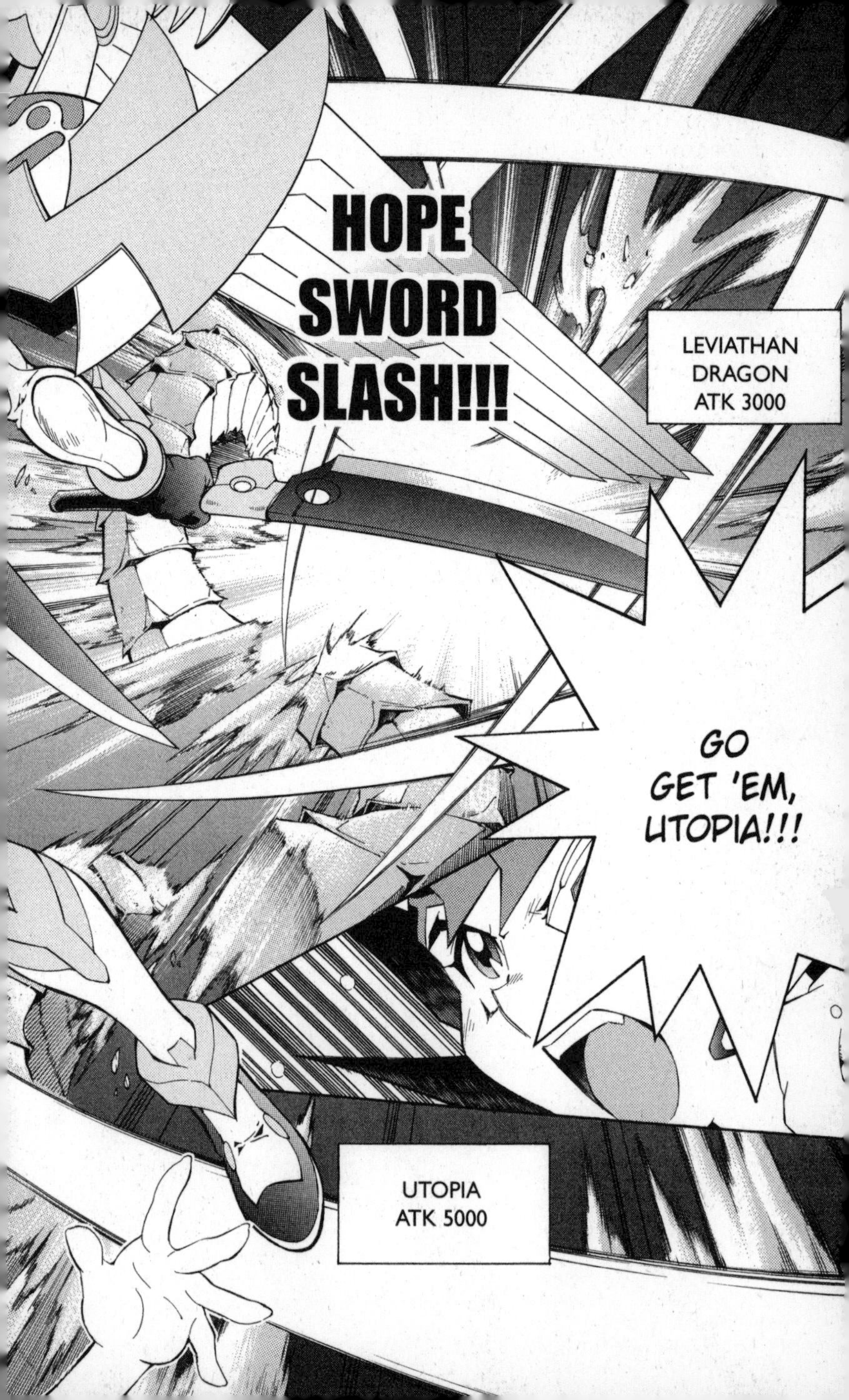
HOPE SWORD SLASH!!!
LEVIATHAN DRAGON ATK 3000
GO GET 'EM, UTOPIA!!!
UTOPIA ATK 5000

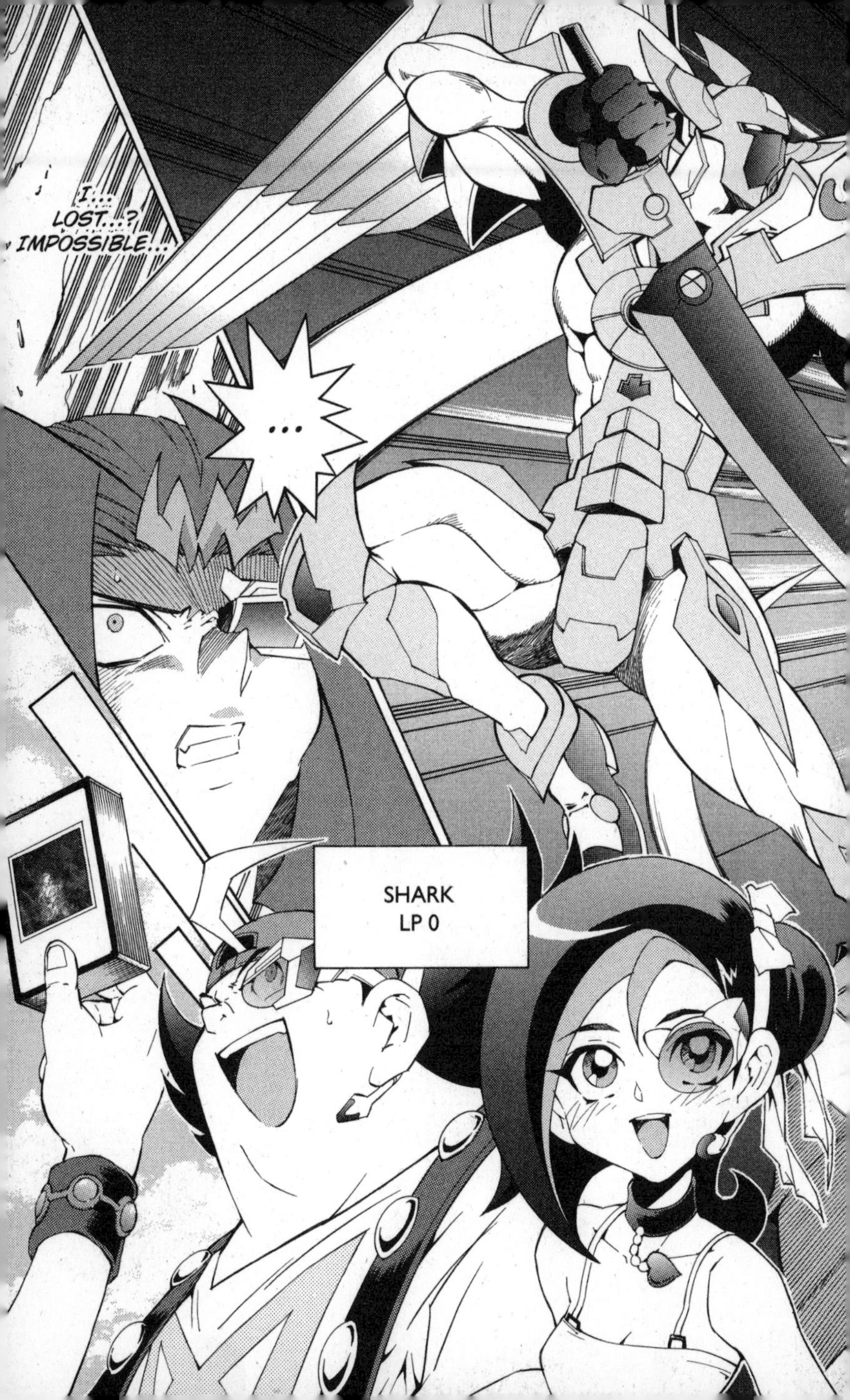
I... LOST...? IMPOSSIBLE...
...
SHARK
LP 0

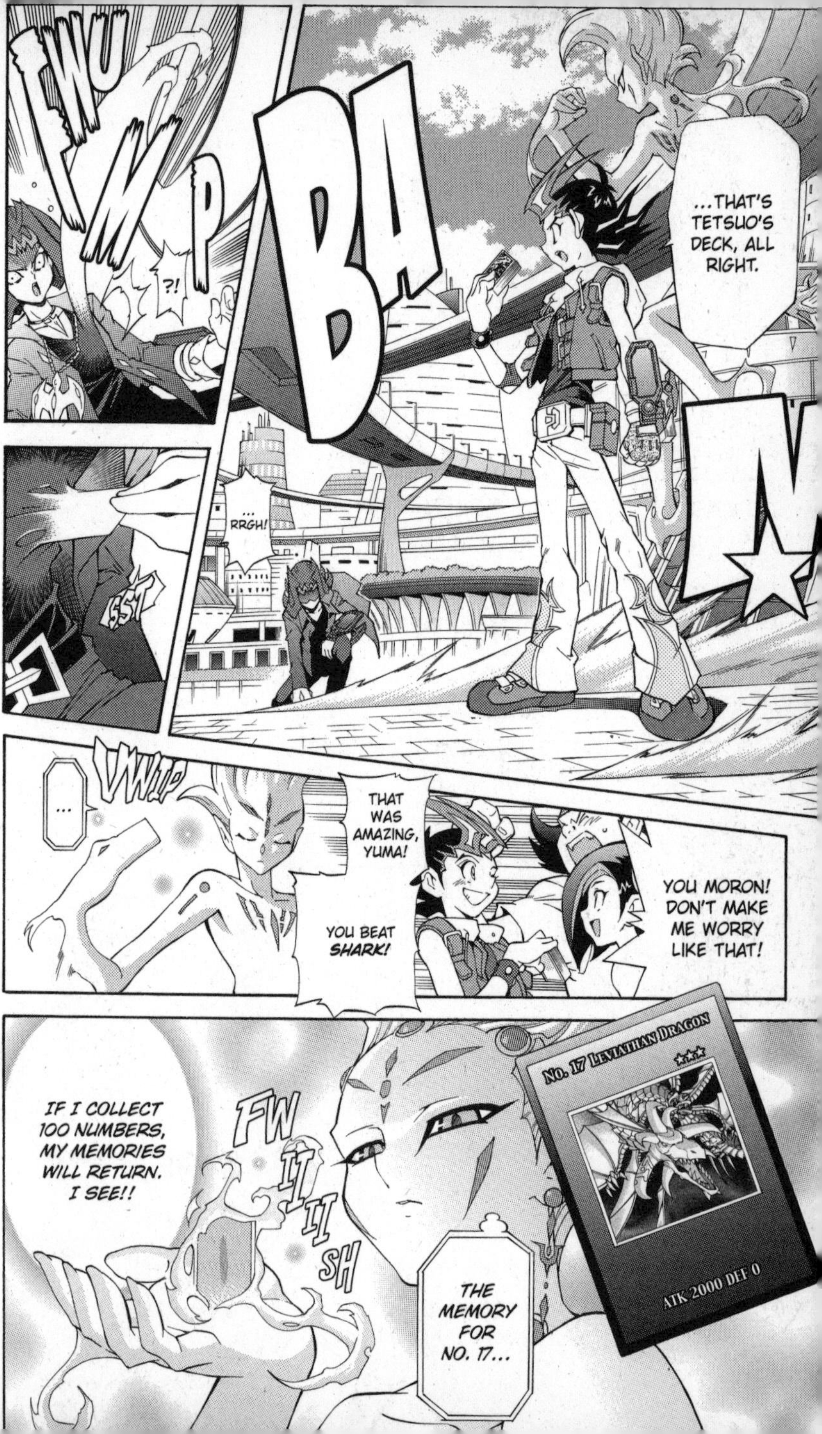
...THAT'S TETSUO'S DECK, ALL RIGHT.
BA
N
... RRGH!
FWUMP
?!
SST
YOU MORON! DON'T MAKE ME WORRY LIKE THAT!
THAT WAS AMAZING, YUMA!
YOU BEAT SHARK!
VWIP
...
No. 17 Leviathan Dragon
ATK 2000 DEF 0
THE MEMORY FOR NO. 17...
FWIIIISH
IF I COLLECT 100 NUMBERS, MY MEMORIES WILL RETURN. I SEE!!

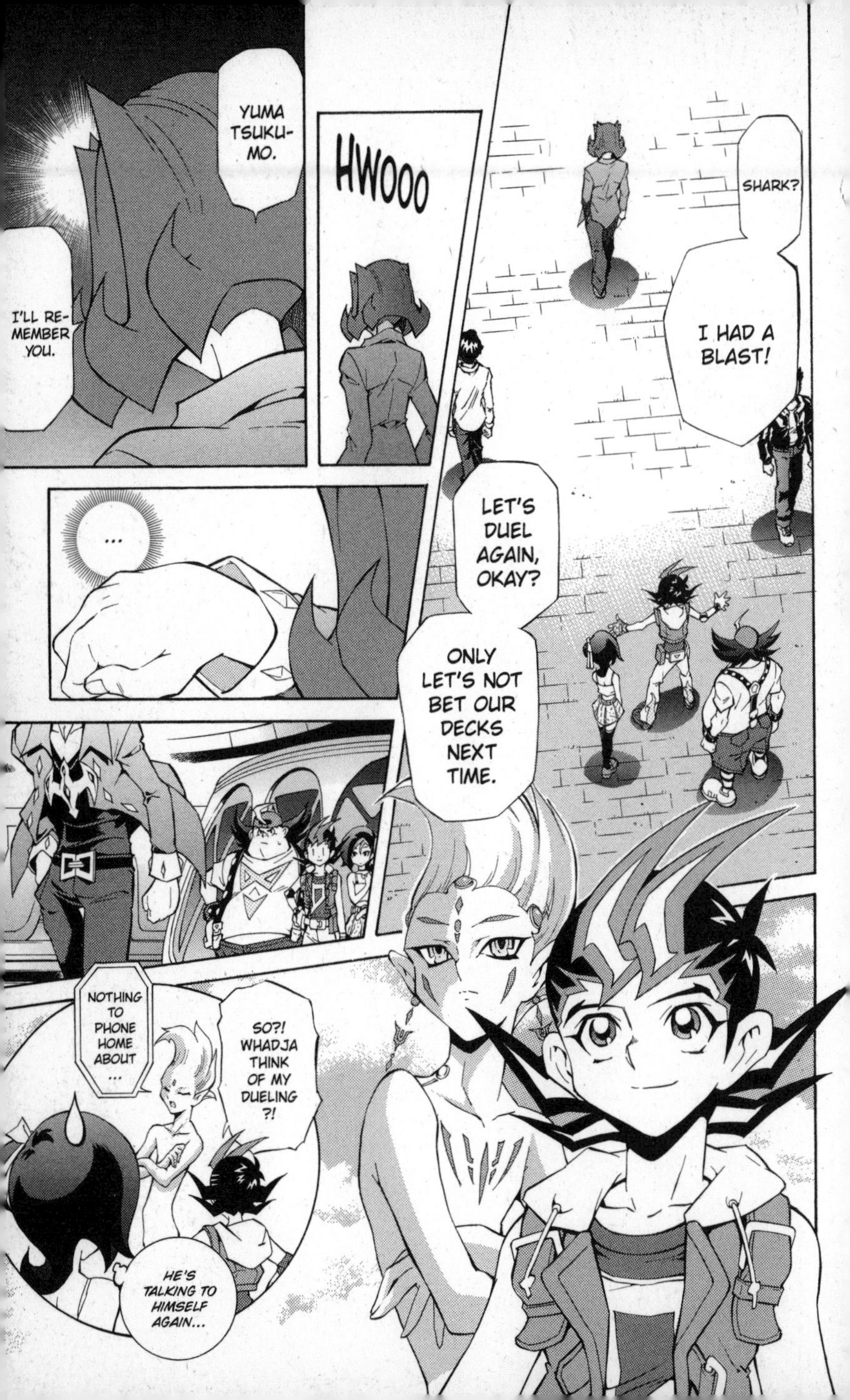
SHARK?
I HAD A BLAST!
LET'S DUEL AGAIN, OKAY?
ONLY LET'S NOT BET OUR DECKS NEXT TIME.
HWOOO
YUMA TSUKUMO.
I'LL REMEMBER YOU.
...
SO?! WHADJA THINK OF MY DUELING?!
NOTHING TO PHONE HOME ABOUT...
HE'S TALKING TO HIMSELF AGAIN...

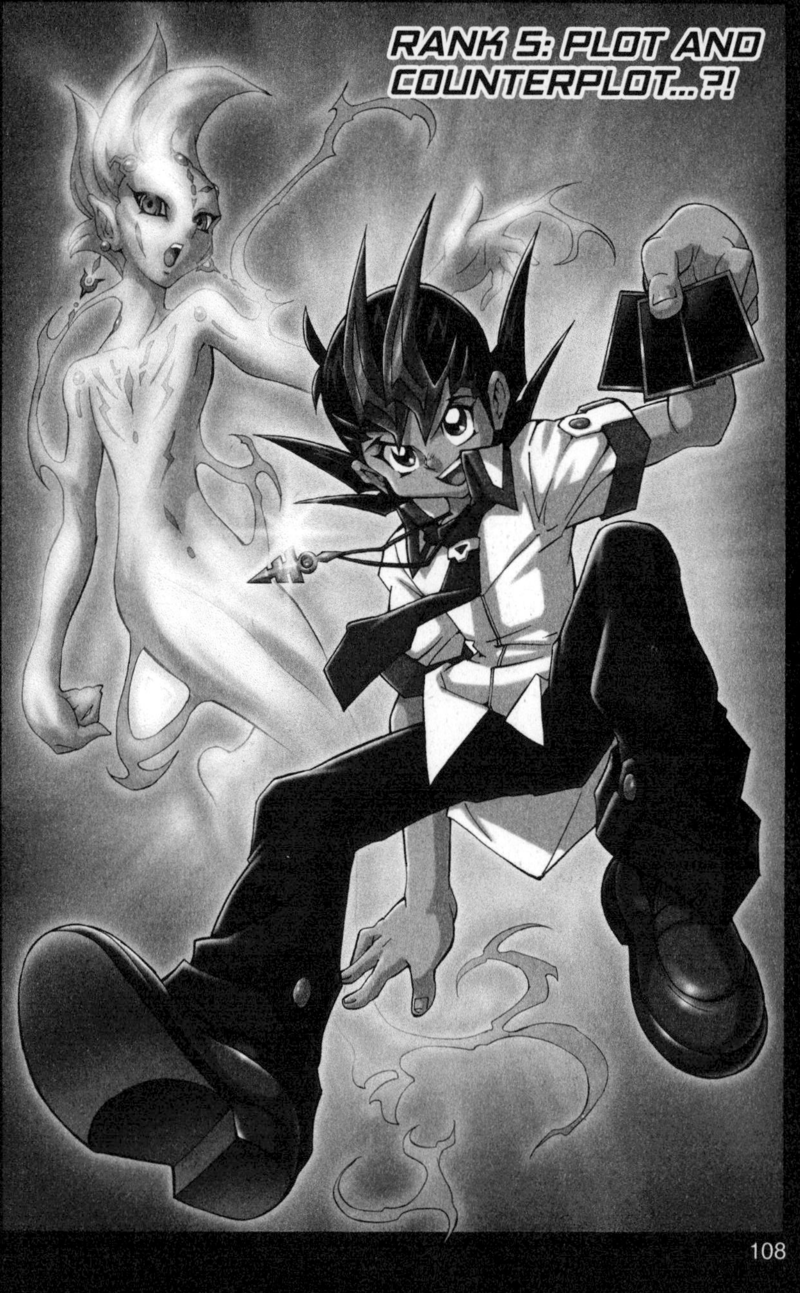
RANK 5: PLOT AND COUNTERPLOT...?!

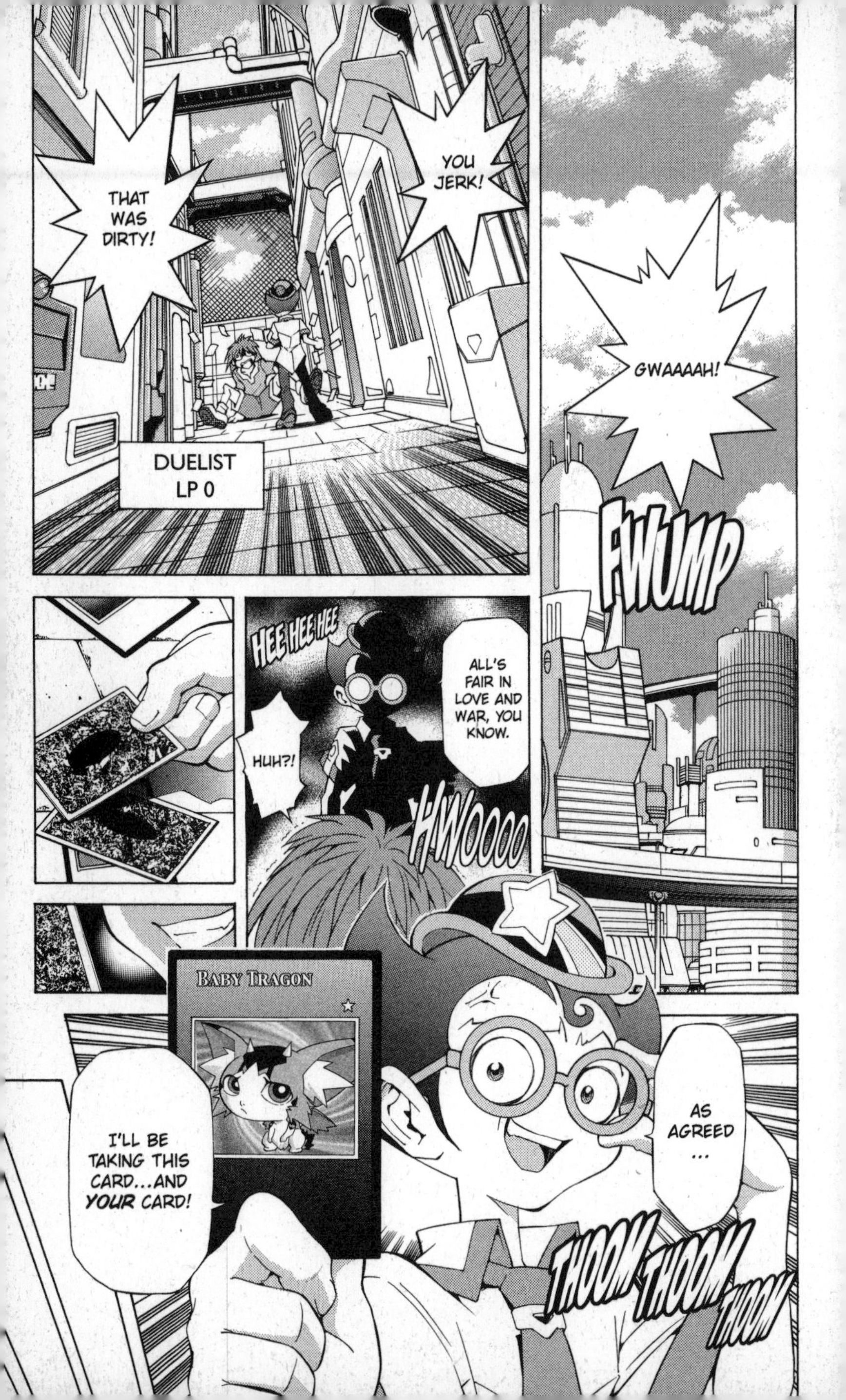
GWAAAAH!
FWUMP
YOU JERK!
THAT WAS DIRTY!
DUELIST
LP 0
HEE HEE HEE
ALL'S FAIR IN LOVE AND WAR, YOU KNOW.
HUH?!
HWOOOO
BABY TRAGON
AS AGREED...
I'LL BE TAKING THIS CARD...AND *YOUR* CARD!
THOOM THOOM THOOM

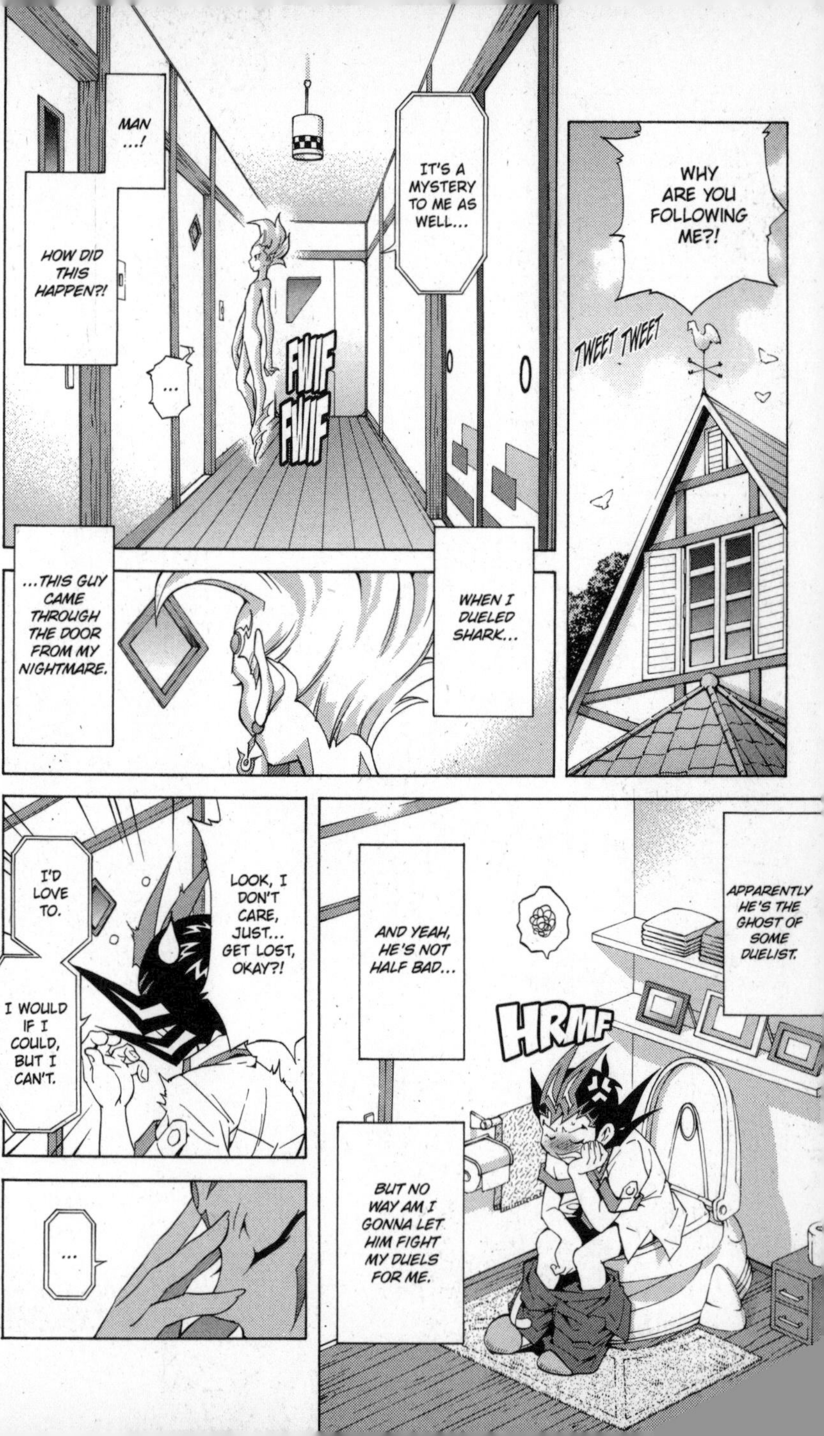
WHY ARE YOU FOLLOWING ME?!
TWEET TWEET
IT'S A MYSTERY TO ME AS WELL...
FWIF FWIF
MAN...!
HOW DID THIS HAPPEN?!
...
WHEN I DUELED SHARK...
...THIS GUY CAME THROUGH THE DOOR FROM MY NIGHTMARE.
APPARENTLY HE'S THE GHOST OF SOME DUELIST.
AND YEAH, HE'S NOT HALF BAD...
HRMF
BUT NO WAY AM I GONNA LET HIM FIGHT MY DUELS FOR ME.
LOOK, I DON'T CARE, JUST... GET LOST, OKAY?!
I'D LOVE TO.
I WOULD IF I COULD, BUT I CAN'T.
...

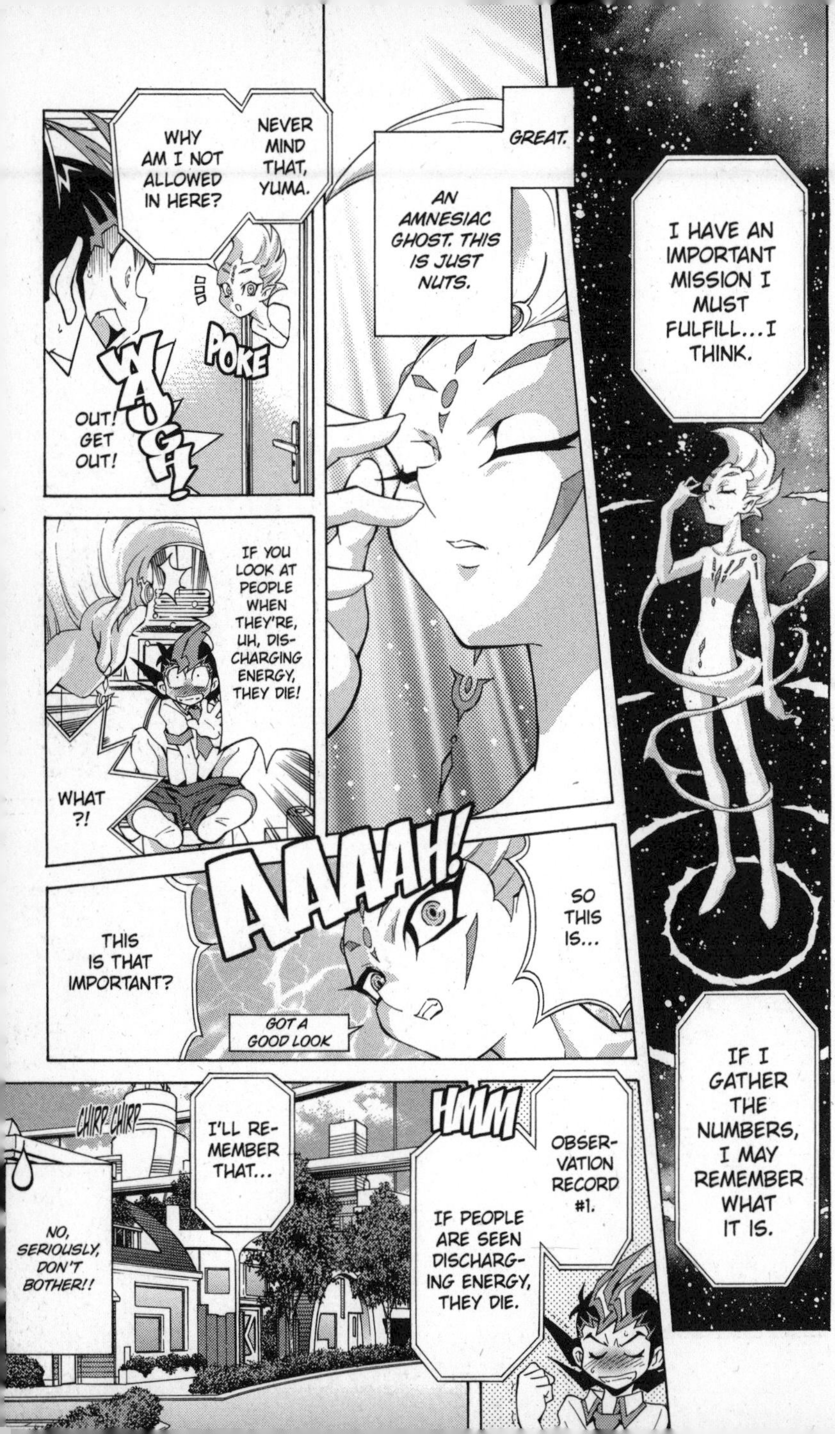
I HAVE AN IMPORTANT MISSION I MUST FULFILL...I THINK.
IF I GATHER THE NUMBERS, I MAY REMEMBER WHAT IT IS.
GREAT.
AN AMNESIAC GHOST. THIS IS JUST NUTS.
NEVER MIND THAT, YUMA.
WHY AM I NOT ALLOWED IN HERE?
POKE
WAUGH!
OUT! GET OUT!
IF YOU LOOK AT PEOPLE WHEN THEY'RE, UH, DIS-CHARGING ENERGY, THEY DIE!
WHAT ?!
SO THIS IS...
AAAAH!
GOT A GOOD LOOK
THIS IS THAT IMPORTANT?
OBSER-VATION RECORD #1.
IF PEOPLE ARE SEEN DISCHARG-ING ENERGY, THEY DIE.
HMM
I'LL RE-MEMBER THAT...
CHIRP CHIRP
NO, SERIOUSLY, DON'T BOTHER!!

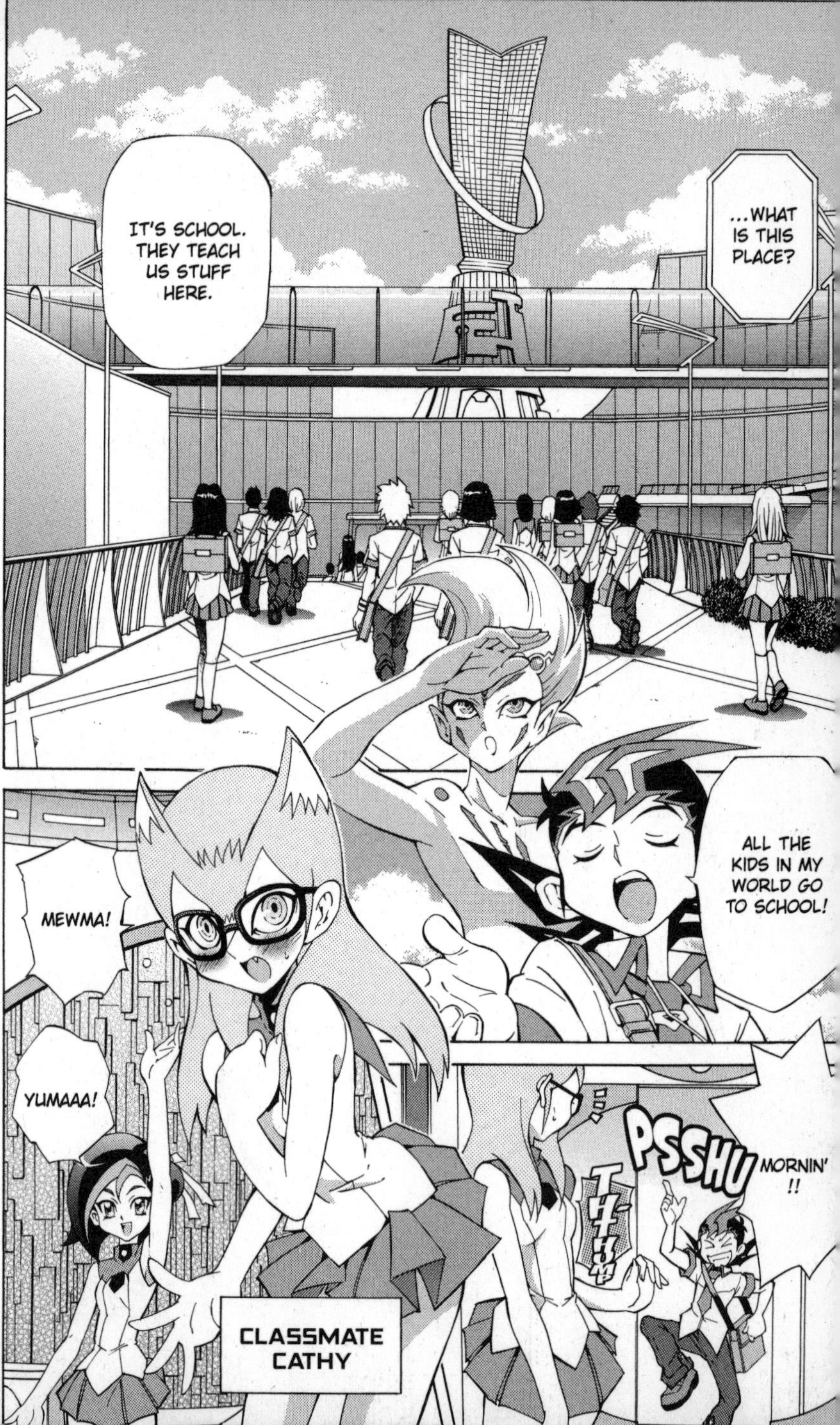
...WHAT IS THIS PLACE?
IT'S SCHOOL. THEY TEACH US STUFF HERE.
ALL THE KIDS IN MY WORLD GO TO SCHOOL!
MORNIN' !!
PSSHU
THUMP
MEWMA!
YUMAAA!
CLASSMATE CATHY

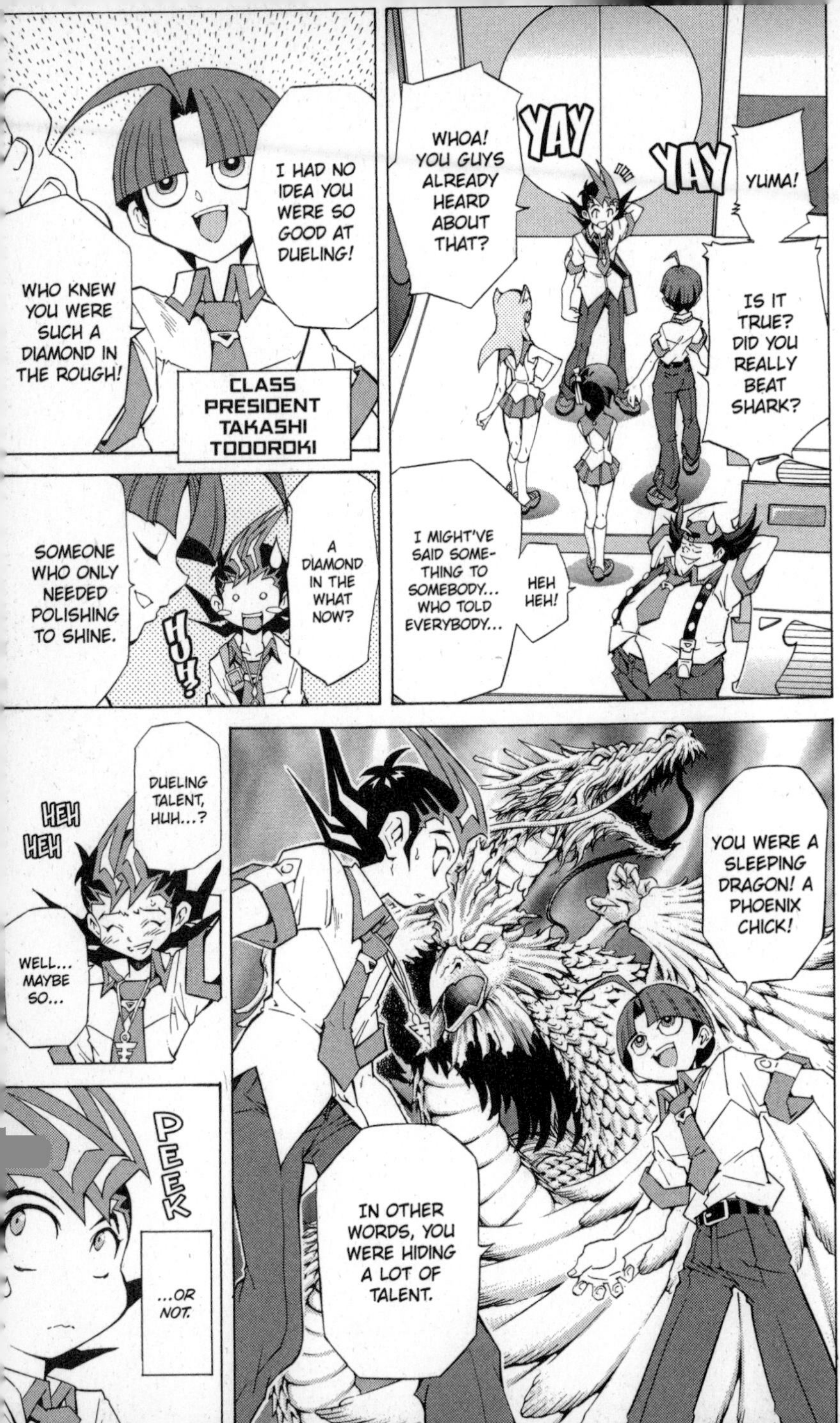
YUMA!
YAY
YAY
WHOA! YOU GUYS ALREADY HEARD ABOUT THAT?
IS IT TRUE? DID YOU REALLY BEAT SHARK?
I HAD NO IDEA YOU WERE SO GOOD AT DUELING!
WHO KNEW YOU WERE SUCH A DIAMOND IN THE ROUGH!
CLASS PRESIDENT TAKASHI TODOROKI
HEH HEH!
I MIGHT'VE SAID SOMETHING TO SOMEBODY... WHO TOLD EVERYBODY...
A DIAMOND IN THE WHAT NOW?
HUH?
SOMEONE WHO ONLY NEEDED POLISHING TO SHINE.
YOU WERE A SLEEPING DRAGON! A PHOENIX CHICK!
IN OTHER WORDS, YOU WERE HIDING A LOT OF TALENT.
DUELING TALENT, HUH...?
HEH HEH
WELL... MAYBE SO...
PEEK
...OR NOT.

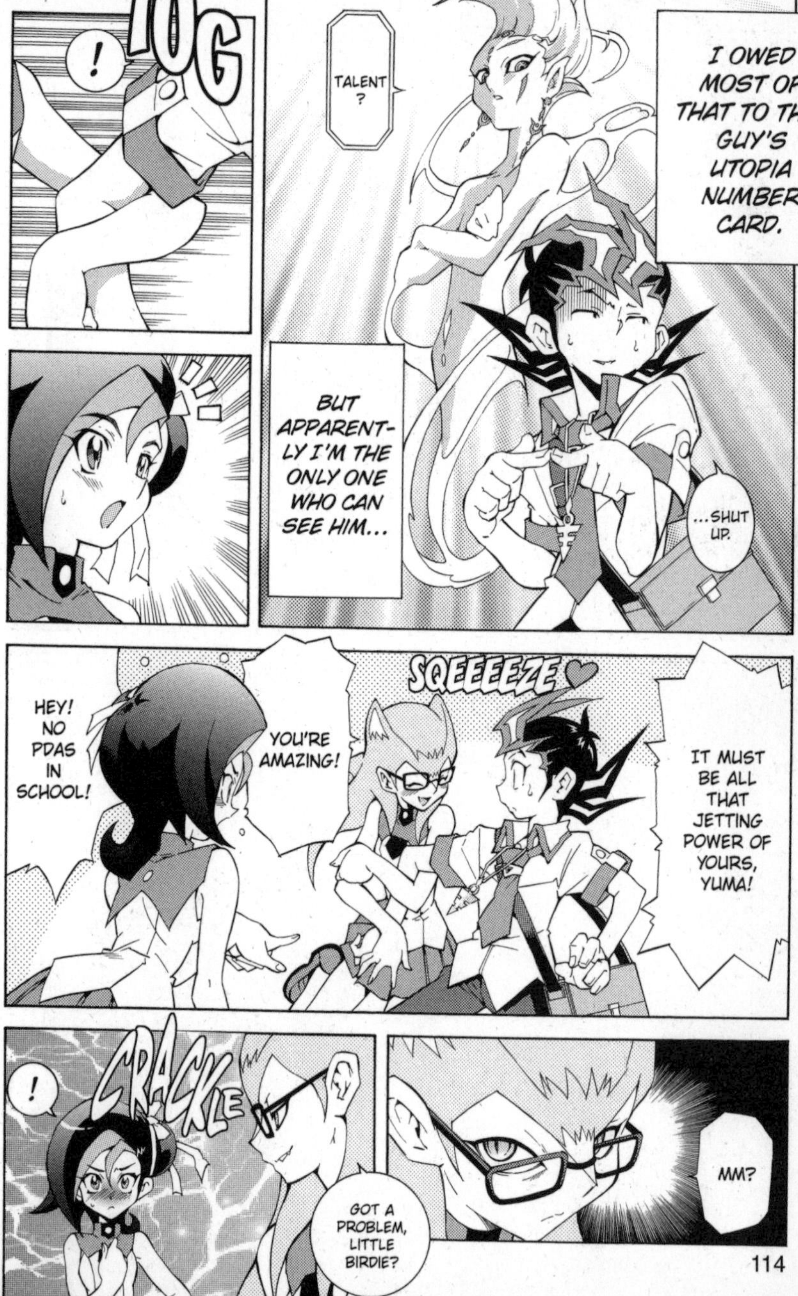
I OWED MOST OF THAT TO THIS GUY'S UTOPIA NUMBER CARD.
TALENT?
...SHUT UP.
BUT APPARENT-LY I'M THE ONLY ONE WHO CAN SEE HIM...
TUG
!
IT MUST BE ALL THAT JETTING POWER OF YOURS, YUMA!
SQEEEEZE
YOU'RE AMAZING!
HEY! NO PDAS IN SCHOOL!
MM?
GOT A PROBLEM, LITTLE BIRDIE?
CRACKLE
!

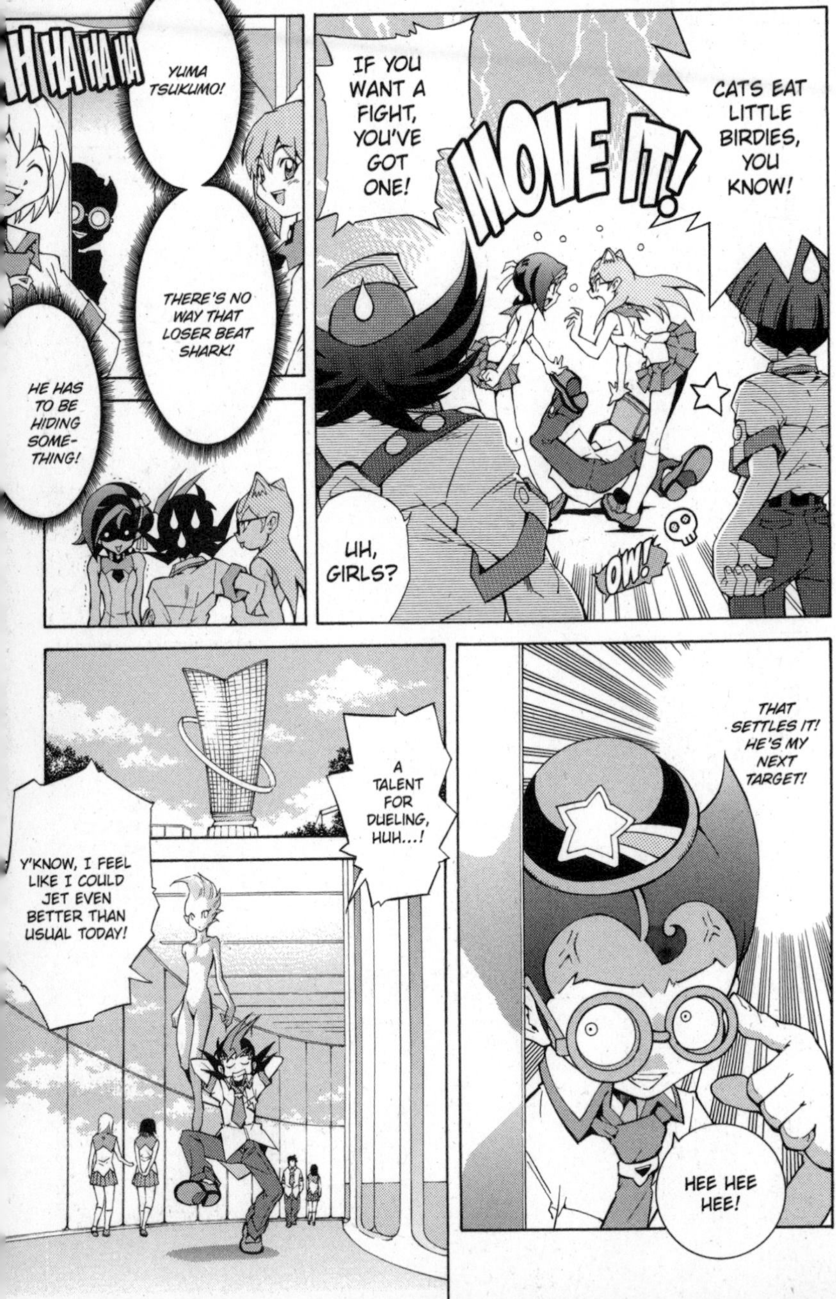
CATS EAT LITTLE BIRDIES, YOU KNOW!
IF YOU WANT A FIGHT, YOU'VE GOT ONE!
MOVE IT!
OW!
UH, GIRLS?
HA HA HA HA
YUMA TSUKUMO!
THERE'S NO WAY THAT LOSER BEAT SHARK!
HE HAS TO BE HIDING SOMETHING!
THAT SETTLES IT! HE'S MY NEXT TARGET!
HEE HEE HEE!
A TALENT FOR DUELING, HUH...!
Y'KNOW, I FEEL LIKE I COULD JET EVEN BETTER THAN USUAL TODAY!

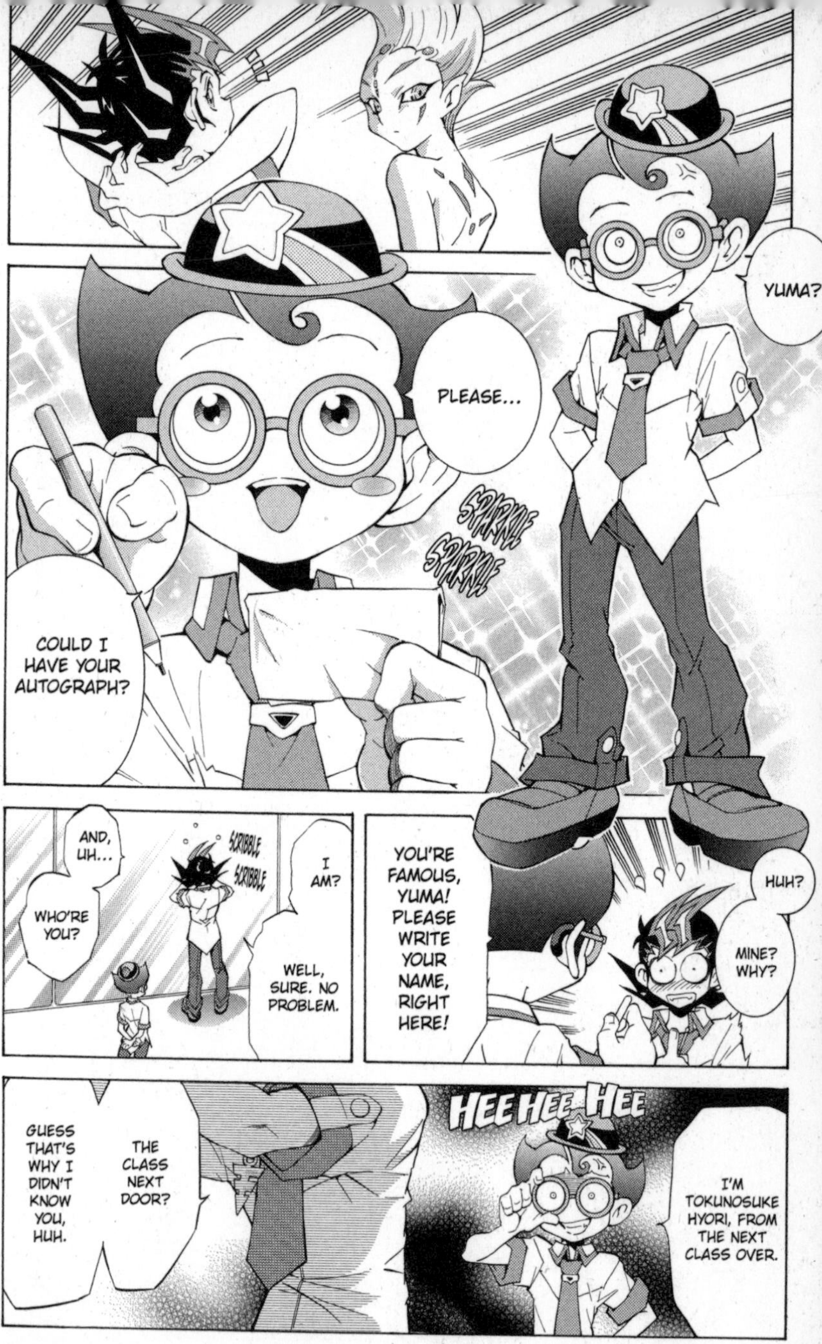
YUMA?
PLEASE...
SPARKLE SPARKLE
COULD I HAVE YOUR AUTOGRAPH?
HUH?
MINE? WHY?
YOU'RE FAMOUS, YUMA! PLEASE WRITE YOUR NAME, RIGHT HERE!
I AM?
WELL, SURE. NO PROBLEM.
SCRIBBLE SCRIBBLE
AND, UH...
WHO'RE YOU?
HEE HEE HEE
I'M TOKUNOSUKE HYORI, FROM THE NEXT CLASS OVER.
THE CLASS NEXT DOOR?
GUESS THAT'S WHY I DIDN'T KNOW YOU, HUH.

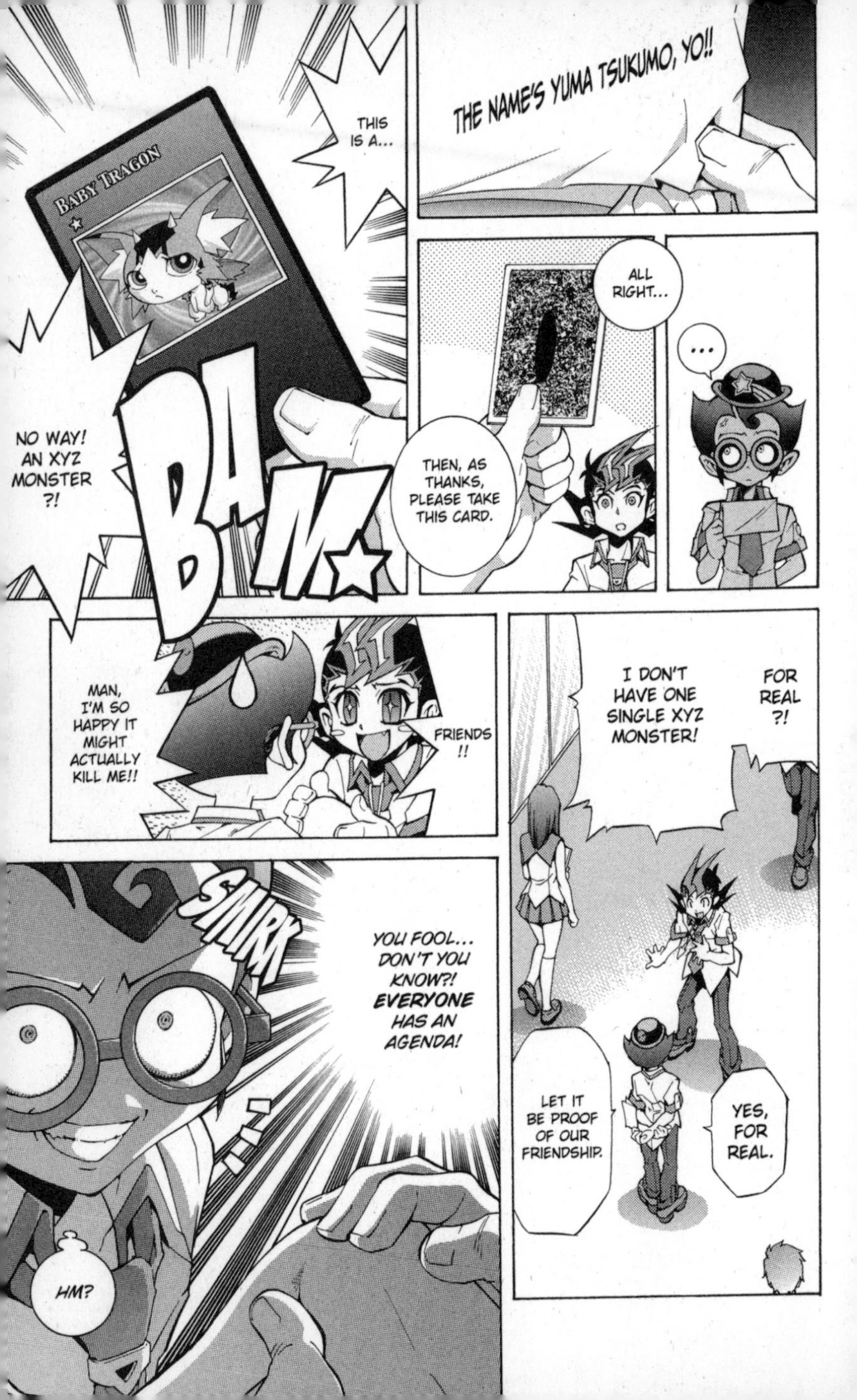
THE NAME'S YUMA TSUKUMO, YO!!
...
ALL RIGHT...
THEN, AS THANKS, PLEASE TAKE THIS CARD.
THIS IS A...
BABY TRAGON
NO WAY! AN XYZ MONSTER?!
BAM☆
FOR REAL?!
I DON'T HAVE ONE SINGLE XYZ MONSTER!
YES, FOR REAL.
LET IT BE PROOF OF OUR FRIENDSHIP.
FRIENDS!!
MAN, I'M SO HAPPY IT MIGHT ACTUALLY KILL ME!!
SMIRK
YOU FOOL... DON'T YOU KNOW?! EVERYONE HAS AN AGENDA!
HM?

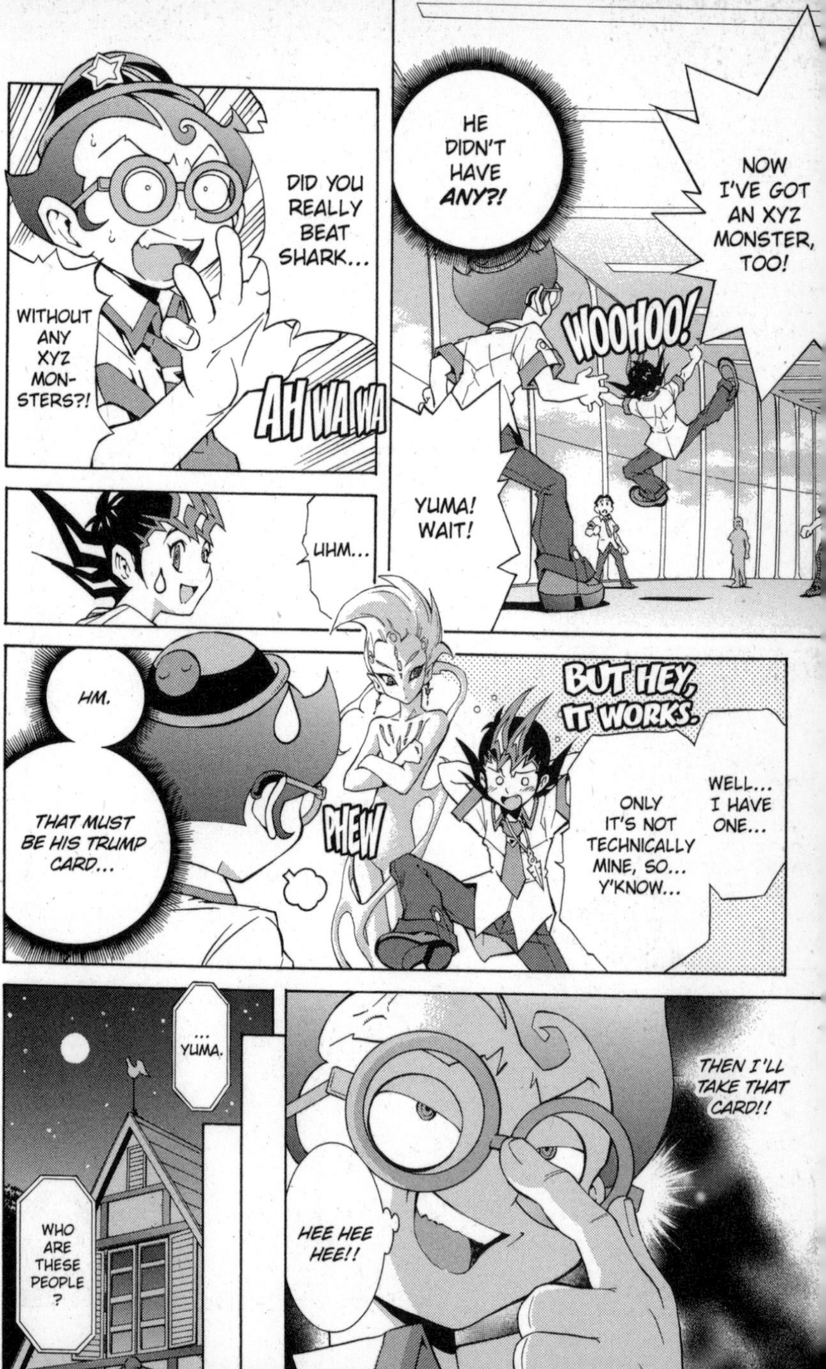
NOW I'VE GOT AN XYZ MONSTER, TOO!
HE DIDN'T HAVE ANY?!
WOOHOO!
YUMA! WAIT!
DID YOU REALLY BEAT SHARK...
WITHOUT ANY XYZ MON-STERS?!
AH WA WA
UHM...
BUT HEY, IT WORKS.
WELL... I HAVE ONE...
ONLY IT'S NOT TECHNICALLY MINE, SO... Y'KNOW...
PHEW
HM.
THAT MUST BE HIS TRUMP CARD...
THEN I'LL TAKE THAT CARD!!
HEE HEE HEE!!
... YUMA.
WHO ARE THESE PEOPLE?

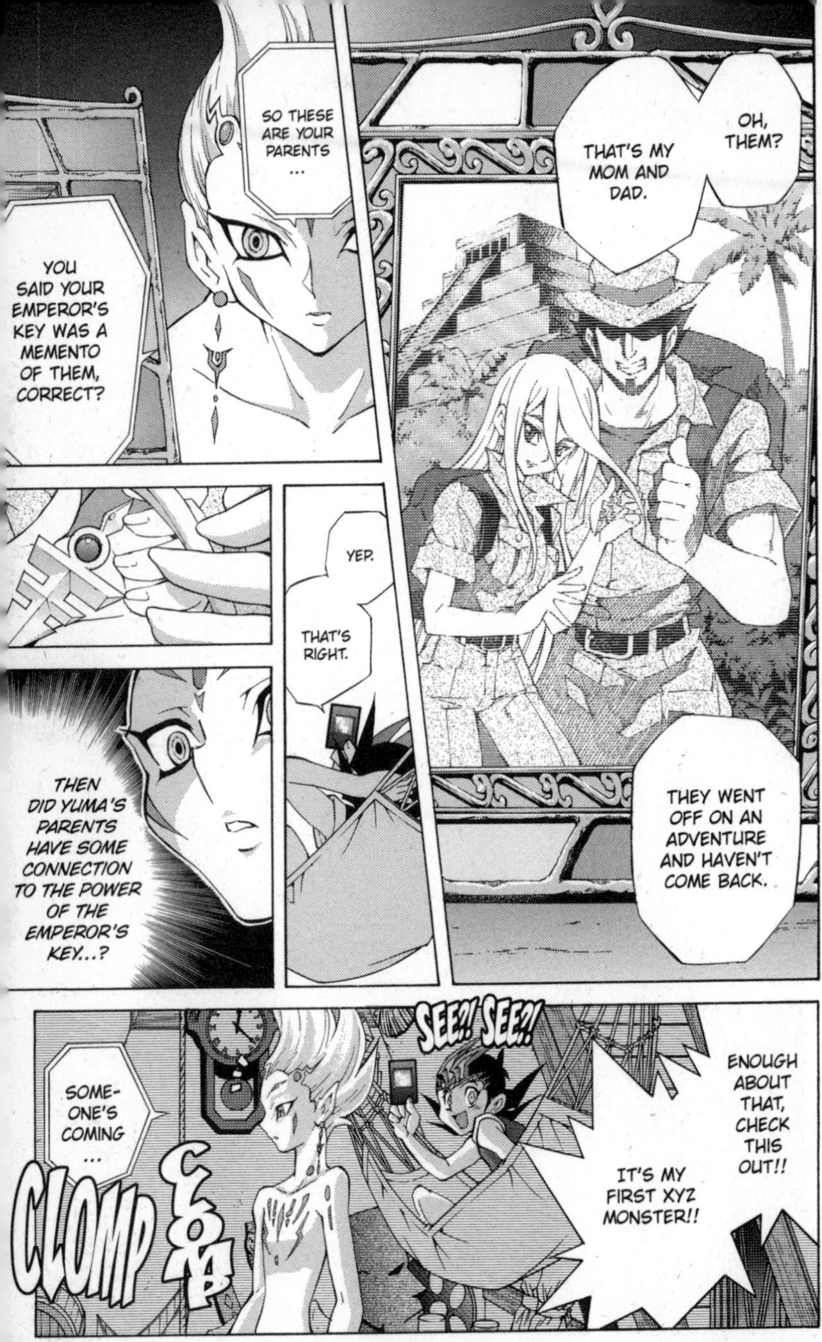
OH, THEM?
THAT'S MY MOM AND DAD.
THEY WENT OFF ON AN ADVENTURE AND HAVEN'T COME BACK.
SO THESE ARE YOUR PARENTS ...
YOU SAID YOUR EMPEROR'S KEY WAS A MEMENTO OF THEM, CORRECT?
YEP.
THAT'S RIGHT.
THEN DID YUMA'S PARENTS HAVE SOME CONNECTION TO THE POWER OF THE EMPEROR'S KEY...?
SEE?! SEE?!
ENOUGH ABOUT THAT, CHECK THIS OUT!!
IT'S MY FIRST XYZ MONSTER!!
SOME-ONE'S COMING ...
CLOMP
CLOMP

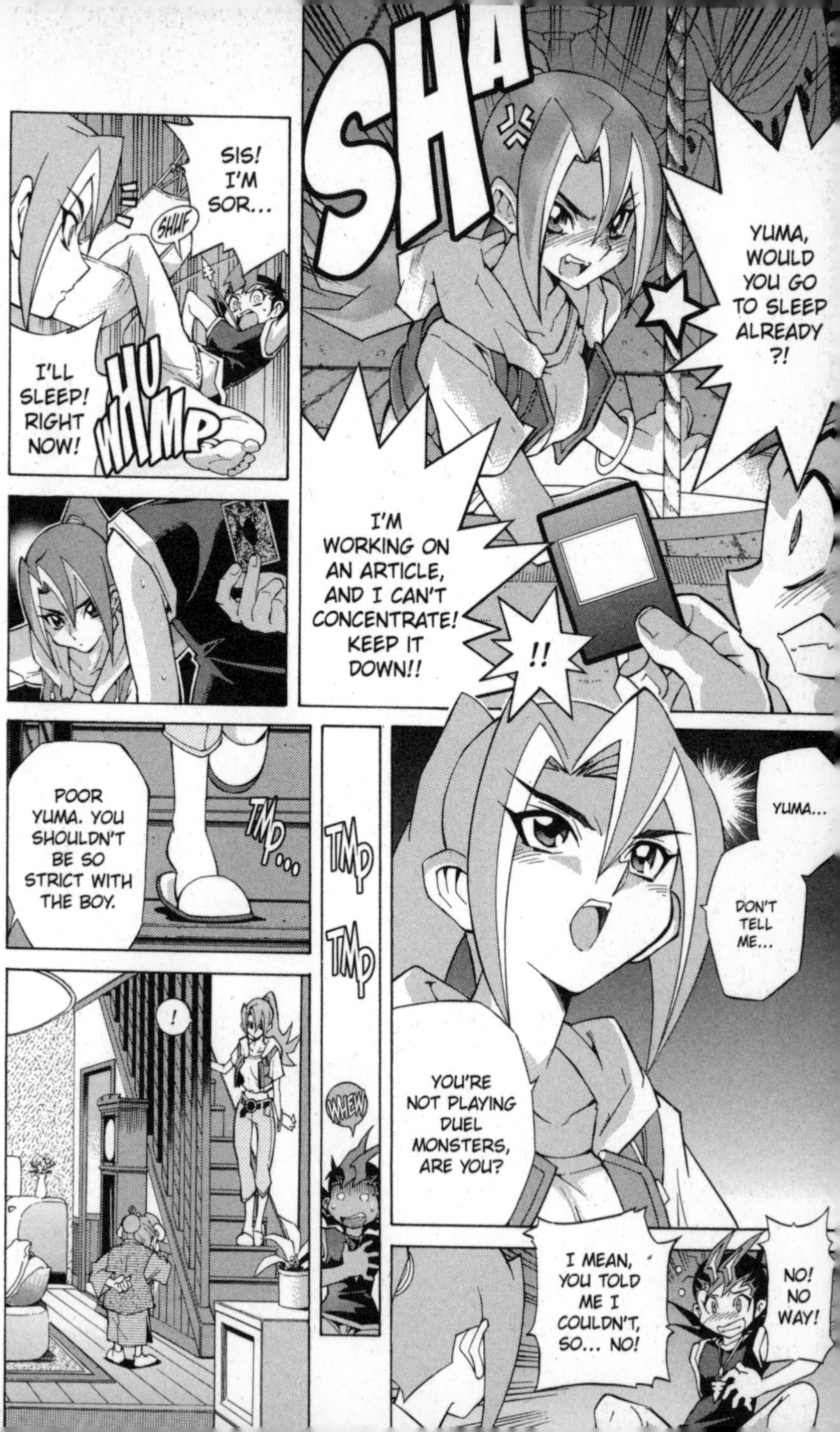
SHA
YUMA, WOULD YOU GO TO SLEEP ALREADY ?!
I'M WORKING ON AN ARTICLE, AND I CAN'T CONCENTRATE! KEEP IT DOWN!!
!!
SIS! I'M SOR...
SHUF
I'LL SLEEP! RIGHT NOW!
YUMA...
DON'T TELL ME...
YOU'RE NOT PLAYING DUEL MONSTERS, ARE YOU?
NO! NO WAY!
I MEAN, YOU TOLD ME I COULDN'T, SO... NO!
TMP
TMP
WHEW
TMP ooo
POOR YUMA. YOU SHOULDN'T BE SO STRICT WITH THE BOY.
!

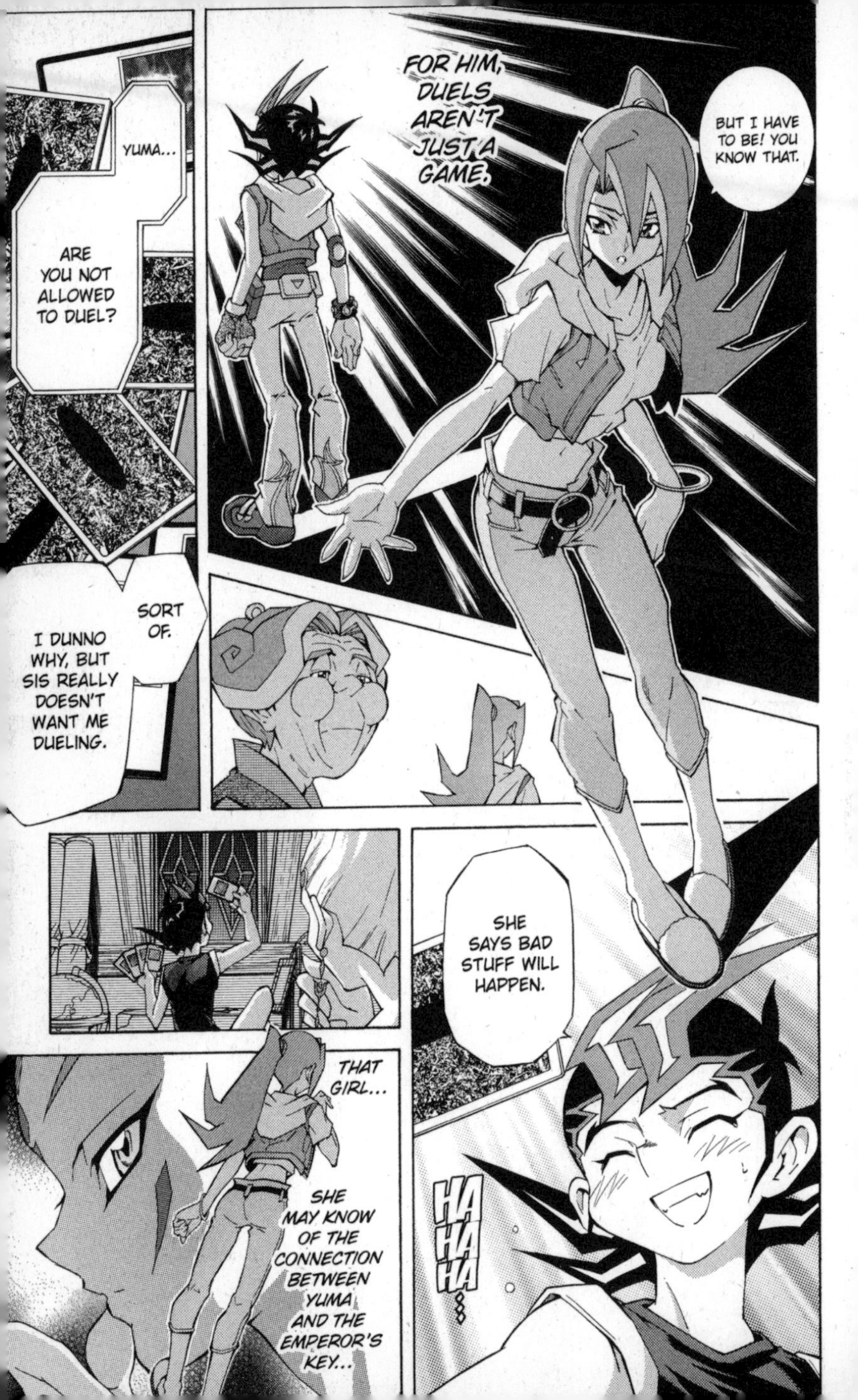

BUT I HAVE TO BE! YOU KNOW THAT.
FOR HIM, DUELS AREN'T JUST A GAME.
YUMA...
ARE YOU NOT ALLOWED TO DUEL?
SORT OF.
I DUNNO WHY, BUT SIS REALLY DOESN'T WANT ME DUELING.
SHE SAYS BAD STUFF WILL HAPPEN.
HA HA HA
THAT GIRL...
SHE MAY KNOW OF THE CONNECTION BETWEEN YUMA AND THE EMPEROR'S KEY...

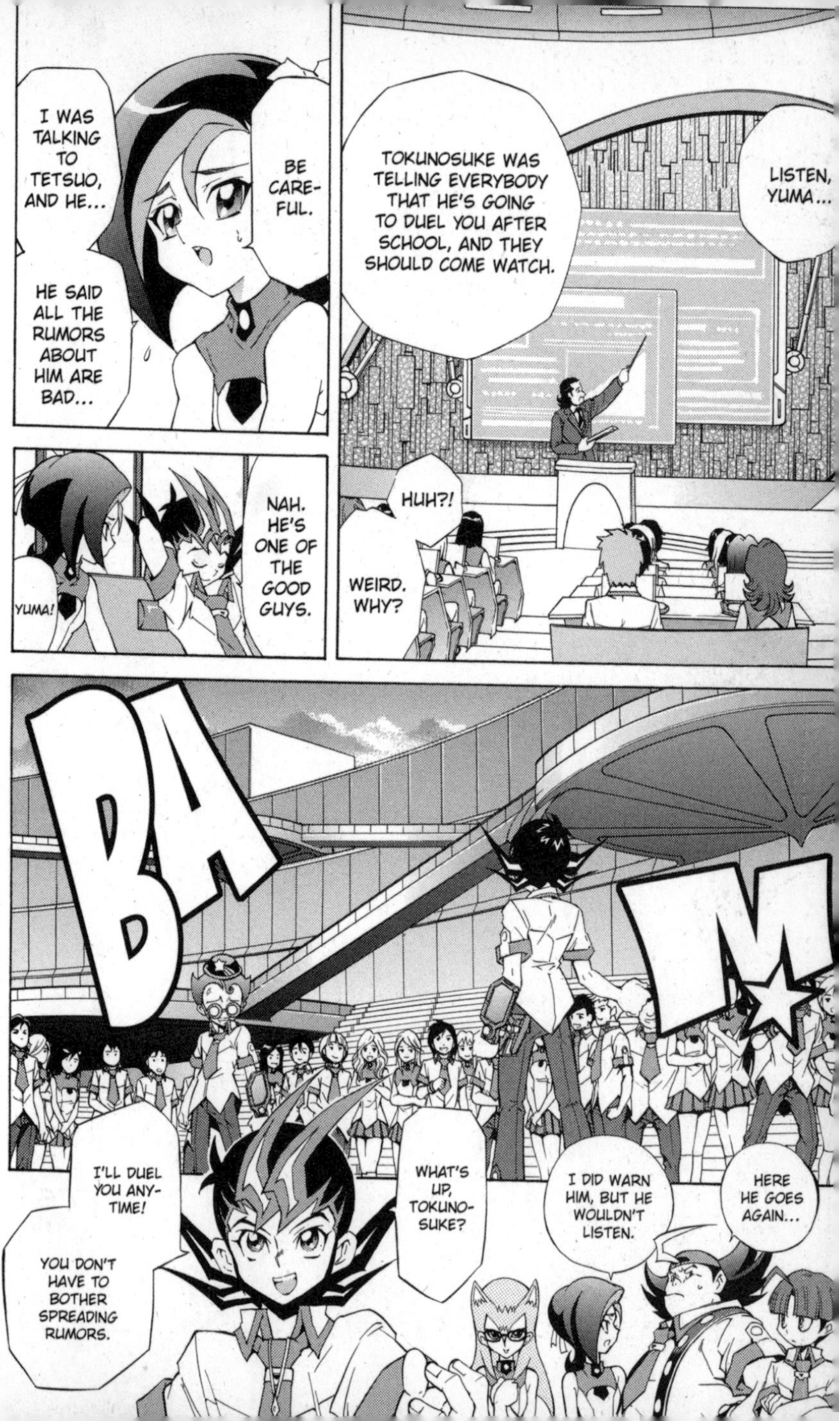
LISTEN, YUMA...
TOKUNOSUKE WAS TELLING EVERYBODY THAT HE'S GOING TO DUEL YOU AFTER SCHOOL, AND THEY SHOULD COME WATCH.
HUH?!
WEIRD. WHY?
BE CARE-FUL.
I WAS TALKING TO TETSUO, AND HE...
HE SAID ALL THE RUMORS ABOUT HIM ARE BAD...
NAH. HE'S ONE OF THE GOOD GUYS.
YUMA!
BAM
HERE HE GOES AGAIN...
I DID WARN HIM, BUT HE WOULDN'T LISTEN.
WHAT'S UP, TOKUNO-SUKE?
I'LL DUEL YOU ANY-TIME!
YOU DON'T HAVE TO BOTHER SPREADING RUMORS.

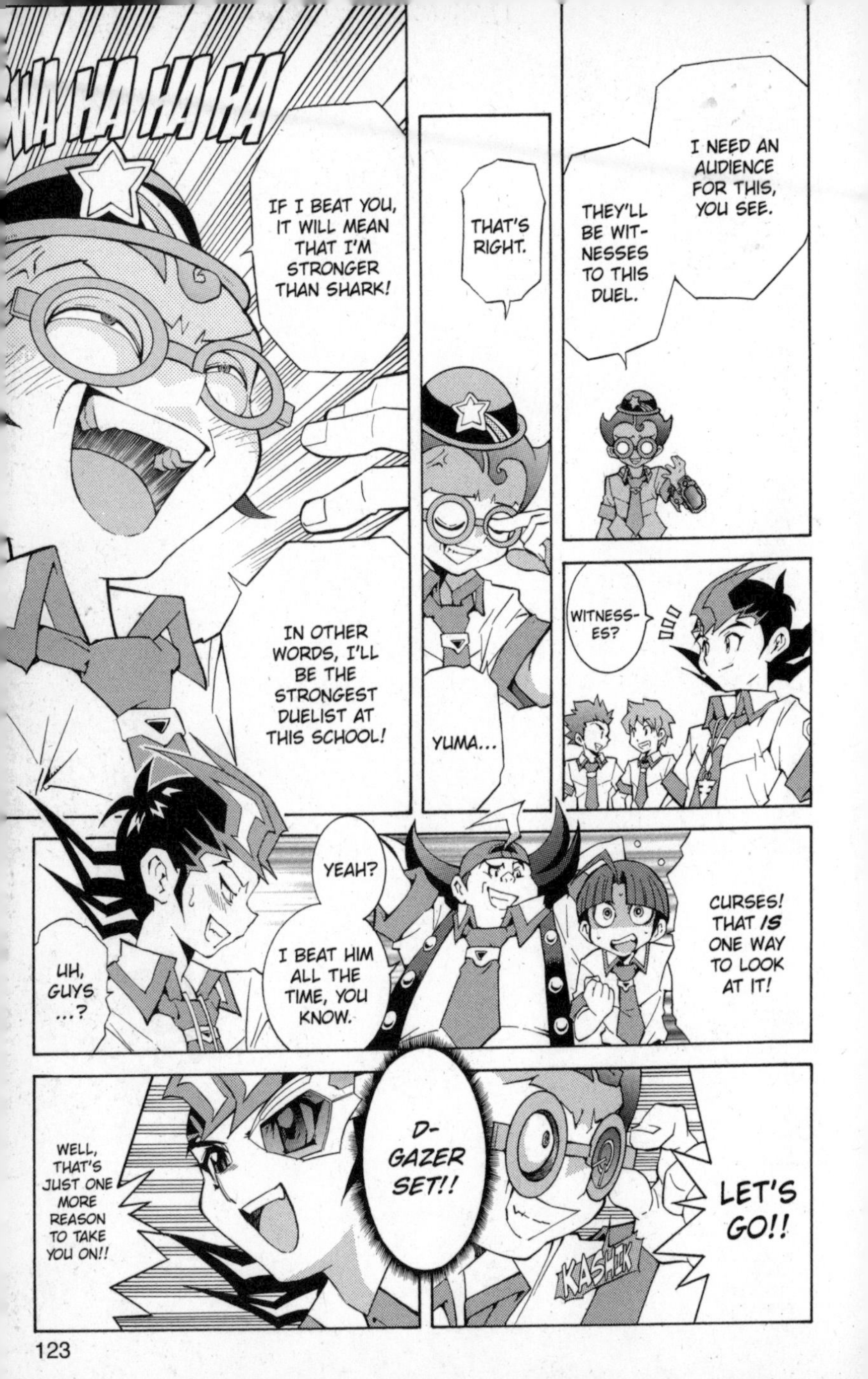

I NEED AN AUDIENCE FOR THIS, YOU SEE.
THEY'LL BE WIT- NESSES TO THIS DUEL.
WITNESS- ES?
THAT'S RIGHT.
YUMA...
WA HA HA HA
IF I BEAT YOU, IT WILL MEAN THAT I'M STRONGER THAN SHARK!
IN OTHER WORDS, I'LL BE THE STRONGEST DUELIST AT THIS SCHOOL!
CURSES! THAT *IS* ONE WAY TO LOOK AT IT!
YEAH?
I BEAT HIM ALL THE TIME, YOU KNOW.
UH, GUYS ...?
LET'S GO!!
KASHAK
D- GAZER SET!!
WELL, THAT'S JUST ONE MORE REASON TO TAKE YOU ON!!

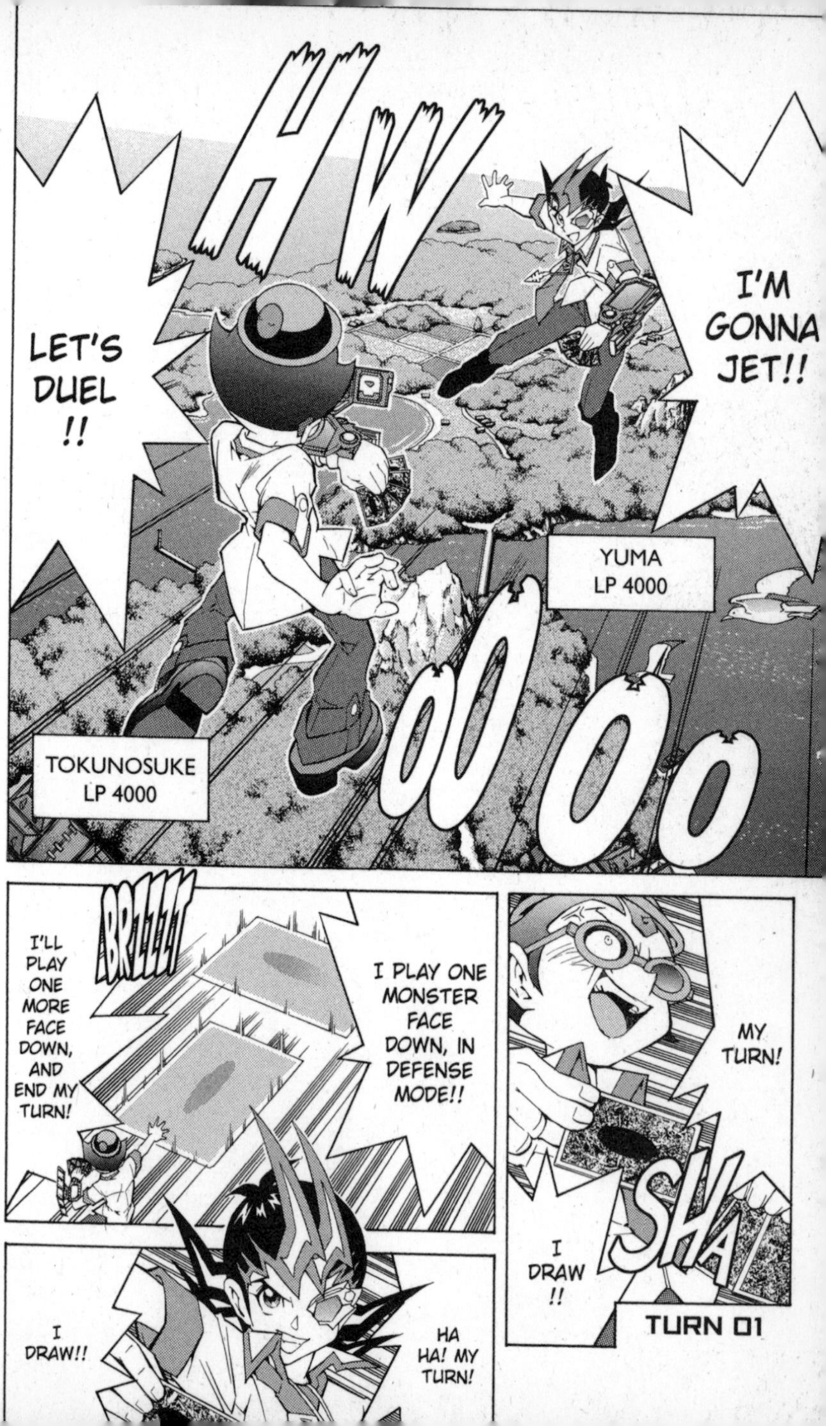
I'M GONNA JET!!
HW
LET'S DUEL!!
YUMA
LP 4000
OOOO
TOKUNOSUKE
LP 4000
MY TURN!
SHA
I DRAW!!
TURN 01
I PLAY ONE MONSTER FACE DOWN, IN DEFENSE MODE!!
BRZZZT
I'LL PLAY ONE MORE FACE DOWN, AND END MY TURN!
HA HA! MY TURN!
I DRAW!!

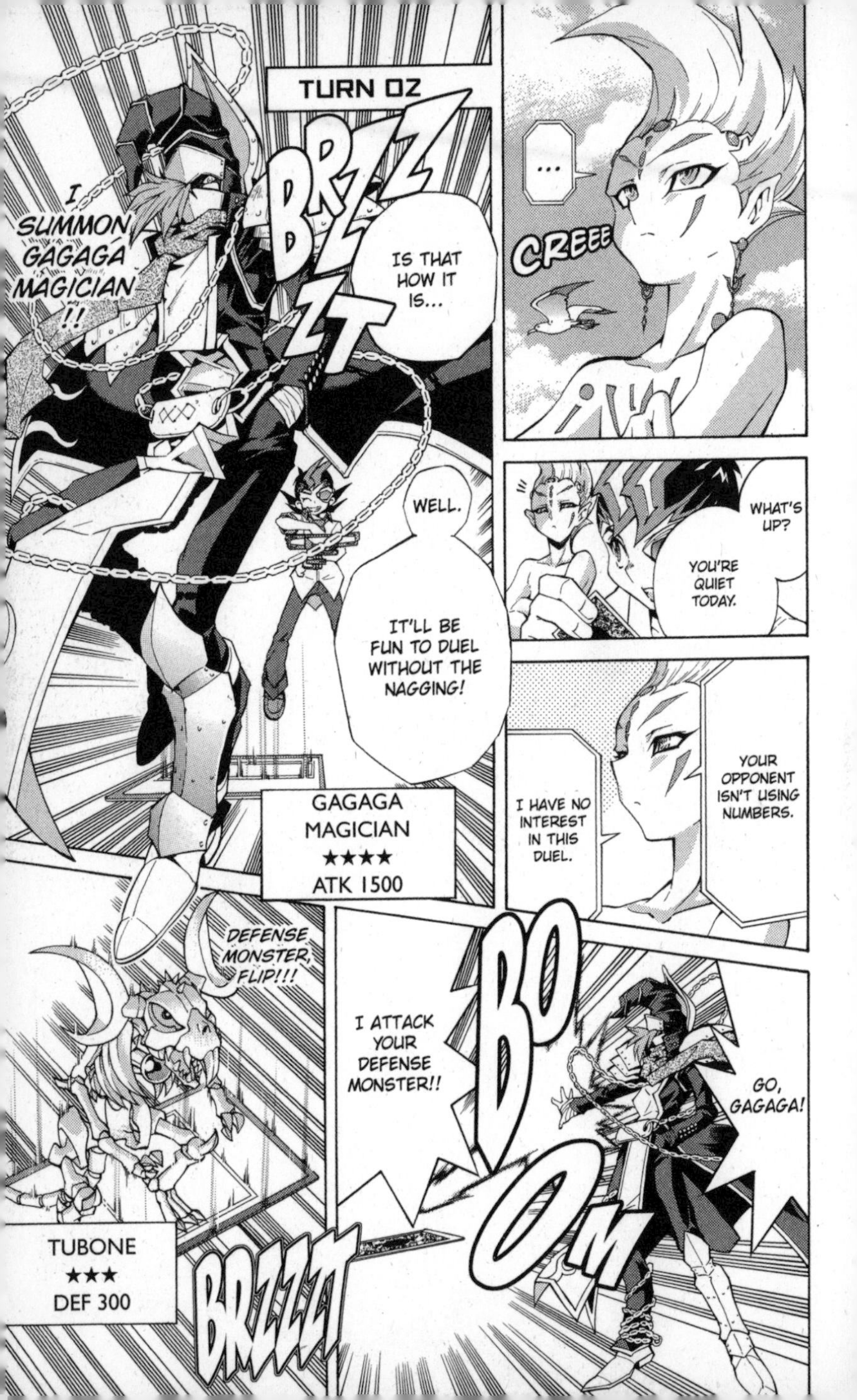
...
CREEE
WHAT'S UP?
YOU'RE QUIET TODAY.
YOUR OPPONENT ISN'T USING NUMBERS.
I HAVE NO INTEREST IN THIS DUEL.
TURN 02
BRZZZT
IS THAT HOW IT IS...
I SUMMON GAGAGA MAGICIAN!!
WELL.
IT'LL BE FUN TO DUEL WITHOUT THE NAGGING!
GAGAGA MAGICIAN ★★★★ ATK 1500
GO, GAGAGA!
BOOM
I ATTACK YOUR DEFENSE MONSTER!!
DEFENSE MONSTER, FLIP!!!
TUBONE ★★★ DEF 300
BRZZZT

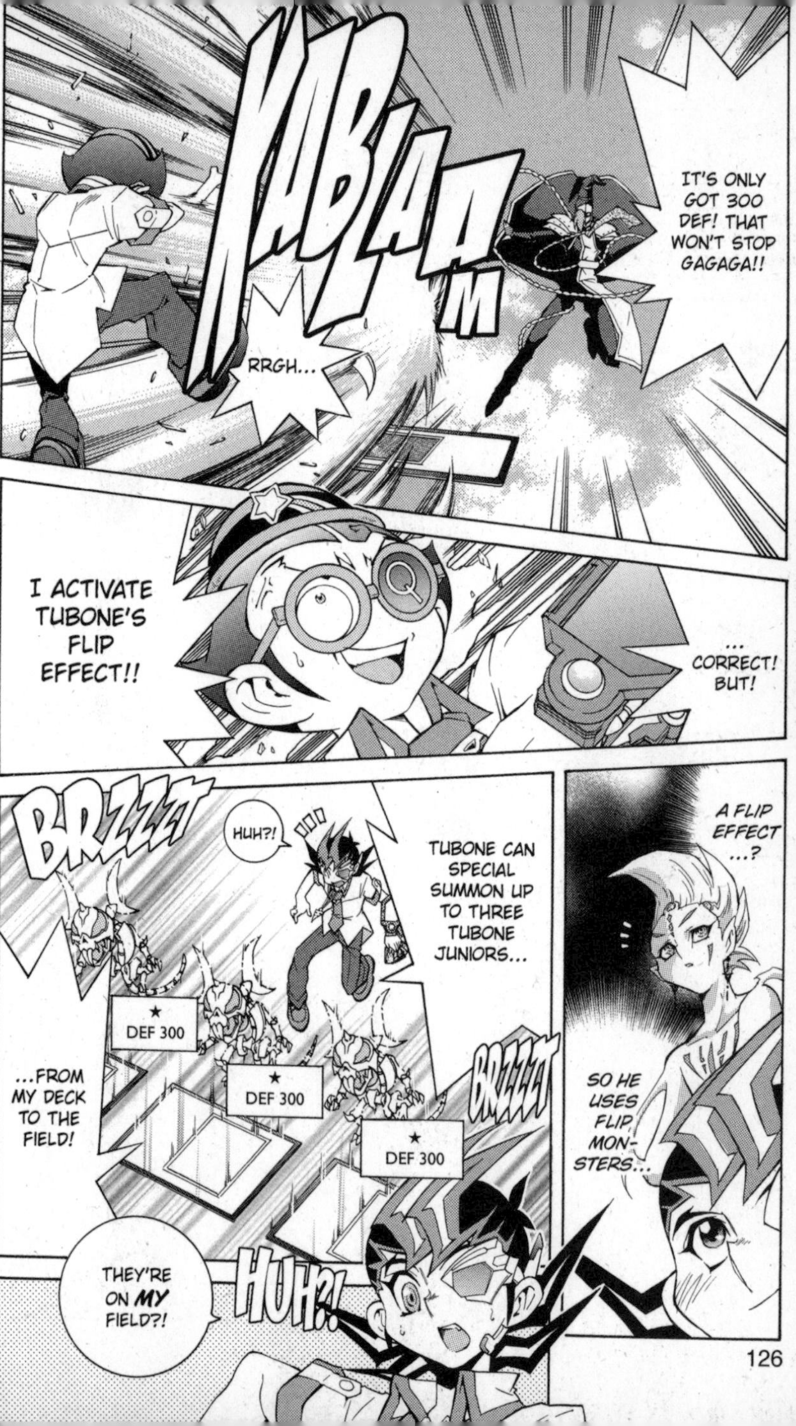
IT'S ONLY GOT 300 DEF! THAT WON'T STOP GAGAGA!!
KABLAAM
RRGH...
... CORRECT! BUT!
I ACTIVATE TUBONE'S FLIP EFFECT!!
A FLIP EFFECT ...?
SO HE USES FLIP MON-STERS...
TUBONE CAN SPECIAL SUMMON UP TO THREE TUBONE JUNIORS...
HUH?!
BRZZZT
★ DEF 300
★ DEF 300
★ DEF 300
...FROM MY DECK TO THE FIELD!
BRZZZT
HUH?!
THEY'RE ON *MY* FIELD?!

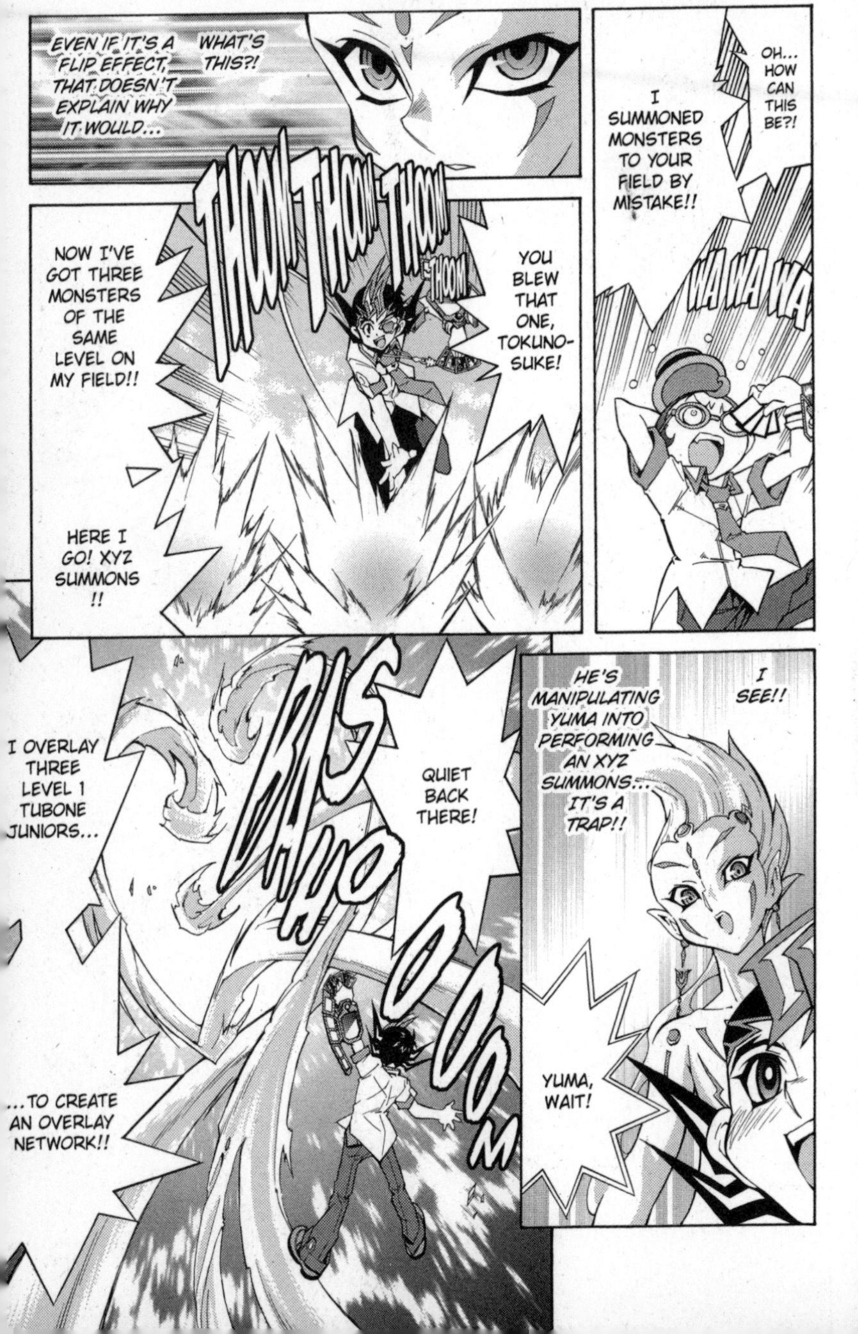
OH... HOW CAN THIS BE?!
I SUMMONED MONSTERS TO YOUR FIELD BY MISTAKE!!
WA WA WA
WHAT'S THIS?!
EVEN IF IT'S A FLIP EFFECT, THAT DOESN'T EXPLAIN WHY IT WOULD...
THOOM THOOM THOOM THOOM
YOU BLEW THAT ONE, TOKUNOSUKE!
NOW I'VE GOT THREE MONSTERS OF THE SAME LEVEL ON MY FIELD!!
HERE I GO! XYZ SUMMONS!!
I SEE!!
HE'S MANIPULATING YUMA INTO PERFORMING AN XYZ SUMMONS... IT'S A TRAP!!
YUMA, WAIT!
QUIET BACK THERE!
BASHOOOOOOM
I OVERLAY THREE LEVEL 1 TUBONE JUNIORS...
...TO CREATE AN OVERLAY NETWORK!!

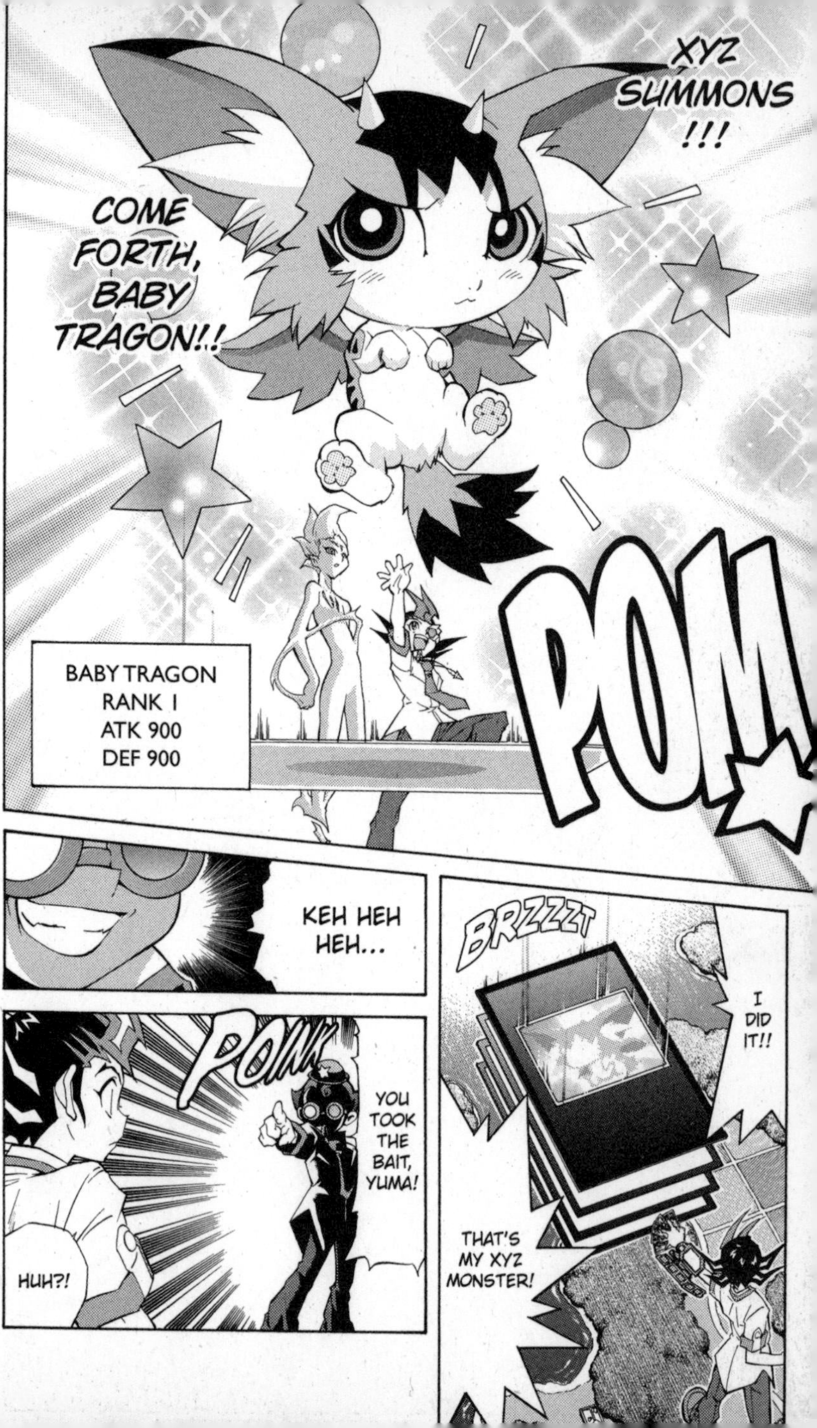
XYZ SUMMONS!!!
COME FORTH, BABY TRAGON!!
BABY TRAGON
RANK 1
ATK 900
DEF 900
POM
BRZZZT
I DID IT!!
THAT'S MY XYZ MONSTER!
KEH HEH HEH...
POMK
YOU TOOK THE BAIT, YUMA!
HUH?!

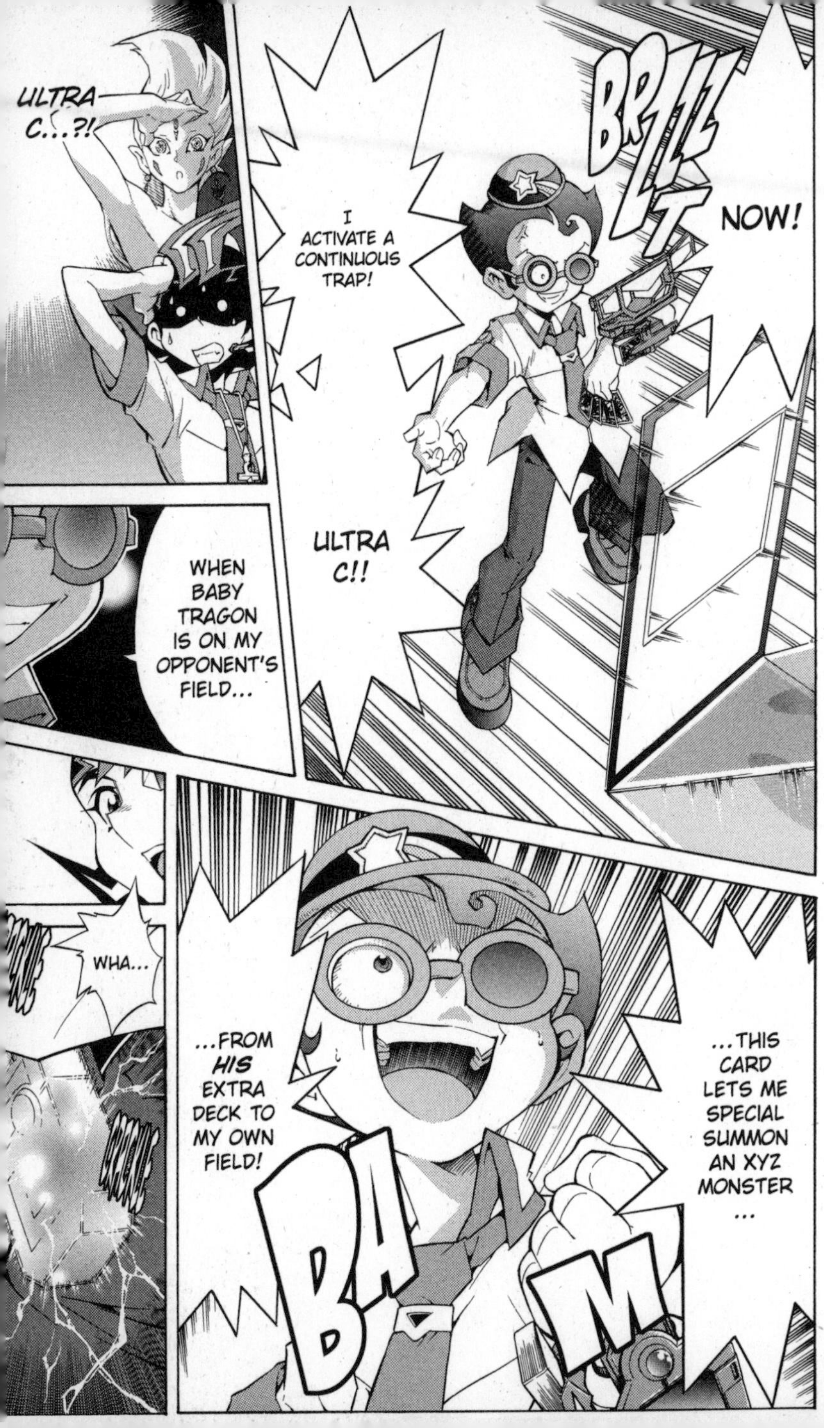
BRZZT
NOW!
I ACTIVATE A CONTINUOUS TRAP!
ULTRA C!!
ULTRA C...?!
WHEN BABY TRAGON IS ON MY OPPONENT'S FIELD...
...THIS CARD LETS ME SPECIAL SUMMON AN XYZ MONSTER ...
...FROM *HIS* EXTRA DECK TO MY OWN FIELD!
BAM
WHA...

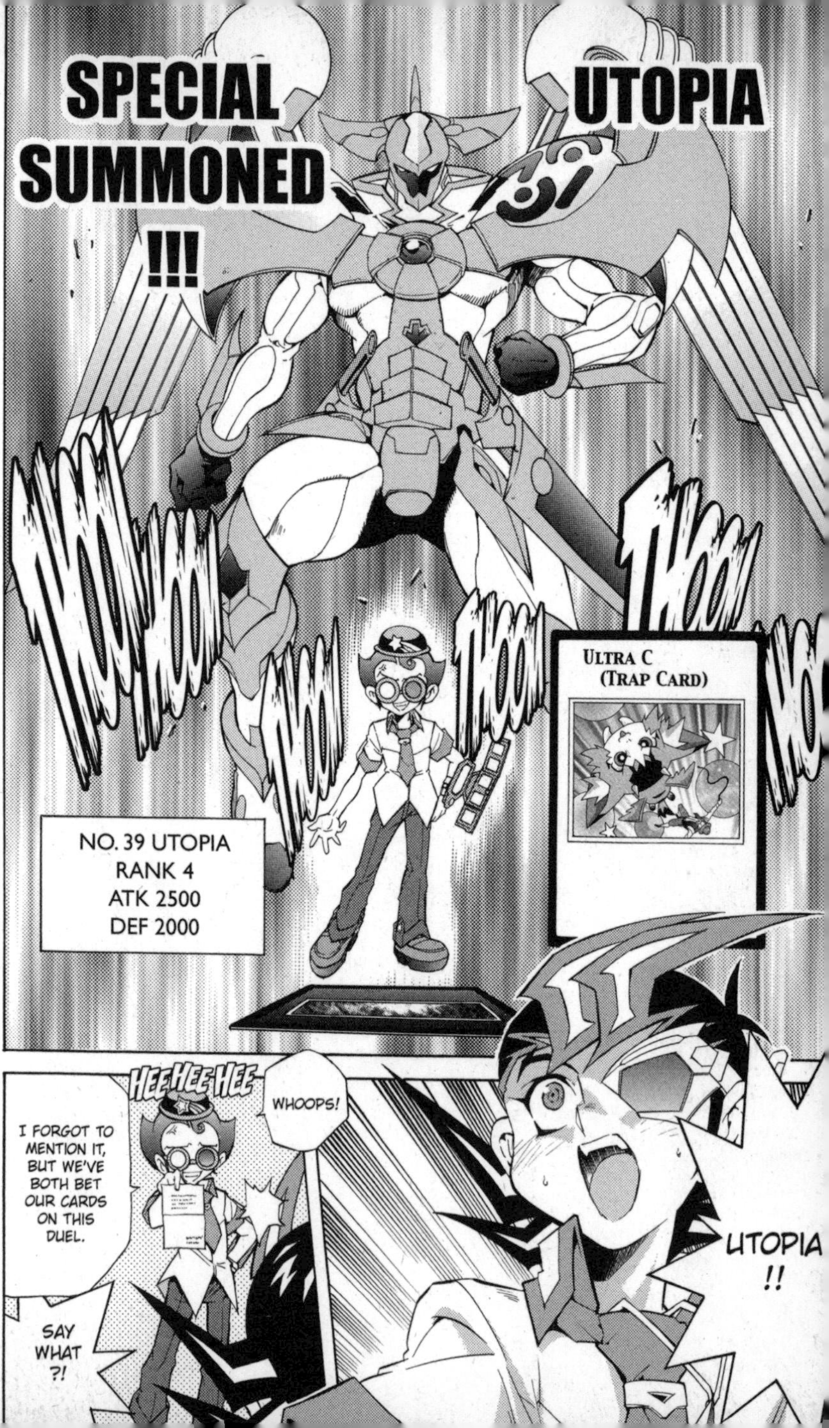
UTOPIA
SPECIAL SUMMONED !!!
THOOM
THOOM
ULTRA C (TRAP CARD)
NO. 39 UTOPIA
RANK 4
ATK 2500
DEF 2000
UTOPIA !!
WHOOPS!
HEE HEE HEE
I FORGOT TO MENTION IT, BUT WE'VE BOTH BET OUR CARDS ON THIS DUEL.
SAY WHAT ?!

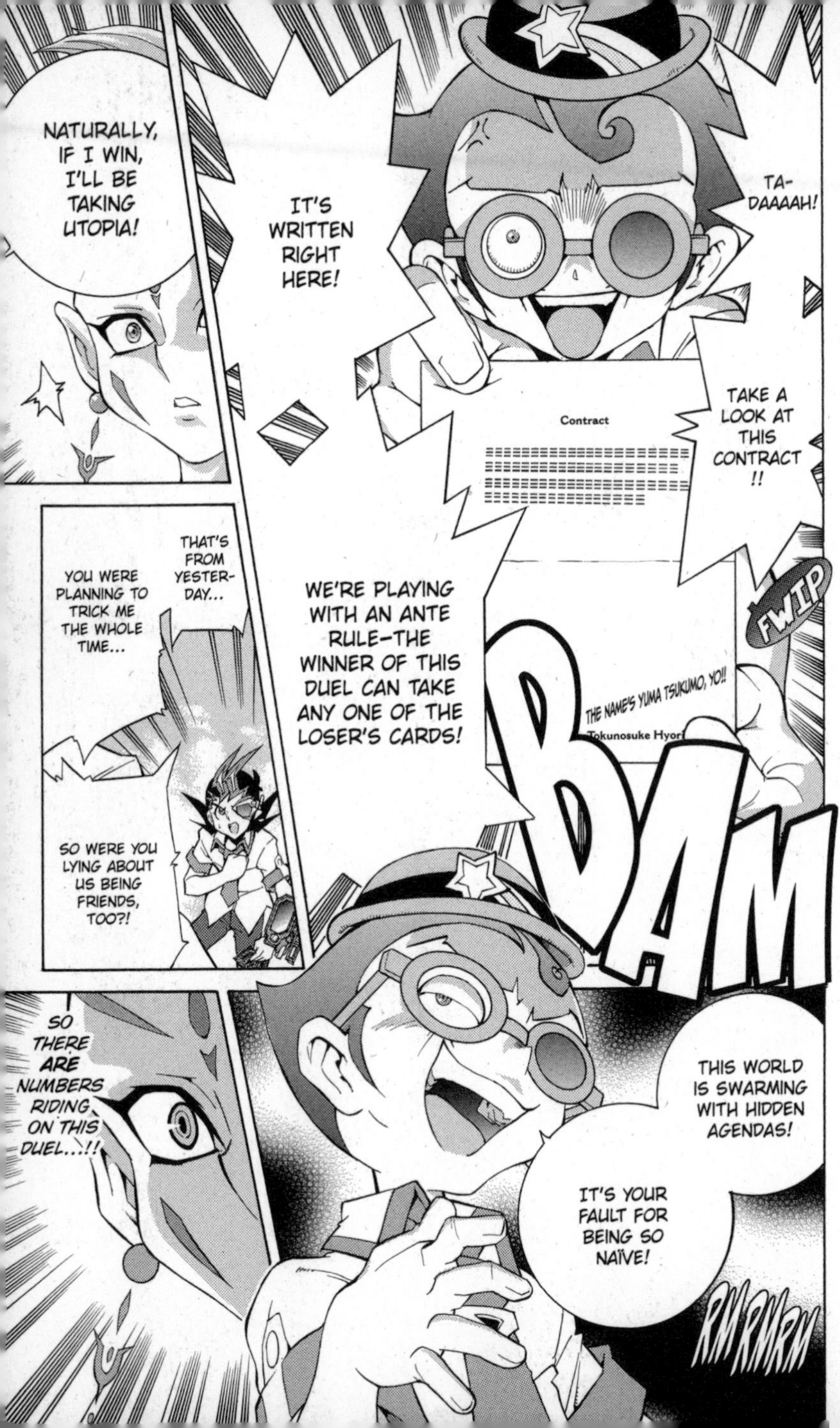
TA-DAAAAH!
IT'S WRITTEN RIGHT HERE!
TAKE A LOOK AT THIS CONTRACT!!
Contract
FWIP
WE'RE PLAYING WITH AN ANTE RULE—THE WINNER OF THIS DUEL CAN TAKE ANY ONE OF THE LOSER'S CARDS!
BAM
THE NAME'S YUMA TSUKUMO, YO!!
NATURALLY, IF I WIN, I'LL BE TAKING UTOPIA!
THAT'S FROM YESTERDAY...
YOU WERE PLANNING TO TRICK ME THE WHOLE TIME...
SO WERE YOU LYING ABOUT US BEING FRIENDS, TOO?!
THIS WORLD IS SWARMING WITH HIDDEN AGENDAS!
IT'S YOUR FAULT FOR BEING SO NAÏVE!
SO THERE *ARE* NUMBERS RIDING ON THIS DUEL...!!

INCREDIBLE
...

I NEVER KNEW A PLACE COULD BE SO CALMING...

HMM...

MY LOST MEMORIES MAY COME BACK TO ME HERE.

BAM

BAM

HEEEEEY!

BATHROOMS OPTIMIZE ONE'S BRAIN FUNCTION.

ASTRAL'S JOURNAL #3

GURGGGLE

ASTRAL'S JOURNAL

#3

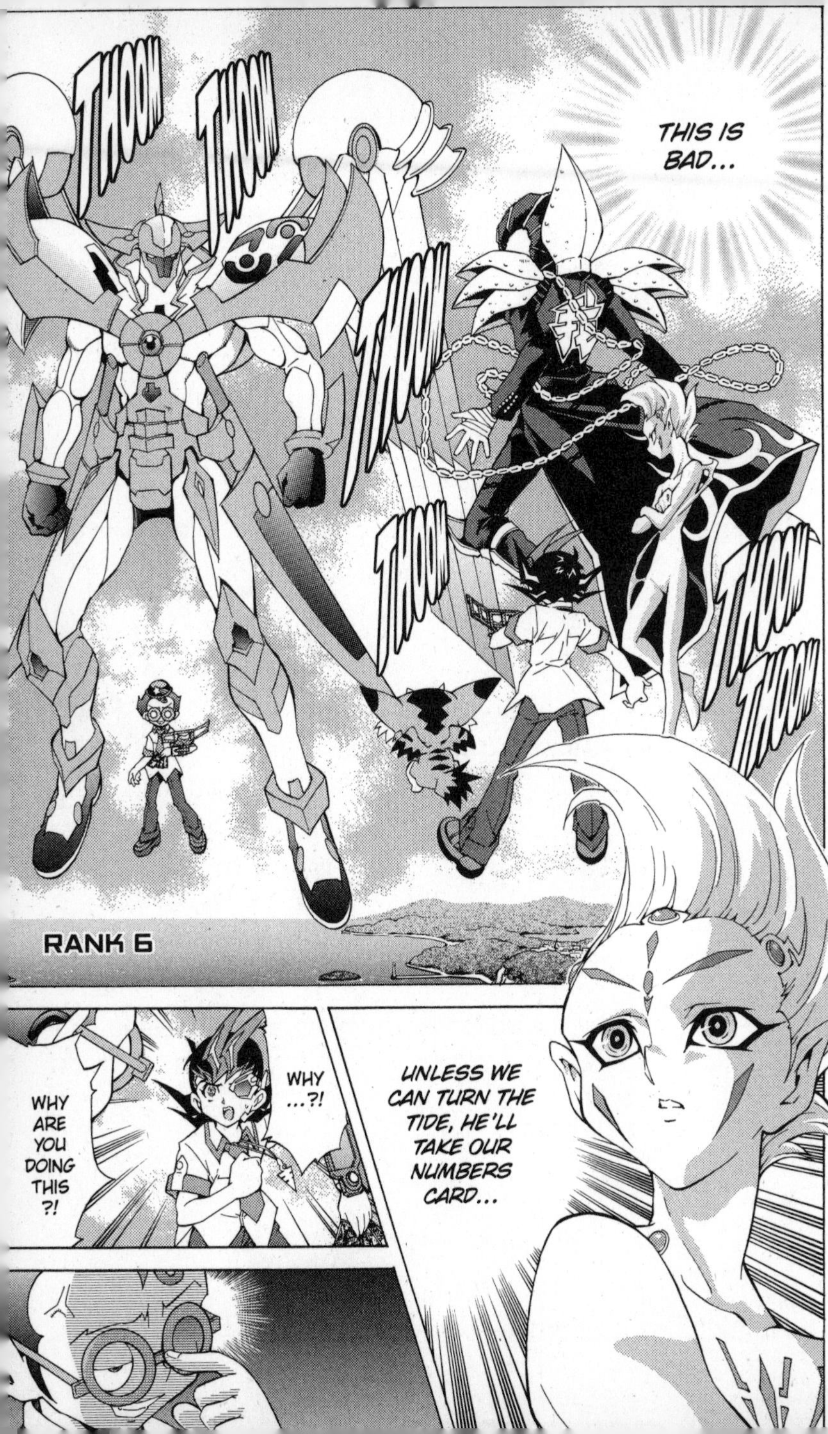
THIS IS BAD...
THOOM THOOM
THOOM
THOOM
THOOM THOOM
RANK 6
UNLESS WE CAN TURN THE TIDE, HE'LL TAKE OUR NUMBERS CARD...
WHY ...?!
WHY ARE YOU DOING THIS ?!

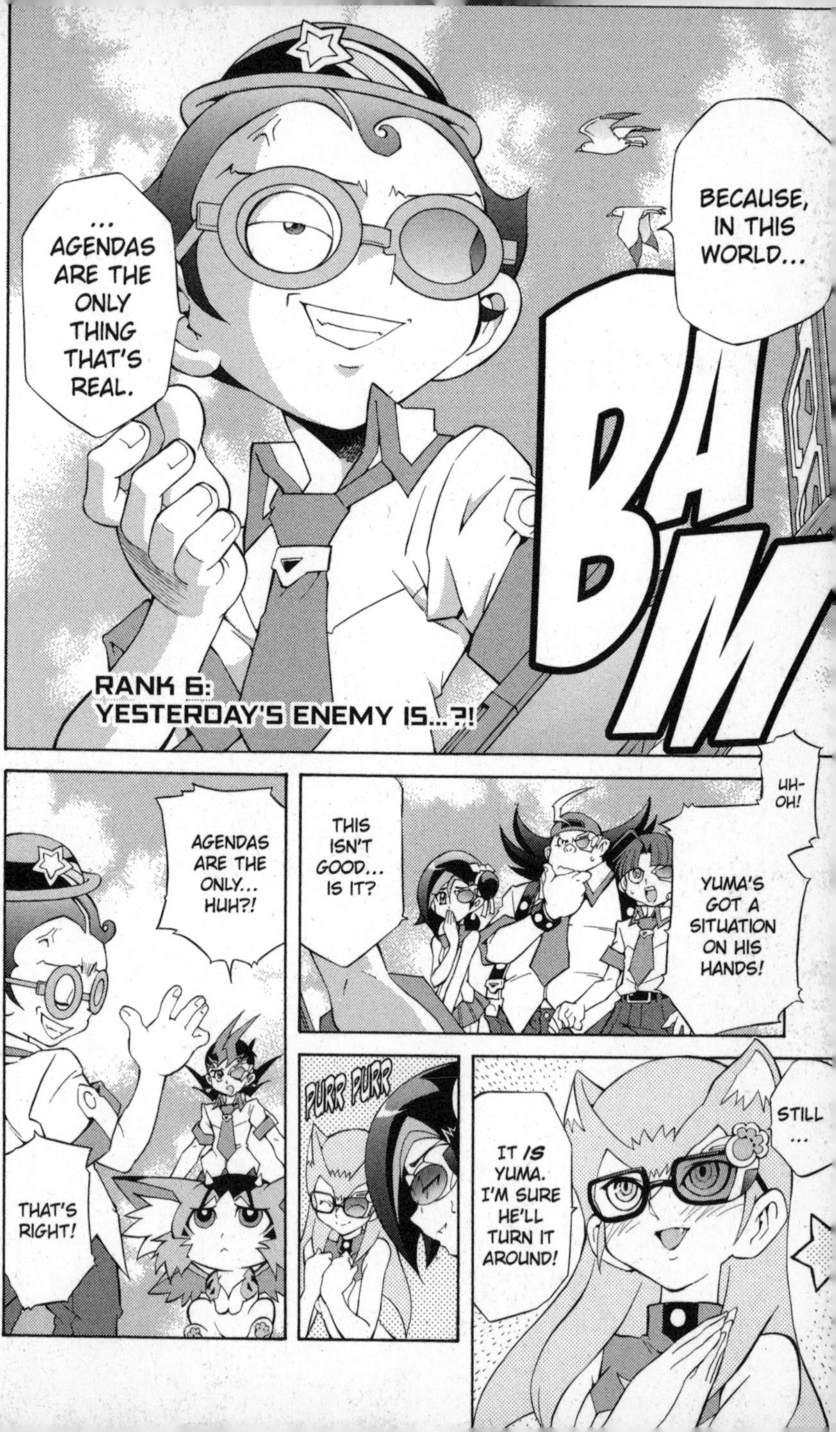
BECAUSE, IN THIS WORLD...
... AGENDAS ARE THE ONLY THING THAT'S REAL.
BAM
RANK 6: YESTERDAY'S ENEMY IS...?!
UH-OH!
YUMA'S GOT A SITUATION ON HIS HANDS!
THIS ISN'T GOOD... IS IT?
STILL ...
IT *IS* YUMA. I'M SURE HE'LL TURN IT AROUND!
PURR PURR
AGENDAS ARE THE ONLY... HUH?!
THAT'S RIGHT!

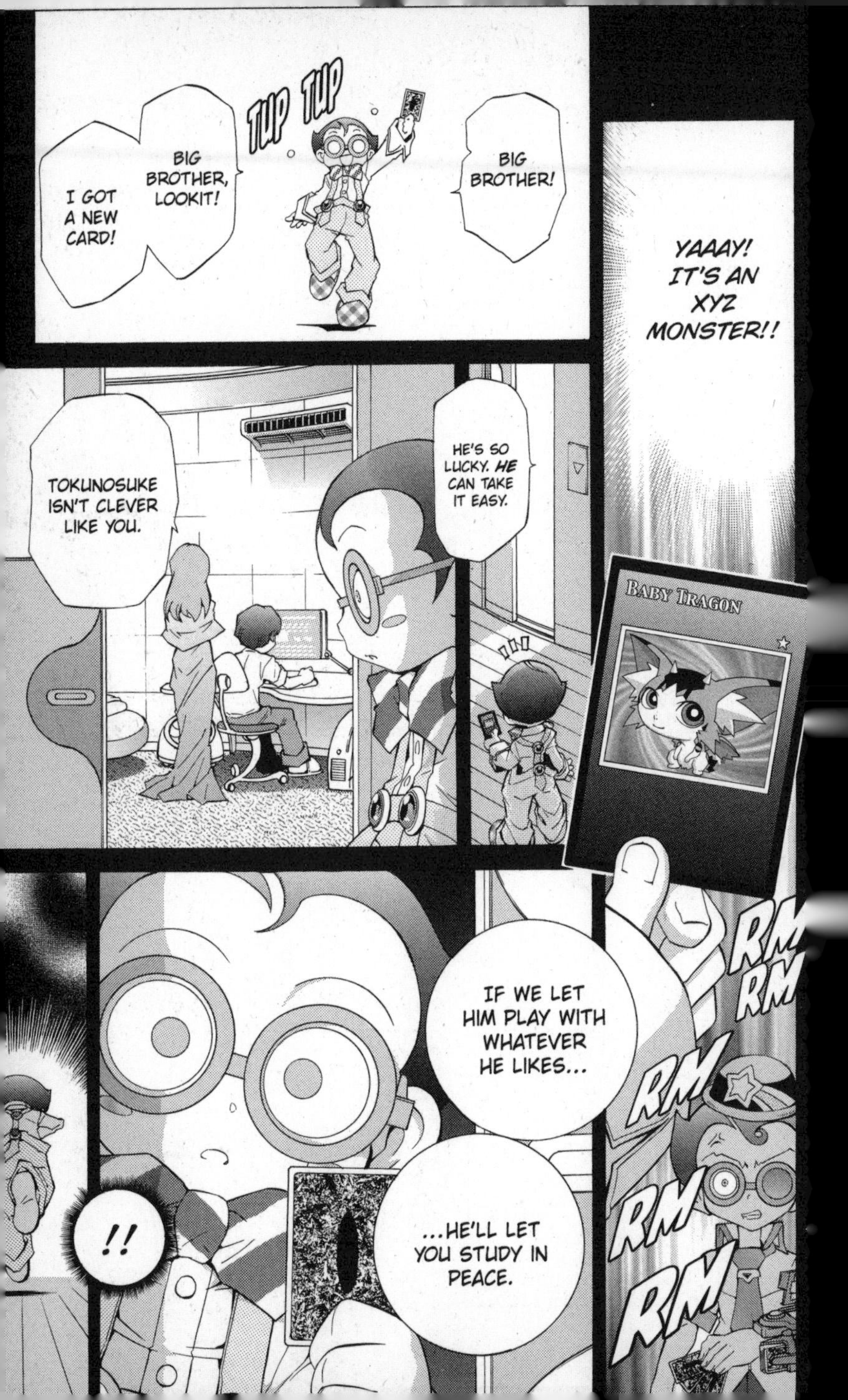
YAAAY! IT'S AN XYZ MONSTER!!
BIG BROTHER!
TUP TUP
BIG BROTHER, LOOKIT!
I GOT A NEW CARD!
HE'S SO LUCKY. HE CAN TAKE IT EASY.
TOKUNOSUKE ISN'T CLEVER LIKE YOU.
BABY TRAGON
RM RM
RM
RM
RM
IF WE LET HIM PLAY WITH WHATEVER HE LIKES...
...HE'LL LET YOU STUDY IN PEACE.
!!

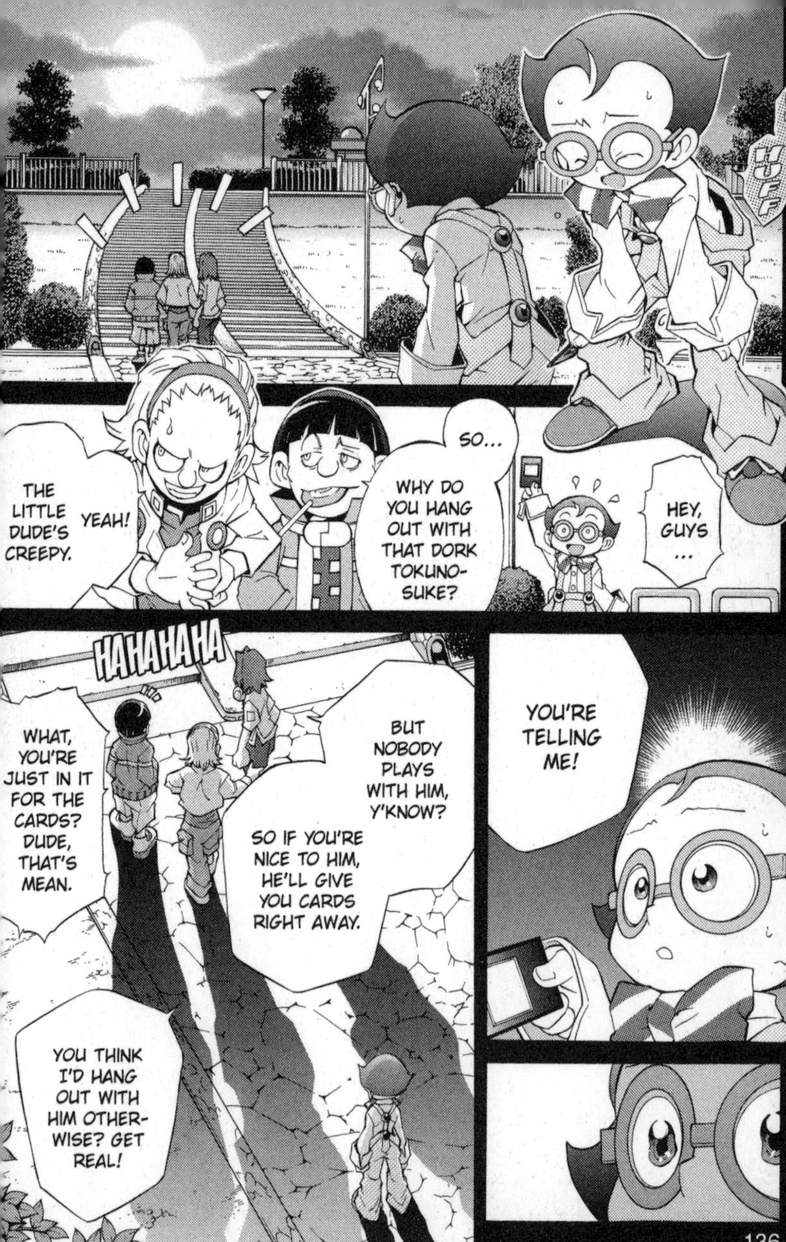
HUFF HUFF
HEY, GUYS ...
SO...
WHY DO YOU HANG OUT WITH THAT DORK TOKUNO-SUKE?
YEAH!
THE LITTLE DUDE'S CREEPY.
YOU'RE TELLING ME!
HAHAHAHA
BUT NOBODY PLAYS WITH HIM, Y'KNOW?
SO IF YOU'RE NICE TO HIM, HE'LL GIVE YOU CARDS RIGHT AWAY.
WHAT, YOU'RE JUST IN IT FOR THE CARDS? DUDE, THAT'S MEAN.
YOU THINK I'D HANG OUT WITH HIM OTHER-WISE? GET REAL!

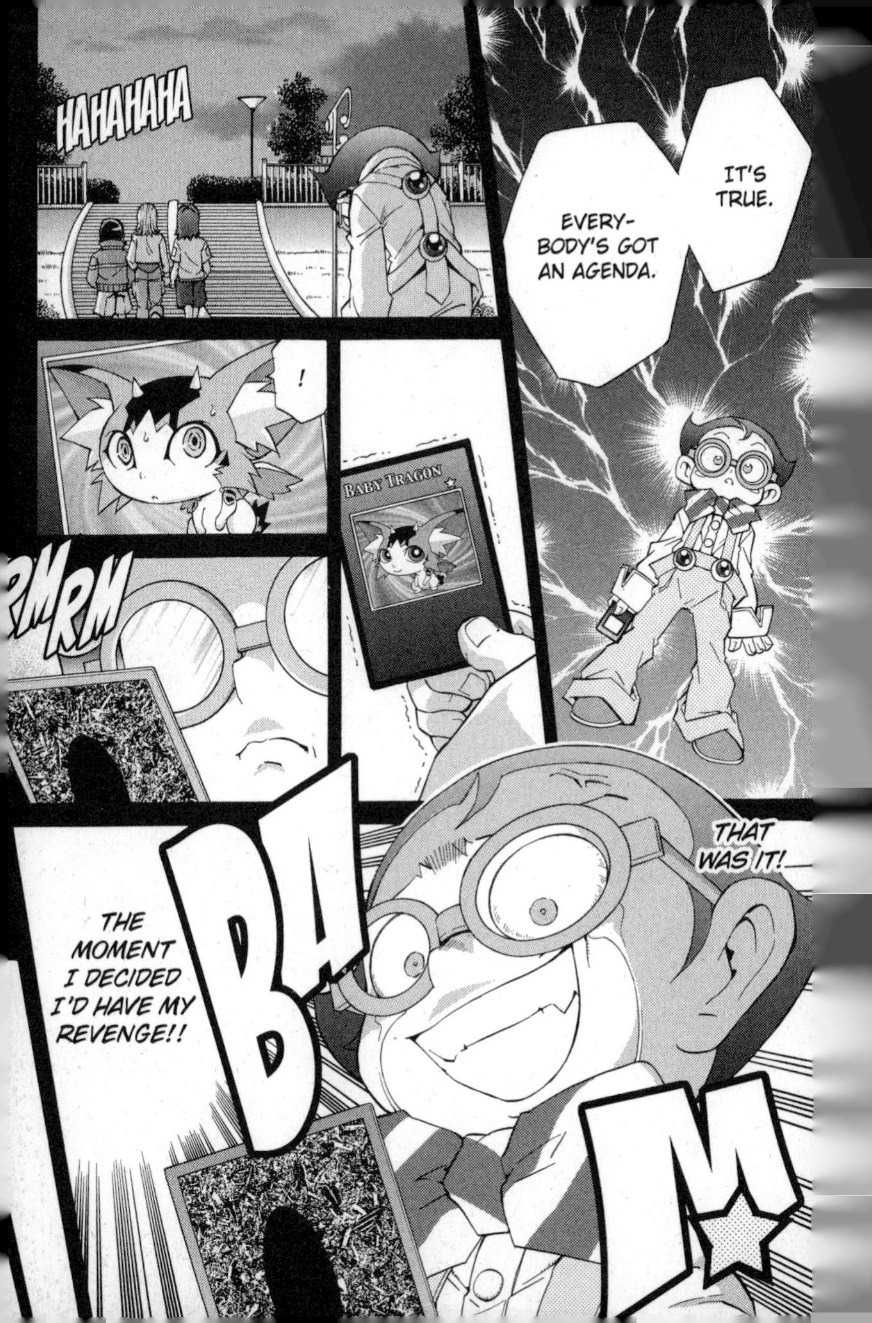
IT'S TRUE.
EVERY-BODY'S GOT AN AGENDA.
HAHAHAHA
BABY TRAGON
!
RMRM
THAT WAS IT!
THE MOMENT I DECIDED I'D HAVE MY REVENGE!!
BAM

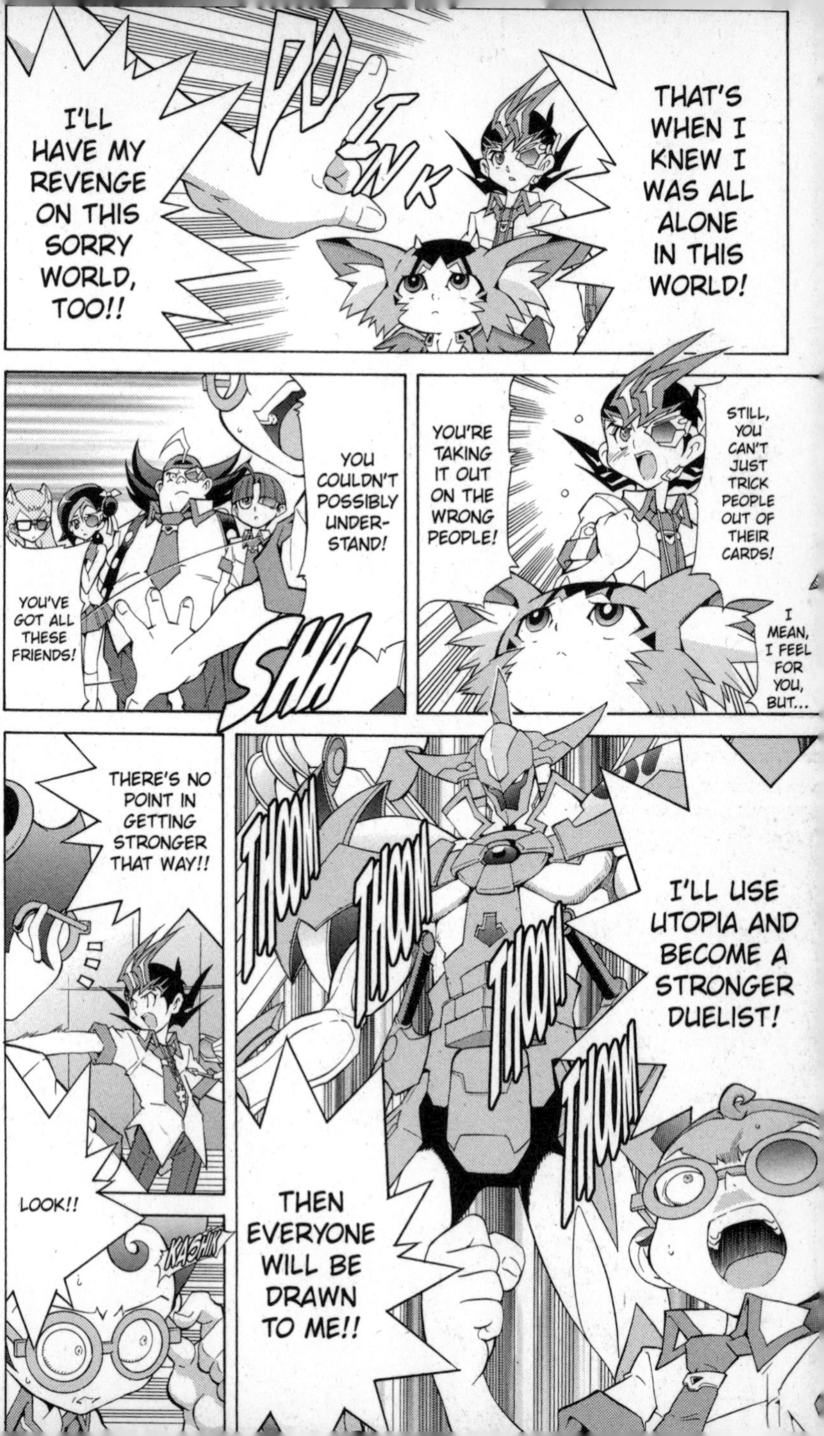
THAT'S WHEN I KNEW I WAS ALL ALONE IN THIS WORLD!
POINK
I'LL HAVE MY REVENGE ON THIS SORRY WORLD, TOO!!
I MEAN, I FEEL FOR YOU, BUT...
STILL, YOU CAN'T JUST TRICK PEOPLE OUT OF THEIR CARDS!
YOU'RE TAKING IT OUT ON THE WRONG PEOPLE!
YOU COULDN'T POSSIBLY UNDER-STAND!
YOU'VE GOT ALL THESE FRIENDS!
SHA
I'LL USE UTOPIA AND BECOME A STRONGER DUELIST!
THOOM
THOOM
THOOM
THOOM
THEN EVERYONE WILL BE DRAWN TO ME!!
THERE'S NO POINT IN GETTING STRONGER THAT WAY!!
LOOK!!
KASHIN

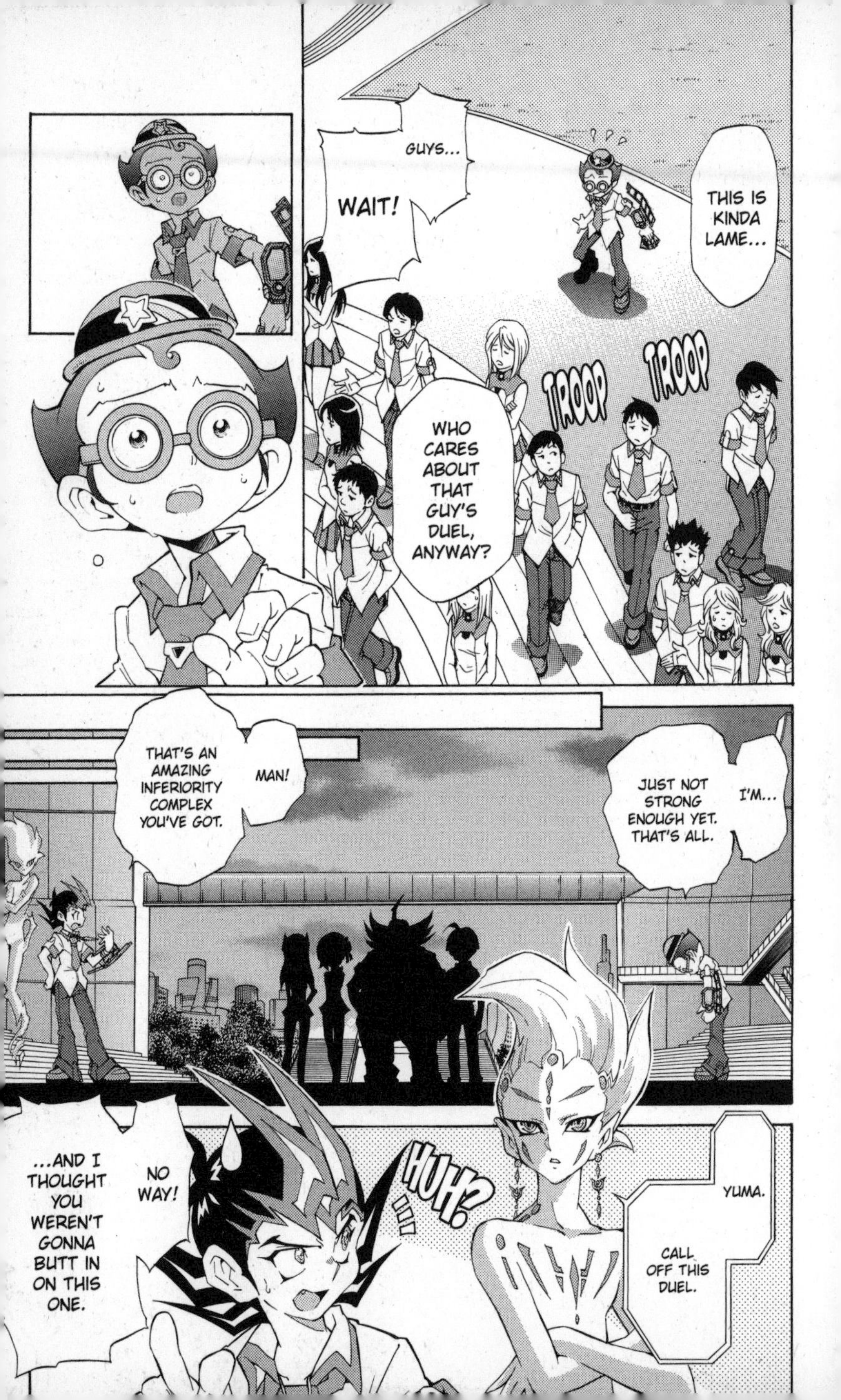
THIS IS KINDA LAME...
WHO CARES ABOUT THAT GUY'S DUEL, ANYWAY?
TROOP
TROOP
GUYS... WAIT!
I'M... JUST NOT STRONG ENOUGH YET. THAT'S ALL.
MAN! THAT'S AN AMAZING INFERIORITY COMPLEX YOU'VE GOT.
YUMA. CALL OFF THIS DUEL.
HUH?!
NO WAY! ...AND I THOUGHT YOU WEREN'T GONNA BUTT IN ON THIS ONE.

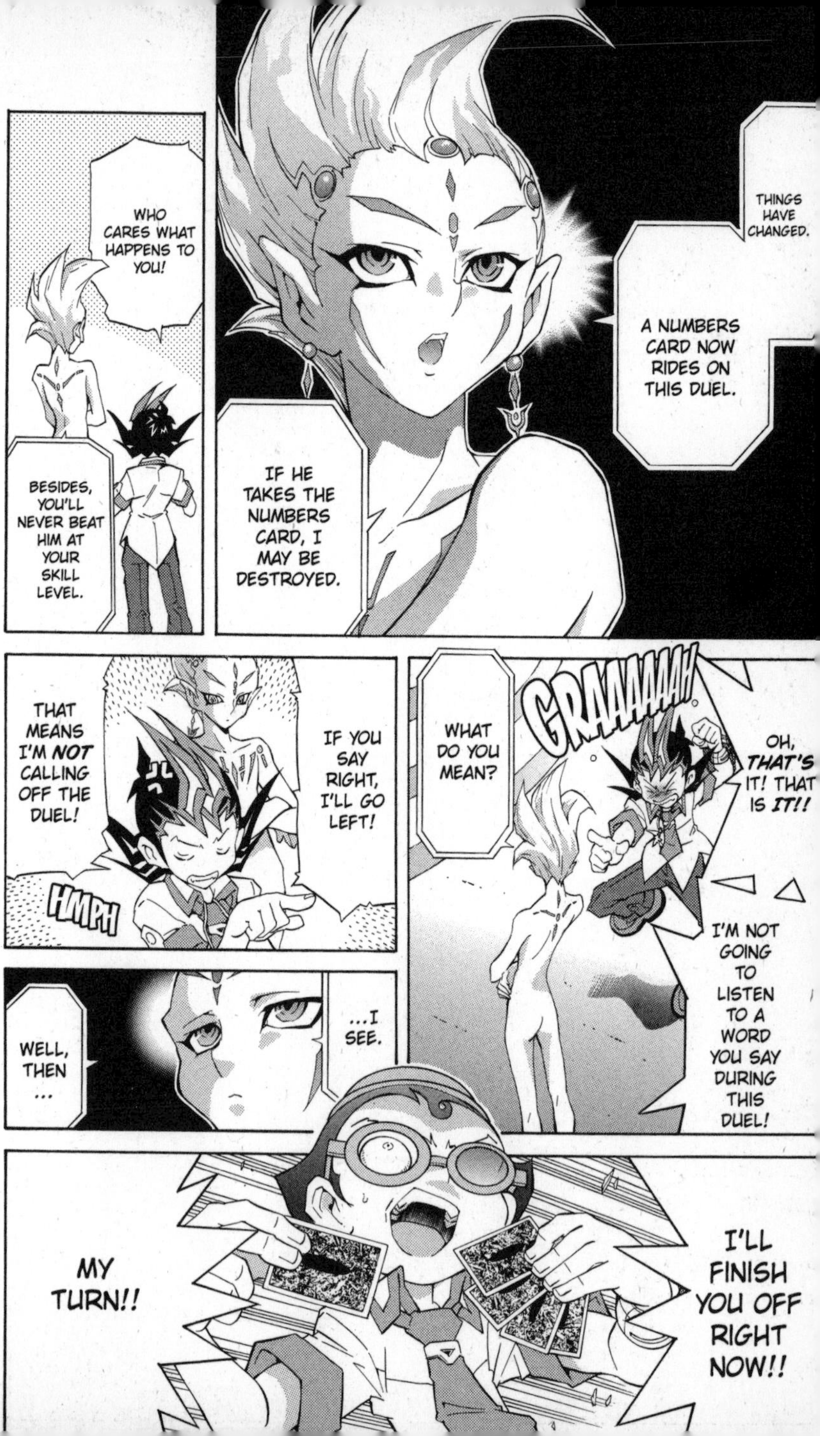

THINGS HAVE CHANGED.
A NUMBERS CARD NOW RIDES ON THIS DUEL.
IF HE TAKES THE NUMBERS CARD, I MAY BE DESTROYED.
WHO CARES WHAT HAPPENS TO YOU!
BESIDES, YOU'LL NEVER BEAT HIM AT YOUR SKILL LEVEL.
OH, ***THAT'S*** IT! THAT IS ***IT!!***
GRAAAAAAH
WHAT DO YOU MEAN?
I'M NOT GOING TO LISTEN TO A WORD YOU SAY DURING THIS DUEL!
IF YOU SAY RIGHT, I'LL GO LEFT!
THAT MEANS I'M ***NOT*** CALLING OFF THE DUEL!
HMPH
...I SEE.
WELL, THEN ...
I'LL FINISH YOU OFF RIGHT NOW!!
MY TURN!!

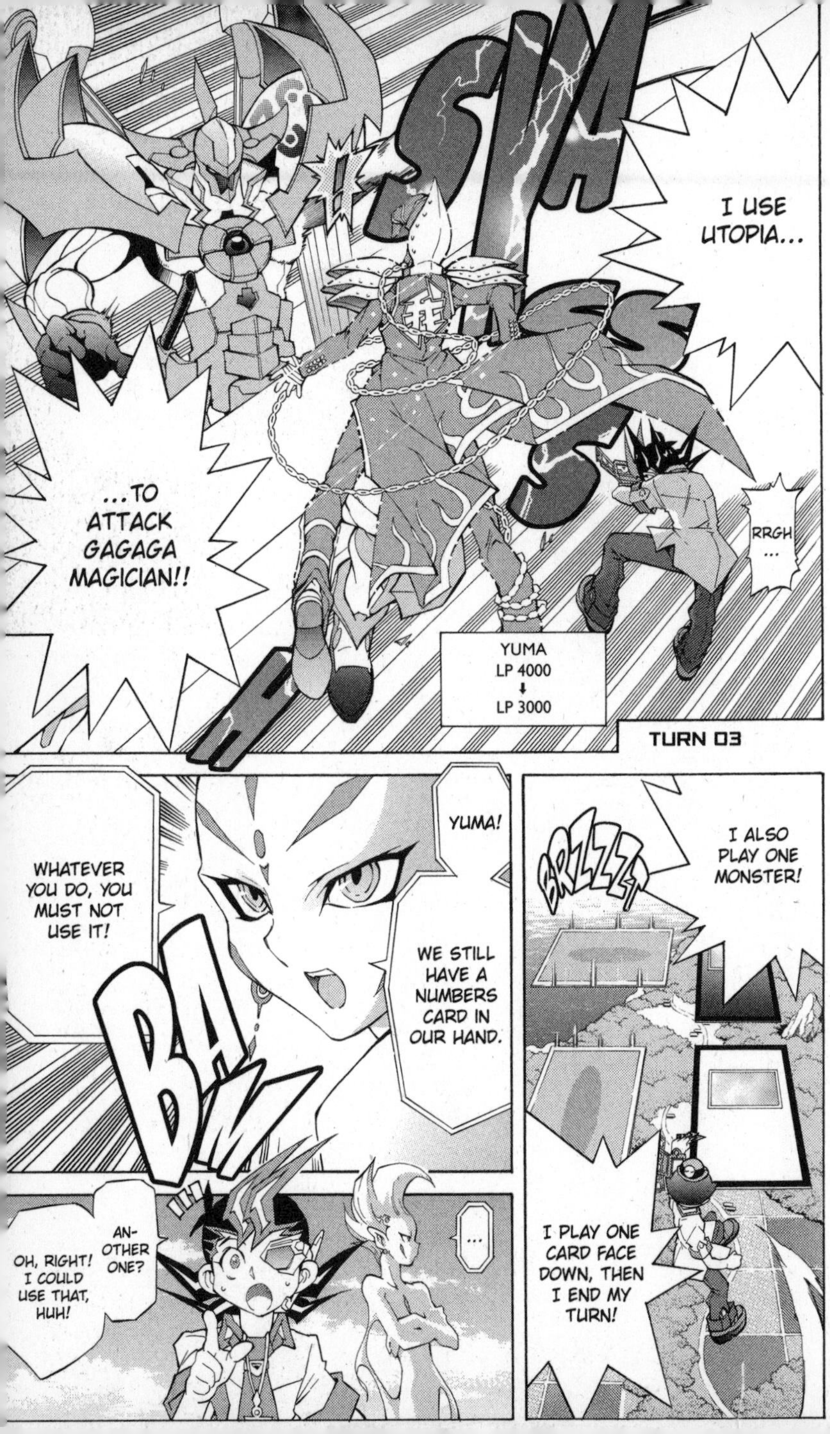
I USE UTOPIA...
!
RRGH...
...TO ATTACK GAGAGA MAGICIAN!!
YUMA
LP 4000
↓
LP 3000
TURN 03
I ALSO PLAY ONE MONSTER!
BRZZZZT
I PLAY ONE CARD FACE DOWN, THEN I END MY TURN!
YUMA!
WE STILL HAVE A NUMBERS CARD IN OUR HAND.
WHATEVER YOU DO, YOU MUST NOT USE IT!
BAM
...
...!!
AN-OTHER ONE?
OH, RIGHT! I COULD USE THAT, HUH!

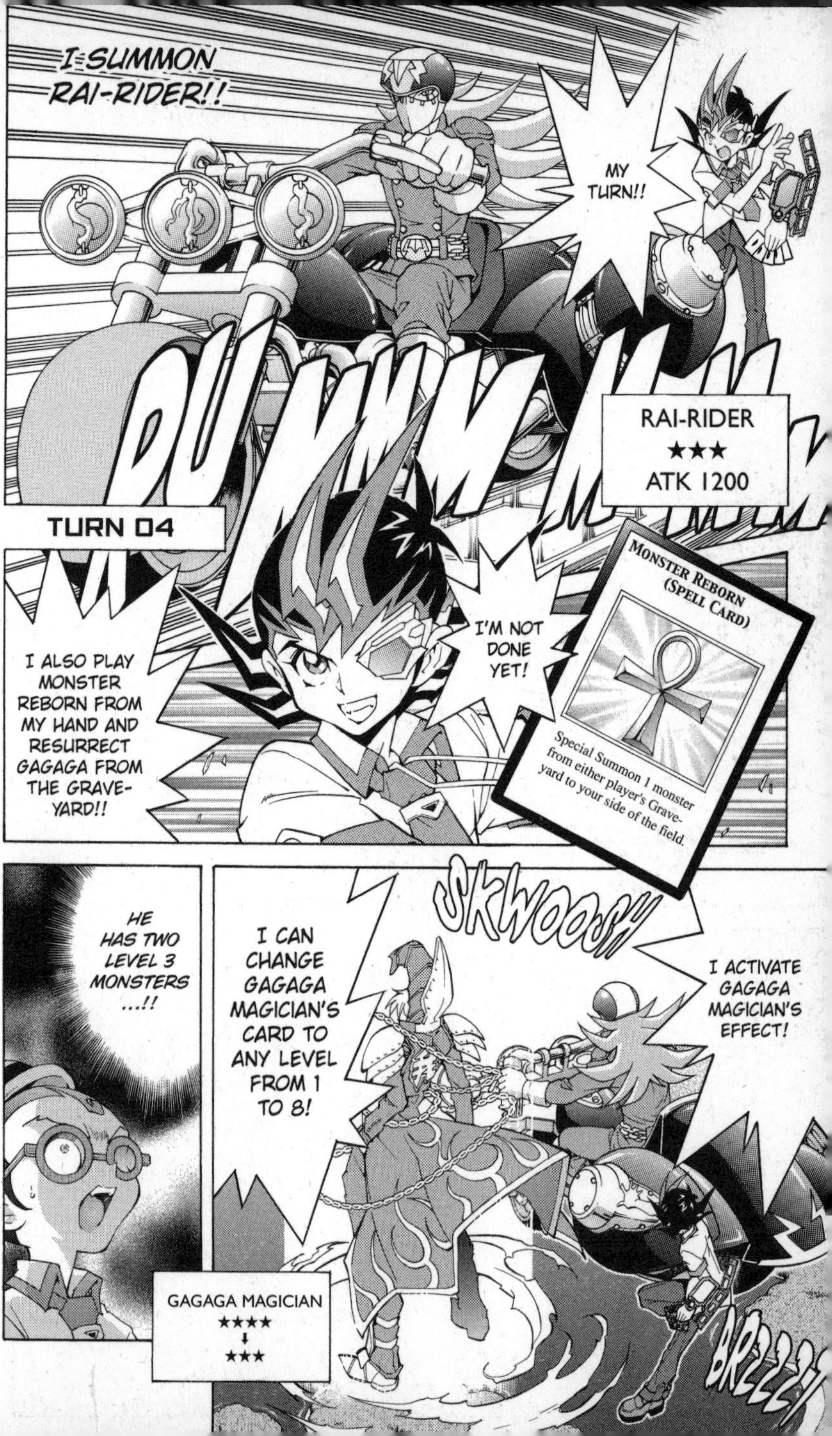

MY TURN!!
I SUMMON RAI-RIDER!!
RAI-RIDER
★★★
ATK 1200
TURN 04
MONSTER REBORN
(SPELL CARD)
Special Summon 1 monster from either player's Graveyard to your side of the field.
I'M NOT DONE YET!
I ALSO PLAY MONSTER REBORN FROM MY HAND AND RESURRECT GAGAGA FROM THE GRAVEYARD!!
SKWOOSH
I ACTIVATE GAGAGA MAGICIAN'S EFFECT!
I CAN CHANGE GAGAGA MAGICIAN'S CARD TO ANY LEVEL FROM 1 TO 8!
GAGAGA MAGICIAN
★★★★
↓
★★★
HE HAS TWO LEVEL 3 MONSTERS ...!!

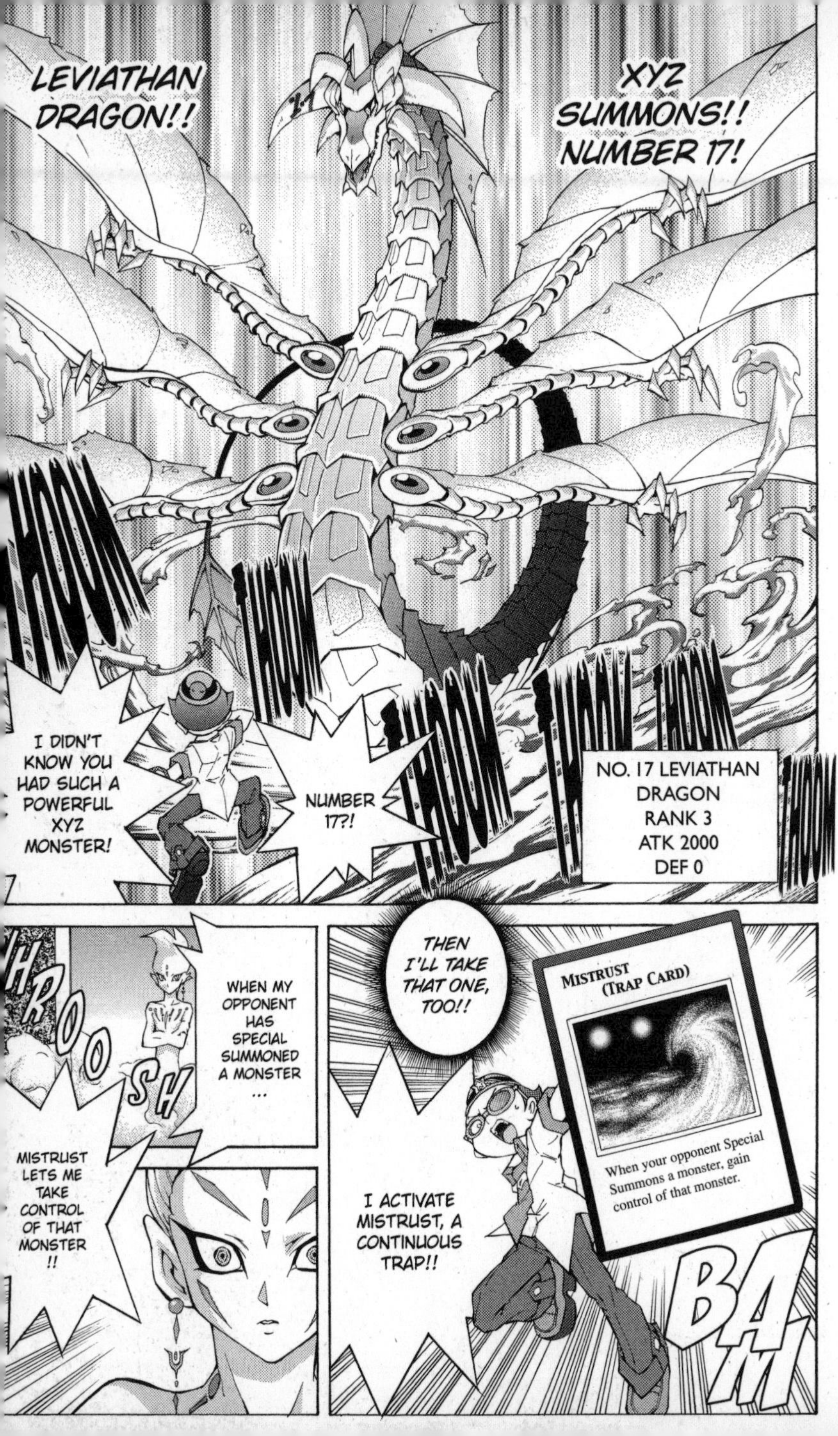

XYZ SUMMONS!! NUMBER 17!
LEVIATHAN DRAGON!!
THOOM
THOOM
THOOM
THOOM
THOOM
THOOM
NO. 17 LEVIATHAN DRAGON
RANK 3
ATK 2000
DEF 0
NUMBER 17?!
I DIDN'T KNOW YOU HAD SUCH A POWERFUL XYZ MONSTER!
THEN I'LL TAKE THAT ONE, TOO!!
MISTRUST (TRAP CARD)
When your opponent Special Summons a monster, gain control of that monster.
I ACTIVATE MISTRUST, A CONTINUOUS TRAP!!
BAM
WHEN MY OPPONENT HAS SPECIAL SUMMONED A MONSTER ...
THROOSH
MISTRUST LETS ME TAKE CONTROL OF THAT MONSTER !!

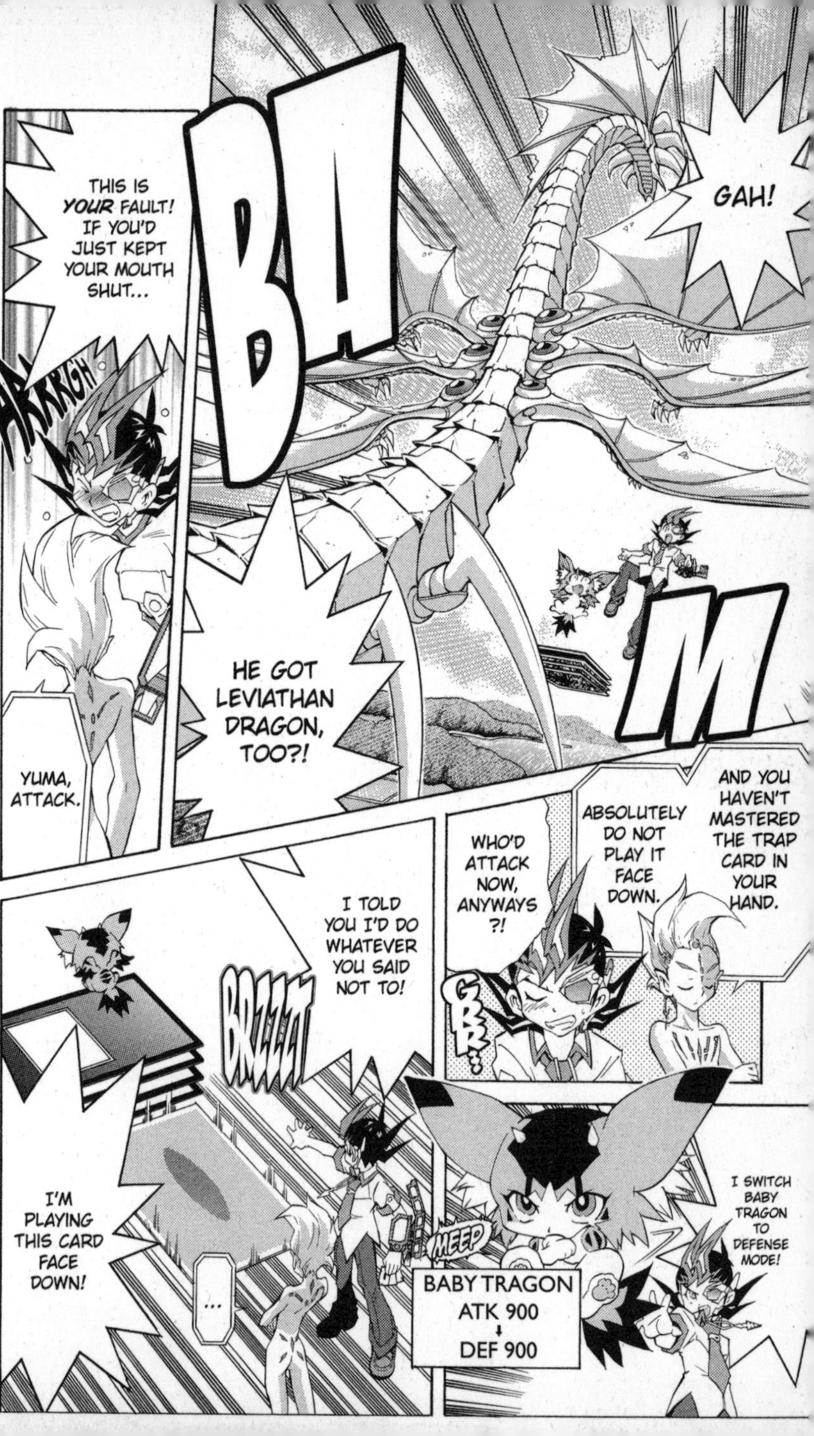
GAH!
BAM
HE GOT LEVIATHAN DRAGON, TOO?!
THIS IS *YOUR* FAULT! IF YOU'D JUST KEPT YOUR MOUTH SHUT...
ARRRGH
YUMA, ATTACK.
AND YOU HAVEN'T MASTERED THE TRAP CARD IN YOUR HAND.
ABSOLUTELY DO NOT PLAY IT FACE DOWN.
WHO'D ATTACK NOW, ANYWAYS?!
GRR...
I TOLD YOU I'D DO WHATEVER YOU SAID NOT TO!
BRZZZT
I'M PLAYING THIS CARD FACE DOWN!
...
I SWITCH BABY TRAGON TO DEFENSE MODE!
MEEP
BABY TRAGON
ATK 900
↓
DEF 900

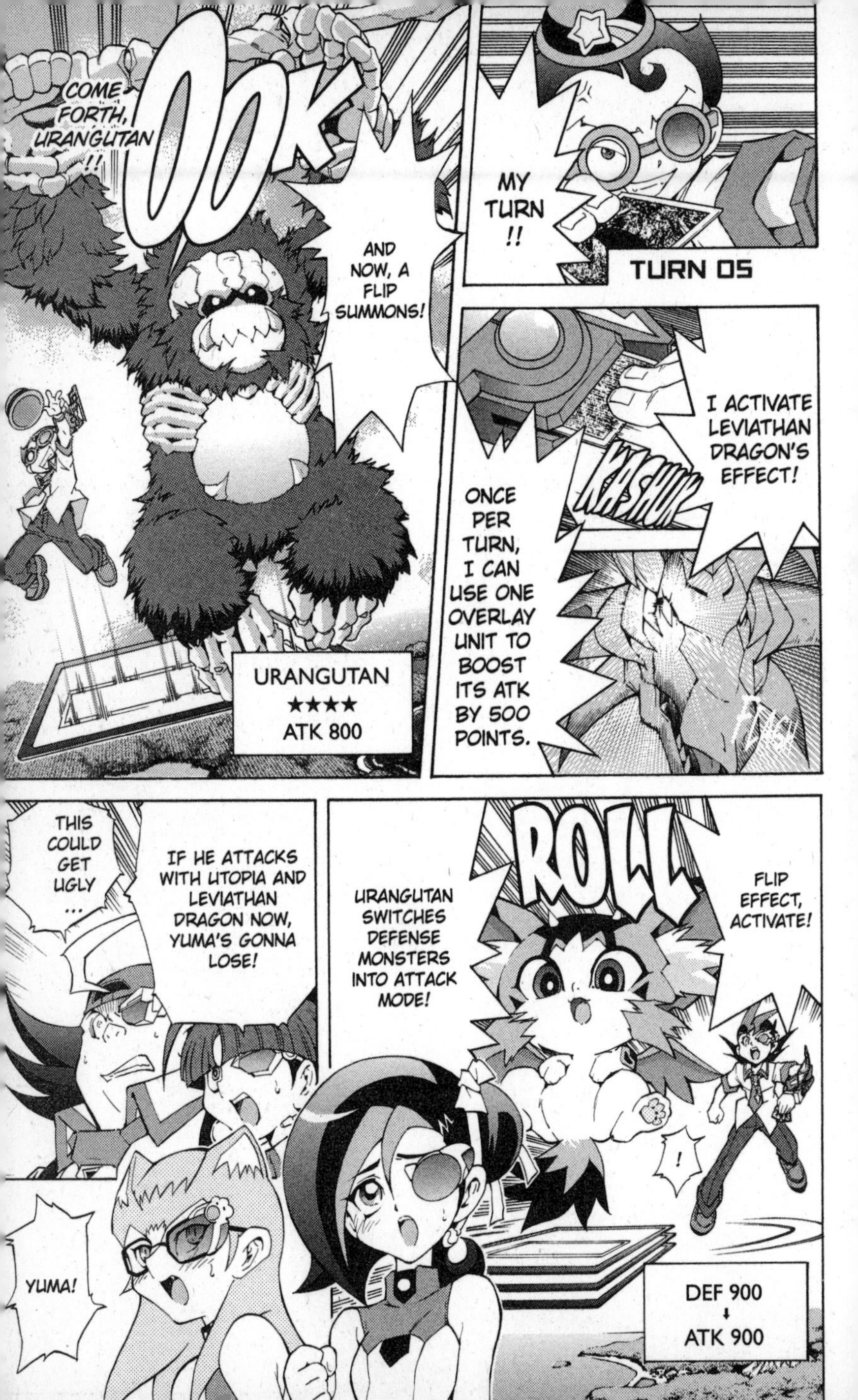
MY TURN !!
TURN 05
I ACTIVATE LEVIATHAN DRAGON'S EFFECT!
KASHUK
ONCE PER TURN, I CAN USE ONE OVERLAY UNIT TO BOOST ITS ATK BY 500 POINTS.
AND NOW, A FLIP SUMMONS!
COME FORTH, URANGUTAN !!
OOOK
URANGUTAN
★★★★
ATK 800
ROLL
FLIP EFFECT, ACTIVATE!
URANGUTAN SWITCHES DEFENSE MONSTERS INTO ATTACK MODE!
!
DEF 900
↓
ATK 900
IF HE ATTACKS WITH UTOPIA AND LEVIATHAN DRAGON NOW, YUMA'S GONNA LOSE!
THIS COULD GET UGLY ...
YUMA!

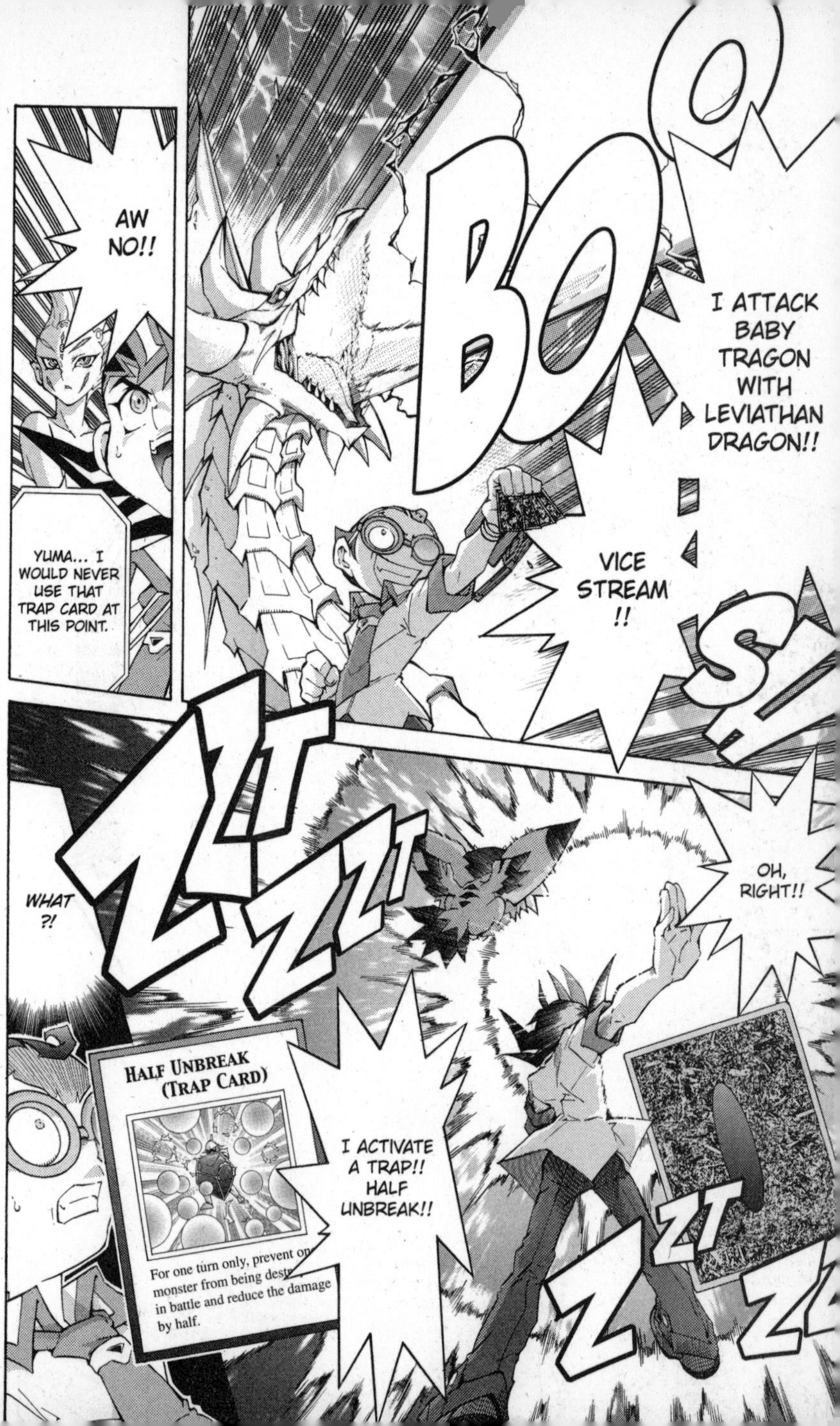
BOO
I ATTACK BABY TRAGON WITH LEVIATHAN DRAGON!!
VICE STREAM!!
AW NO!!
YUMA... I WOULD NEVER USE THAT TRAP CARD AT THIS POINT.
OH, RIGHT!!
ZZT
I ACTIVATE A TRAP!! HALF UNBREAK!!
HALF UNBREAK (TRAP CARD)
For one turn only, prevent on monster from being destr in battle and reduce the damage by half.
ZZZT
WHAT?!

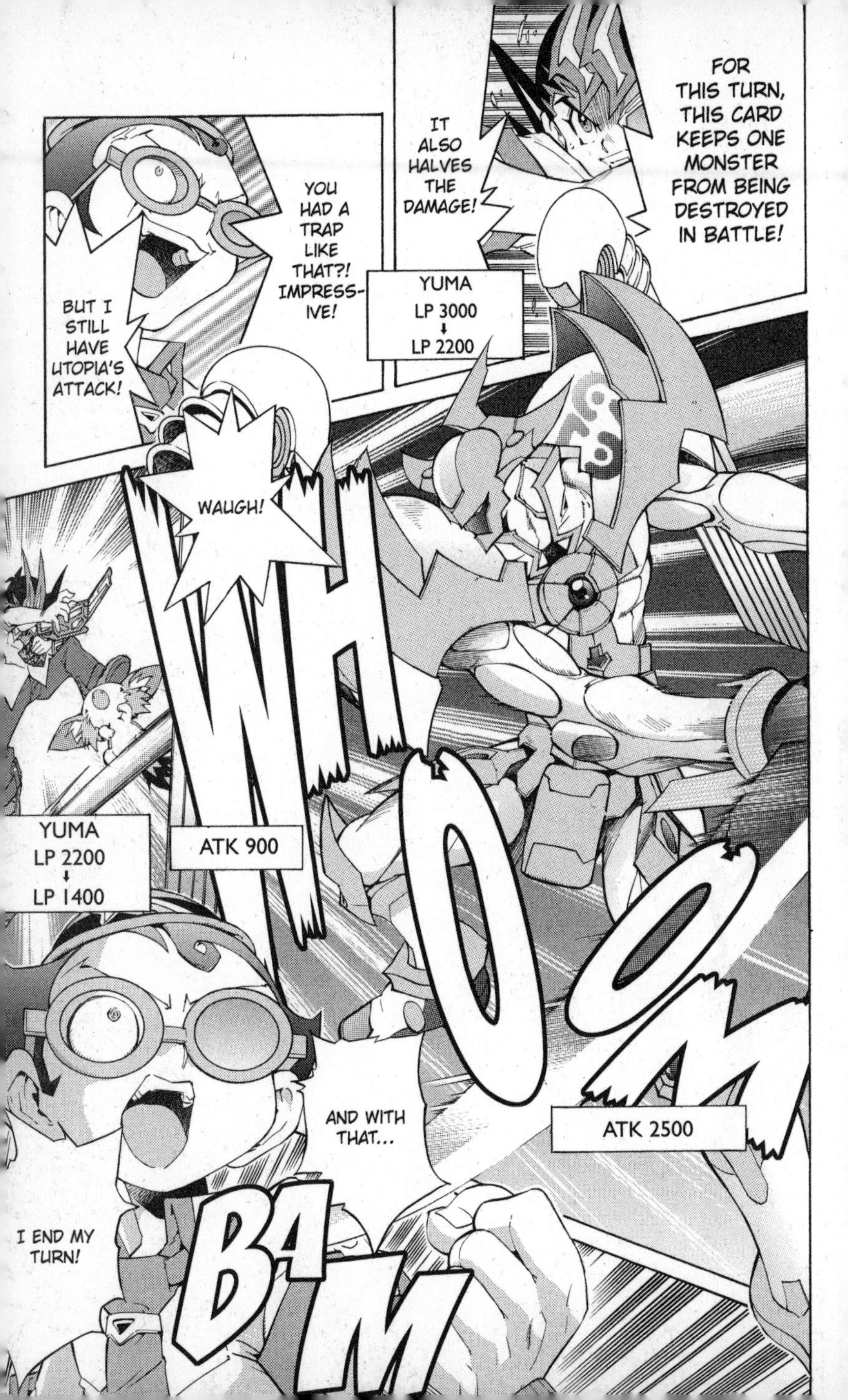
FOR THIS TURN, THIS CARD KEEPS ONE MONSTER FROM BEING DESTROYED IN BATTLE!
IT ALSO HALVES THE DAMAGE!
YUMA LP 3000 ↓ LP 2200
YOU HAD A TRAP LIKE THAT?! IMPRESS-IVE!
BUT I STILL HAVE UTOPIA'S ATTACK!
WHOOM
WAUGH!
ATK 2500
ATK 900
YUMA LP 2200 ↓ LP 1400
AND WITH THAT...
I END MY TURN!
BAM

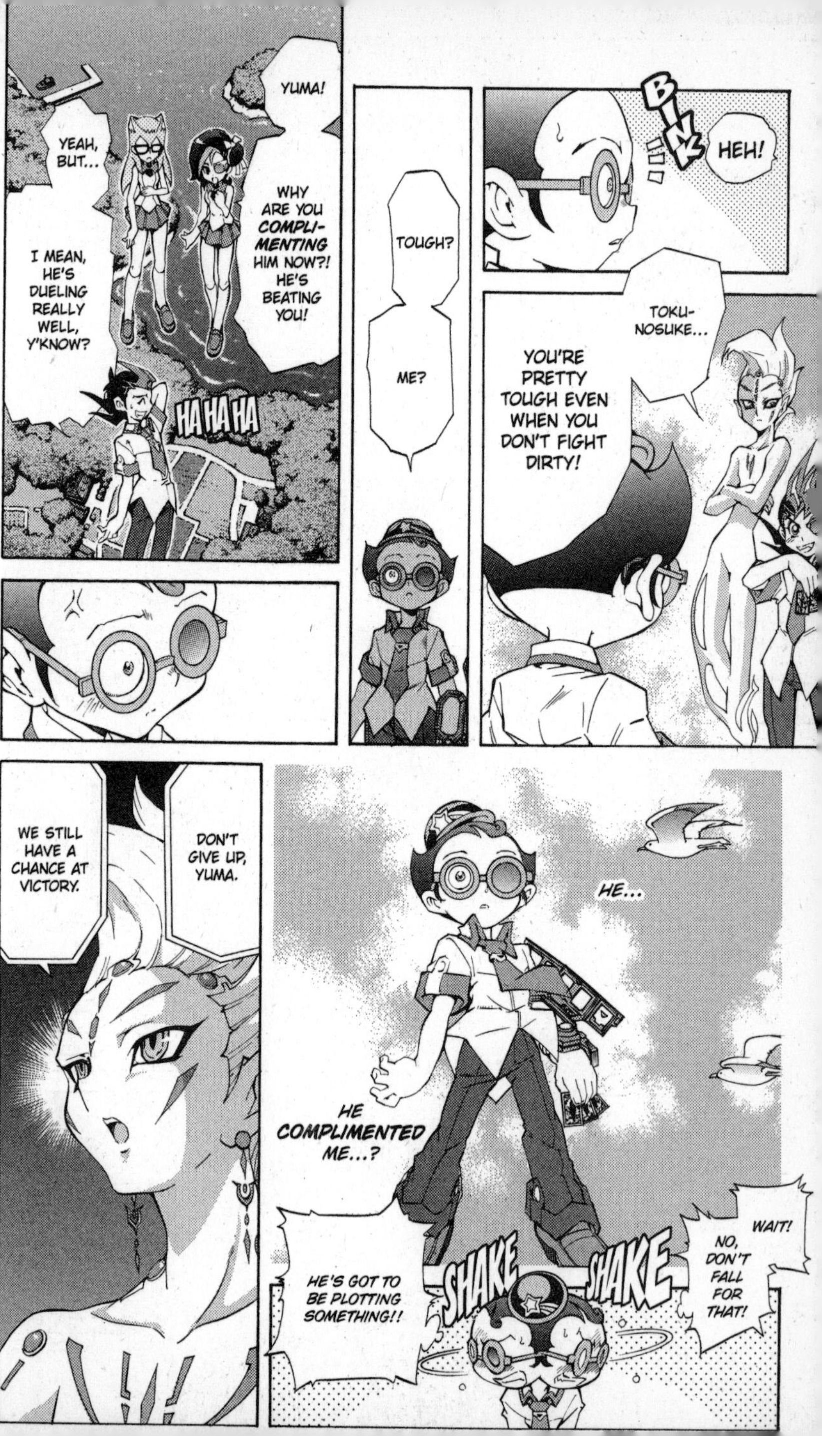
BINK
HEH!
TOKU-NOSUKE...
YOU'RE PRETTY TOUGH EVEN WHEN YOU DON'T FIGHT DIRTY!
TOUGH?
ME?
YUMA!
WHY ARE YOU COMPLIMENTING HIM NOW?! HE'S BEATING YOU!
YEAH, BUT...
I MEAN, HE'S DUELING REALLY WELL, Y'KNOW?
HA HA HA
HE...
HE COMPLIMENTED ME...?
WAIT!
NO, DON'T FALL FOR THAT!
SHAKE
SHAKE
HE'S GOT TO BE PLOTTING SOMETHING!!
DON'T GIVE UP, YUMA.
WE STILL HAVE A CHANCE AT VICTORY.

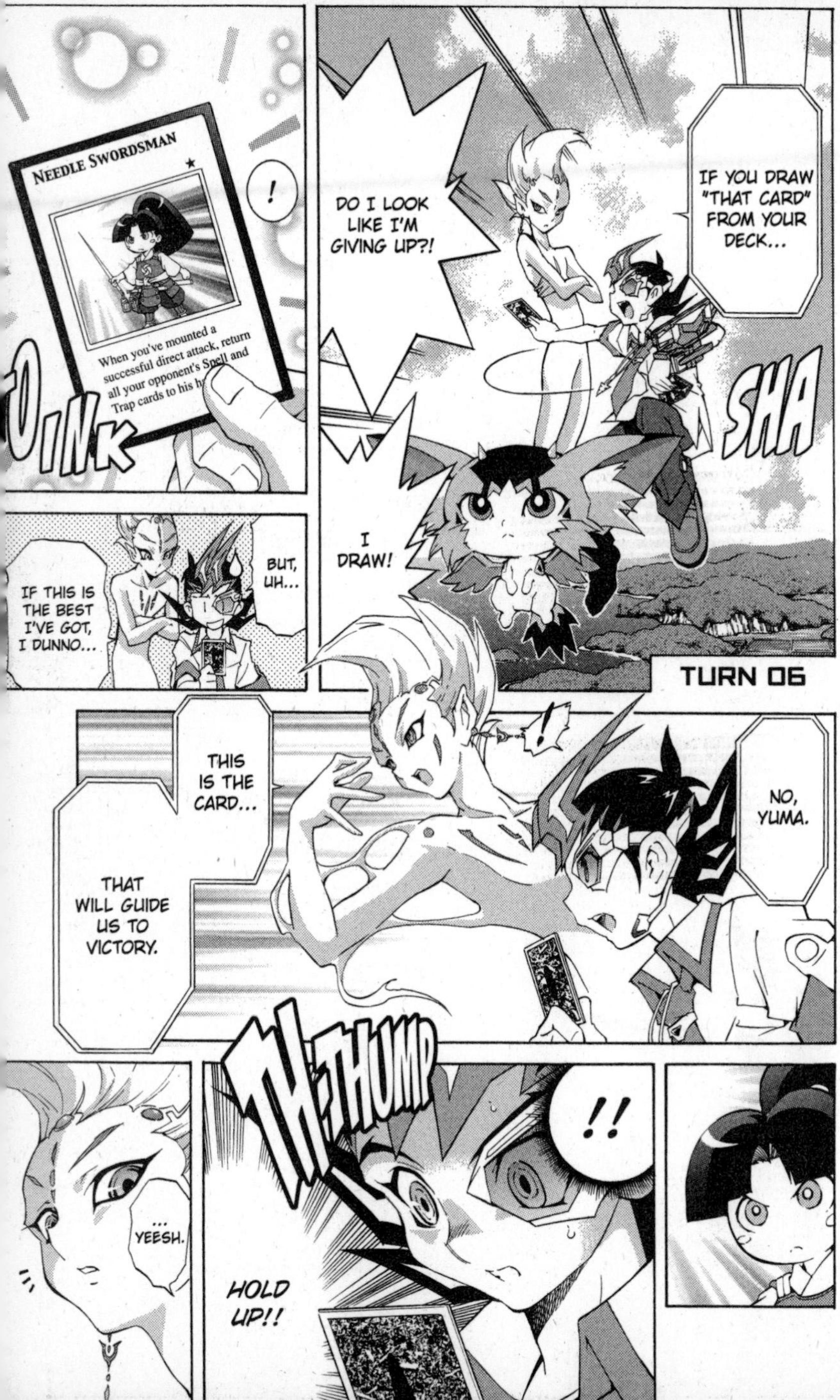

IF YOU DRAW "THAT CARD" FROM YOUR DECK...
DO I LOOK LIKE I'M GIVING UP?!
SHA
I DRAW!
TURN 06
!
NEEDLE SWORDSMAN
When you've mounted a successful direct attack, return all your opponent's Spell and Trap cards to his h
TOINK
BUT, UH...
IF THIS IS THE BEST I'VE GOT, I DUNNO...
NO, YUMA.
THIS IS THE CARD...
THAT WILL GUIDE US TO VICTORY.
!!
TH-THUMP
HOLD UP!!
... YEESH.

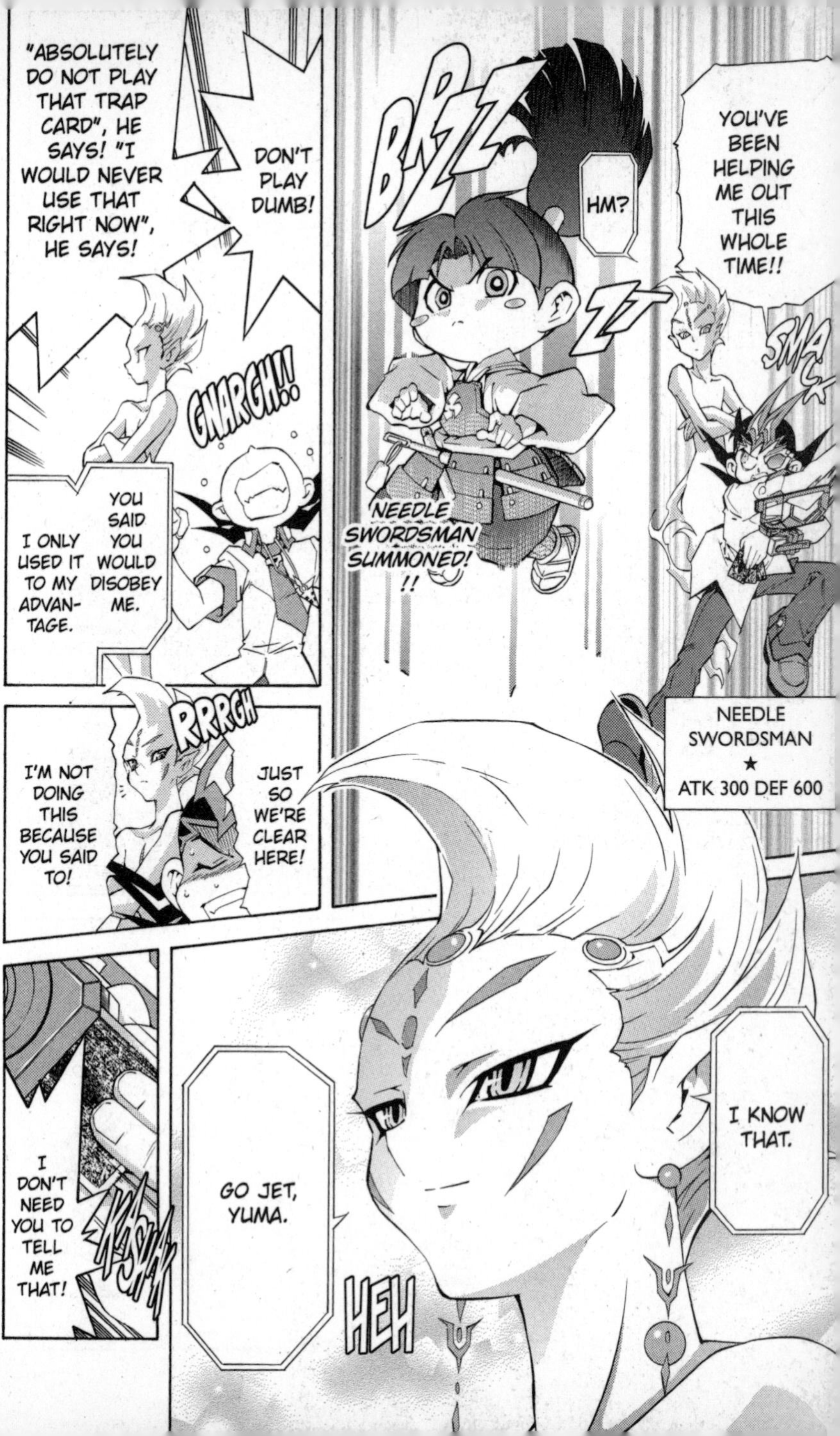
YOU'VE BEEN HELPING ME OUT THIS WHOLE TIME!!
SMACK
BZZ
HM?
ZT
NEEDLE SWORDSMAN SUMMONED!!!
NEEDLE SWORDSMAN ★ ATK 300 DEF 600
"ABSOLUTELY DO NOT PLAY THAT TRAP CARD", HE SAYS! "I WOULD NEVER USE THAT RIGHT NOW", HE SAYS!
DON'T PLAY DUMB!
GNARGH!!
YOU SAID YOU WOULD DISOBEY ME.
I ONLY USED IT TO MY ADVANTAGE.
RRRGH
JUST SO WE'RE CLEAR HERE!
I'M NOT DOING THIS BECAUSE YOU SAID TO!
I KNOW THAT.
GO JET, YUMA.
HEH
KASHAK
I DON'T NEED YOU TO TELL ME THAT!

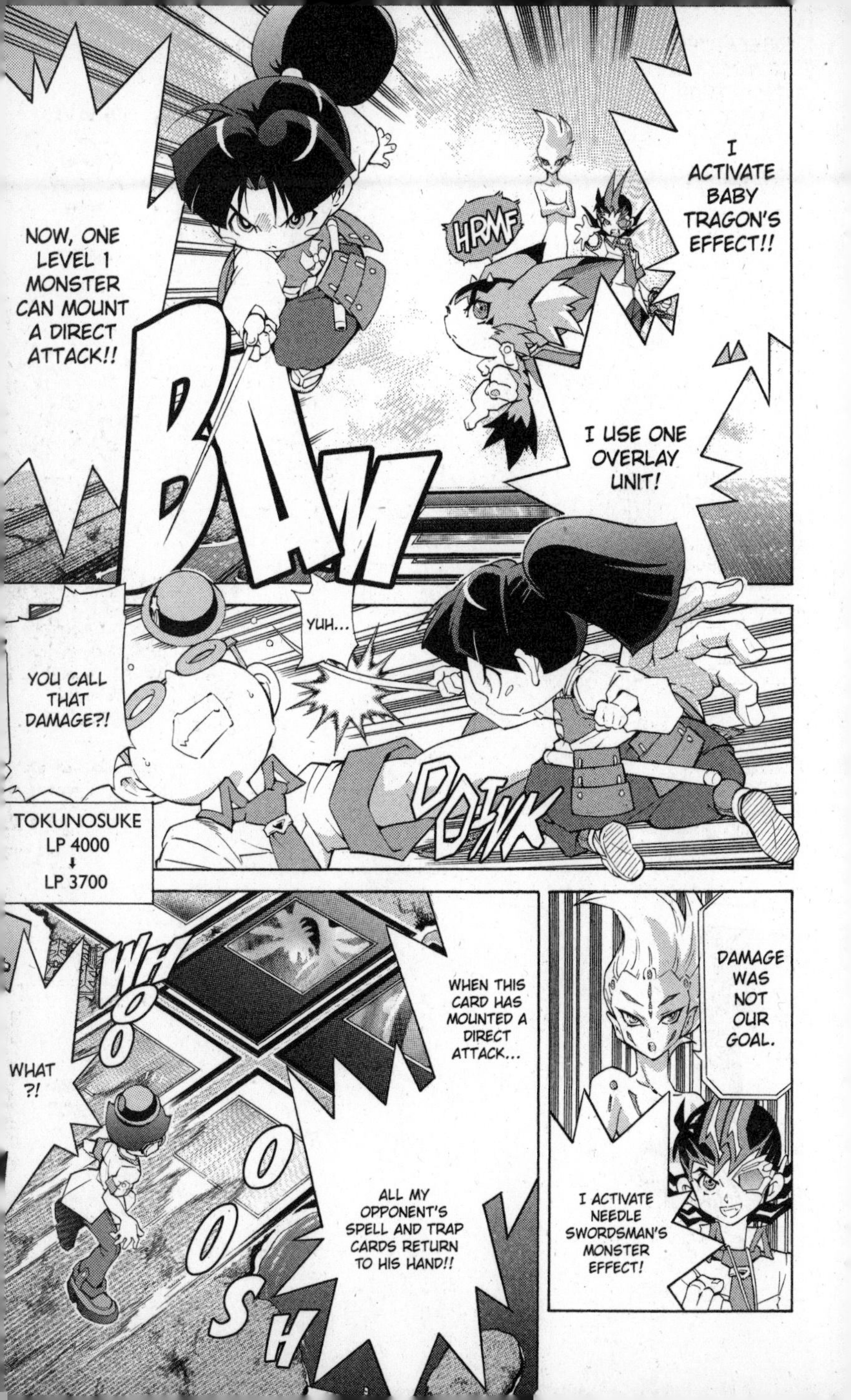
I ACTIVATE BABY TRAGON'S EFFECT!!
HRMF
I USE ONE OVERLAY UNIT!
NOW, ONE LEVEL 1 MONSTER CAN MOUNT A DIRECT ATTACK!!
BAM
YUH...
YOU CALL THAT DAMAGE?!
DOINK
TOKUNOSUKE LP 4000 ↓ LP 3700
DAMAGE WAS NOT OUR GOAL.
I ACTIVATE NEEDLE SWORDSMAN'S MONSTER EFFECT!
WHEN THIS CARD HAS MOUNTED A DIRECT ATTACK...
ALL MY OPPONENT'S SPELL AND TRAP CARDS RETURN TO HIS HAND!!
WHOOOOOSH
WHAT?!

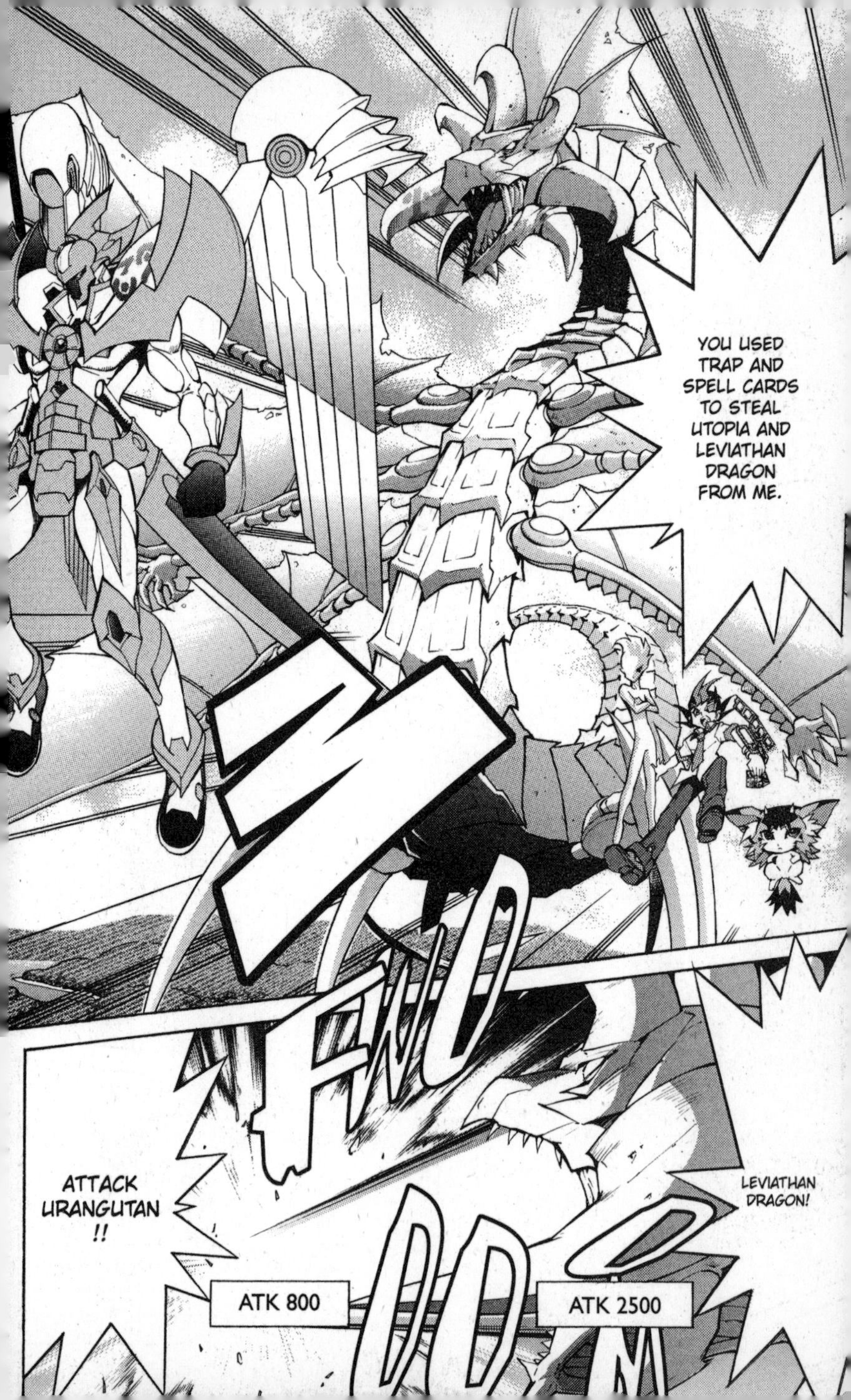
YOU USED TRAP AND SPELL CARDS TO STEAL UTOPIA AND LEVIATHAN DRAGON FROM ME.
LEVIATHAN DRAGON!
ATTACK URANGUTAN !!
ATK 2500
ATK 800

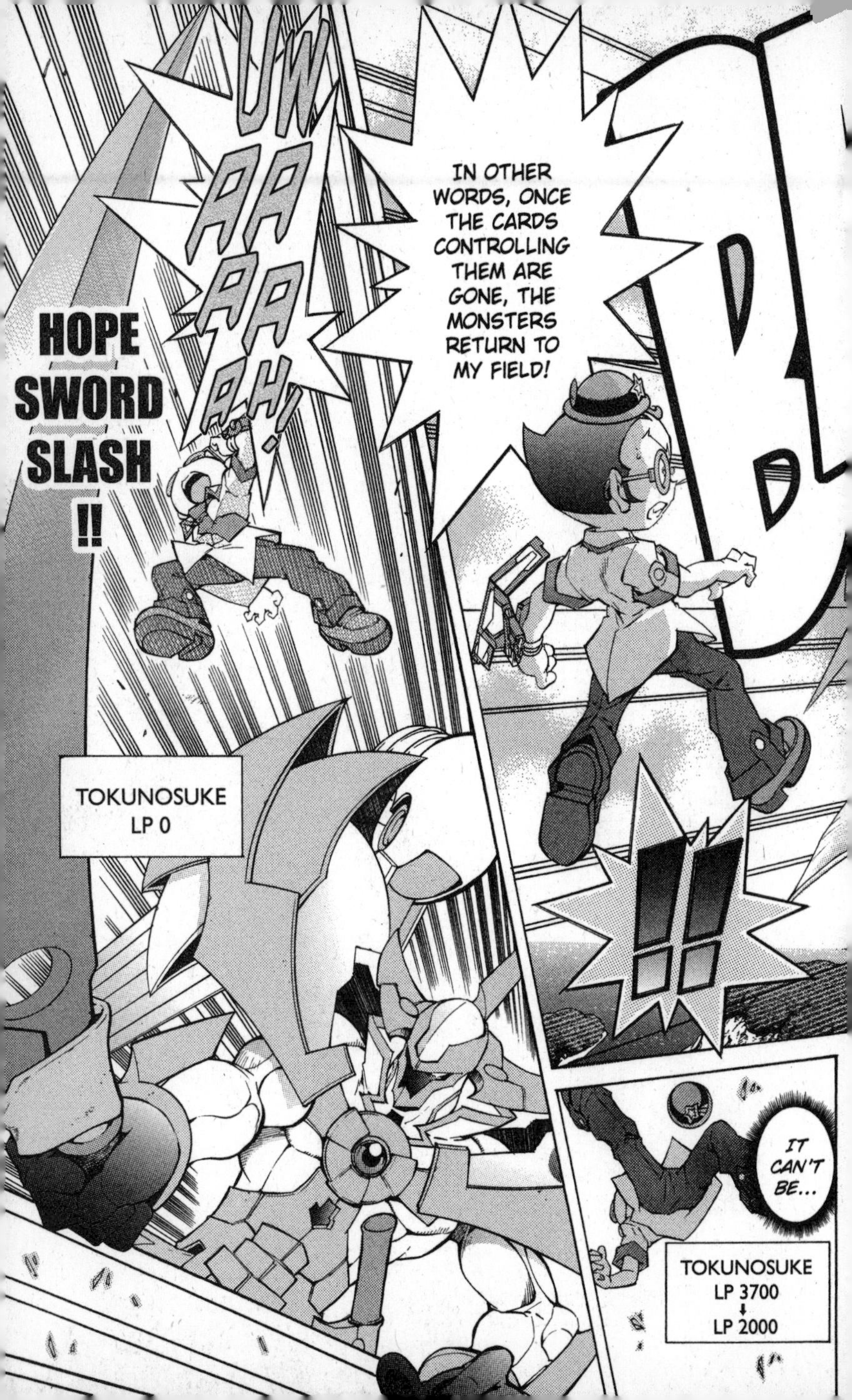
IN OTHER WORDS, ONCE THE CARDS CONTROLLING THEM ARE GONE, THE MONSTERS RETURN TO MY FIELD!
!!
IT CAN'T BE...
TOKUNOSUKE
LP 3700
↓
LP 2000
UWAAAAAAH!
HOPE SWORD SLASH!!
TOKUNOSUKE
LP 0

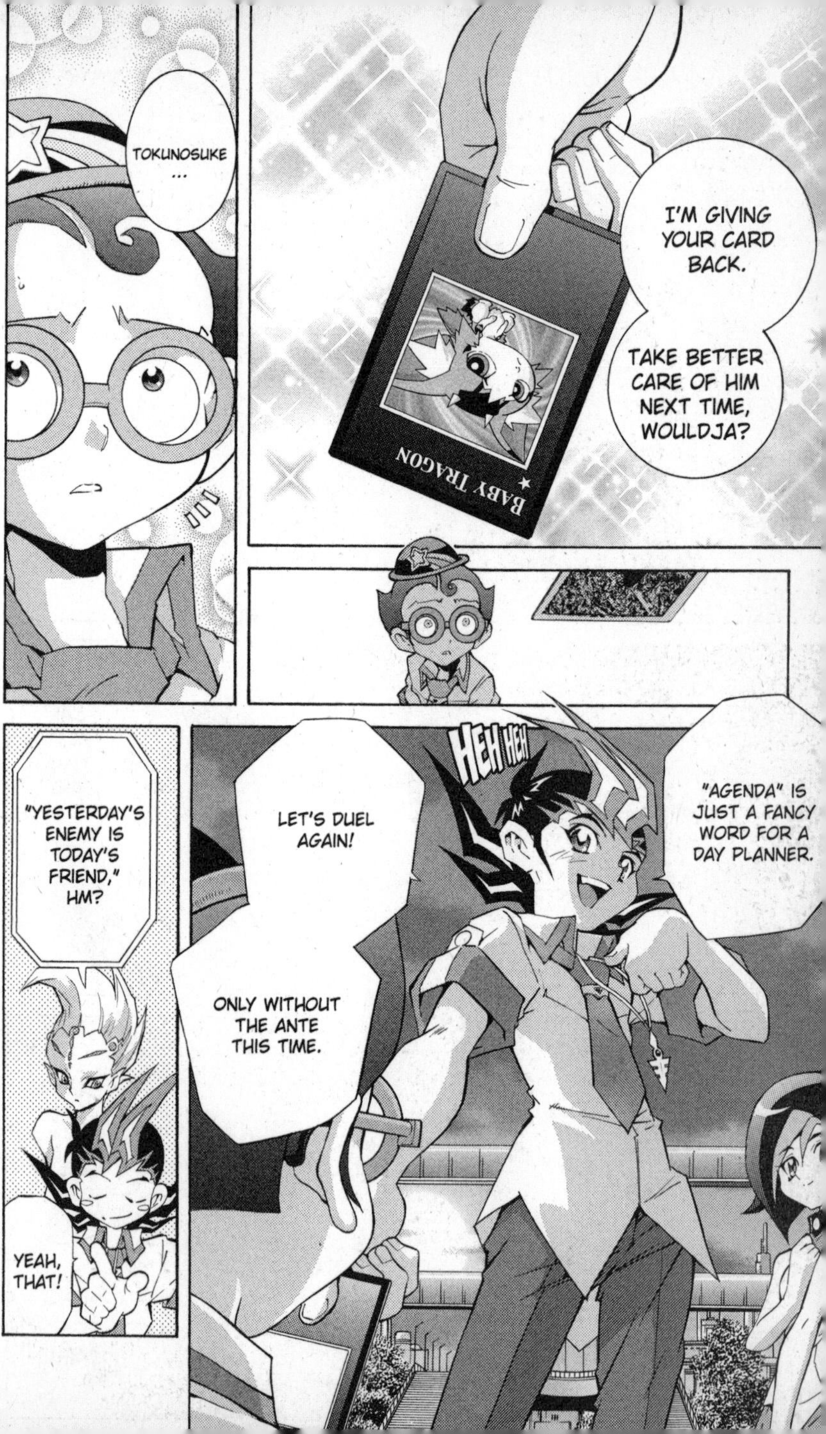
I'M GIVING YOUR CARD BACK.
TAKE BETTER CARE OF HIM NEXT TIME, WOULDJA?
BABY TRAGON
TOKUNOSUKE ...
"AGENDA" IS JUST A FANCY WORD FOR A DAY PLANNER.
HEH HEH
LET'S DUEL AGAIN!
ONLY WITHOUT THE ANTE THIS TIME.
"YESTERDAY'S ENEMY IS TODAY'S FRIEND," HM?
YEAH, THAT!

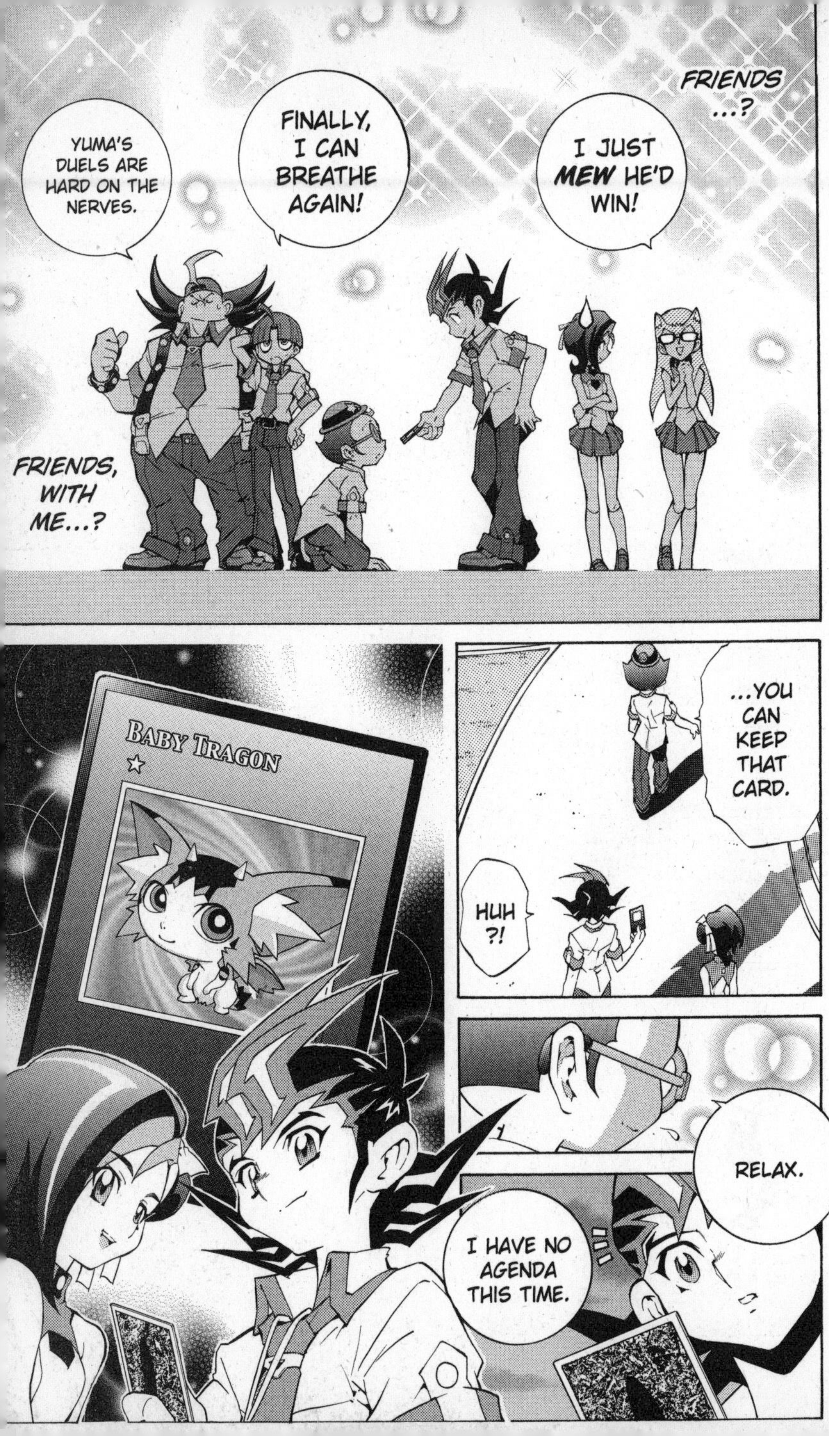
FRIENDS ...?
I JUST *MEW* HE'D WIN!
FINALLY, I CAN BREATHE AGAIN!
YUMA'S DUELS ARE HARD ON THE NERVES.
FRIENDS, WITH ME...?
...YOU CAN KEEP THAT CARD.
HUH ?!
RELAX.
I HAVE NO AGENDA THIS TIME.
BABY TRAGON

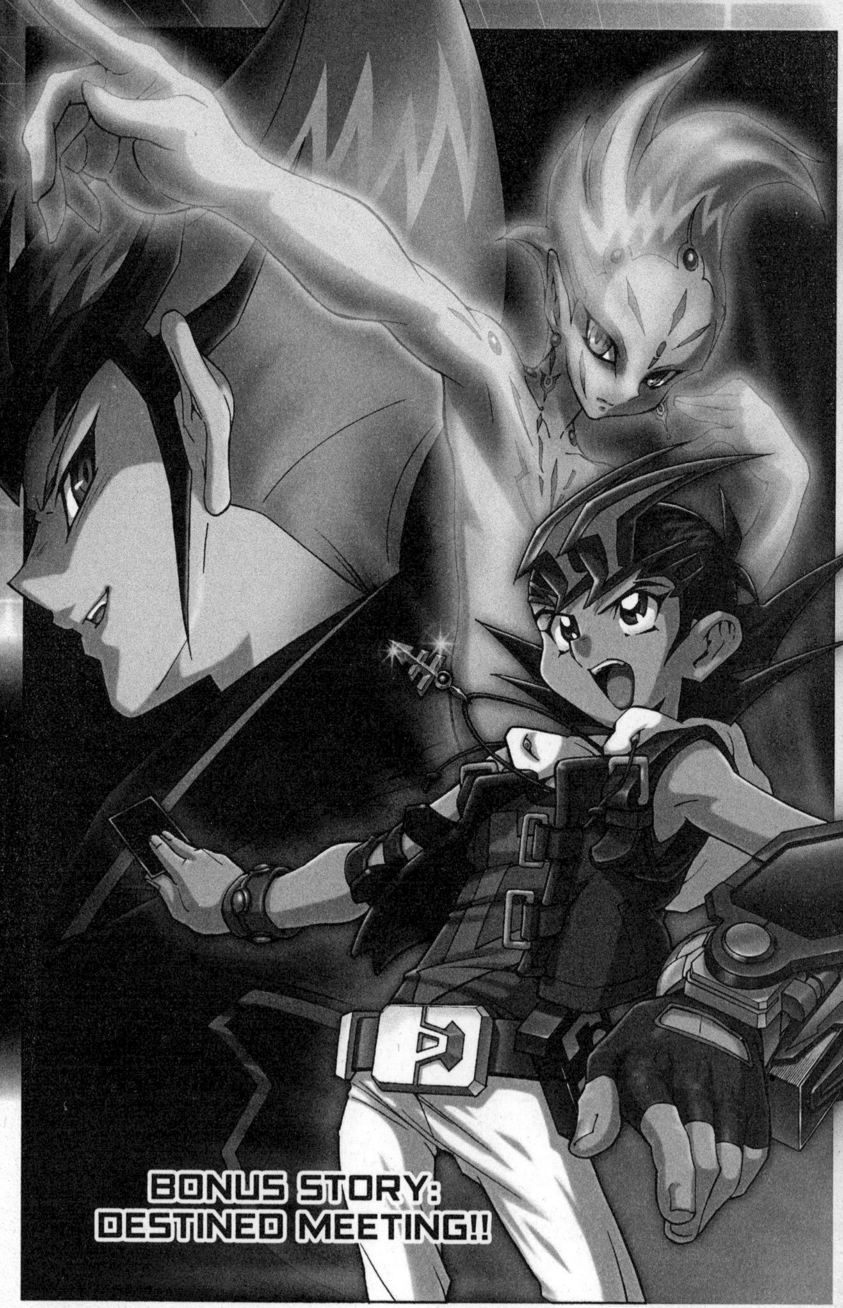
BONUS STORY:
DESTINED MEETING!!

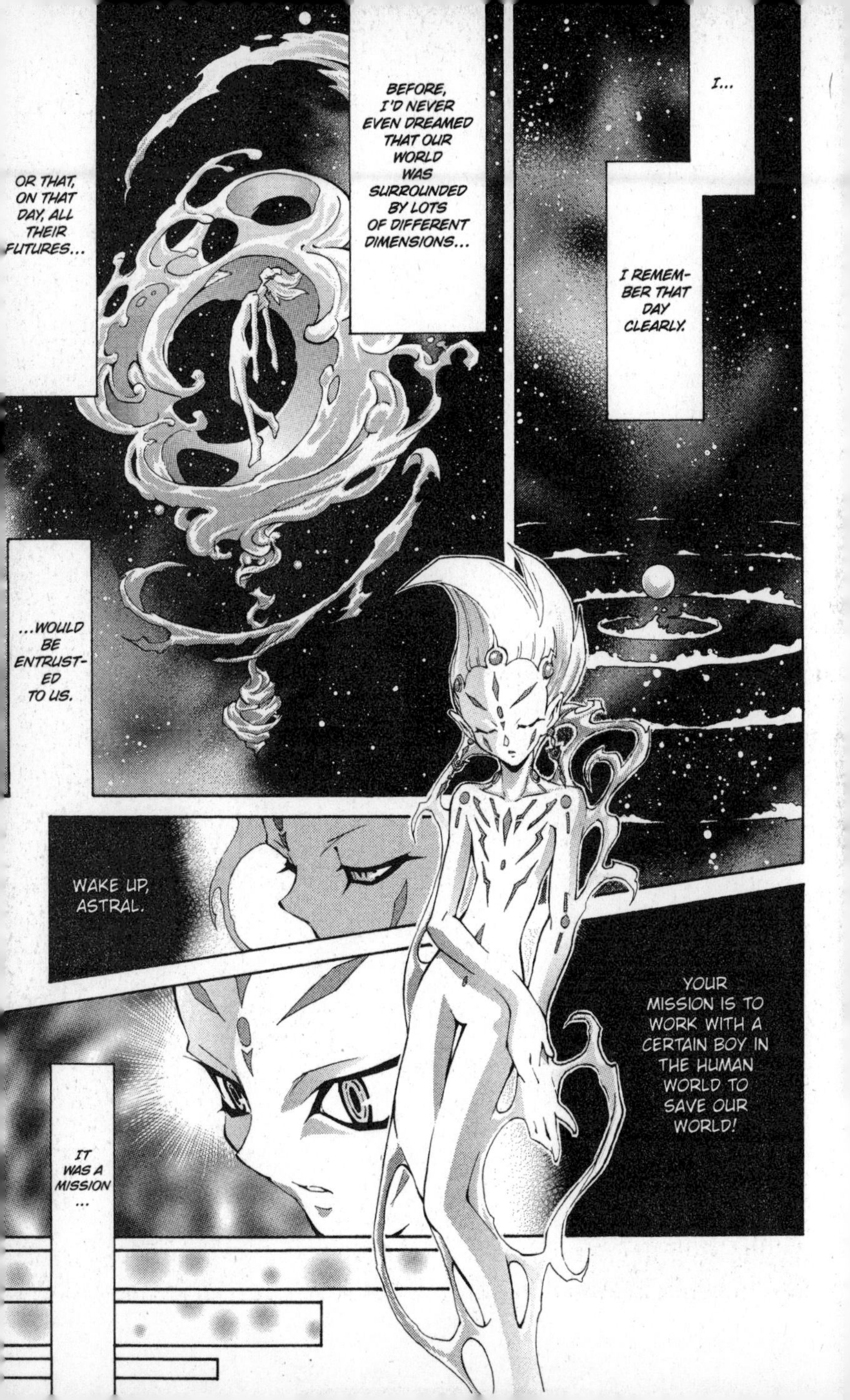
I...
I REMEMBER THAT DAY CLEARLY.
BEFORE, I'D NEVER EVEN DREAMED THAT OUR WORLD WAS SURROUNDED BY LOTS OF DIFFERENT DIMENSIONS...
OR THAT, ON THAT DAY, ALL THEIR FUTURES...
...WOULD BE ENTRUSTED TO US.
WAKE UP, ASTRAL.
YOUR MISSION IS TO WORK WITH A CERTAIN BOY IN THE HUMAN WORLD TO SAVE OUR WORLD!
IT WAS A MISSION...

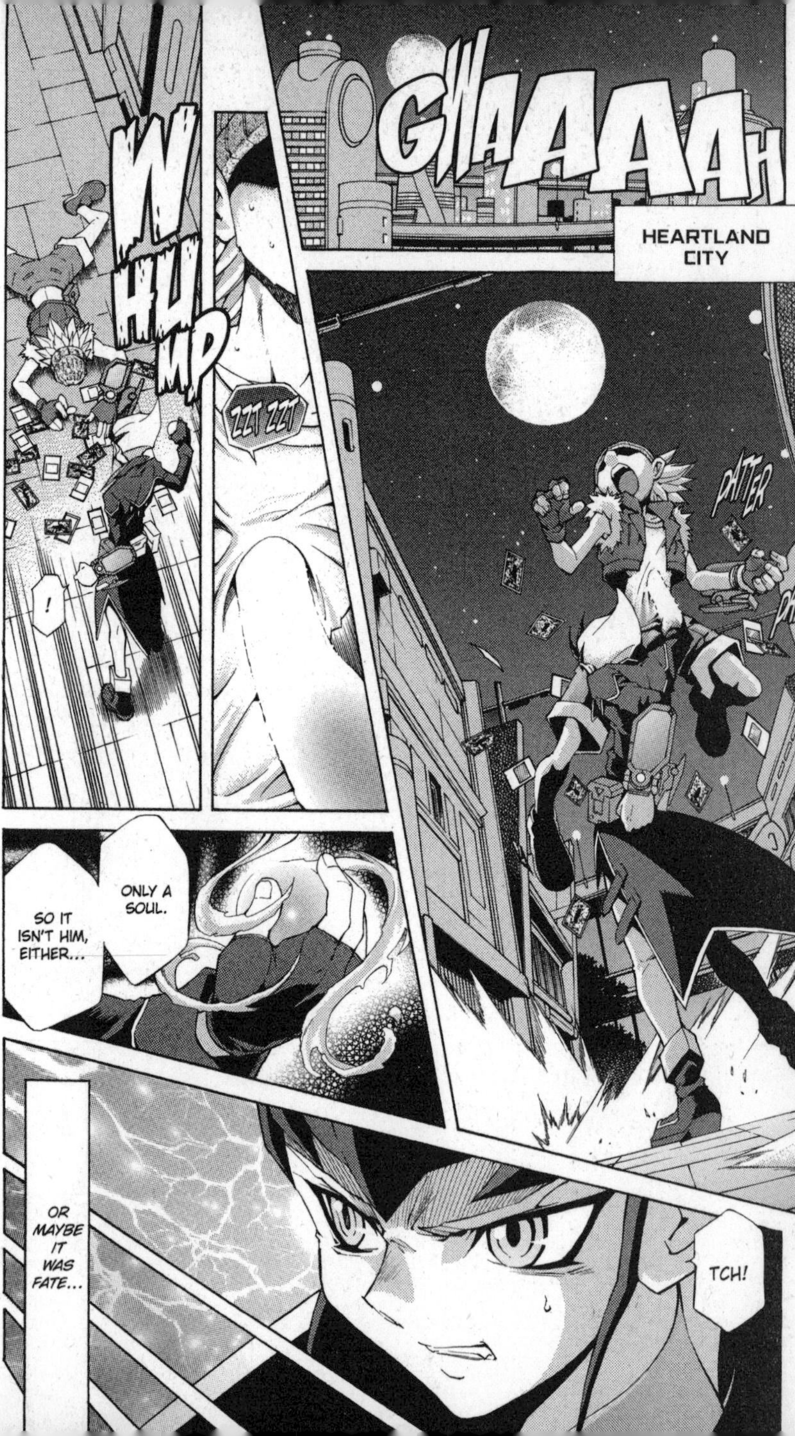
GWAAAAAH
HEARTLAND CITY
PATTER
PATTER
ZZT ZZT
WHUMP
!
ONLY A SOUL.
SO IT ISN'T HIM, EITHER...
TCH!
OR MAYBE IT WAS FATE...

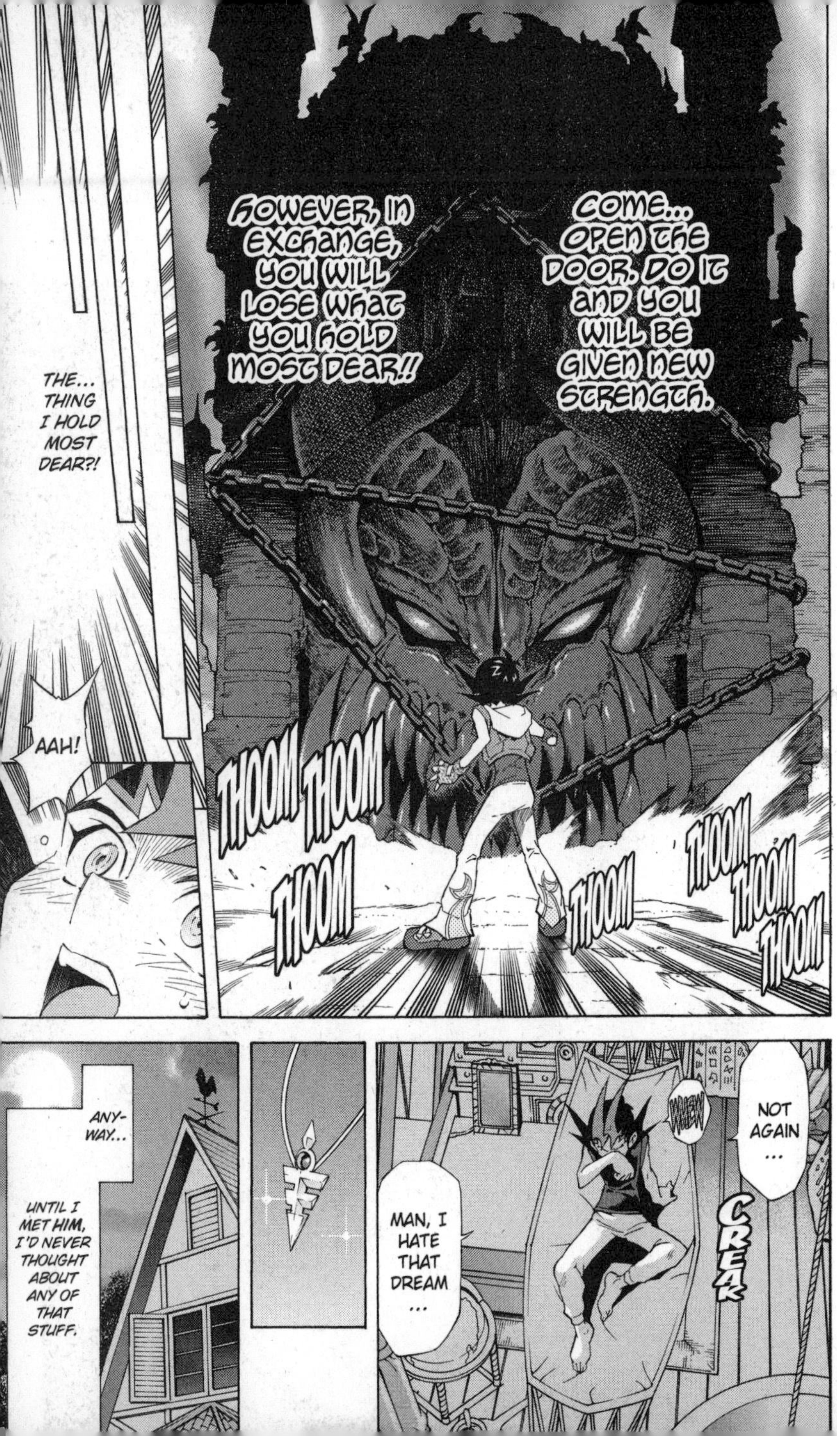
COME... OPEN THE DOOR. DO IT AND YOU WILL BE GIVEN NEW STRENGTH.
HOWEVER, IN EXCHANGE, YOU WILL LOSE WHAT YOU HOLD MOST DEAR!!
THOOM THOOM THOOM
THOOM THOOM THOOM
THOOM THOOM THOOM
THE... THING I HOLD MOST DEAR?!
AAH!
NOT AGAIN...
WHEW
CREAK
MAN, I HATE THAT DREAM...
ANY-WAY...
UNTIL I MET HIM, I'D NEVER THOUGHT ABOUT ANY OF THAT STUFF.

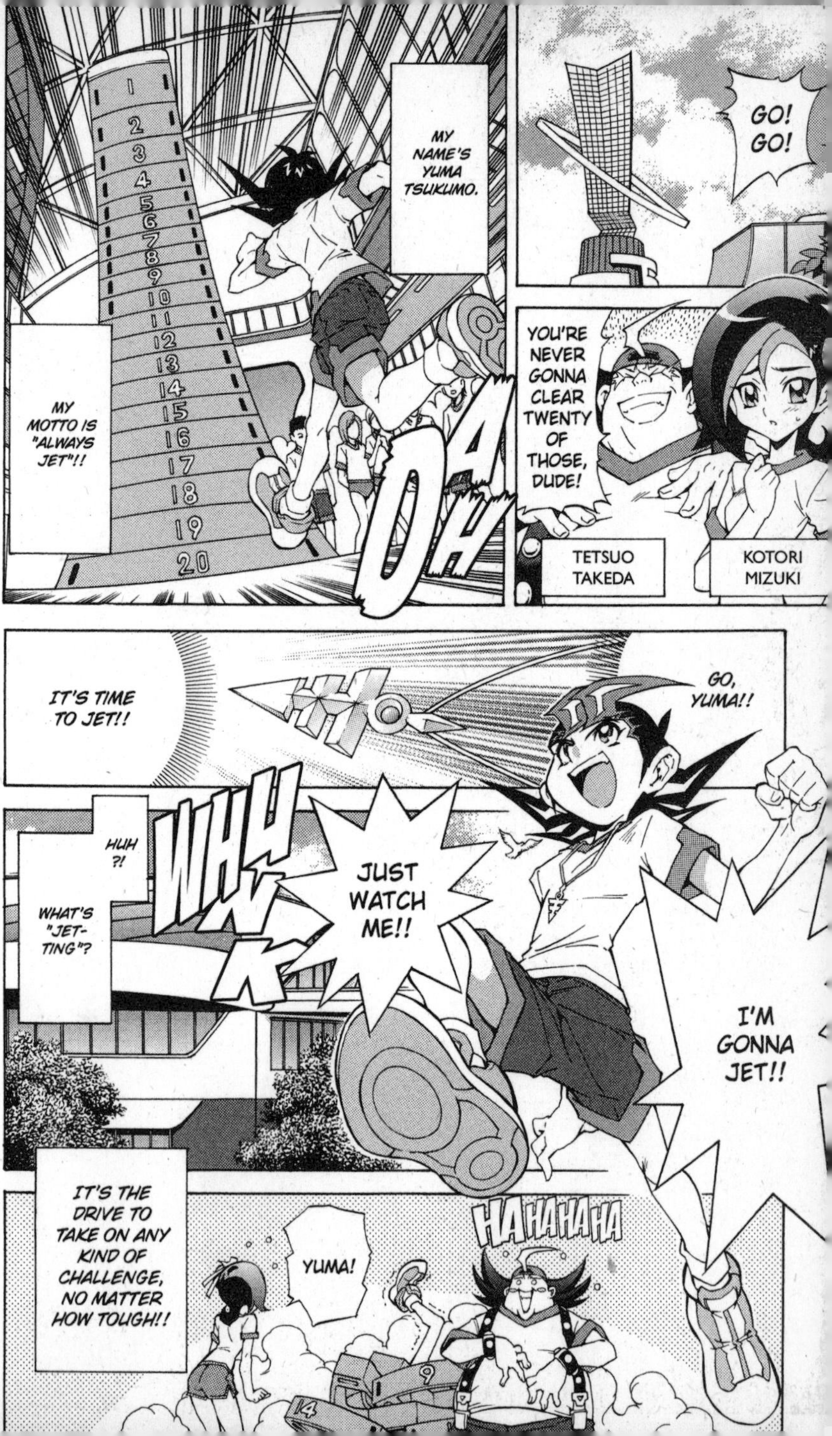
GO! GO!
YOU'RE NEVER GONNA CLEAR TWENTY OF THOSE, DUDE!
TETSUO TAKEDA
KOTORI MIZUKI
MY NAME'S YUMA TSUKUMO.
MY MOTTO IS "ALWAYS JET"!!
1 2 3 4 5 6 7 8 9 10 11 12 13 14 15 16 17 18 19 20
GO, YUMA!!
IT'S TIME TO JET!!
I'M GONNA JET!!
JUST WATCH ME!!
WHUNK
HUH ?!
WHAT'S "JET-TING"?
HAHAHAHA
YUMA!
IT'S THE DRIVE TO TAKE ON ANY KIND OF CHALLENGE, NO MATTER HOW TOUGH!!

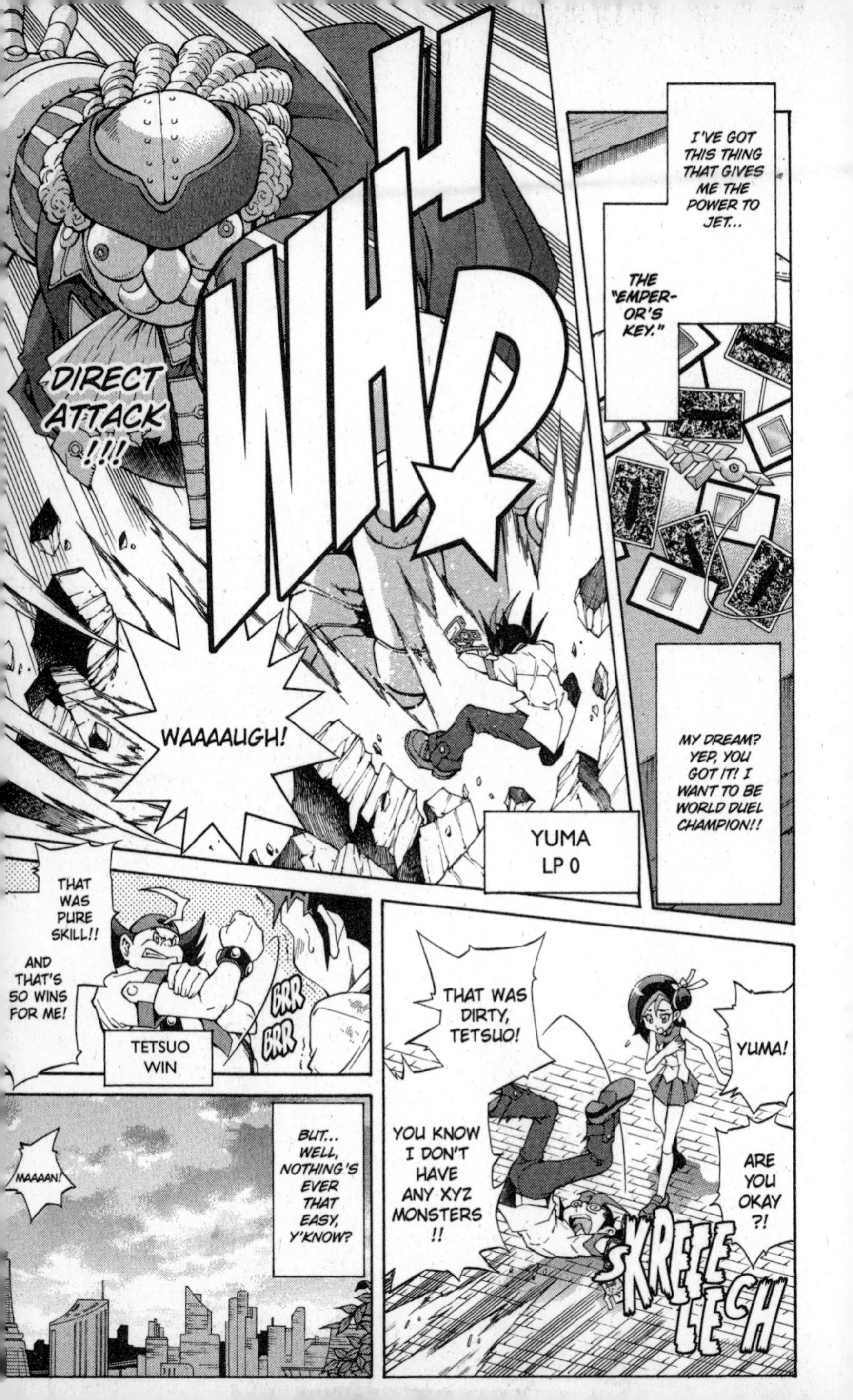
I'VE GOT THIS THING THAT GIVES ME THE POWER TO JET...
THE "EMPEROR'S KEY."
MY DREAM? YEP, YOU GOT IT! I WANT TO BE WORLD DUEL CHAMPION!!
DIRECT ATTACK!!!
WAAAAUGH!
YUMA LP 0
YUMA!
ARE YOU OKAY?!
THAT WAS DIRTY, TETSUO!
YOU KNOW I DON'T HAVE ANY XYZ MONSTERS!!
SKREEECH
THAT WAS PURE SKILL!!
AND THAT'S 50 WINS FOR ME!
BRR BRR
TETSUO WIN
BUT... WELL, NOTHING'S EVER THAT EASY, Y'KNOW?
MAAAAN!

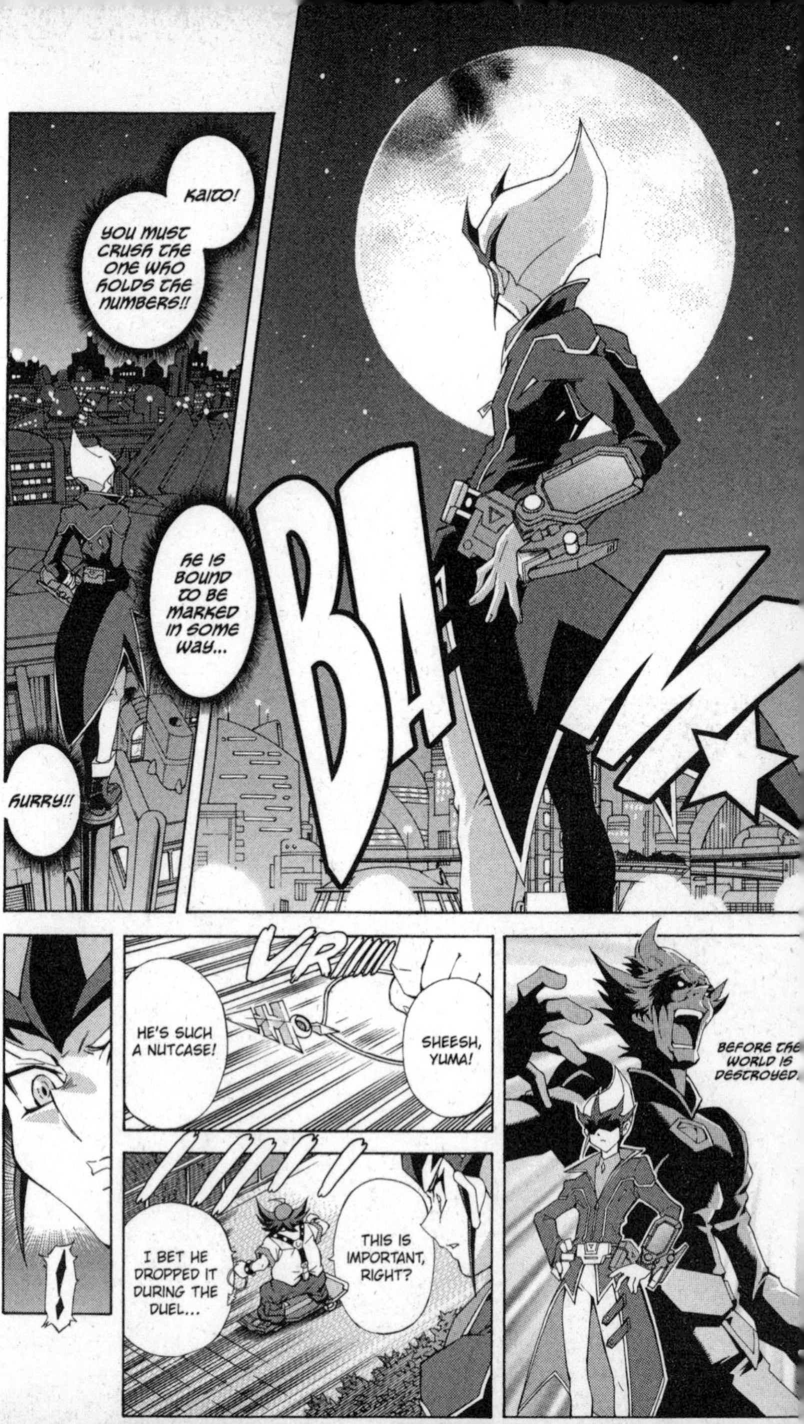
BAM
KAITO!
YOU MUST CRUSH THE ONE WHO HOLDS THE NUMBERS!!
HE IS BOUND TO BE MARKED IN SOME WAY...
HURRY!!
BEFORE THE WORLD IS DESTROYED.
VR
SHEESH, YUMA!
HE'S SUCH A NUTCASE!
THIS IS IMPORTANT, RIGHT?
I BET HE DROPPED IT DURING THE DUEL...
!

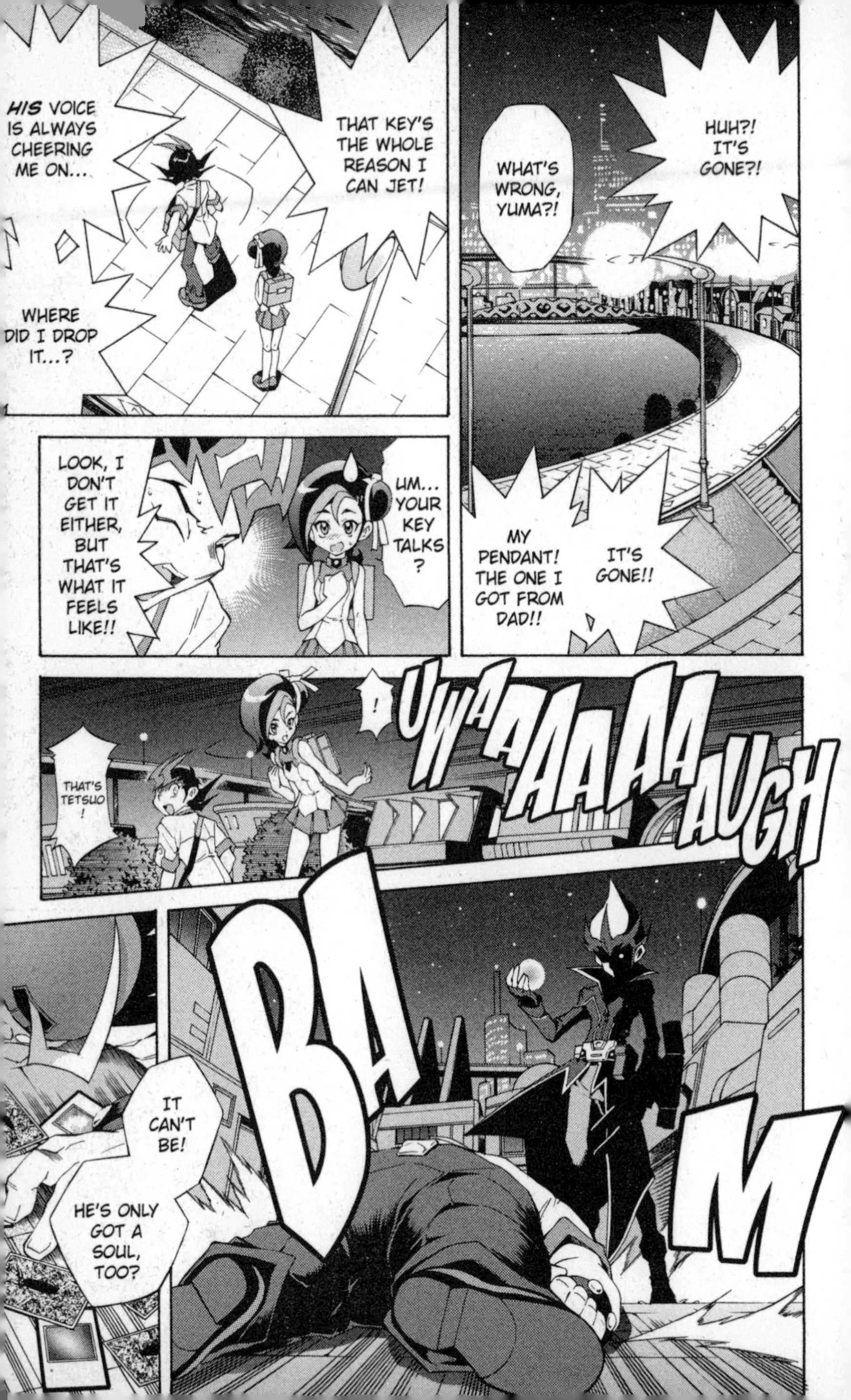
HUH?! IT'S GONE?!
WHAT'S WRONG, YUMA?!
IT'S GONE!!
MY PENDANT! THE ONE I GOT FROM DAD!!
THAT KEY'S THE WHOLE REASON I CAN JET!
HIS VOICE IS ALWAYS CHEERING ME ON...
WHERE DID I DROP IT...?
UM... YOUR KEY TALKS?
LOOK, I DON'T GET IT EITHER, BUT THAT'S WHAT IT FEELS LIKE!!
UWAAAAAAAUGH
!
THAT'S TETSUO!
BAM
IT CAN'T BE!
HE'S ONLY GOT A SOUL, TOO?

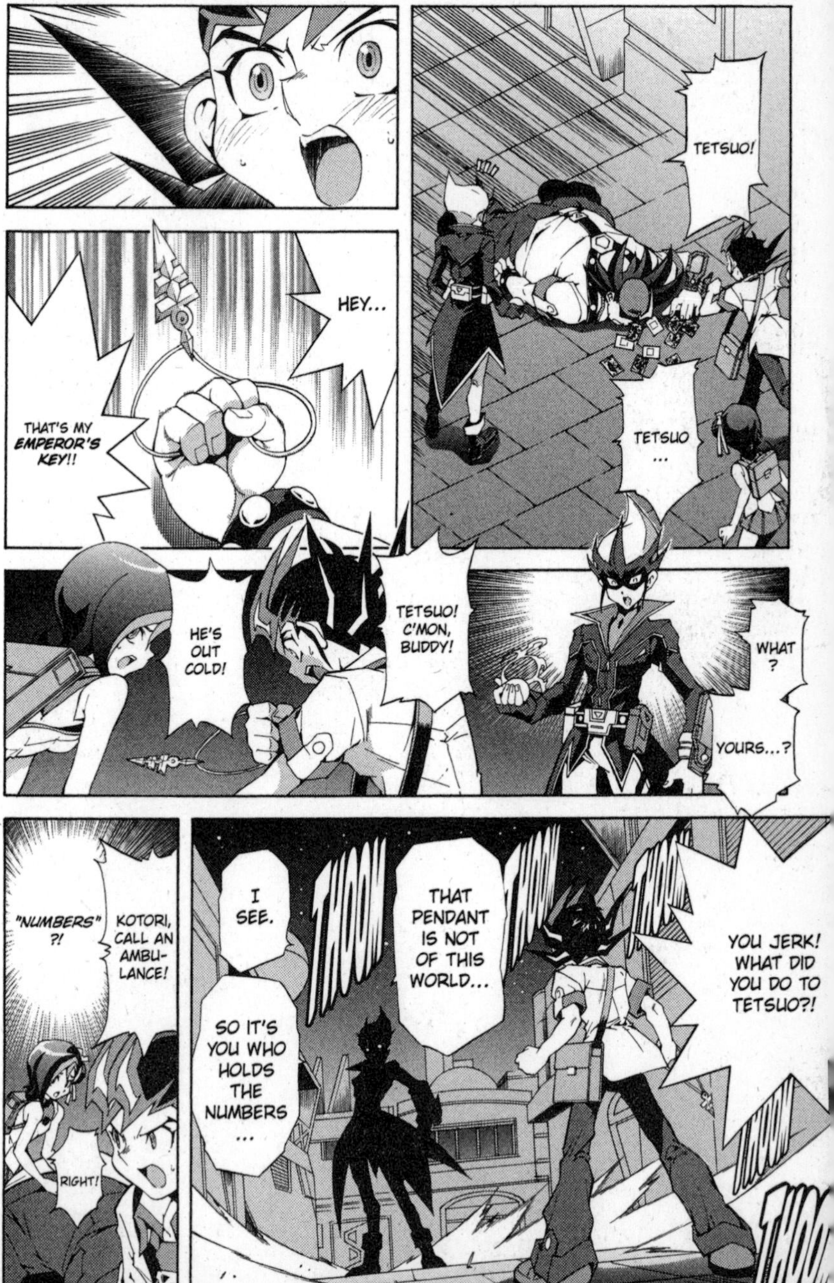
TETSUO!
TETSUO ...
HEY...
THAT'S MY EMPEROR'S KEY!!
WHAT ?
YOURS...?
TETSUO! C'MON, BUDDY!
HE'S OUT COLD!
YOU JERK! WHAT DID YOU DO TO TETSUO?!
THOOM
THAT PENDANT IS NOT OF THIS WORLD...
I SEE.
SO IT'S YOU WHO HOLDS THE NUMBERS ...
KOTORI, CALL AN AMBULANCE!
"NUMBERS" ?!
RIGHT!

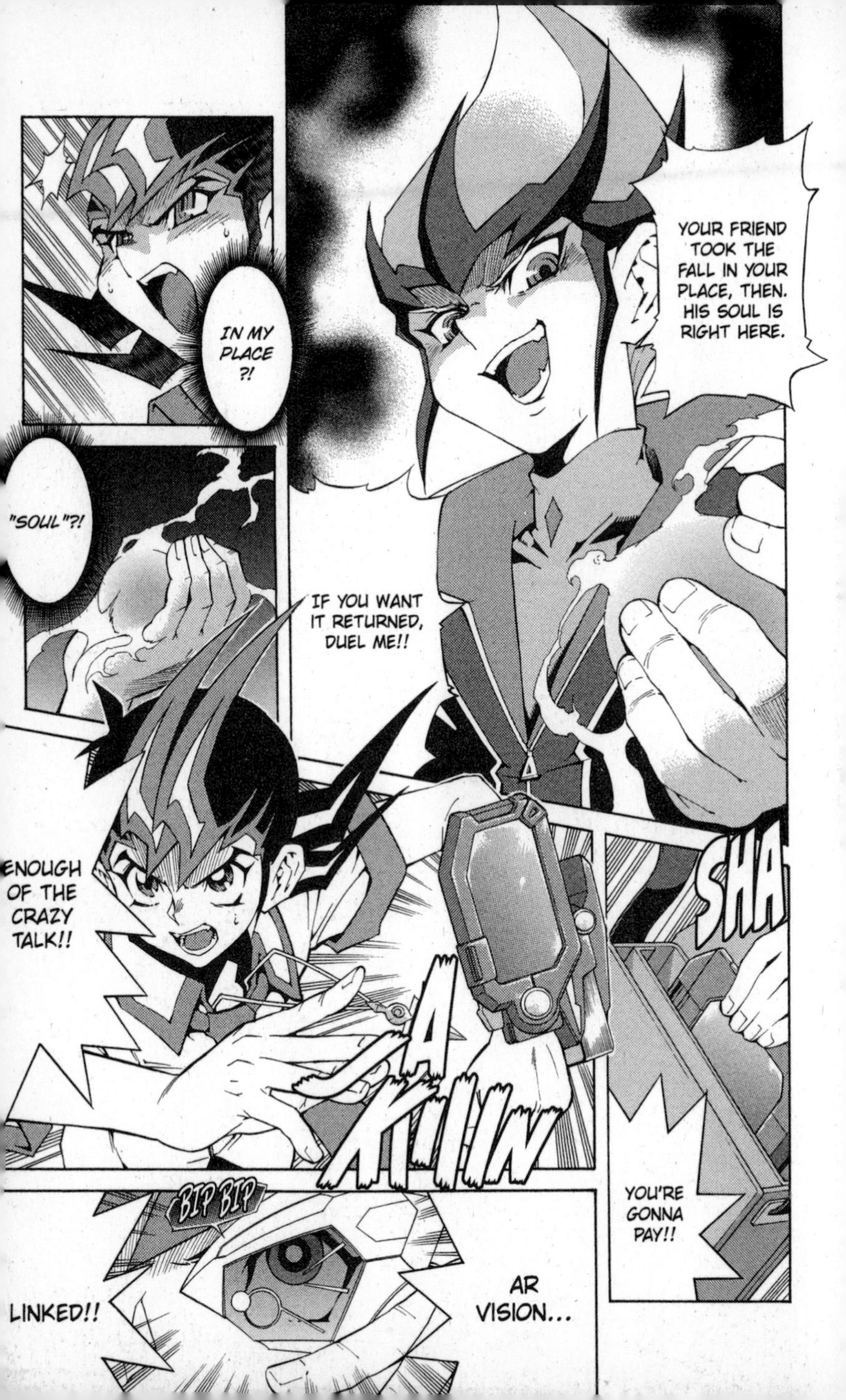

YOUR FRIEND TOOK THE FALL IN YOUR PLACE, THEN. HIS SOUL IS RIGHT HERE.
IN MY PLACE?!
"SOUL"?!
IF YOU WANT IT RETURNED, DUEL ME!!
SHA
YOU'RE GONNA PAY!!
ENOUGH OF THE CRAZY TALK!!
A
KIIIN
BIP BIP
AR VISION...
LINKED!!

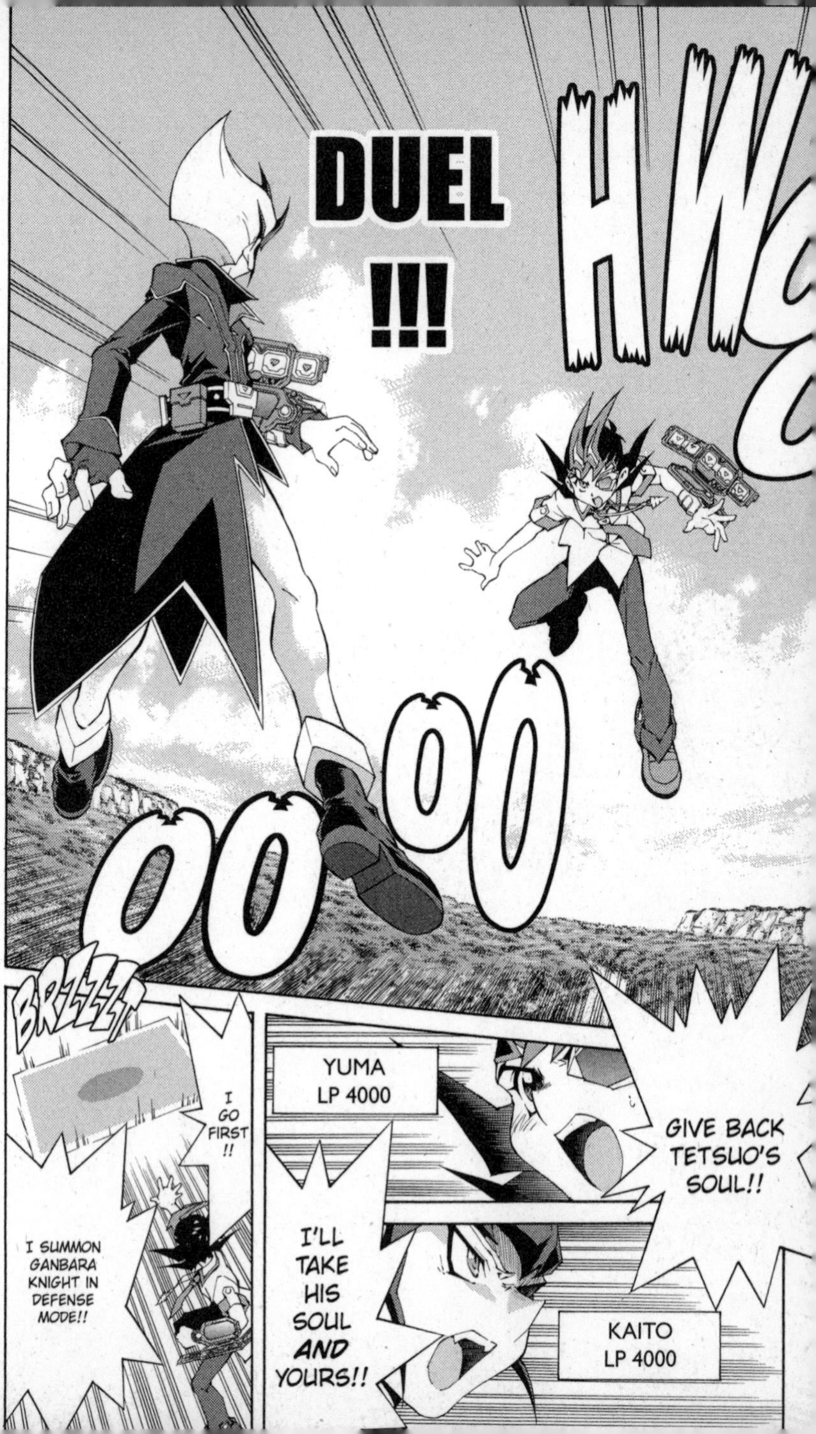
DUEL !!!
GIVE BACK TETSUO'S SOUL!!
YUMA LP 4000
KAITO LP 4000
I'LL TAKE HIS SOUL *AND* YOURS!!
BRZZZT
I GO FIRST !!
I SUMMON GANBARA KNIGHT IN DEFENSE MODE!!

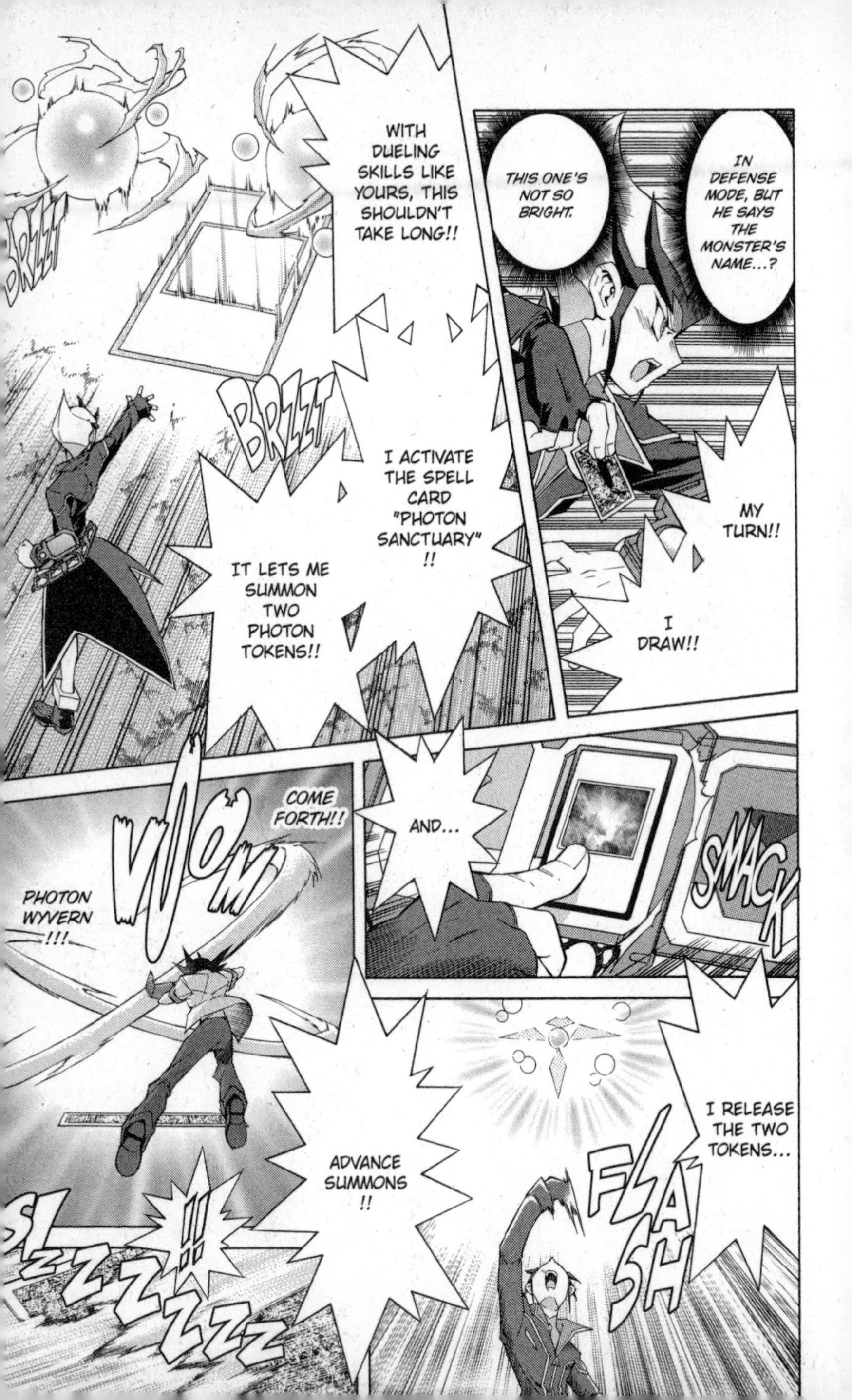
IN DEFENSE MODE, BUT HE SAYS THE MONSTER'S NAME...?
THIS ONE'S NOT SO BRIGHT.
MY TURN!!
I DRAW!!
WITH DUELING SKILLS LIKE YOURS, THIS SHOULDN'T TAKE LONG!!
BRZZZT
I ACTIVATE THE SPELL CARD "PHOTON SANCTUARY"!!
IT LETS ME SUMMON TWO PHOTON TOKENS!!
BRZZZT
SMACK
AND...
I RELEASE THE TWO TOKENS...
FLASH
ADVANCE SUMMONS!!
COME FORTH!!
VOOM
PHOTON WYVERN!!!
!!
SZZZZZZZ

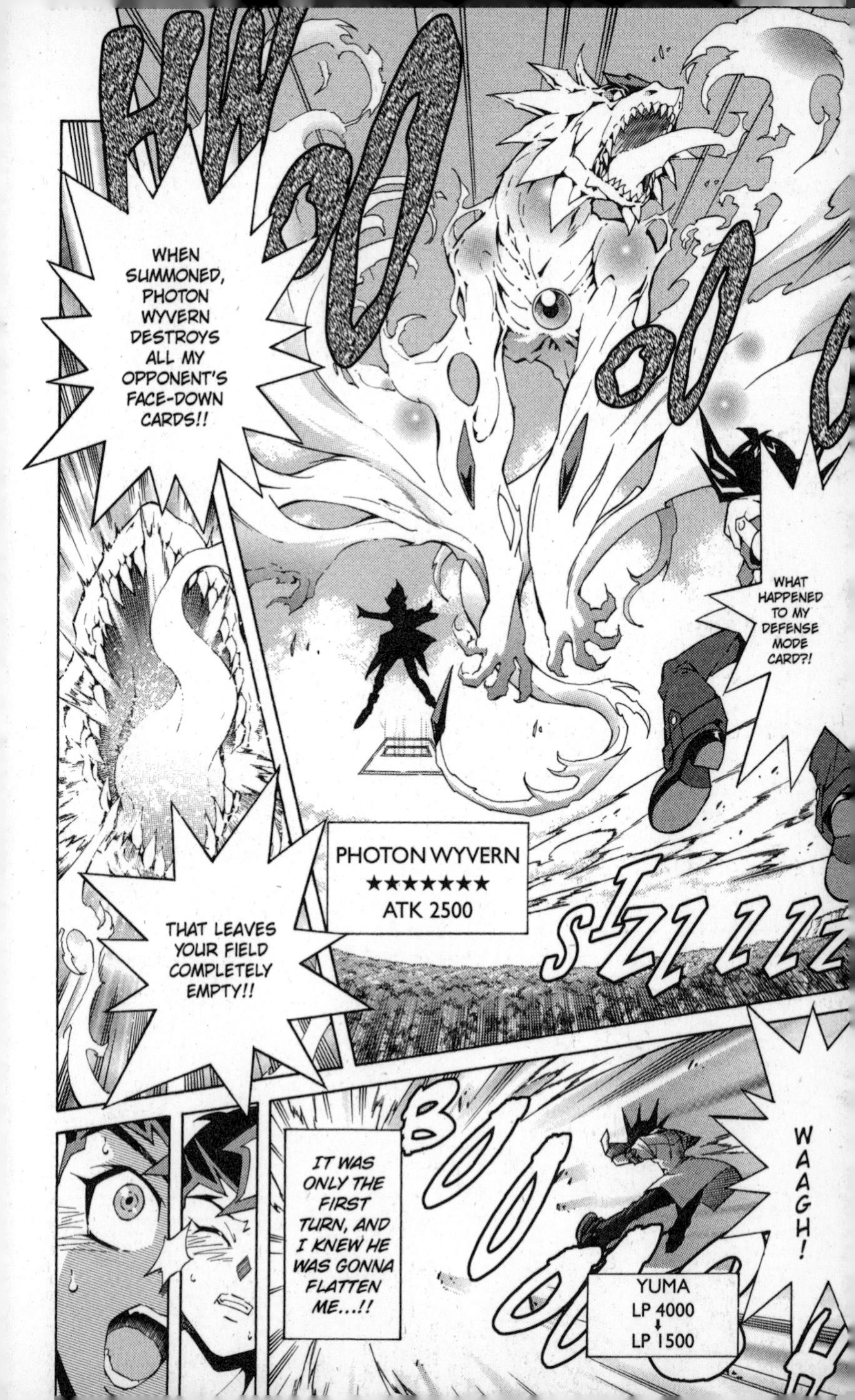

HWOOOOO
WHAT HAPPENED TO MY DEFENSE MODE CARD?!
WHEN SUMMONED, PHOTON WYVERN DESTROYS ALL MY OPPONENT'S FACE-DOWN CARDS!!
PHOTON WYVERN ★★★★★★★ ATK 2500
SIZZZZ
THAT LEAVES YOUR FIELD COMPLETELY EMPTY!!
WAAGH!
BOOOOOO
YUMA LP 4000 LP 1500
IT WAS ONLY THE FIRST TURN, AND I KNEW HE WAS GONNA FLATTEN ME...!!

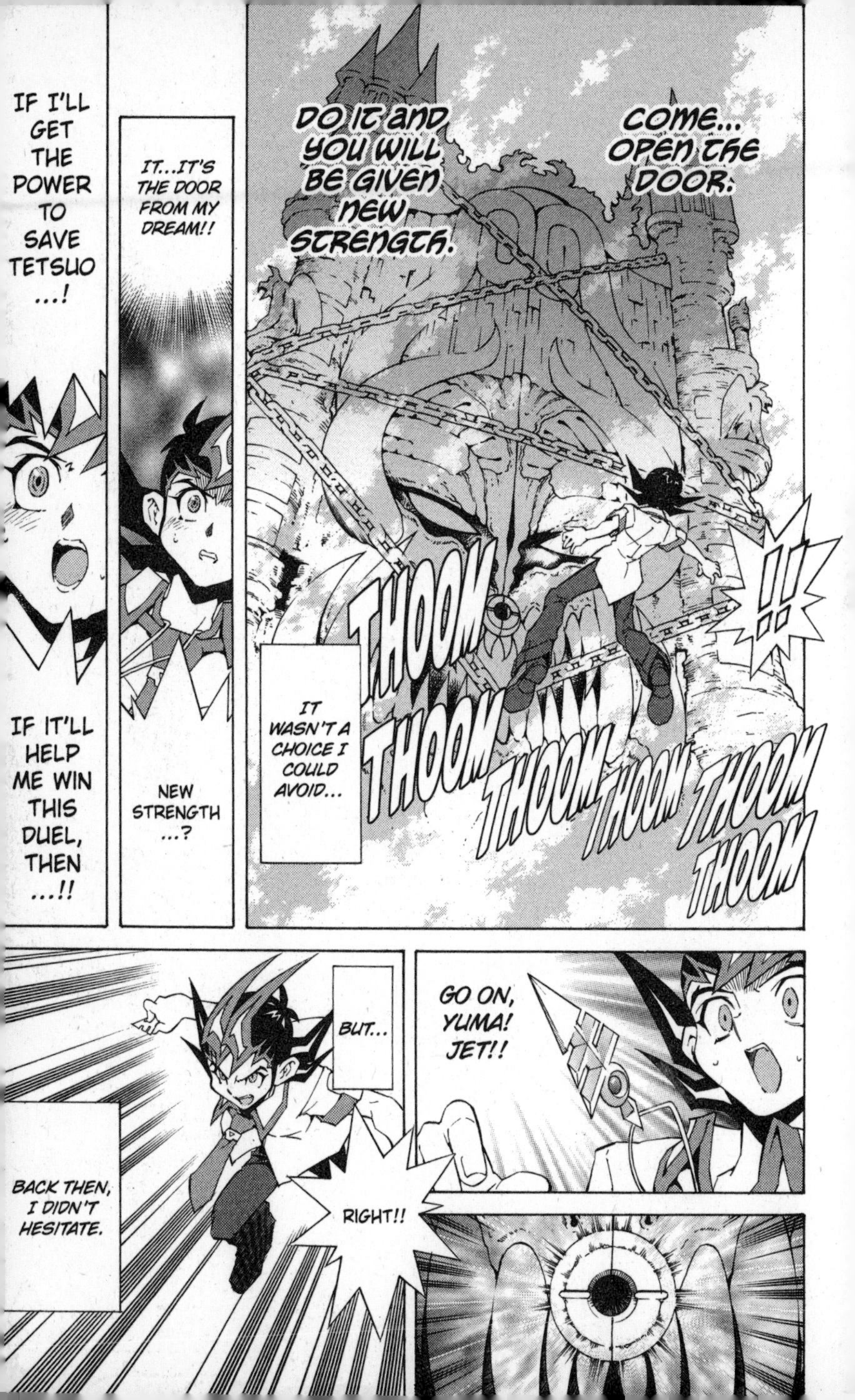
COME... OPEN THE DOOR.
DO IT AND YOU WILL BE GIVEN NEW STRENGTH.
!!
THOOM
THOOM
THOOM
THOOM
THOOM
THOOM
IT WASN'T A CHOICE I COULD AVOID...
IT...IT'S THE DOOR FROM MY DREAM!!
NEW STRENGTH ...?
IF I'LL GET THE POWER TO SAVE TETSUO ...!
IF IT'LL HELP ME WIN THIS DUEL, THEN ...!!
GO ON, YUMA! JET!!
BUT...
RIGHT!!
BACK THEN, I DIDN'T HESITATE.

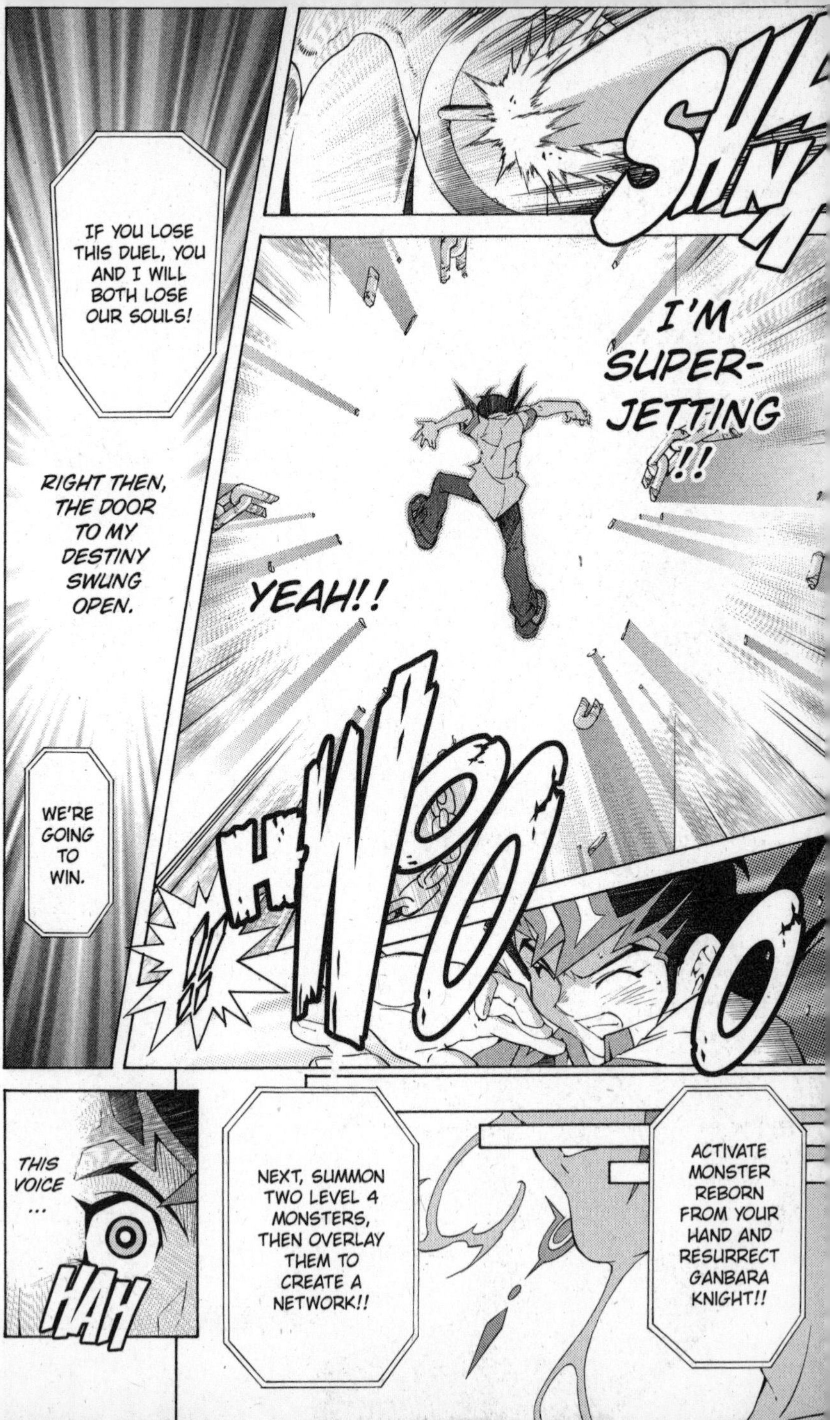

SHN
I'M SUPER-JETTING!!
YEAH!!
HWOOO!!
IF YOU LOSE THIS DUEL, YOU AND I WILL BOTH LOSE OUR SOULS!
RIGHT THEN, THE DOOR TO MY DESTINY SWUNG OPEN.
WE'RE GOING TO WIN.
ACTIVATE MONSTER REBORN FROM YOUR HAND AND RESURRECT GANBARA KNIGHT!!
NEXT, SUMMON TWO LEVEL 4 MONSTERS, THEN OVERLAY THEM TO CREATE A NETWORK!!
THIS VOICE...
HAH

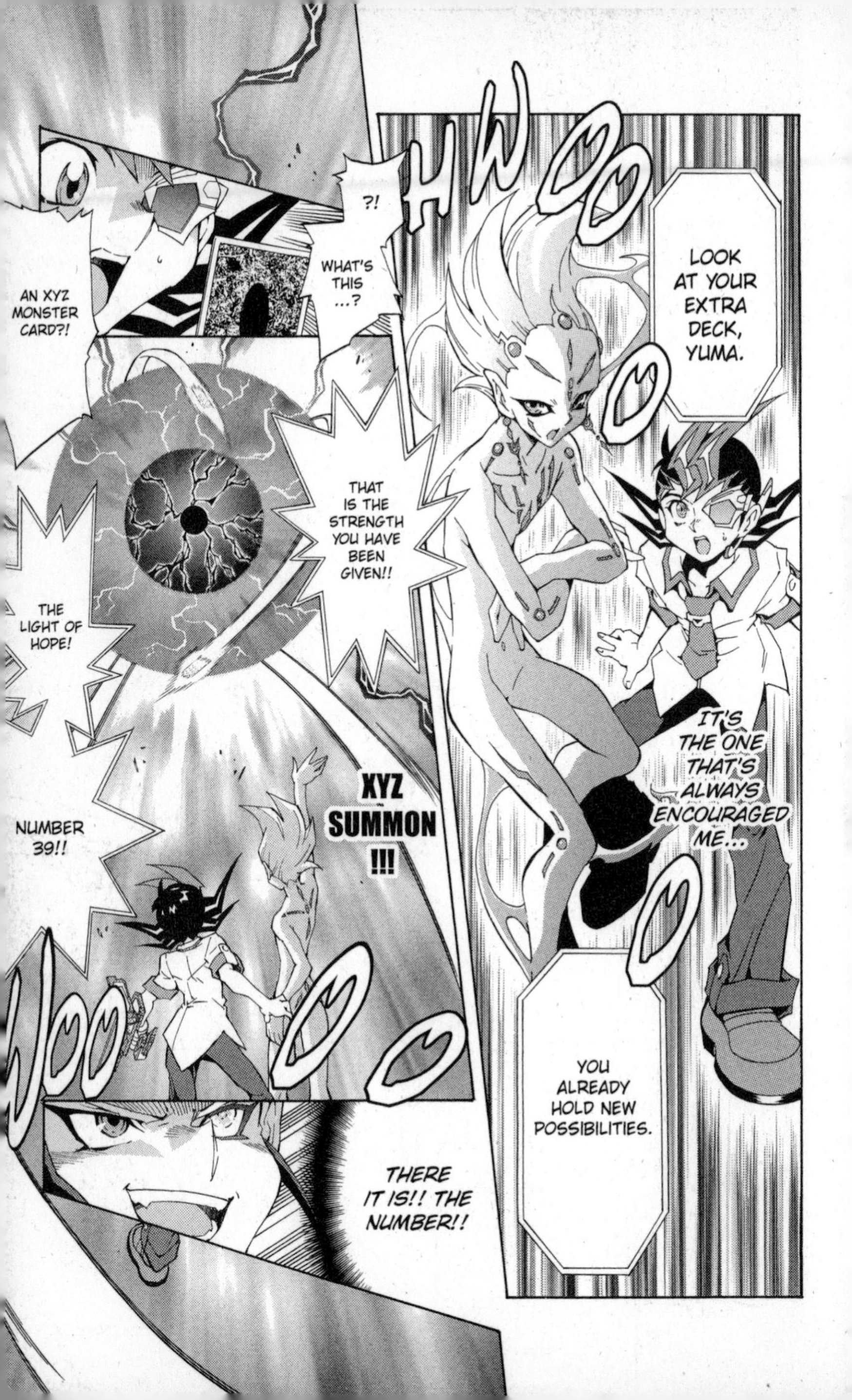
HWOOOO
LOOK AT YOUR EXTRA DECK, YUMA.
IT'S THE ONE THAT'S ALWAYS ENCOURAGED ME...
YOU ALREADY HOLD NEW POSSIBILITIES.
?!
WHAT'S THIS ...?
AN XYZ MONSTER CARD?!
THAT IS THE STRENGTH YOU HAVE BEEN GIVEN!!
THE LIGHT OF HOPE!
XYZ SUMMON !!!
NUMBER 39!!
WOOOO
THERE IT IS!! THE NUMBER!!

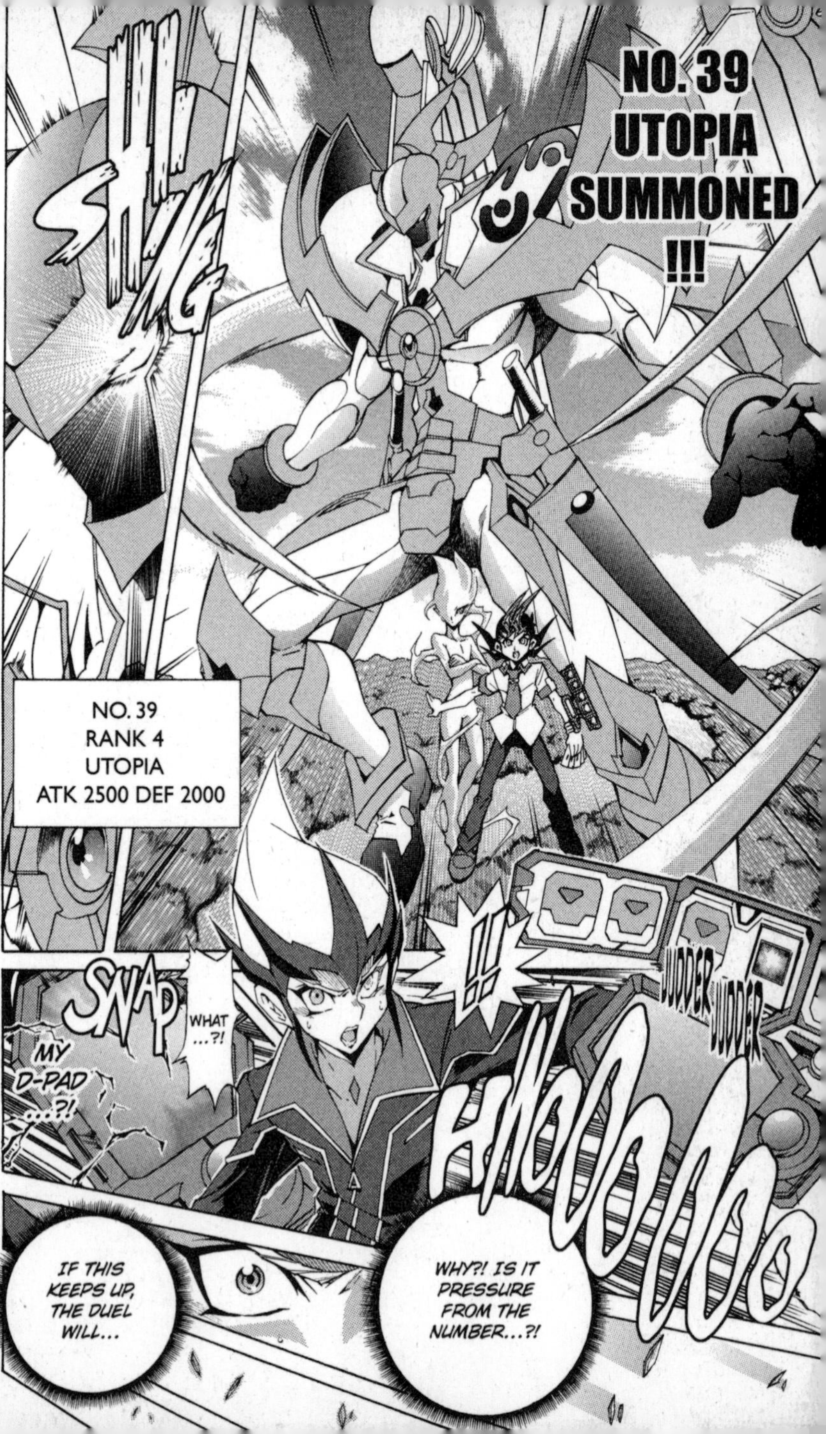
NO. 39 UTOPIA SUMMONED !!!
SHING
NO. 39
RANK 4
UTOPIA
ATK 2500 DEF 2000
!!
JUDDER JUDDER
HWOOOOOO
WHAT ...?!
SNAP
MY D-PAD ...?!
WHY?! IS IT PRESSURE FROM THE NUMBER...?!
IF THIS KEEPS UP, THE DUEL WILL...

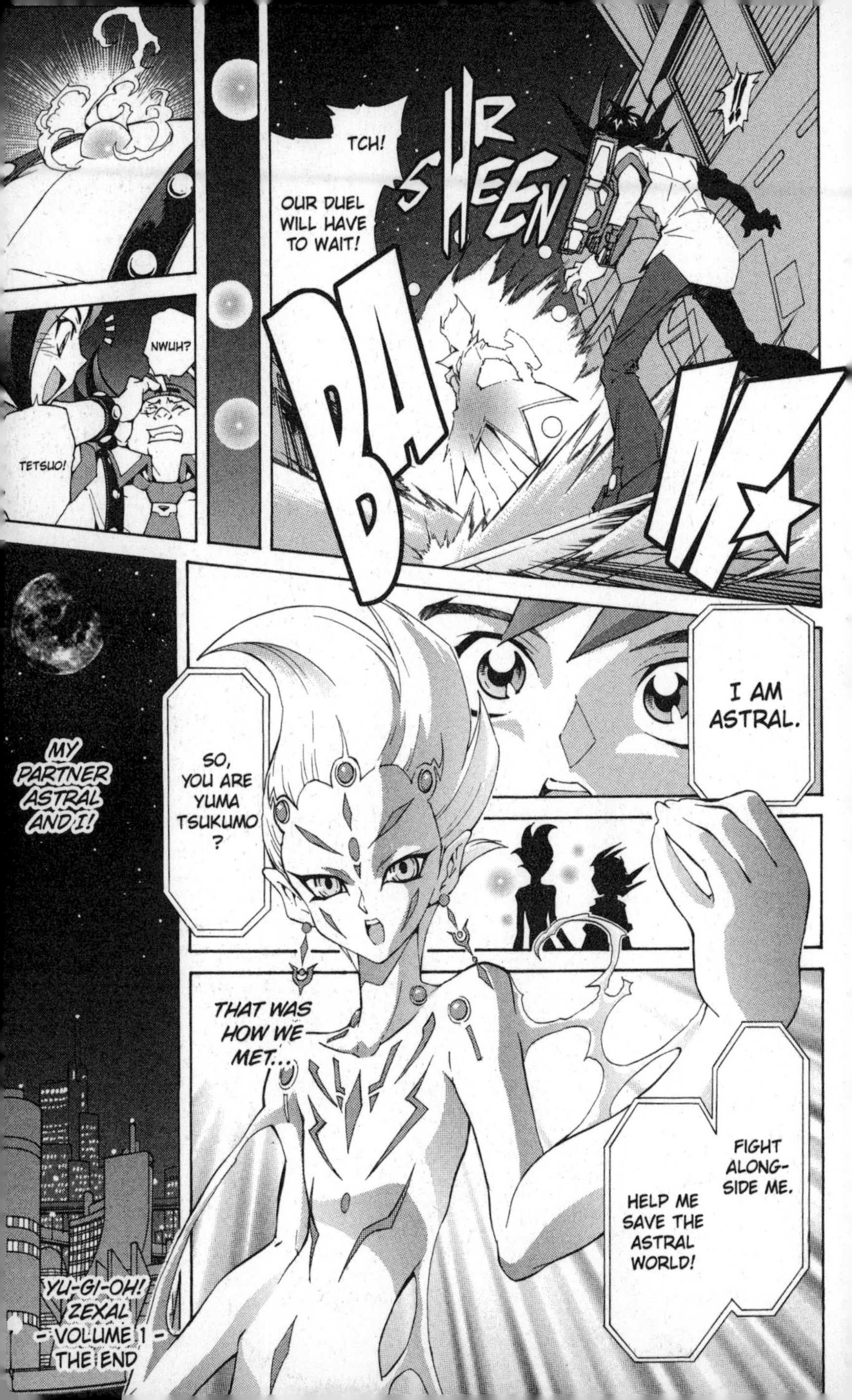
!!
SHEEN
TCH!
OUR DUEL WILL HAVE TO WAIT!
BAM
NWUH?
TETSUO!
I AM ASTRAL.
SO, YOU ARE YUMA TSUKUMO?
FIGHT ALONG-SIDE ME.
HELP ME SAVE THE ASTRAL WORLD!
THAT WAS HOW WE MET...
MY PARTNER ASTRAL AND I!
YU-GI-OH! ZEXAL
-VOLUME 1-
THE END

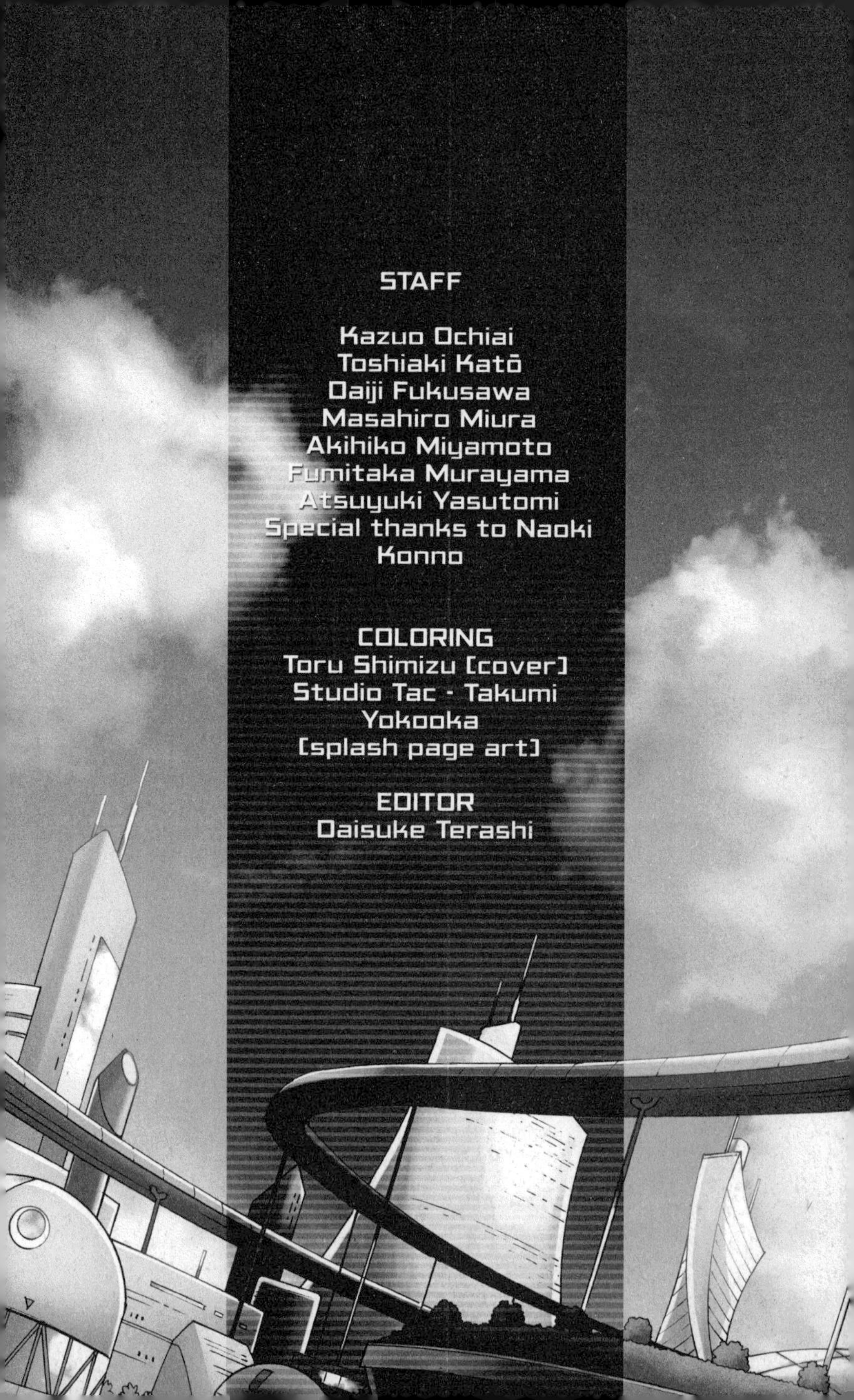

STAFF

Kazuo Ochiai
Toshiaki Katō
Daiji Fukusawa
Masahiro Miura
Akihiko Miyamoto
Fumitaka Murayama
Atsuyuki Yasutomi
Special thanks to Naoki Konno

COLORING

Toru Shimizu [cover]
Studio Tac - Takumi Yokooka
[splash page art]

EDITOR

Daisuke Terashi

YOU ARE READING IN THE WRONG DIRECTION!!

Whoops! Guess what? You're starting at the wrong end of the comic!

DISCARD

...It's true! In keeping with the original Japanese format, *Yu-Gi-Oh! ZEXAL* is meant to be read from right to left, starting in the upper-right corner.

Unlike English, which is read from left to right, Japanese is read from right to left, meaning that action, sound effects and word-balloon order are completely reversed... something which can make readers unfamiliar with Japanese feel pretty backwards themselves. For this reason, manga or Japanese comics published in the U.S. in English have sometimes been published "flopped"—that is, printed in exact reverse order, as though seen from the other side of a mirror.

By flopping pages, U.S. publishers can avoid confusing readers, but the compromise is not without its downside. For one thing, a character in a flopped manga series who once wore in the original Japanese version a T-shirt emblazoned with "M A Y" (as in "the merry month of") now wears one which reads "Y A M"! Additionally, many manga creators in Japan are themselves unhappy with the process, as some feel the mirror-imaging of their art alters their original intentions.

We are proud to bring you Shin Yoshida and Naohito Miyoshi's *Yu-Gi-Oh! ZEXAL* in the original unflopped format. For now, though, turn to the other side of the book and let the duel begin...!

–Editor